ONWARD, CHRISTIAN SOLDIERS

*The Growing Political Power of Catholics
and Evangelicals in the United States*

DEAL W. HUDSON

THRESHOLD
EDITIONS

New York   London   Toronto   Sydney

THRESHOLD EDITIONS
A Division of Simon & Schuster, Inc.
1230 Avenue of the Americas
New York, NY 10020

First Threshold Editions hardcover edition March 2008

THRESHOLD EDITIONS and colophon are trademarks of Simon & Schuster, Inc.

For information about special discounts for bulk purchases,
please contact Simon & Schuster Special Sales at
1-800-456-6798 or business@simonandschuster.com.

Designed by Ruth Lee-Mui

Manufactured in the United States of America

10   9   8   7   6   5   4   3   2   1

ISBN-13: 978-1-4165-2442-7
ISBN-10:   1-4165-2442-8

This book is dedicated to

FRANK AND DAVID HANNA

ACKNOWLEDGMENTS

MANY PEOPLE, FRIENDS AND FAMILY, HAVE MADE THIS BOOK possible. Frank and David Hanna, to whom this book is dedicated, saw the importance of funding the *Crisis* Catholic Voter Project, which led to a paradigm change of understanding Catholics in politics and, eventually, this study encompassing both Evangelicals and Catholics.

My book agent, Alex Hoyt, first saw the merit of my project, and Mary Matalin, general editor of this series, was gracious in taking it under her wing.

I want to thank present and former members of the board of the Morley Publishing Group Inc.: Denis Coleman, Cortes de Russy, Sim Johnston, John Sites, Peter Flanigan, Pat Cipillone, Alan Carson, Sean Fieler, John Klink, Jeff Wallin, Jack Kelly, Jane Mary Garvey, Leo Linbeck III, Bill Simon, Admiral Jeremiah Denton, Helen Anne Bunn, Lisa Correnti, Barbara Henkels, Paul Henkels, Ed Marzec, and Madelon Talley.

Much gratitude to my students at St. John's Catholic Parish in McLean, Virginia, who discussed these issues with me over many months, especially religious education director Laura Pennefather.

The staff of the Morley Publishing Group provided encouragement and help: Brian Saint-Paul, Zoe Romanowsky, Margaret Cabaniss, Christina Jopson, Trang Lam, Elena Cardenas, Agnes Bunagan, Mary McPherson, Matthew Wray, Ann Waterman, Eden Simmons, Lisa Brown, Mary Hundt, and Elizabeth McGuirk.

Others who have encouraged and supported my work include Gene Zurlo, Chris Donahue, William Cousins, Jack Whelan, Pat O'Meara, Pat Beach, Barksdale Hortenstein, Steve Clune, Bill Plunkett, Ralph Reed, Cookie Adler, John Garvey, Alejandro Bermudez, Teri Bohlinger, Marjorie Campbell, Bill Campbell, Steve Castleton, Rose Bente Lee, John Saeman, Carol Saeman, Jerry Trautschold, Veronica Daigle, Carl Davis, Lois Davis, Michael Hall, Dana Gioia, Ed Moy, Tim Goeglein, Matthew D. Smith, J. R. Sanchez, Michael Starr, Russ Shaw, Bonnie Moran, Mattie Smith, Grover Norquist, Samah Norquist, Chuck Piola, John F. Cannon, Father Benedict Groeschel, Father Frank Pavone, Ray LeBlanc, Mike Ferrier, Mary Garaventa, Jim Kelly III, Michael Gleba, Matt Schlapp, Martin Gillespie, Steve Wagner, Bishop Robert Vasa, Archbishop Jose Gomez, Bishop Alan Vigneron, Senator Mack Mattingly, Representative Chris Smith, Senator Rick Santorum, Senator Sam Brownback, Representative Henry Hyde, Senator Mel Martinez, Secretary Jim Nicholson, Governor Frank Keating, Michael Schwartz, Paul Weyrich, and Robert D. Novak.

This book could not have been completed without Brenda Steele, who patiently corrected consecutive drafts, making suggested revisions along the way. Carol McKinley read early drafts, transcribed interviews, provided research, and suggested valuable edits. Kathleen Jerabek helped me with my other writing and reporting during the time devoted to this book.

Most of all, I want to thank my wife, Theresa, my daughter, Hannah, and my son, Ciprian, for their love and understanding.

CONTENTS

FOREWORD

NOTHER BOOK BEARS THE TITLE *ONWARD, CHRISTIAN SOLDIERS,* but its title ends with a question mark. My title has no question mark. The political movement started by religious conservatives who came to be known as the Religious Right is, as I will argue, motivated by and expressive of an authentic, and mainly Christian, faith.

Written by a Georgetown University professor, *Onward, Christian Soldiers? The Religious Right in American Politics* is an excellent, comprehensive overview of the religious conservative movement which has gone through several editions, the most recent in 2006.[1] The question mark in the title of Clyde Wilcox's book is appropriate for a university scholar writing for other scholars and classroom students. Wilcox, for the most part, does a good job of maintaining the scholarly neutrality symbolized by his question mark.

There is another difference between the two books. This is not a comprehensive history of the religious conservative movement. This history,

---

1. Clyde Wilcox and Carin Larson, *Onward Christian Soldiers? The Religious Right in American Politics* (Washington, D.C.: Georgetown University Press, 2006).

both its grassroots activism and its political strategy, has already been told.[2] I'm writing for two reasons: to persuade skeptics that religious conservatives are not unreasonable extremists, and to defend religious conservatives in politics against the charge that they have no business having a voice in the democratic process.

---

2. In addition to Wilcox, there is a vast and growing literature: William Martin, *With God on Our Side: The Rise of the Religious Right in America* (New York: Broadway Books, 1996); Jerome L. Himmelstein, *To the Right: The Transformation of American Conservatism* (Berkeley: University of California Press, 1990); Steve Bruce, *The Rise and Fall of the New Christian Right: Conservative Protestant Politics in America, 1978–1988* (Oxford: Clarendon Press, 1988); Geoffrey Layman, *The Great Divide: Religious and Cultural Conflict in American Party Politics* (New York: Columbia University Press, 2001); Kenneth J. Heineman, *God Is a Conservative: Religion, Politics, and Morality in Contemporary America* (New York: New York University Press, 1998); Godfrey Hodgson, *The World Turned Right Side Up: A History of the Conservative Ascendancy in America* (Boston: Houghton Mifflin, 1996).

A PERSONAL INTRODUCTION

I N 1966, I WAS A JUNIOR IN HIGH SCHOOL. THAT YEAR, THE EASTER issue (April 8) of *Time* magazine displayed the question "Is God Dead?" on its cover in large red letters against a black background. A professor of theology from Emory University, Thomas J. Altizer, published *The Gospel of Christian Atheism.*[1] The best-selling book on religion that year, *The Secular City,* was published a year earlier by Harvey Cox, a Harvard theology professor. Cox described the retreat of organized religion before the onslaught of unbelief.[2] The following year, Joseph Fletcher, another Harvard theology professor, published *Situation Ethics: The New Morality,* calling into question all traditional moral strictures except one: the duty to love one another.[3]

These three books declared the uncertainty of the time regarding religion. The only certainty these books acknowledged was that religion would never be the same after the forces of secularization, relativism, and atheism had left their marks.

---

1. The first book in English on the "death of God" was actually by Gabriel Vahanian, *The Death of God* (New York: George Braziller, 1961), but it was Altizer who got the credit. In 1966, he wrote *The Gospel of Christian Atheism* (Philadelphia: Westminster Press, 1966) and, along with William Hamilton, *Radical Theology and the Death of God* (Indianapolis: Bobbs-Merrill, 1966).

2. Harvey Cox, *The Secular City: Secularization and Urbanization in Theological Perspective* (New York: Macmillan, 1965.

3. Joseph Fletcher, *Situation Ethics: The New Morality* (Philadelphia: Westminster—John Knox Press, 1967).

To those of us who were children in the 1950s, God, religion, and morality were taught without qualification. The confusions of the adult world were not passed on. But by the time we became teenagers, what seemed enduring truths were up for grabs.

Years later, when I heard our parents described as belonging to the Greatest Generation, I wondered if we had grown up at a disadvantage. Did we pale in comparison because our parents were bolstered by certainties that we lacked? They fought a war united against undisputed evil. Conversely, the war in Southeast Asia divided the nation. Our parents' confident convictions about religion and about morality became suspect.

Like our parents, we grappled with the specter of insecurity. But ours was overlaid with moral and spiritual ambiguity. As children, we crouched under our school desks in preparation for nuclear war. The president, who was shot while riding down a city street in an open automobile, had narrowly avoided a nuclear confrontation with the Soviet Union only thirteen months earlier. A few years later, another president resigned from office, leaving respect for governmental authority at a historic low.

Isolated thinkers and savants such as Friedrich Nietzsche had only talked about overthrowing the virtues—we were actually doing it. In place of the old virtues, we created lifestyles. Birth-control pills, psychedelic drugs, and ear-splitting music blew holes in the traditional boundaries of acceptable behavior.

Like many of my peers, I felt ambivalent toward the changes—with wider boundaries came an unspoken expectation that everyone should explore them or be left behind, unenlightened. As a seventeen-year-old leaving home to live at a university of 40,000 students, I grappled less with my newfound freedom than with the expectation of exploiting it.

In the midst of this tumult, I turned to the study of philosophy. Instead of the prelaw program at the University of Texas that my parents had approved, I enrolled in classes such as Philosophy of Art, Greek Philosophy, Philosophy of Science, Love and the *Divine Comedy*, Philosophy of Law, and Philosophical Theology. Family and friends were aghast, assuming the worst about the influence of philosophy. I was sure to join a band of ponytailed, pot-smoking hippies.

Something surprising happened. After two years in college, I chose to become a traditional Christian. The course on Philosophical Theology, taught by an Episcopal priest, had enthralled me. It forced me to think about what it meant to be religious and to have faith. We studied the work of Paul Tillich, who is not much read now but was renowned as the theologian who systematized and integrated Christianity and existentialism. Tillich argued that all of us necessarily have an "ultimate concern," whether it is in God or something else. Tillich made faith in God a reasonable endeavor, since it made no sense to be concerned about anything that was less than ultimate.

Eventually, I got to know a group of Evangelical friends and was deeply impressed by their genuine love for one another, so I gave organized religion another try. My adolescent years as a Presbyterian had been personally helpful but evoked in me nothing like the urgency I experienced in the presence of great thinkers such as Tillich or the witness of Evangelicals seeking to give their lives over to Jesus Christ. Like others of my generation, I wanted to understand and experience for myself what truth is and what was going to guide my life.

After attending a Southern Baptist church for a few months, I walked the aisle, saying publicly that I was becoming a Christian. My Presbyterian parents thought I was already a Christian, since I had been duly baptized and attended church regularly. Of course, they were right, but the physical act of walking the aisle was, in fact, something different: I was declaring in the midst of '60s confusion that I was committed to the world of beliefs and values being left behind by a culture embracing the "death of God" and the "secular city."

I returned to campus the day after my conversion to attend my weekly philosophy seminar with the campus radical, Dr. Larry Caroline. Caroline was a Marxist in the midst of a public fight with Dean John Silber, who wanted to deny him tenure. Dr. Caroline had announced at the beginning of his class that all students would receive an A, whether or not they attended class or turned in any assignments. He divided the class into small groups, and we met weekly in students' apartments, usually smelling of their pot and incense.

It was Dr. Caroline's habit to begin each session asking what the students had been doing the previous week, so I knew that I was facing a moment of truth. My turn came, and I blurted out that I had walked the aisle to become a Christian. I gritted my teeth for the reaction. There were half-turned faces and muffled giggles, but Dr. Caroline quickly spoke up with great warmth and kindness, congratulating me for making a firm decision about the direction of my life. Few things are more delightful than discovering that stereotypes are false.

I have met more Larry Carolines along the way. I needed to, since some years later, I would convert once again, this time to Roman Catholicism. That conversion began at my first graduate school, Princeton Theological Seminary. There I studied theology for three years and started a student ministry for Southern Baptist students at Princeton University. A small group of Evangelicals were enrolled at the seminary in the early '70s, along with another group who were evading the draft. The combination of earnest Evangelicals, buttoned-down Presbyterians, and radicals espousing the new radical theology created a sometimes contentious environment.

The friendly religious disputes of my undergraduate days turned bitter during my three years in seminary. We argued, and at times almost came to blows, over the future of religion and traditional values. One side insisted that organized religion was dying, along with its outdated morality. The other side—which I belonged to—tried to convince them, and ourselves to some extent, that people still needed a traditional biblical worldview and morality.

This argument is still far from settled. But the resurgence of traditional Christianity in American culture has surprised those on all sides of the argument. Evangelicals and socially conservative Catholics have emerged as a far more powerful cultural and political force than anyone predicted at the time. Certainly, there would be a remnant, even the most liberal among us conceded, but to become the most powerful religious force in contemporary American culture? It wasn't possible, or so it seemed.

As a young man, I argued for traditional Christianity, but now my arguments come from a Roman Catholic perspective. After seminary, I chose not to pursue the ministry but went on to earn my doctorate at Emory University in Atlanta. I became a philosophy professor, first at a Baptist college and then at a Catholic one. I taught for fifteen years before becoming a journalist and publisher in Washington, D.C. Throughout those years, the issues that animated my high school and college years have remained the same. They are transposed into new forms of argument and ideological conflicts, but at the core they are identical. The most recent iterations were seen in the public arguments about the role of religious faith in the 2004 presidential campaign, followed by the furor over President George W. Bush's first nominee, a practicing Catholic, to the Supreme Court. The temperature of that public discussion has been rising for years.

The questions that keep surfacing are these: What is the future of organized religion and its traditional morality in the face of secularism? What impact will—or should—religion have on culture and politics? Are the traditional teachings of Christianity still relevant? Are these traditional teachings actually the cause, not the cure, of social ills such as war, discrimination, or simple unhappiness? Finally, where do the citizens of the United States themselves come down on these questions?

Those who embraced the "death of God" and the "secular city" predicted that in the future, all religions would take completely different forms. This transformation would be necessary, they argued, because people no longer respond to the old dogmas and rituals, perceiving them with incredulity. In the theological phraseology of that day, the religious worldview would have been "demythologized." The myths being expunged would include the virgin birth, the incarnation and resurrection of Jesus Christ, and the three-story universe of heaven, hell, and Earth. Intercessory prayer would be thrown out, too. A prominent Anglican bishop of the time wrote a controversial book, *Honest to God,* which dismissed the traditional idea of petitionary prayer to a God "up there" and replaced it with a secular theology. For example, in Bishop John Robinson's secularized spirituality, a prayer to God for rain to make crops grow becomes the help given farmers to build an irrigation ditch.[4] Robinson explained at the time that he was seeking an existentialist theology along the lines of Paul Tillich and Dietrich Bonhoeffer, the Lutheran theologian who had been executed by Adolf Hitler for participation in an assassination plot. Perhaps I was a poor student, but both Tillich and Bonhoeffer led me toward a supernatural faith that promises the gift of grace and salvation.

My small role in these battles was as a college professor—nine years at a Baptist college in Atlanta, Mercer University, and six years at Fordham University, a Catholic Jesuit institution in the Bronx. On both campuses, I was known as a conservative who taught the "great books," especially the tradition stretching from Aristotle to Saint Thomas Aquinas and their later interpreters.

The focal point of my research and teaching was the idea of happiness. The first time I seriously studied Aristotle's *Ethics,* I noticed that his understanding of a happy life was inseparable from one that could be called morally good as well. Aristotle's usage and the contemporary understanding of happiness as "feeling good" were miles apart. If my generation promoted anything, it was the cultivation of self-gratification and satisfaction, and I began to doubt that this alone could be called happiness. The more I thought about it, the more I became obsessed with finding out why the meaning of happiness had changed so drastically between the ancient world and the modern. I found out that nearly all the ancient philosophers agreed that you could not call a person happy whom you could not also judge to be morally good. To underline the point, Greek and Roman philosophers argued about whether it was possible for a person to be called happy while being tortured. Most of them answered yes, since torture does not remove the goodness of its victim. That perspective provokes astonishment, if not outright laugh-

4. John A. T. Robinson, *Honest to God* (Philadelphia: Westminster Press, 1963).

ter, today, among people who have never questioned the identification of happiness other than with good feelings.

Over ten years, I studied the history of happiness, locating the moments when the meaning was gradually stripped of its moral expression. In *Happiness and the Limits of Satisfaction* (Rowman & Littlefield, 1995), I published my findings to an academic audience. But personally, I thought I had clarified the source of some basic confusion that had dogged me since my years at college and the seminary and, I believe, had dogged my entire generation.

I mention these academic orientations and preoccupations as a way of saying that whatever form of conservatism I possess was not shaped directly by politics. My reading of the great books, from Homer onward, and my religious conversion shaped me as a conservative. A so-called great books education has no necessary political slant. In fact, my political orientation was very different from that of my friend and mentor, Mortimer J. Adler, who was virtually identified with the study of great books during his lifetime. Adler was a classic liberal in his politics, and during my three years as Adler's fellow at the Aspen Institute in the mid-'90s, we constantly bickered over the political ramifications of the books we both loved. Our discussions always went along well until we got into politics, and then we parted company. On the basic concepts of rights and freedom, Adler seemed to lose sight of his metaphysical realism. Both of these ideas will play a central role in the story I tell. The Catholic vision of the Western tradition, like the study of great books, can inform a wide spectrum of political opinion but cannot justify relativism in ethics or the exile of faith from the public arena.

My education in the great books became increasingly refracted through the Catholic intellectual tradition, particularly that of modern interpreters of Aquinas, such as Jacques Maritain and Etienne Gilson. The names of these two philosophers are hardly recognized now, but during the '40s and '50s, they were major figures in Catholic colleges and seminaries. Like Adler, also an interpreter of Aquinas, Maritain and Gilson were committed liberals. Maritain and Gilson both played important roles in drafting the Universal Declaration of Human Rights (1948).

Maritain even championed the work of the political radical Saul Alinsky to Pope Paul VI as a model of Church renewal.

More than anything else, however, it was their modern interpretations of Saint Thomas Aquinas that helped to keep his thought alive in the twentieth century. Maritain and Gilson, along with other neo-Thomists, are now viewed as relics of the pre-Vatican II era. This attitude tells us more about those who have distorted the meaning of Vatican II than the actual continuity of Catholic teaching over the past century. Indeed, as a Catholic journalist and commentator, I have found myself grappling with false representations of Vatican II more than any other issue. As I will argue, those who completely invested in the bogus understanding of the Council were the last to recognize what happened in the Catholic Church.

Apart from the politics of the left or the right, what all these philosophers had in common was confidence in the capacity to know the moral virtues and values grounded in human nature. This moral knowledge should guide both human life and the governing of human communities. In short, they believed that truth exists and can be known. Their confidence in an ethical knowledge that is universal and common to all human persons in all cultures contradicted the growing acceptance of "situation ethics" or, as it was also known, moral relativism.

In the thirty years between the time I attended college and the mid-'90s, when I left teaching, a revolution occurred in academic circles. Some label this the arrival of postmodernism, but it is easily described without the label. It is the belief that there is no possibility of knowing the truth about human nature that would lead to an ethics for everybody or, in other words, a common morality. Most teachers of the humanities in colleges and universities embrace this position in one form or another.

It's a bit more difficult to describe what they changed from. Some professors were simple traditionalists; others had become modernists. Modernism was much more subtle than its destructive offspring, postmodernism. Moderns, such as the poet T. S. Eliot, believed that truth and human goodness existed but could be glimpsed only partially or in fragments. But they still believed that a common meaning, a common purpose of human life, was "out there" to discover and to put into words and images. The revolution that I witnessed among college professors and their students was the last gasp of modernism, the belief that human existence had a common meaning. It's no accident that during this period, the great books were gradually eliminated from many college classrooms, and the entire notion of teaching a "Western tradition" was rejected as an artificial construct. This radical shift confirmed my choice of philosophical and religious affiliations.

This shift, however, had a concurrent impact on politics and, particularly, political discourse. The liberals of my college days, such as Caroline and Adler, based their opinions on a foundation of knowledge beginning with the nature of human life. They did not think they were creating moral values out of a void. Liberals such as Maritain and Adler regarded human rights as something required by a respect for human nature. Someone might differ with them, as I did, about the application of those rights, but we agreed that they were rooted in nature. Both conservatives and liberals in those days believed in the possibility of knowing human nature, making genuine discussion possible between them.

The political and religious differences I describe in this book have become increasingly vicious because the two sides no longer share a starting point. Arguments require exposing assumptions, and if those assumptions are diametrically opposed, then conversation inevitably breaks down. The talking heads shouting over each other on cable news shows illustrate this problem every day.

In the fall of 1994, I left teaching and became the publisher and editor of *Crisis* magazine in Washington, D.C. *Crisis,* a conservative Catholic monthly, was twelve years old. It was founded to do battle with the liberal wing of the Catholic Church but had never evolved beyond a small but dedicated readership. The magazine's location in Washington provided a unique platform from which to address the world of policy and politics from a Catholic perspective.

Shortly after taking over the magazine, I realized that *Crisis* needed to pay greater attention to practical politics in addition to the problems of dissent within the Catholic Church. In chapter eight of this book, I discuss at length how I became involved, as a consequence of this editorial decision, in an actual campaign and grassroots activism. It began with an invitation to attend a briefing on outreach to Catholic voters hosted by the Republican National Committee. My dissatisfaction with what I heard there led me to seek funding for a special report on the Catholic voter to be published in *Crisis*. I wanted to see if there were any hard data showing that successful political outreach to Catholics could be based on their commitment to the central social teachings of their faith. I floated the idea to several conservative Catholics in Washington who had the political background to do the research, and they agreed.

The outcome of the 1996 election firmly demonstrated that the GOP Catholic outreach was not effective. Senator Robert Dole received only 37 percent of the Catholic vote, a huge drop from previous national elections.

The findings of the *Crisis* Catholic Voter Project began to be published in November 1998, along with commentaries by Robert Novak, William McGurn, and Michael Barone. The research established that the steady migration of Catholic voters from the Democratic Party since the Kennedy presidency was most closely correlated to church attendance. In fact, we found that the real Catholic vote was a subgroup of all the Catholics who voted. The Catholic vote consisted of religiously active Catholics, not those who called themselves Catholic and never or rarely attended church. Catholics made up about 28 percent of all the voters in a national election, but religiously active Catholic voters were half of that number, about 14 million voters.

Catholics were moving toward the Republican Party because of the issues that coincided with the social teachings of the Church: concern for moral decline, priority of the family, education of children, and protection of innocent life. (A complete account of the polling and analysis will be found later in this book.) The Republican Party platform and candidates were appealing to religiously active Catholics who were primarily concerned about social issues centered on life and the family. The secular left either neglected these issues or represented positions that contradicted what practicing Catholics were taught in their parishes.

The articles in *Crisis* had unforeseen consequences. A month after they were published, I received a call from Bush's chief campaign strategist, Karl Rove. He asked if I would come to Austin to meet him and then-Governor Bush to talk about the articles. I spent a day with Rove, met Bush, and heard him give one of his early campaign stump speeches to Republicans from the South Carolina legislature. Shortly after, I agreed to become the informal and unpaid advisor to the campaign on outreach to Catholics. Never in my life had I imagined, or hoped, that I would become involved in politics.

The key to Catholic outreach in the Bush campaign was the creation of a national network that would support the candidate in his effort to communicate with Catholic voters. The campaign followed the main recommendations of the Catholic Voter Project: that practicing Catholics would respond to a candidate who supported values taught by their faith. This network became the mouthpiece to the Catholic grassroots for Governor Bush.

After the 2000 election, I became the volunteer chair of the new Catholic outreach of the Republican National Committee. Rove then asked me to select the members of the first-ever White House Catholic Working Group. The Working Group held weekly conference calls with White House personnel over the next four years, including the president and other members of the administration.

As the "chief Catholic surrogate" for the White House, it was my job to decide who was invited to meetings and events with the president and who was not. In short, I was the Catholic gatekeeper. Being new to the political world, I had little appreciation of how my new responsibilities would make me a target for attack.

Members of the Catholic Working Group advised on policies and appointments. For example, we pressed the White House for greater attention to life issues and, for the most part, were pleased with the results. But during the build-up to the Iraq invasion, a few of us begged the White House to presell the invasion to the Vatican, which it failed to do, seriously endangering the 2004 election. This was one of the few times the White House failed to act on one of our strong recommendations.

Much of Bush's first term was devoted to launching his faith-based initiative. I convened the first comprehensive meeting of Catholic leaders to discuss the faith-based initiative with the president and four members of his cabinet. However, it was primarily my role as writer and pundit that gave me the opportunity to explain my support for Bush and the reasons I thought other Catholics should do the same.

During the first term, I faced the resistance of the Catholic establishment to supporting a Republican administration. The head of the United States Conference of Catholic Bishops wrote a letter to President Bush protesting the existence of the Catholic Working Group, saying that the White House should deal solely with the Bishops' Conference. The bishops' news agency, the Catholic News Service, displayed a consistent bias against the Republican White House at every opportunity, as did most of the other media. These struggles became part of my routine until three months before the 2004 election.

I was at the vanguard of a sea change in political and religious history. Catholics were ripe to switch from the Democratic to the Republican Party. They were following in the footsteps of Evangelical voters of the '70s and '80s because issues of life and family values were on the brink of judicial extinction. A coalition of Catholic and Evangelical voters could successfully elect any national candidate they united to support—in sheer numbers, such a coalition was simply too large and too strategically placed to defeat.

Who would have thought in the midst of the late '60s or early '70s that religiously active Catholics and Evangelicals would emerge, thirty years later, with such cultural and political clout? The predictions of the death of God, the secularization of American culture, widespread moral relativism—all these have failed to claim the heart of America. This country has become more religious, not less, since the '60s. The religious organizations that have grown are both more traditional and very demanding, morally and spiritually, of their adherents. And these adherents have found ways to be heard in the midst of media dominated by bias on both coasts.

European nations have developed the kind of cultural and moral environments once predicted for the United States: low church attendance, little or no religious presence in the public arena, acceptance of moral relativism, rejection of all attempts to interject strong moral or religious arguments into politics, and a pervasive attitude that religion has become irrelevant. Why didn't the United States become like Europe? Our nation appeared to be poised on the brink of moving in that direction, but it never did. This is the story of why it did not happen and will not happen.

ONWARD, CHRISTIAN SOLDIERS

1

1979

I N 1976, *NEWSWEEK* FAMOUSLY ANNOUNCED THE "YEAR OF THE Evangelical."[1] Most people were not familiar with Evangelical piety at the time. To them, the headline seemed exactly right. For the first time, a self-professed Evangelical Christian—Jimmy Carter—was about to make his home in the White House. His candidacy was attracting the support of religious voters nationally. Most notable was the effect Carter was having on Evangelical pastors and communities across the South, where Republicans already had made serious inroads since the civil rights and busing controversies of the '60s. It appeared that religiously motivated voters, turned off by the '72 George McGovern candidacy, were returning to the Democratic Party.

The *Newsweek* headline introduced the country to the growth of the Evangelical movement. The mention of an Evangelical evoked an image of a Bible-toting hick who talked about "being saved" in a Southern accent. Carter didn't fit this stereotype, *and* he was a liberal. His politics were formed out of the crucible of the civil rights movement. "Carter is not a strict Evangelical," *Time* had written several months earlier.[2] Little

1. *Newsweek*, October 26, 1976.
2. *Time*, May 10, 1976.

explanation was given for this observation, which would turn out to be decisive for Carter's presidency. The article briefly mentions Carter's fondness for the theologian Reinhold Niebuhr, a figure unknown to the general public but whose influence on Protestant clergy in America was immense. A professor at Union Theological Seminary from 1928 to 1960, Niebuhr had a career that encompassed successive periods in American religion, from the Social Gospel of the '20s to the mainstream Protestant liberalism of the postwar period.

Carter was particularly taken with one sentence from Niebuhr: "The sad duty of politics is to establish justice in a sinful world." This reveals the fundamental difference of outlook between Carter and the Evangelicals he was supposed to represent. The federally enforced notion of justice was precisely what was fueling the coming revolution of the religious conservatives against Washington. Carter was an Evangelical whose White House activism aroused a slumbering giant known as the Religious Right.

Niebuhr's call for political elites to correct injustice, protect civil rights, and challenge structures of inequality was the dominant voice of religion in politics at the time. This kind of religious activism was not new in American politics; it was the bread and butter of the National Council of Churches and mainstream Protestantism. The fact that a Southerner, Carter, had become its principal spokesman was not new, either. The country was only a decade beyond the civil rights movement led by Dr. Martin Luther King Jr. What was new was that Carter— Southern *and white*—had unified other Southern Evangelicals behind his Democratic candidacy. The liberal base of the Democratic Party, uncomfortable with his public piety, made common cause with Evangelicals, still at odds with the party over civil rights issues. Evangelicals were about to learn a political lesson. They had signed on to support one of their own, or at least they thought so.

BREAKING WITH CARTER

Eight days before the election, Pat Robertson put his arms around a Sunday-school teacher from Plains, Georgia, on his nationally broadcast television program, *The 700 Club,* and called him "my Christian brother." After Evangelical voters were decisive in putting the Georgia governor into office, their brother soon disappointed and alienated them. Carter turned out not to be so Evangelical after all, at least by the standards of Fundamentalists and Pentecostals, such as Robertson, who had helped to make him president.

Carter's religious convictions were those of a mainstream Protestant, but he walked and talked like an Evangelical. He quoted the Bible more freely than any presidential candidate since William Jennings Bryan, but his religiously infused political passion for justice was formed by the civil rights movement, not by the culture wars that were stirring in the grass-roots of religious conservatives. Carter cared little for social issues such as abortion, homosexuality, and the militant feminism that had inflamed pockets of resistance around the country and were making activists out of conservative Christians.

In the late '70s, most of these Christians were Democrats from Democratic states, but President Carter was tone-deaf to the sense of cultural crisis in conservative religious communities across the country. His success as a candidate in winning the support of religious voters was short-lived. Through its actions, Carter's administration drove the conservative Christians back toward the Republican Party. It had shed its pro-abortion inclination just in time to receive them with open arms under the leadership of Ronald Reagan.

Carter's missteps were many, but they were unavoidable given his political vision. His zeal for imposing "justice" on segregated communities led to a showdown between the IRS and Christian schools in the South. He allowed the Internal Revenue Service to threaten these private schools, newly created since the busing days of the '60s, with the loss of their nonprofit status on the grounds of being segregated. Longtime activists and organizers credit this one initiative, more than any other, with the beginning of the Religious Right.

Nothing revealed Carter's distance from the Evangelicals who supported him more than his infamous 1979 White House Conference on Families. From the moment he allowed the conference to be renamed "On Families" from "On the Family" a train wreck was inevitable for the Carter administration. The name of the conference, which was created to rebuild religious support for Carter's reelection campaign, was changed under pressure from Democratic Party ideologues. As it turned out, Carter's sense of the justice that needed to be imposed on the "sinful world" comported better with the feminists in the Democratic Party left over from the McGovern campaign than with the Southern Baptists, Fundamentalists, Pentecostals, and conservative Catholics who had rallied to his candidacy.

Religious conservatives had a much different notion of the sins that needed to be addressed by their political representatives. Protecting the traditional family, not questioning it, was a first principle of their political vision. They felt they had no choice but to protect themselves against the Evangelical in the White House the way they had defended themselves against the Equal Rights Amendment. The struggle against the ERA, which began in 1972, already had created a loose network of Evangelicals, Mormons, conservative Catholics, and Jews who saw the amendment as a threat against the family and traditional gender roles and a pretext for abortion rights. Phyllis Schlafly, a Catholic activist, had rallied a coalition of religious conservatives to kill the ERA by 1979. Carter's "Conference on Families" succeeded in reenergizing the same troops for another battle. Schlafly, along with other religiously motivated activists, led the fight to subvert the left-wing agenda of the White House conference held in all fifty states during 1979.

Religious conservatives had demonstrated their grassroots muscle in the states where the ERA was defeated. Schlafly and others were ready to defend their values and way of life as not being the source of any social flaws. They were ready to bring their regional grassroots leaders to Washington. Two years earlier, as part of her anti-ERA effort, Schlafly had organized a successful counterdemonstration to another federally funded effort to challenge the traditional family, the Conference on Women in Houston. But Carter's White House Conference on Families, coupled with the IRS attack on Christian schools, made the White House and Congress the source of opposition for the newly created network of religious conservatives.

Evangelicals scratched their heads in disbelief as the Sunday-school teacher from southern Georgia provided a public platform for McGovernites to attack the man-woman-child norm of the family. With the White House itself calling into question the meaning of "the family" on the heels of Roe v. Wade (1973), the IRS investigation of Christian schools, and the feminist threat of ERA still hanging in the air, a cultural all-out attack on the core beliefs of religious conservatives was under way. Taken together, these initiatives were seen as nothing less than a declaration of war on their way of life and possibly something even more sinister: an assault on the content of faith itself. Sensitive to the threat of atheism from their anti-Communist days, the network continued to mobilize.

"The Religious Right was a reactionary movement with two strands: anti-Communism and the sexual revolution of the 1960s," says Tim Goeglein, a senior advisor to President George W. Bush. Goeglein knows a great deal about the politics of religious conservatives. Over the years, he has participated in thousands of conference calls and events involving the movers and shakers in the religious conservative movement. As associate director of coalitions for President Bush, Goeglein worked 24/7 with Catholic and Evangelical leaders to relay their concerns to the Bush administration. Before that, Goeglein, a Missouri Synod Lutheran, worked on the Senate staff for Senator Dan Coates (R-Idaho), who was a leading religious conservative.

His knowledge of the broader cultural horizons of the debate makes Goeglein a particularly interesting and succinct commentator. "Everything that has come out of the movement can be seen as a product of those reactions to the Communist threat and the sexual revolution. This," he explained, "was the reason the movement loved Reagan and hated Clinton." Reagan had firmly established his credentials as an anti-Communist during his years in Hollywood and later as governor of California. But it was as a social conservative that Reagan presented himself in the 1980 presidential campaign.

Conversely, "The reason the Religious Right's hatred for Bill Clinton was so venomous," Goeglein explained, "is that Bill Clinton was a proxy for '60s behavior; he embodied the same issues that created the movement in the first place. The Clinton presidency was eight years of feeling confirmed about its views of the sexual revolution. We would wake up each morning wondering what we missed in the White House soap opera of the previous twenty-four hours. The Clinton years," he added, "are a big part of the explanation why Governor George W. Bush could get such enthusiastic cooperation from religious conservatives during the 2000 presidential campaign."

I asked Goeglein if this animus toward Bill Clinton would carry over to Senator Hillary Clinton. "If Hillary is elected president, the Religious Right will reemerge so powerfully it will make its first iteration look like a cakewalk," he said. "It's important to remember that the most powerful leader of the Religious Right came to prominence because he was the anti–Dr. Spock, that is, Dr. James Dobson, founder and president of Focus on the Family." By the time Dobson wrote his groundbreaking book *Dare to Discipline* (1982), the ideas of Dr. Benjamin Spock and his imitators had become the establishment view. Dobson's name and message became supercharged after an appearance on *The Phil Donahue Show* where he tangled with the liberal Catholic host about the raising of children. Dobson's steady rise to movement leadership underlines the centrality of family issues as the hub of Religious Right concerns. "Dobson's Focus on the Family," as Goeglein put it, "has become the bricks and mortar of the Religious Right since the days of the Moral Majority and the Christian Coalition."[3]

ORGANIZING THE MOVEMENT

The Carter fiasco made Evangelicals realize they had no leverage against the president they helped to elect. Without outside groups such as the labor unions, they had no mechanism to apply pressure and deliver

3. The story of Dobson's rise to influence is told by Dan Gilgoff in *The Jesus Machine: How James Dobson, Focus on the Family, and Evangelical America Are Winning the Culture War* (New York: St. Martin's Press, 2007).

votes. The Carter campaign and election had brought Evangelicals onto the national stage; their preeminence as a religious force had finally been recognized. Also publicly recognized was an unexpected cost to mainstream Protestants: a significant loss of membership.

The disaffection with Carter made the year 1979, not 1976, the historical turning point for religious conservatives, both Catholic and Evangelical. They were not going to make that mistake again. Just as Clinton made Bush possible, so Carter paved the road to the White House for Reagan.

But at that moment in time, Evangelicals did not have an organization like the National Council of Churches to work their message through the media. What ongoing lobbying presence Evangelicals had in Washington, was either ineffective or out of step, just as Carter was, as a result of their growing discontent over social issues. It was during this time that two powerful Christian organizations emerged that would represent the needs and wishes of conservative Christians in the years to come.

Gary Jarmin's name is not as well known as those of other Religious Right leaders. He is president of Christian Voice, an organization he helped to create in 1979. Jarmin was present at the beginning and was a significant and innovative player throughout the growth of the Religious Right through the Reagan years. His organization continues to thrive, having registered nearly 350,000 voters in the 2004 campaign. Jarmin comes across as an affable veteran of D.C. politics and looks more like a career lobbyist than the Evangelical ministers he's organized over thirty years. Sitting in his office in Alexandria, Virginia, he spoke to me of the frustrations that led to the founding of Christian Voice.

Christian Voice was founded the year before the Moral Majority. The two fledgling organizations shared space in the same building on Capitol Hill in Washington in the early 1980s. A Baptist from California, Jarmin came to D.C. in 1971, eventually becoming legislative director of the American Conservative Union, founded in 1964. "I remember constantly encountering many of these prominent liberal clergymen, from mostly mainline denominations," said Jarmin. "All of these people would gather on Capitol Hill and were taking a very liberal or hard left line. It was frustrating. You would hear these guys running around lobbying members of Congress, testifying at committee hearings, presuming to represent all of Christendom. You'd have the National Council of Churches pretending to represent all of their denominations. You'd have the Baptist Committee guy talking as though he represented all Baptists in the U.S., and of course, you knew darn well that what was really represented there was a minority slice of opinion in those churches. In fact, I felt that I represented the political views and attitudes of most mainstream Protestants, Evangelicals, or Baptists. I found this very frustrating."

Jarmin continued to complain aloud about "all the liberals running around Capitol Hill pretending to represent all of Christendom" and was eventually introduced to someone who was doing something about the same problem in California. In 1974, Robert Grant started a group called American Christian Cause, and, like Anita Bryant in Florida, he fired one of the first flares of Religious Right activism, fighting the pornography and the homosexual lobby on the West Coast. Jarmin saw in Grant's activism the opportunity to start an "effective lobby for pro-family Christian values around the country." When the two finally met in 1977, they agreed that the conservative Christian community had no voice in Congress and decided to create one. "That's how the name came about. We were really the first Moral Majority." According to Jarmin, the first two major news stories about the Religious Right, in *Newsweek* and on *60 Minutes*, were both about Christian Voice.

"We made a decision at the beginning not to get a big name, like a Falwell, Bakker, or Swaggart. We wanted to make sure we were as broad-based and as eclectic as possible in terms of representing the Christian community. Fundamentalists, Pentecostals, mainstream Protestants, and Catholics—everyone would feel welcome and support what we did. If we picked one well-known leader of a particular domination or faction within a denomination, that would really limit our appeal to only those people," Jarmin told me.

Grant and Jarmin had correctly realized the need for someone to represent conservative Christians in Washington. Their timing in founding Christian Voice was impeccable. They sensed that it was only a matter of time until the culture "inside the Beltway" would step over the line and so outrage Evangelicals that they would be shaken loose from their disdain of politics. At the very moment he and Grant were getting organized, it happened.

Jarmin pointed to the IRS's threat against Christian schools in 1978 as the "spark that set off the powder keg." "Nothing gets Christian pastors mobilized faster than when their churches are being threatened. Suddenly, there was a genuine threat, Caesar coming in to take away the tax-exempt status of a church school, an appendix of a church, not a separate entity. By going after the schools, the government was in effect going after the Church. Evangelical Christians perceived the action as governmental interference with their civil right to teach and pass on to their children Christ-guided principles of how to distinguish right from wrong, sin from virtue."

Fortunately, the Carter administration's regulation was never fully promulgated or implemented. But the mere fact that the IRS was proposing and circulating this for public comment was enough to provide insight into their intention. For the conservative Christian movement, it was a blessing in disguise. There was probably nothing the left could have said or done that felt more like hitting the Christian community over the head with a two-by-four. The community was stirred and suddenly understood that the government was presenting a real threat to Christian education. Schools mobilized, associations suddenly got involved, and it became an integral part of an emerging Christian Right.

Christian Voice also anticipated the work of the Christian Coalition by using candidate scorecards and spreading them through networking in church groups. Jarmin recalled, "We were the first ones to do scorecards. I used to do ratings for the American Conservative Union, so I came up with the idea of doing them for Christian Voice. We used them in 1980 to target about thirty-two members of Congress." Initially, Jarmin encountered resistance from the churches. "We had two major challenges. One was what we considered bad theology. This was the attitude that good Christians are not going to associate with politics or get tainted by that. We'll all hang by our fingertips and wait for Jesus to come. We went to the ministers and said, 'Jesus taught us to be salt and light; we have to take dominion of our communities. There may be certain things we have to render unto Caesar, but our children won't be one of them.'"

The second challenge was the ministers' fear of violating the IRS, which was already threatening to strip the nonprofit status from their Christian schools. "We showed them the law. Sometimes they would check with their attorneys and get back to us, and they'd say it was okay. So first, we had to get them in the pot, and then we had to turn up the temperature. Next, we had their members register to vote. Then we said, 'Don't you think it would be a good idea to let them know where the candidates stand on our family biblical values?'"

FROM FEMINISM TO SECULARISM

One historian of the Religious Right, Ruth Murray Brown, calls 1979 the year of "transition between the first anti-feminist phase of the movement and the second anti-secularist Christian America phase."[4] It was the Carter administration's hostility toward Evangelical culture and values that propelled this evolution. After the founding of Christian Voice came Jerry Falwell's Moral Majority, Beverly LeHaye's Concerned Women for America, and Ed McAteer's Religious Roundtable. (James Dobson's fifteen-minute weekend radio show, *Focus on the Family*, was founded in 1977 but started expanding in 1979 when staff was hired to answer letters from listeners.) And since pollster George Gallup had just announced that the number of U.S. Evangelicals had grown from 40 million to 70 million between 1946 and 1979, there were plenty of potential voters for the new organizations to recruit.[5]

4. Ruth Murray Brown, *For a "Christian America": A History of the Religious Right* (Amherst, Mass.: Prometheus Books, 2002), 141.

5. These numbers are the result not only of population growth but of a reduction in market share of adherents to mainline Protestant denominations versus a dramatic rise in the percentage of Evangelicals. Between 1940 and 2000, United Methodists went down 56 percent, Episcopals 51 percent, Presbyterians (U.S.) 60 percent, while Southern Baptists were up 37 percent, Church of God in Christ 129 percent, Assemblies of God 221 percent, and Pentecostal Assemblies of the World 2,375 percent. See Roger Finke and Rodney Starke, *The Churching of America, 1776–2005: Winners and Losers in Our Religious Economy* (New Brunswick, N.J.: Rutgers University Press, 2005), 246.

These groups, and the others to follow, would combine to lead the majority of Evangelicals from the Democratic Party to the Republican. But in 1979, Evangelical Christians were not nearly as united in their theological and political perspectives as they would become in later elections. The Southern Baptist Convention, then and now the largest Protestant denomination in the United States, had significant pockets of liberal leadership expressing support for women's ordination, abortion, and laxer views of biblical interpretation. Major seminaries of the SBC, such as Southern Seminary in Louisville, Kentucky, and Southeastern Seminary in Wake Forest, North Carolina, were seen as under the control of liberal trustees, resulting in the hiring of faculty who did not believe in the "inerrancy" of Scripture. There was growing alarm that the SBC was going down the same road as mainline denominations in conforming to the latest political concerns of the secular culture.

The Carter years in the White House had an impact on the president's own religious denomination as well. At the annual meeting of the Southern Baptist Convention in Houston in 1979, a group of conservative pastors and laymen, including Paul Pressler, Reverend Paige Patterson, and Reverend Adrian Rodgers, met to create a plan to rid the SBC of its liberal leadership. By the time they were through, the Jimmy Carters of the SBC would be gone from positions of power and, for the most part, from the Convention itself. With the election of Rodgers at the Houston convention, a ten-year effort began effectively to purge the Southern Baptist Convention of liberals and unify it under conservative leadership by using Rodgers's power over the SBC's Committee on Committees. Consequently, several moderate-to-liberal Baptist organizations and seminaries were created, such as the Cooperative Baptist Fellowship in 1990 and McAfee School of Theology at Mercer University in 1994.

The changes at the SBC were a watershed for religious conservatives. As Ralph Reed, first executive director of the Christian Coalition, put it, "I consider the purging of the Southern Baptist Convention and the election of John Paul II the two most significant events for social conservatives in this country." John Paul II's papacy, whose first full year was 1979, would overcome much of the lingering anti-Catholic suspicion among Evangelicals toward Catholics. The pope's pro-life message inspired a de facto political coalition between conservative Catholics and Evangelical organizations such as Moral Majority, Christian Coalition, and Focus on the Family; their swelling numbers created outposts in non-Evangelical areas of the country.

A CATHOLIC STARTS THE MORAL MAJORITY

As Evangelicals' discontent with Jimmy Carter grew, they began to pin their hopes on a candidate without any Evangelical bona fides, who didn't speak with the Evangelical cadences that gave Carter his appeal. Nevertheless, this man, Ronald Reagan, became the president who empowered an entire generation of religious conservatives, enabling them to become the political movement known as the Religious Right. After a single term of Carter's presidency, Evangelicals voted decisively for Reagan. A *New York Times* and CBS voter exit poll showed that white "born-again" Protestants voted 61 percent for Reagan, 34 percent for Carter.

Prominent Evangelical leaders such as Falwell, Robertson, Grant, McAteer, LeHaye, and Dobson, along with other nationally known Evangelicals such as Reverend James Robison in Texas, Oral Roberts in Oklahoma, and Campus Crusade founder Bill Bright, threw themselves into the Reagan campaign as if the very future of our nation depended on it. Oddly enough, the strategy for bringing these Evangelical preachers and laymen into politics was the brainchild of a Catholic, Paul Weyrich, a conservative strategist who later became a deacon in the Melkite rite (the Melkite Greek Catholic Church is an Eastern rite Catholic church in communion with the Roman Catholic Church and the pope).

Beginning in 1979 and continuing to the 1980 election, Weyrich and his colleagues Howard Phillips and Connie Marshner traveled coast-to-coast recruiting ministers by explaining both what was at stake and how a nonprofit church could become political without risking tax exemption. It was a hard sell. Evangelicals had stayed out of politics since the *Scopes* trial debacle in 1925, believing such an active grappling with worldly matters beneath their spiritual mission. Yet when they realized that the power of the federal government and the judiciary was legitimizing the taking of human life, putting its religious schools and churches at risk, redefining the meaning of the family and sexuality, and forcing the teaching of secular and relativistic morality in public education, there was nothing to do but stand and fight.

Throughout the '70s, there had been bursts of Christian activism among ERA opponents and in local controversies in Florida, West Virginia, and California. But the event that galvanized the leadership occurred in February 1979 at a rally in Dallas held by Robison. A local television station, WFFA in Dallas, had taken the evangelist off the air because of his remarks about homosexuals who Robison claimed recruited children for sex acts. Twelve thousand attended a rally to protest the station's action and defend Robison's right to speak from a Christian perspective. (Future Arkansas Governor Mike Huckabee worked for Robison at the time and helped organize the meeting.)

Weyrich was asked to speak at the rally. As he recalls, Robison introduced him by saying, "Weyrich is a brother Cath-o-lic, and if any of you want to leave, do it now, because I don't want you in the room." Only six people left. Weyrich said this was the first time he witnessed the barrier between Evangelicals and Catholics begin to break down. Following the rally, WFFA put the show back on the air. But the rally itself, with its success, was not what galvanized Evangelical leadership; it was the meeting afterward.

Weyrich was surprised when Ed McAteer came up to him after his speech and told him that he had organized a meeting of ministers and lay leaders, including Jerry Falwell and prominent Dallas minister W. A. Criswell, and wanted him "to tell them what they needed to do." Weyrich went and took with him a Dallas pollster named Lance Torrance. This was fortunate. Speaking extemporaneously, he told the group, "I have talked to any number of you, and you are telling me that you can't get involved in the political process because your congregations will not support both your church activities and any political activities you might engage in. . . . We need to find out if this is the case now." Weyrich then introduced Torrance, saying, "We need to take a poll. What is it going to cost?"

Weyrich raised the required amount, $30,000, on the spot, commissioning the survey from Dick Wirthlin's D.C. firm to find out whether members of Evangelical churches wanted their leaders involved in the political process, whether they would continue to support their contributions to the church, and whether they were prepared for the inevitable negative reaction. The most important question to be asked, according to Weyrich, was, "Since you have been told that it is a virtual sin to be involved in politics, are you willing to become political, based upon what is going on in the country?"

The results of the Weyrich-commissioned survey were delivered at a Religious Roundtable meeting in late December in Washington. Shortly after the Robison rally, McAteer had created the Religious Roundtable, and attendance at the first meeting included most of the future leaders of the Religious Right, including Pat Robertson, Jerry Falwell, Howard Phillips, James Robison, and Beverly LeHaye. The survey showed that church members were *demanding* that their leaders be involved in the political process. Jan Vandelhausen from Wirthlin, who made the presentation, said he had never seen polling results that showed such a sense of urgency. Evangelicals would support financially *both* their churches and a political effort.

Other denominations were not as ready to engage in the culture war. Results showed that the groups least inclined to become politically active were mainline Protestants, followed closely by Catholics. But Evangelicals, especially the Southern Baptists, were, as Weyrich recalled, "off the charts," as were the Missouri synods of Lutherans and Mormons. "That was life-changing, when these guys saw that. They fell over themselves to start some activity or to involve themselves," Weyrich remembered.

The success of his postrally meeting in Dallas and the survey results encouraged McAteer to continue his briefings, which culminated in the now-famous speech of candidate Ronald Reagan at a Religious Roundtable meeting in Dallas in 1980. It was at this gathering that Reagan said, "I know you cannot endorse me, but I endorse you." Weyrich further recollected, "We gave him a ten-minute standing ovation. I've never seen anything like it. The whole movement was snowballing by then." Connie

Marshner, who was also there, told me she had "never heard such a loud noise."

Ed McAteer, as a salesman for Colgate Palmolive, had made it a point to meet the Evangelical ministers in whatever town he visited. He offered to introduce Weyrich to his network of ministers around the country. Thus, Weyrich met pastors such as Robison, Falwell, Robertson, Charles Stanley, and Adrian Rodgers and important laymen such as Paul Pressler, who later led the purging of liberals from the Southern Baptist Convention.

It was in one of these meetings with Jerry Falwell that the idea of the Moral Majority was born. In May 1979, McAteer and Weyrich had flown on a private plane to Lynchburg, Virginia, along with attorney Alan Dye, who was there to explain the legalities of setting up a political organization. Howard Phillips did not arrive at the meeting on time, and Weyrich, knowing that Falwell was a fanatic about starting meetings on time, began the meeting. Weyrich said, "Out there is a moral majority . . ." Falwell interrupted and said, "What did you say about a moral something?" Weyrich, stumbling, said, "You mean the moral majority?" Falwell turned to an associate and said, "If we have an organization, that will be its name."

The Moral Majority was founded a month later, in June 1979.

There was no overt display of religious conservatism in 1979 among U.S. Catholics to match the turbulence of Evangelicals entering politics. Catholics who had led the pro-life movement since the '60s had joined, with the help of the Catholic bishops, to create National Right to Life, but it would be years before NRL would have a significant voice in politics.

The Catholic left was in its ascendancy, and there was no core group of laymen, as in the SBC, who had the power to challenge it. By the late '70s, political and theological liberalism became the dominant voice in Catholic colleges, universities, publications, and associations. Pro-life Catholics were becoming alienated from their bishops and the Catholic Conference and, just as Evangelicals did, gave up on Jimmy Carter. Catholics, disgusted with the turning away from life issue at the Conference, started to send money to Falwell's Moral Majority.

These same Catholic pro-lifers soon would find themselves in the awkward position of being judged not pro-life enough by American bishops. Leading bishops, emboldened by radical changes in the Church, extended the pro-life agenda to housing, health care, education, and welfare assistance, among other things. Catholic activists who simply wanted to overturn *Roe* v. *Wade* by passing the Human Life Amendment were excluded from the centers of Catholic power because they wouldn't embrace the liberal agenda. The bishops themselves created an office in 1973 devoted specifically to passing the Human Life Amendment, but by 1979, few Catholics were aware that it existed.

THE U.S. CATHOLIC CHURCH MOVES LEFT

The United States Conference of Catholic Bishops in Washington, D.C., and the United States Catholic Conference were created in 1966 on the heels of the Second Vatican Council (1962–65). The two-part structure of the conferences was originally intended to provide more input from parts of the Church not officially connected to the bishops. As Russell Shaw, who worked at the conferences for eighteen years, put it, "The USCC was intended in the minds of the people who created it to evolve into a national pastoral council, a structure involving the collaborative interaction of bishops, priests, religious, and lay people in hammering out and implementing the Church's sociopolitical program in the United States."

In other words, the dual structure of the conferences was to encourage the adoption of a collaborative model for the U.S. Church and weakening of the centuries-old hierarchical model. It is no accident that in 1967, twenty-six Catholic college presidents met at the Land O' Lakes Conference Center in Wisconsin to declare their "independence" from the Church hierarchy.[6] The so-called spirit of Vatican II was blowing through the creation of the Catholic Conference and the Land O' Lakes statement. A quarter-century later, Catholic dissident groups such as

6. George A. Kelly, *The Battle for the American Church* (Garden City, N.Y.: Image Books, 1981), 62.

Call to Action and Voice of the Faithful still would be insisting on the democratization of the Church, which was assumed in the mid-'70s to be just around the corner.

Both Catholic conferences were closely aligned with the Democratic Party from their inception, which is only to be expected given the historic relationship of Catholics and Democrats. According to the only major study of the public-policy positions of the bishops, 1979 marked the year that the U.S. Conference of Catholic Bishops and the U.S. Catholic Conference declared their adoption of "liberal policy prescriptions," as exemplified in their 1979 pastoral letter, "Brothers and Sisters to Us":[7]

> The structures of our society are subtly racist, for these structures reflect the values which society upholds. They are geared to the success of the majority and the failure of the minority. Members of both groups give unwitting approval by accepting things as they are. Perhaps no single individual is to blame. The sinfulness is often anonymous but nonetheless real. The sin is social in nature in that each of us, in varying degrees, is responsible. All of us in some measure are accomplices. As our recent pastoral letter on moral values states: "The absence of personal fault for an evil does not absolve one of all responsibility. We must seek to resist and undo injustices we have not caused, lest we become bystanders who tacitly endorse evil and so share in guilt in it."[8]

For the bishops, sin was not confined to the individual person. Sin now existed in social structures—and every individual who lived within these structures was guilty of "anonymous sin," whatever that is. Thus, it was no longer enough for someone to cultivate love for God and one's neighbor; suddenly, it was necessary to change social "structures." People

7. Michael Warner, *Changing Witness: Catholic Bishops and Public Policy, 1917–1994* (Washington, D.C.: Ethics and Public Policy Center, 1995), 104.

8. "Brothers and Sisters to Us," U.S. Catholic Bishops Pastoral Letter on Racism, 1979. The quote within the quote is from "Live in Christ Jesus," issued by the bishops in 1976.

are not the only racists; social structures themselves are racist. And, of course, it falls to the federal government to reengineer society through its various means of redistributing income and giving preferential treatment to groups claiming discrimination. Catholics were left in the odd position of overcoming their sin by demanding that the federal government use its power to restructure society according to the vision of the Bishops Conference. One wonders if voting against Jimmy Carter in 1980 or Walter Mondale in 1984 should have been a matter for the confessional. No matter, it wouldn't be long before the same staff would be advocating changes in social structures that led to abortion rather than focusing on changing the laws that permitted it.

Conference staff and leading bishops at this time were animated by this egalitarian ideology that eventually alienated the longtime base of Catholic voters from the Democratic Party—the proof of which was to be seen shortly in the surprise victory of Ronald Reagan over Jimmy Carter in 1980. The now well-known description of the Conferences as "the Democratic Party at prayer" was elicited by eight years of unrelenting attacks on the Republican administration by Catholic bishops and Conference staffers.

The representation of the faith by the Conference in the late '70s was replaced with a social service and civil rights mission. The Conference contributed to the public misperception that pro-lifers were not active in feeding, clothing, and educating the poor. That being pro-life was represented, in and of itself, as a dereliction of Catholic duty made it possible to depict pro-lifers as "sinful." The USCCB began a crusade to make the catechetical and scriptural teachings on the sanctity of life a political and in fact "Republican" issue that should be alienated from Catholic theology and academics.

These two conferences, which essentially operated as one, replaced the National Catholic Welfare Conference, founded in 1919. The intent of the newly created organizations in Washington was to provide the U.S. bishops with a more effective and visible lobbying arm to Congress and the White House. The NCWC had relied on the traditional and inherently conservative understanding of Catholic social teaching based on the natural-law tradition as articulated by Saint Thomas Aquinas and his later interpreters, especially Pope Leo XIII.

The new Bishops Conference and especially the staffers at the U.S. Conference didn't have much time for Aquinas, Leo XIII, or his magisterial encyclical *Rerum Novarum* (1891). The U.S. Catholic Church was, at this moment, looking only ahead, not backward. It was enveloped in a progressive, sometimes revolutionary mood following Vatican II. At the Bishops Conference and the Catholic Conference, the Thomism (shorthand for the philosophy of Saint Thomas Aquinas) of preceding generations was deemed unsuitable to address the complex realities of the modern world, particularly the need to cooperate with non-Catholics in pursuit of social change. (The battle of the legacy of Thomism and its reliance on natural law is analogous to the battle over the interpretation of Scripture among Southern Baptists that arose in the mid-'80s resulting in a purge that strengthened the Religious Right.) Thomistic Catholic theology, with its carefully preserved hierarchies of knowledge and authority, had been taught to the generation of bishops and staff who controlled the Catholic conferences in Washington. But Thomism gave way to a politicized theology focused on the "sinful" social structures and the need for greater social activism.

The move toward social activism meant that the voice of the Catholic bishops, as expressed through the Conference, was going to become less effective as it sought to address more and more issues. And as they lobbied on particular pieces of legislation, at several steps distant from traditional Catholic social teaching, their moral authority was diminished. As a result, "American bishops in the NCCB now hesitated to assert that the Catholic faith holds truth for all society. They were even more reluctant to criticize the ideological sources of error or vice, or to insist that true social progress and its source and end is in Christ."[9]

The kind of perspective proposed by Reinhold Niebuhr and embraced by Jimmy Carter was the bread and butter of the Catholic left, but it was now being radicalized by large doses of Marxism through the influence

---

9. Warner, *Changing Witness,* 167.

of liberation theology. Catholic pro-lifers were told that social structures were responsible for abortion—not activist judges, not feminists—and it was the duty of all Catholics to change them.

Jerry Falwell later estimated that one-third of his seven million Moral Majority members were Catholics. They had nowhere else to go. The actions of the American bishops and their conference staffers were driving pro-life Catholics into political collaboration with Evangelicals, two groups who for years had looked upon each other with near disdain. Ralph Reed estimated that 25 percent of his Christian Coalition members were Catholics. Even today, large numbers of Catholics support organizations led by Evangelical ministers: American Family Association and Focus on the Family.

There were still many bishops who had not embraced the shift to the left, but with the creation of a center of operations in Washington, those bishops, now viewed as "conservative" or "pre-Vatican II," watched helplessly as liberal or radical staffers produced documents on every left-wing issue. This rejection of the politicization of the Catholic theology in the style of a "social gospel" had been a mainstream Catholic position since early in the century.[10] Those voices now found themselves in the minority. Conference staffers were alarmed by the election of Ronald Reagan in 1980 and for the next eight years did everything they could to thwart his administration. As Michael Warner so judiciously puts it, "During the 1980s, the leaders of the NCCB and the USCC consciously resolved to play a 'prophetic' role in confronting the errors of the Reagan administration."[11] The bishops' major pastoral letters of the '80s, one on war and peace, another on justice and the economy, were aimed at the heart of the Reagan agenda, with the hope that Catholic voters would return to the Democratic Party. (They didn't, at least not until Bill Clinton's defeat of George H. W. Bush in 1992.)

The beginning steps toward the new liberal paradigm for Catholic social teaching were taken by its first president, Bishop John F. Dearden;

10. Thomas E. Woods, *The Church Confronts Modernity: Catholic Intellectuals and the Progressive Era* (New York: Columbia University Press, 2004), 146–47.

11. Warner, *Changing Witness*, 148.

the first general secretary, Bishop Joseph Bernardin; the first assistant general secretary, Father James S. Rausch; and the first director of the Office of International Justice and Peace, Father J. Brian Hehir. They became the major architects for the new model of political theology focused on the issue of social justice. Among these figures, it was Rausch, not Bernardin, as is commonly thought, who was the most committed to a liberalizing agenda. Rausch, who became the second general secretary, was a strong proponent of liberation theology and made its principal assumption the foundation of subsequent policy pronouncements by the bishops: "All inequalities of wealth and power that are not immediately tied to some greater service for the common good are oppressive."[12] Their interpretation of the "preferential option of the poor" made what had been understood as an act of charity into an obligation of justice and a first principle of public policy.

Later on, Bernardin, with the aid of Hehir, devised a "consistent ethic of life" known as the "seamless garment" that defined being pro-life to include positions on poverty reduction, housing, education, health care, war, and nuclear deterrence. His motivation for this, according to Russ Shaw, was not an attempt to bury the defense of unborn life under a plethora of other issues. Bernardin had been badly burned in 1976, when he was tasked by the bishops with interviewing candidates Jimmy Carter and President Gerald Ford. Bernardin was surprised and disappointed to discover that Carter refused to support the Human Life Amendment, and he said so. When he said publicly that he was "encouraged" by Ford's support for the amendment, the Conferences erupted with anger toward Bernardin. As Shaw remembers, "Bernardin found out that you could never expect support from Catholic conservatives." The seamless-garment approach, Bernardin hoped, would force the left to embrace the defense of life as part of *their* consistent ethic of life.

One Catholic pro-life activist put it this way: "Realistically speaking, the bishops made their own bed. Who was the party of the first part in abandoning support? The bishops abandoned us. They should have

12. Ibid., 99.

expected no more support in the public square than they gave. By then, our families were under siege on the parish level and we were frantically trying to keep our children from embracing the dissent they ignored." Archbishop Rembert Weakland of Milwaukee expressed the view of many bishops and Conference staffers when he said later that Catholic pro-lifers needed "a laxative and a hug." [13]

In spite of Bernardin's intentions, the broadening of the pro-life position enabled the Catholic Conferences to back away from the abortion issue and distance themselves from pro-life activists who were demanding more action from the bishops. The USCC message to the pro-life community was clear: "If you are not visibly active in promoting these programs of redistribution then you are not truly pro-life." The American bishops, who truly can be credited for helping to lead the pro-life movement after *Roe* v. *Wade,* gradually withdrew from grassroots involvement to attend to what they considered larger matters. John Cardinal O'Connor of New York City, the pope's point man in the United States, was one obvious exception among others, including Bernard Cardinal Law of Boston.

While the American bishops were moving left, there was a different wave of change in the Vatican. The election of Reagan may have alarmed the Conference staff in Washington, D.C., and led to a series of anti-Reagan pastoral letters, but the election of Karol Cardinal Wojtyla as pope in late 1978 had consequences they could not thwart.

The liberal establishment in the United States was surprised by the choice of the first Polish pope and didn't know what to expect. But with John Paul II's first encyclical, *Redemptor Hominis* (1979) and his first trips to the United States and Latin America, it was clear the new pontiff was going to challenge the new politicized theology that had taken hold in the Americas. At the same time, he was not going to countenance dissent on issues such as abortion, contraception, or female priests. On his first trip to the United States, John Paul II proclaimed on the Mall in Washington, D.C., "No one ever has the authority to destroy unborn

13. Ibid., 148.

life." In Chicago, he spoke in support of the ban on contraception and addressed the lack of confession.

John Paul II set out to restore the traditional moral and social teaching of the Catholic Church, which he called the "culture of life." In this act of restoration, which he considered the true "spirit" of Vatican II, John Paul II empowered a movement of religious conservatism among Catholics that started down the political path cleared by the Evangelicals in the late '70s and early '80s.

There were no Catholic movements or organizations to match the Evangelicals' Moral Majority or the Christian Broadcasting Network. But there were scores of small entrepreneurial apostolates that arose to reassert Catholic orthodoxy in the face of Catholic institutions that were openly practicing and endorsing dissent from Church teaching. These apostolates enjoyed little, if any, support from the Catholic bishops. They were driven by charismatic and determined individuals who overcame the opposition and hostility of many bishops and staff from the Catholic Conference. Some of these apostolates became quite influential; Lyman Stebbins's Catholics United for the Faith, Father Paul Marx's Human Life International, Judie Brown's American Life League, Father Joseph Fessio's Ignatius Press, Mother Angelica's Eternal Word Television Network, and an organization for Catholic CEOs called Legatus, created by Domino's Pizza founder Tom Monaghan.

Monaghan, before he started building Ave Maria University in Naples, Florida, became something of a Medici figure in the renaissance of Catholic orthodoxy. His office complex in Ann Arbor, Michigan, Domino's Farms, had an entire wing reserved for Catholic apostolates, including the Thomas More Society, the Spiritus Sanctus Academies, and Legatus. So strong was Monaghan's influence that a group of Dominican nuns, led by Mother Assumpta Long, started a community on property adjacent to Monaghan's headquarters. Without Monaghan's support, many of the new conservative apostolates, including Mother Angelica's EWTN, would not have survived.

CONSERVATIVE CATHOLIC
LEADERS EMERGE

Other conservative apostolates, along with many of the bishops appointed after 1979, would become the outposts of John Paul II's message to American Catholics. Normally, this would be the work of colleges, universities, seminaries, media, and intellectuals. But in the late '70s, these were almost entirely in the hands of the Catholic left. National leadership figures emerged, such as Father Richard Neuhaus, editor of *First Things;* Mary Ann Glendon, professor at Harvard Law School; Robert George, political philosophy professor at Princeton University; Mary Ellen Bork, wife of Judge Robert Bork; Kate O'Beirne, a writer for *National Review;* Bill Donohue, president of the Catholic League for Religious and Civil Rights; and Scott Hahn, formerly a Protestant minister who became a best-selling author for Doubleday. New publications such as *Crisis, Catholic World Report, Fidelity, Lay Witness,* and *This Rock* took up the cause. Largely Catholic pro-life groups such as American Life League, National Right to Life, and Human Life International and orthodox colleges such as Christendom College, St. Thomas Aquinas College, University of Dallas, St. Thomas More, Magdalen College, Ave Maria College (now a university), Ave Maria School of Law, and Father Michael Scanlon's revived Franciscan University of Steubenville led in the work of evangelizing the culture following the inspiration of John Paul II. It was at Franciscan University that charismatic Catholics found an institution to welcome them. The movement of charismatic renewal among Catholics had begun with the Word of God community in Ann Arbor, Michigan, founded by Ralph Martin. The Word of God community became very important in the creation of an Evangelical subculture in the U.S. Catholic church supporting the leadership of John Paul II.

In the early days of his pontificate, John Paul II not only confronted the left in the Church, starting with the Jesuits, but also protected and encouraged these orthodox apostolates. These included the charismatic renewal movements and organizations such as Opus Dei and the Legionnaires of Christ. The pope came to the aid of Mother Angelica and

EWTN when it was unpopular with some bishops and the U.S. Catholic Conference. His popularity reinforced the leadership of Bill Donohue in fighting anti-Catholic prejudice at the Catholic League for Religious and Civil Rights. Most of all, John Paul II legitimized the work of pro-life activists who fought abortion directly through legislation and judicial review. His teaching of a culture of life directly challenged the left's political message of the "seamless garment" favored by the Bishops Conference, an approach that put the prohibition of abortion on a par with issues such as ending homelessness. As a result, Catholic politicians in the Democratic Party found it more difficult to pretend their pro-abortion stance conformed to Catholic teaching.

Reagan's appeal to Catholics in the 1980 campaign, and throughout his terms in office, accelerated the migration of Catholics into the GOP. His appeal to Catholics was more natural than it had been with Evangelicals—after all, one of his most famous roles had been that of the "Gipper" in a film about Notre Dame football coach Knute Rockne. Many Catholic voters just assumed he was Catholic or Irish or both. Among Catholic voters, there was a similar sense of alienation from the Democratic Party over social issues that had disaffected Evangelicals. Out of Reagan's message of patriotism and traditional values, the so-called Reagan Democrat was born, a usually ethnic, usually Catholic, usually Northern or Midwestern version of the Evangelical voter who could not stomach the ideological drift of the Democratic Party. The Bishops Conference would find out that Reagan Democrats could not be won back to the Democratic Party with liberal pastorals on peace and economic justice.

The year 1979 was a tipping point, when Democrats lost their allegiance to the party of their parents and began identifying with the GOP as social or religious conservatives. It was the Reagan Democrats, mostly Catholic, and the Southern Democrats, mostly Evangelical, who would provide the Republican Party with an entirely new generation of voters to have an impact on elections into the twenty-first century.

2

WAS PAT BUCHANAN RIGHT?

"THERE IS A RELIGIOUS WAR GOING ON IN OUR COUNTRY FOR THE soul of America. It is a cultural war, as critical to the kind of nation we will one day be as was the Cold War itself." The date was August 17, 1992, the place the Republican National Convention in Houston. Pat Buchanan, defeated by Vice President George Bush in a bitter primary, was in the midst of a speech scheduled during primetime on Monday night. It was a chance to deliver his message to the entire nation.

A year earlier, a University of Virginia sociologist, James Davidson Hunter, published *Culture Wars: The Struggle to Define America*.[1] Hunter had announced in the academic community the same conflict broadcast to the nation by Buchanan in his convention speech. Since then, the notion of culture wars has become the shorthand describing the clash between secular liberalism and religious conservatism.

Hunter provided the intellectual construct to understand the issues dividing the nation, but it was Buchanan who took the gloves off and used the spotlight of a national political convention to name what would eventually divide America into red and blue states. Buchanan called it a

---

1. James Davidson Hunter, *Culture Wars: The Struggle to Define America* (New York: Basic Books, 1991).

"religious war" because it was *about* religion; Hunter called it a "culture war" because the regional differences created by differing forms of religious practice were exposed.

History has proven both of them correct. The religious war produced a cultural fault line. It opened quietly at first, but once Buchanan brought the fact of that war into the open, the ensuing debate opened the chasm even wider.

Barry Lynn agrees with Buchanan: "Buchanan's rhetoric was strident and his remedies unthinkable—but he was right about the existence of this 'war.' Our side did not start it, but it does exist."[2] Lynn, as executive director of Americans United for the Separation of Church and State, has been one of the leading critics of the Religious Right for more than a decade. He contends that it's a mistake to pretend this war over religion doesn't exist: "We'll just end up whistling past the graveyard of our Bill of Rights and religious freedom if we take that road." Lynn delineates the two sides of the dispute. For Buchanan, the war is about religious citizens having their say and retaining their influence on public policy. For Lynn, it's about religious people keeping their religious opinions to themselves. Religious freedom for one is the freedom to have influence; for the other, it is the freedom from being influenced.

Lynn's first principle is the "wall of separation" mentioned by Thomas Jefferson is his famous letter to the Danbury Baptist Association in 1802. Putting aside the validity of the wall as a constitutional principle, here is how Lynn explains the importance of separating church and state: "The wall means no one can force your children to pray in public schools against your wishes. It means your schoolchildren will learn modern biology, not Bible stories masquerading as science. It means religious groups must rely on moral suasion, not the raw power of the state to convince people to adopt their views. It means religious organizations must pay their own way in this world, not rely on government-provided handouts coerced from the taxpayer."[3]

2. Barry W. Lynn, *Piety and Politics: The Right-Wing Assault on Religious Freedom* (New York: Harmony Books, 2006), 4.
3. Ibid., 17.

On first reading, this list of complaints left me wondering if all that divide us are particular issues—school prayer, evolution, the faith-based initiative. Then I went back to the statement "religious groups must rely on moral suasion, not the raw power of the state" and realized how much Lynn had left unsaid. A basic disagreement with religious conservatives about religious liberty underlies the entire discussion. Lynn characterizes the use of the democratic process by the Religious Right as enlisting "the raw power of the state." Liberal critics such as Lynn are always contradicting themselves. They believe steadfastly in big government, big entitlement programs, and activist judges to enact the policies that Congress or the state legislatures fail to pass. But when it comes to any legislation or government program that embodies conservative values, they start yelling about the imposition of religion. The 1947 *Everson* v. *Board of Education* decision enshrined this form of bad argument. Drafted by Justice Hugo Black, this decision incorporated Jefferson's notion of the wall of separation into American jurisprudence. The issue before the Supreme Court was whether or not local school boards should pay the transportation costs of students to private (i.e., Catholic) schools. By a 5–4 decision, the Court ruled against it. Justice Black stretched the notion of establishing a religion to the much broader idea of aiding or benefiting religion:

> The "establishment of religion" clause of the First Amendment means at least this: Neither a state nor the Federal Government can set up a church. Neither can pass laws which aid one religion, aid all religions, or prefer one religion over another. Neither can force nor influence a person to go to or to remain away from church against his will or force him to profess a belief or disbelief in any religion. No person can be punished for entertaining or professing religious beliefs or disbeliefs, for church attendance or non-attendance. No tax in any amount, large or small, can be levied to support any religious activities or institutions, whatever they may be called, or whatever form they may adopt to teach or practice religion. Neither a state nor the Federal Government can, openly or secretly, partici-

pate in the affairs of any religious organizations or groups and vice versa. *In the words of Jefferson, the clause against establishment of religion by law was intended to erect "a wall of separation between Church and State."*

Without Black's tenuous argument, secularists such as Lynn lack the rationale to protest against religious influence on legislation and public policy. Black himself was a former member in the '20s of the Robert E. Lee Klan No. 1 cell of the Ku Klux Klan in Birmingham, Alabama. Anti-Catholicism and anti-Semitism were KKK specialties in addition to racism. That Black would reach into a private letter of Thomas Jefferson to extract the "wall of separation" language suggests a strong animus was in play in writing the *Everson* decision. Federal and state aid to parochial schools had been a contentious issue in American politics for a century, and Black obviously wanted to end the debate.

Lynn's organization was founded in 1947 as Protestants and Other Americans United for Separation of Church and State, a watchdog group against the growth of Catholic influence. There is no reason to think that Lynn is anti-Catholic, though he still has the unfortunate habit of referring to the "Roman Catholic Church of the Middle Ages" as the model of what he opposes.[4] Lynn wants to talk about the imposition of an alien standard, but what about his imposition of a secular standard of government in the thirteenth century? One thing that can be said for Lynn, however, is that he is consistent. He is one of the few on the left who didn't welcome the publication of *God's Politics* by Religious Left leader Jim Wallis. Democrats hailed Wallis's work as the long-awaited answer to the Religious Right, but Lynn wrote: "I read the book as a misguided attack on both secular values and groups that seek to base U.S. public policy on something other than the interpretation of their favorite holy scripture."[5] Lynn's reaction is indicative of the split that will take place in the Democratic Party as it tries to straddle the war over religion.

Most Democratic Party leadership has grown comfortable support-

4. Ibid., 43.
5. Ibid., 167.

ing the kinds of attacks on religious conservatives that became common after the Buchanan speech. There were already numerous anti-Religious Right groups, the first of which was Norman Lear's People for the American Way, founded in 1981. But in 1994, the Anti-Defamation League published *The Religious Right: The Assault on Tolerance and Pluralism in America.* Given the respect afforded to this organization, the release of this study dramatically raised the ante. The ADL accused the Religious Right of being undemocratic, exclusionist, hysterical, paranoid, and coercive, and that's only in the first two pages.

By basing its study on this definition, the ADL ensured that its analysis could ignore the religious, philosophical, moral, and scientific concerns that animated the movement. Instead, the organization asserted misleading generalizations, such as its depiction of the Religious Right as "an array of politically conservative religious groups and individuals who are attempting to influence public policy based on a shared cultural philosophy that is antagonistic to pluralism and church/state separation."[6] It's laughable to think that those in the Religious Right would recognize themselves as aligned behind a "shared cultural philosophy." It was their faith and their overlapping religious creeds that united them and provided the core concerns that motivated their political action.

Throughout its study, the ADL avoided debating the issues of greatest concern to religious conservatives in favor of championing the cause of pluralism, as if that were some sort of value in and of itself. And its account of the separation of church and state became just another tactic to avoid debate on moral issues by disqualifying religiously held values from having influence on public policy and legislation. The ADL study would become the template for dozens of Religious Right critics to follow, especially in the years following the 2000 presidential victory of George W. Bush.

6. *The Religious Right: The Assault on Tolerance and Pluralism in America* (New York: Anti-Defamation League, 1994), 7.

DEFINING THE TERMS

In defending the Religious Right against its critics, I use "Religious Right" to refer to those who identify themselves with the movement and ignore the pejorative meaning the phrase may convey to others. "Religious conservatives" is used to denote a larger group of religious leaders and voters who do not identify with the movement but share a religious foundation for their similar values, issue priorities, and voting habits. The ADL study correctly mentions Reverend Billy Graham, and Reverend Robert Schuller as examples of this group. Graham has avoided mixing politics with religion since he was tangled up for defending Nixon after the Watergate break-in. But his deliberate cultivation of U.S. presidents, beginning with Harry Truman, was a foreshadowing of the Religious Right.[7] Schuller, privately a Republican, enjoyed his regular access to the White House but avoided any public expression of a political preference.

Sometimes religious conservatives are called social conservatives when their values and issue priorities are viewed without regard for religious beliefs or motivation. But for consistency's sake, I will use "social conservatism" only when referring to those voters who apply secular and philosophical rather than theological principles as the basis for their values and public policy. This includes conservatives who are pro-life but not primarily for theological reasons. Spokesmen for the Religious Right prefer to use "social conservatives" for tactical reasons when referring to themselves and other religious conservatives. Social conservatism has become the code word for the Religious Right when talking in polite company.

Some social conservatives think they would be better off if the Religious Right were driven from the field. They are fooling themselves if they think that their more philosophical approach, sometimes called a natural-law perspective, would not suffer as a result. The natural-law

---

7. Graham, working through Congressman John McCormack, got a meeting in the summer of 1950 with Truman in the White House. Truman, however, was angry when Graham revealed all the details of the meeting to reporters and posed for photographers with three associates in prayer in front of the executive residence; see William Martin, *With God on Our Side: The Rise of the Religious Right in America* (New York: Broadway Books, 1996), 30.

tradition of accepting the moral order as discovered in nature is under-stood and accepted almost exclusively in traditional religious communi-ties. Anything that weakens the existence of that religious presence in politics would undermine the social conservative approach as well—it's the religious community that demands attention be given to scientific findings that bolster its value claims.

The new, younger leaders among religious conservatives want to stay away from the "Religious Right" for more than the tactical reasons men-tioned earlier. Drew Ryun is a son of five-term Congressman Jim Ryun (R-Kansas), who was defeated in 2006. Drew Ryun and his twin brother, Ned, have been political operatives in the GOP since they graduated from college in 1996. Drew is the director of government affairs for the American Center for Law and Justice and served with the Republican National Committee as head of Evangelical outreach for the 2004 elec-tion. He told me, "The 'Religious Right' brings back visions of the Moral Majority, Jerry Falwell, and hellfire-and-brimstone imagery. That's not where we are now." As will be discussed in a later chapter, Ryun's desire to distance himself from the Religious Right is shared by many of the influential pastors in the megachurch network. For Ryun, it's not just a matter of terminology but a statement of fact: "We are not on the right— we are Evangelical Christians and conservative Catholics in the main-stream of America. That's what we should be called, the mainstream." Ryun's view that religious conservatism is mainstream America was shared by the movement leaders, young and old, whom I interviewed. From this, one may deduce that an attack on the Religious Right is an at-tack on mainstream America, not on a small extreme element living on the margins.

Although secular liberals might dispute who represents the so-called mainstream, they do agree that religious conservatives inhabit a cultural domain very distinct from their own. Secular liberal culture is consid-ered alien and hostile to religious conservatives, while the culture of reli-gious conservatives is considered oppressive and condemning to secular liberals. As a result, attacks on religious conservatives in politics can be traced to differences in opinion located well beyond the dimension of public policy. The differences can be traced all the way down the line to issues of cosmology and issues of ultimate concern. This explains why any "person of faith" who seeks public office makes the hard-core secularists on the left jittery.

As the Democratic Party seeks to rebuild its relationship with the faith community, a deep division will open wide on the political left. Democratic candidates and legislators will be given the green light to talk about their faith, about the importance of religion, about what faith means for health care, poverty, and education. Pity the Democrat who openly questions abortion on demand, fetal stem-cell research, or gay marriage. Then the cordiality between the secularists and religionists on the left will be blown apart. The Democrats will allow the Religious Left a place at the table as long as they do not question any of the sacred cows of feminist and gay activists.

The same division has existed in the Republican Party ever since the overthrow of the Northeast establishment represented by Nelson Rockefeller during the Barry Goldwater era. The religious presence in the New Right was in the background during that period, but with the election of Reagan, GOP leaders got into the habit of biting their tongues. In interviews with three former employees of the Republican National Committee, one each from the '80s, '90s, and 2000s, this ongoing tension was confirmed. Outreach to religious conservatives in the RNC was always a matter of compromise on how many resources were going to be put into the effort and how conservative and specific the message would be.

Drew Ryun echoed these sentiments. He doesn't think the GOP is destined to maintain its close relationship with religious conservatives, "because the people who run the Republican Party don't have any religion. It's pragmatism that keeps the marriage together." I asked him what it would take for the marriage to last. Ryun answered, "Religious people would rather have sympathy, not pragmatism. If sympathy happened, the marriage would last longer." By sympathy, Ryun means an affirmation of social conservatism by Republicans that matches its historic embrace of fiscal conservatism—in other words, using the term coined in

1956 by *National Review* editor Frank Meyer, a true "fusionism." Ryan
Sager has explained how the fusionism that kept religious conservatives
in the Republican fold for decades is in danger of falling apart.[8]

Now and then, pragmatism breaks down, and someone from the GOP
will fire away, such as Senator John McCain after his loss in the 2000
South Carolina primary. McCain was on the verge of winning the Republican nomination, when religious conservatives, led by Ralph Reed,
delivered the Evangelical vote for Governor Bush. A week later, McCain
called Falwell and Robertson "agents of intolerance" who had a "cor-
rupting influence" on American politics. The next day, McCain threw
coal on the fire by decrying "the evil influence that they exercise over the
Republican Party."

In preparing for his next presidential bid, however, McCain evidently
realized that he couldn't win the nomination without Religious Right
support. Thus, in the recent past, he has seemed to change his position
accordingly. After reaching out to Falwell, McCain was invited to deliver
the May 2006 commencement speech at Liberty University in Lynchburg, Virginia. That Falwell would give McCain a pulpit, so to speak, at
Liberty University is evidence of the political maturity of the religious
conservative leadership.

NEEDING THE RELIGIOUS RIGHT

Patrick Hynes is a political consultant in his mid-thirties who got fed up
with the maligning of the Religious Right during the Terri Schiavo affair
and decided to write his own book, *In Defense of the Religious Right: Why
Conservative Christians Are the Lifeblood of the Republican Party and Why
That Terrifies the Democrats* (2006).

Hynes warned the "Republican bigwigs" who would like to jettison
the Religious Right: "The Religious Right is the Republicans' indispensable voting bloc, representing thirty million conservative Evangelicals
and Roman Catholics. Without the Religious Right, the GOP would

8. Ryan Sager, *The Elephant in the Room: Evangelicals, Libertarians, and the Battle to Control the
Republican Party* (Hoboken, N.J.: John Wiley, 2006), 8.

never have obtained power in Congress in 1994, and they never would have reasserted their control over Washington in 2004."[9]

Hynes called 2004 "the year in which the Religious Right established itself as the most consequential voting bloc in the nation ... the people standing between the modern Democratic Party and its hopes of ever again becoming the nation's dominant political faction."[10] Hynes pointed out that those who tried to downplay the "moral values" interpretation of that election were turning their eyes from the most obvious factor that brought religious conservatives to the polls in record numbers. Bush, for example, lost the popular vote by 500,000 votes in 2000 but won by more than 3 million in 2004.

Nearly half of Bush's 61 million votes came from conservative Christian voters, according to Hynes. Working from a Pew Center study of the 2004 election, Hynes calculated the size of the Religious Right voting bloc as follows: 80 percent of the 28 million Evangelicals (or 21 million) voted for Bush. When added to the nearly 7 million religiously active Catholics who also voted for Bush, it appears that at least 28 million conservative Christians voted Republican. Though this is not quite the 30 million figure Hynes estimated, his point was made nonetheless. Conservative Christians, therefore, are as important to the GOP as the African-American vote and the labor vote combined is to the Democratic Party.[11]

Hynes had a unique explanation of what brought the moral-values voters to the polls in such high numbers. "It's a mistake," he said, "to focus on the mega-church phenomenon, as influential as it may be, because only 13 percent of Evangelicals belong to those churches. No, what the analysts miss is that every night across America small gaggles of believers gather in a neighbor's living room or in some other mutually convenient place. They're there to worship, but this isn't church."[12] Through

9. Patrick Hynes, *In Defense of the Religious Right: Why Conservative Christians Are the Lifeblood of the Republican Party and Why That Terrifies the Democrats* (Nashville, Tenn.: Nelson Current, 2006), 27.

10. Ibid., 132.

11. Ibid., 145–46.

12. Ibid., 139.

Bible studies, prayer meetings, marriage-prep meetings, youth groups, young singles groups, and seniors groups, the Evangelical churches have a long tradition of organizing weeknight meetings in private homes and in rooms outside the sanctuary in the local church. These meetings are integral to the sense of community that pervades Evangelical fellowships. It's central to their ability to attract people who don't go to church or who go to churches that fail to meet their emotional needs. Hynes reported that in his work as a Republican consultant to numerous campaigns, he found that political messaging and political organizing were taking place through these small groups on an ad hoc but dependable basis. Evangelicals, through their natural affinity for ministering within small-group meetings, have effectively created a national network that was electrified by the Bush candidacy, seen as an antidote to the Clinton years.

In his book, Hynes probably went farther than anybody else in making the case for what Drew Ryun claimed about religious conservatism and the mainstream. Hynes implied, but did not say, that critics are so thrown off by the intensity of Religious Right feelings about social issues that they miss the similarity with what is going on in the mainstream. "[T]he fact remains on issue after issue, conservative Christians and mainstream Americans are on the same side of virtually every social and moral debate in our public dialogue." [13] Hynes then analyzed poll results on the disputed hot-button issues between the Religious Right and its liberal critics. Whether it is removing "under God" from the Pledge of Allegiance, removing signs that list the Ten Commandments from public buildings, giving equal time to the teaching of creationism and intelligent design, rejecting gay marriage, limiting abortion on demand, government funding for embryonic stem-cell research, or pulling life support from Terry Schiavo, most Americans come out on the side of the Religious Right. [14] His point was not that most Americans are religious conservatives but that the majority of Americans agree with many

13. Ibid., 180.
14. Ibid., Chapter 7.

of their values and are thus attracted to a broad social conservative message.[15]

Democrats are beginning to recognize this, but they refuse to recognize, at least publicly, what is at the root of the conflict. The discord between liberals, both secular and religious, and the Religious Right is about *what* they believe and the *right* to be heard in public. As we have seen, it was acceptable for Jimmy Carter to be inspired by his faith "to establish justice in a sinful world," but it's a threat to democracy for conservative Christians to protect innocent life in accordance with their core religious principles.

State-sponsored religion was specifically rejected by the Founding Fathers in the First Amendment to the Constitution. This does not mean that that civil law is free of religious influence. American courthouses prosecute theft, larceny, perjury, slander, or murder as a result of such "theocratic" concepts as "Thou shalt not steal," "Thou shalt not lie," and "Thou shalt not kill."

Political liberals who cite religious influence are never accused of having theocratic aspirations, imposing their values, or being coercive. When any of the many religious lobbyists in Washington, D.C., such as the United Conference of Catholic Bishops or the National Council of Churches, visit members of Congress to urge a higher minimum wage or more funding for Medicare, they are not seen as a threat against the separation of church and state. These criticisms are reserved for those people of faith who seek public policy and legislation regarding human life, family, marriage, children, and education.

Anyone educated in the '60s, as I was, is likely to have been taught that traditional religion was in its death throes and a post-Christian era had begun. Theologians and philosophers were quoted in the pages of major newsmagazines and newspapers announcing the victory of secularism and relativism. The views of obscure theologians such as Thomas J.

15. This recognition that conservatism inhabits the American mainstream is corroborated by two English journalists who recently published a study of conservatism in the United States with the purpose of explaining: "[T]he center of gravity of American opinion is much further to the right—and the whole world needs to understand what that means." John Micklethwait and Adrian Wooldridge, *The Right Nation: Conservative Power in America* (New York: Penguin, 2004), 11.

Altizer, Harvey Cox, and Joseph Fletcher became part of public debate. Altizer, a professor at the then-conservative Candler School of Theology at Emory University, was forced to leave his teaching post. His use of Friedrich Nietzsche's phrase "God is dead" and Fletcher's "situation ethics" gave Evangelical preachers of the late '60s all the ammunition they needed to fire away at the encroachment of secular atheism.

The Evangelical preachers won, and the secular academics lost. Instead of passing away, traditional religion thrived in the wake of the '60s, especially the Evangelical Christianity that flourished in the '70s and '80s. As a result, those who today espouse traditional religion far outnumber those who do not. They still believe in the existence of God, the supernatural world of heaven and hell, miracles, the authority of Scripture, and the objectivity of the moral order. Traditional Christians believe that Jesus Christ is both human and divine and that only through Christ can a person achieve salvation and eternal life.

Evangelical voters who hold these beliefs delivered more than 75 percent of their votes for Republican George W. Bush in 2004, while Roman Catholic voters who regularly attend mass gave 56 percent. Though lagging behind Evangelicals, the trajectory of religiously active Catholic voters supporting the GOP has been steadily growing. Self-identified Catholics who do not attend mass usually vote the same as the general public. Their lack of involvement in parish life makes them an easier target for the influence of secularism.

EFFECTS OF SECULARISM

The growth of secularism, so evident in the '60s, failed to retard the growth of Evangelicalism, but it left its mark on American religion. Many mainstream Protestants, Roman Catholics, and Jews no longer believe in the tenets of a traditional religion. Their beliefs have been refracted through several generations of psychology beginning with Freudianism, philosophy beginning with existentialism, and the politics of the left. In this nontraditional faith, the promise of eternal life has been replaced by several worldly goals, both personal and political. Personal happiness in the form of psychological happiness has become the mantra of liberal religionists. But "feeling good" about oneself is not to be pursued in isolation from the familiar retinue of liberal political causes. In fact, the two goals have become fused into one. Instead of merely relieving poverty as a goal worthy in itself, poverty has to be relieved so that the poor can also share in the "good feeling" that is personal happiness. The right to the pursuit of happiness in America has become the right to have happiness in the form of entitlements. The notion of an afterlife has been accommodated into this worldview by transposing the fear of hell and the hope of heaven into a fear of poverty and the hope of economic justice. The conditions of sin and guilt have been solved by positive thinking, eschewing all regret, and nurturing self-esteem.

The earthly priorities of psychology and politics, in short, have superseded the three-level cosmology in which the pilgrim soul sought forgiveness for earthly sins and the company of God, not Satan, for eternity. Part therapeutic, part political, nontraditional religion seeks to balance the demands of nurturing psychological happiness with advancing the claims of women, sexually liberal feminists, and homosexuals, while seeking economic justice for the poor.

The religious war in this country divides believer from believer and the traditional believers from secularists.

There is still another player in the religious war who is hardly ever mentioned: the mainstream Protestant Republican conservatives who dominated the GOP before the coming of the Evangelicals. These are the kind of Republicans who championed the first challenges to antiabortion laws prior to *Roe* v. *Wade* in 1973. The dominant religion in the Republican Party was not always Evangelical. The notion of "country club Republican" is synonymous with urban Episcopalians and suburban Presbyterians who recoil at Evangelical enthusiasm. (The odd relationship that developed between President Dwight Eisenhower and the young Billy Graham provides the best picture of the tension between the past and present of the Republican Party.)

Evangelicals made common cause with the Republican Party but not without meeting ongoing resistance. Those who talk about the "take-over" of the Republican Party are greatly exaggerating. They don't recognize the old mainline Protestant distrust of Evangelicals that still exists among GOP leadership and bureaucracy. This is a distrust that has been exacerbated into outright hostility by some of the successful forays of Evangelicals into local party politics.

Kevin Phillips, for example, was once the golden boy among Republican strategists, scoring big with his 1969 book, *The Emerging Republican Majority*.[16] In that seminal book, Phillips was one of the first to recognize the significance of religious conservatives migrating to the GOP. Evidently, Phillips's electoral playbook worked far too well. By 2006, he published *American Theocracy*, dedicated to "the millions of Republicans, present and lapsed, who have opposed the Bush dynasty and the disenlightenment in the 2000 and 2004 elections."[17] The unraveling of an enlightened politics is a result, according to Phillips of "an elected leader who believes himself in some way to speak for God; a ruling party that represents religious true believers and seeks to mobilize the churches; the conviction of many voters in the Republican party that government should be guided by religion; and on top of it all, White House implementation of domestic and international political agendas that seem to be driven by religious motivation and biblical worldviews."[18]

Phillips's diatribe against the influence of religious conservatives expressed the often repressed views of many Republicans. There are more than a few GOP regulars who hope that religious conservatives will somehow fall from their recently attained heights. Every election result is being scrutinized, both by the left and by GOP moderates, for proof that the era of the Religious Right is coming to an end.

Pat Buchanan was not surprised by the indignation elicited from the Republican establishment for his 1992 convention speech. Many Republican operatives, reflecting the old Protestant ethos, reacted to Buchanan's speech with hysteria, worried that it would ruin Vice President

---

16. Kevin Phillips, *The Emerging Republican Majority* (New York: Arlington House, 1969).

17. Kevin Phillips, *American Theocracy: The Peril and Politics of Radical Religion, Oil, and Borrowed Money in the 21st Century* (New York: Viking, 2006), viii.

18. Ibid., xiii–ix.

Bush's appeal to moderate voters. Subsequent polling showed the post-speech conflagration was unfounded. What Buchanan called the "Houston Myth" saw Bush's level of support rise by 10 percent the next day.

Eight years later, it was George W. Bush's tacit acknowledgment of Buchanan's wisdom that led to his election and reelection to the White House. Then-Governor Bush made it clear to the steady stream of religious leaders invited to meet with him in Austin during the primary campaign that he would speak humbly but directly about his faith in God and his habits of prayer and Bible reading.

BUSH TESTS HIS MESSAGE

What disturbed the left so much about the candidacy and presidency of George W. Bush was his repeated references to personal faith. His faith was explicitly connected to his pro-life commitment, and he did not hide it. I witnessed one of the earliest challenges to Bush's pro-life position during his campaign for the presidential nomination in 2000. Karl Rove had invited me to Austin to discuss an article published in *Crisis* magazine on the Catholic vote. After meeting with Rove in the morning, I was invited to have lunch at the governor's mansion with some members of the South Carolina legislature who were there to hear the governor's stump speech.

Bush spoke for ten minutes and asked for questions. One of the first hands to go up was that of a middle-aged female legislator who expressed her admiration for the governor but wondered if he would explain his denial of "a woman's right to choose." Realizing this was the kind of challenge that would make or break his candidacy with religious conservatives, I watched Bush closely to see how he would respond.

He took a breath, smiled, and said he respected people who differed with him on this issue but that "faith" taught him that he had to respect life, that it was "sacred." He added that he thought "abortion was bad for America," and that if he was elected president, he would do all he could to reduce the number of abortions.

The face of the legislator never scowled as she listened to his explanation; she seemed content to accept his simple explanation based on a straightforward admission of a value received from his religious faith. When Bush paused for her reaction, she said she appreciated his honesty and would be supporting him in spite of their difference on this issue.

It was clear to me at that moment that Bush could be the next president of the United States. He had demonstrated that he could publicly stand with social conservatives on issues such as abortion but speak with humility and compassion. ("Compassionate conservatism" was only in the planning stages at this time.) The issue of tone would be especially important when reaching out to Catholic voters.

Bush's promises to his religious coalition and his manner of presenting himself as a man of faith made it clear that he had a position to take on the importance of religion in America, as well as the role of religion in politics. He had no intention of hiding his personal beliefs, and even further, he intended to pursue policies that would conform to the values of religious conservatives. Interestingly, Buchanan and his hard-core followers never believed Bush could be their champion in America's religious war. Bush was seen as having neither a strong commitment to the pro-life cause nor the populist strain that Buchanan represented. Buchanan, like Alan Keyes after him, showed not just that the wars, both cultural and religious, were between two sides but that each side contained its own internal disputes.

HOW CULTURE COUNTS

But as the divide between the left and the Religious Right has widened, the phrase "culture wars" has remained a helpful rhetorical marker for the religious and political dynamics that created the map of red and blue states. The juxtaposition of "culture" with "wars" explains how deep passions can erupt suddenly and without warning. It also explains why neither side attempts to rein in the ensuing invective. Whatever wall it is that has been breached needs to be defended to the last breath. It's just that important.

Culture, after all, is like air; we breathe it in order to live, but we are unaware of it until, for some reason, we are unable to take a breath. Culture provides a kind of invisible frame to our lives, a default perspective governing, at an unconscious level, the way the most mundane or global occurrences are understood.

People are rarely self-aware of the culture that refracts their thinking, unless something, usually some kind of traumatic experience, forces them to take a long look at themselves. No doubt, the use of "culture war" terminology for many people brings their unspoken first principles to a conscious level. The media firestorm following Buchanan's pronouncement of a "religious war" raised public awareness in an unprecedented way.

Still, the notion of culture wars always should be kept in the background when examining the current religious war. It reminds us that these battles are not always fought at a conscious level. No matter how aware a person is of the culture that shapes his perspective, culture will direct thought and judgment. It's the nature of human existence that our thinking is mediated through concepts and images collected from experience. Unlike the angels (who are said to know by direct illumination from God), human beings think through the senses, which is where they are inevitably enmeshed in a culture.

Our culture may consist of overlapping, even clashing elements, especially in the age of electronic media and the Internet. But it is a culture nonetheless, and people will do their best to forge some kind of unity out of what they encounter. Individuals do not create cultures. Communities construct cultures through the communication of shared meaning and value. If a culture has any staying power, a vision of life will arise inevitably as well. That vision represents what human life is supposed to be about, the bottom line or first principles that govern thought and action.

Within the dominant culture, there will be myriad subcultures consisting of individuals and families with beliefs and behaviors that distinguish them. Religious conservatives have learned to create and nurture these subcultures by adding the sophisticated use of education and media to their local church communities.

Religious conservatives are acculturated in the midst of an often vibrant and emotionally supportive church life. Over the past forty years, religious conservatives have protected their communities by the formation of a vast subculture, complete with nearly every institution necessary to sustaining a shared life. It doesn't take very much effort for an Evangelical Christian living in the right place, with access to cable television and radio, to exist entirely in a conservative Christian subculture.

Christian radio is a prime example. Evangelicals now run more than 2,000 of the nation's 13,000 radio stations. Country music and news talk are the only formats that are larger, and Christian radio is threatening to overtake country music in the near future. According to the National Association of Religious Broadcasters, a group of more than 1,500 organizations representing Christian radio, television, Internet, and film, Christian radio stations reach nearly half of all the adults living in the United States. The Barna Group, which specializes in polling for Evangelicals, finds that 46 percent of all U.S. adults listen to a Christian radio broadcast in a typical month, and one out of six adults listens every day. Ninety-six percent of Evangelicals consume some form of Christian media each month. Arbitron, the radio industry standard for measuring audiences, reported in 2005 that religiously formatted radio stations were the fastest growing in the country: 14 percent over a five-year period, compared with 4 percent growth in stations as a whole.

Salem Communications, the leading Evangelical radio organization, started with about 200 stations and now airs on 1,100 (seven times those that broadcast National Public Radio programs). USA Radio has more than 800 and can be heard on two XM satellite radio stations and Armed Forces Radio. Many mainstream stations are picking up Salem's programming. [19]

Many Christians, whether Evangelical or from other faith traditions, are turning to religious broadcasting networks for their news and entertainment. Christian Broadcasting Network (CBN) began *News Watch* following the September 11, 2001, attacks. Family Net TV, owned by the

19. Mariah Blake, "Stations of the Cross: How Evangelical Christians Are Creating an Alternative Universe of Faith-Based News," *Columbia Journalism Review* (May–June 2005).

North American Mission Board of the Southern Baptist Convention, hired its own news staff in 2004. Family Net TV is a twenty-four-hour, seven-day-a-week cable network viewed by some 30 million households.

Trinity Broadcasting Network (TBN) is the world's largest religious network and is the most watched of all religious broadcasting. Its five networks, airing twenty-four hours a day, provide religious programming for Protestants, Catholics, and Messianic Jews. Aside from news and world events, TBN offers worship, variety, movies, health, music, and programming for children, youth, and young adults. It is the seventh-largest broadcast group in the United States and is affiliated with all major cable and satellite companies.

Evangelicals now control six television networks, including three direct-broadcast satellite networks. Among these, Sky Angel is the only Christian-owned and -operated direct-to-home satellite television system in the United States and carries nothing but thirty-six channels of Christian radio and television. This multichannel TV service was founded twenty-five years ago by Robert Johnson Sr., who wanted a Christian-controlled telecommunications system that would give its viewers news and family programming adhering to Christian family values and biblical teaching.

Christian television audiences are still far behind in the ratings when compared with secular networks, though approximately 1 million households view each of the most popular Christian shows on a daily basis. While this number doesn't compare with that of viewers who watch top-rated secular shows, it continues to grow as more and more Christians turn to faith-based programming to meet the needs of their families and themselves.

Catholic radio's 150-plus stations can hardly compare with the more than 2,000 Evangelical stations, but in the arena of television, conservative Catholics have produced a powerhouse, comparable to a Dobson or a Robertson: the Eternal Word Television Network (EWTN) and its shortwave radio broadcast, Eternal Word Radio Network.

EWTN was founded in a suburb of Birmingham, Alabama, on August

15, 1981, by Mother Angelica. She came to the South from her native Ohio to start a religious order but ended up creating the largest and most influential religious media apostolate in the world. She started by developing short written religious teachings. These tracts became so popular that she began receiving requests to speak, and eventually, she and her fellow nuns created a series of videos of her talks that were aired on Pat Robertson's Christian Broadcasting Network. Mother Angelica was so well received that she decided to start her own TV studio on the monastery property.[20]

Programming started slowly, with only four hours a day devoted to *Mother Angelica Live,* mass, talk shows, and reruns of Catholic programs. Expansion soon followed. In the 1990s, EWTN began producing more of its own programs, aired mass daily, and took a strong stance on providing programming from a traditional and conservative Catholic perspective. Today, Catholic programming is broadcast by EWTN twenty-four hours a day in both English and Spanish over shortwave radio to 125 million homes in 140 countries via more than 4,800 cable systems, wireless cable, DBS, low-power TV, and individual satellite users. In 2004, Sirius satellite radio picked up EWTN as well. All of this is done without advertising and at a cost of $30 million annually, which is covered entirely by charitable donations. Most of the 150 Catholic radio stations in the United States carry the EWTN satellite feed that they can broadcast without cost. In a little more than twenty-six years, the TV and radio station founded by a lone Catholic nun in a blue-collar suburb of Birmingham, Alabama, has become the largest religious media network in the world.

Today's EWTN programming includes a weekly news show, *The World Over,* created and hosted by Raymond Arroyo, who formerly worked for Pat Robertson at CBN. Arroyo regularly discusses Catholic teaching and its relationship to politics, often with political figures, such as former

20. Raymond Arroyo, *Mother Angelica: The Remarkable Story of a Nun, Her Nerve, and a Network of Miracles* (New York: Doubleday, 2005). The importance of Arroyo's book goes beyond the life and work of Mother Angelica; this is the first serious biography of a major figure in the revival of orthodox Catholicism in America. Others surely will follow.

Senator Rick Santorum, who fly to Alabama from D.C. to appear on the show. Arroyo's news department also offers a daily news service. Other regulars have included Father Frank Pavone, head of Priests for Life; Father George Rutler; Jeff Cavins; Father Michael Scanlon; Father John Corapi; Father John McCloskey; Scott Hahn; Marcus Grodi; Father Benedict Groeschel; and Father Mitch Pacwa. There are thousands of Catholics in the United States whose bookcases are filled with the books and recorded lectures of these EWTN hosts. EWTN is the Catholic subculture par excellence, and it goes unnoticed by those who comment on trends in Catholic America.

Mother Angelica's poor health now prevents her from active participation in most of EWTN's projects, but she has become *the* symbol for the Catholic subculture that resists the liberal elites within the Catholic Church and supports the political efforts of religious conservatives and the Religious Right. The staff and hosts of EWTN carefully avoid politicizing their programming, but their daily emphasis on the orthodox social teaching of the Catholic Church, with the priority of life issues, has been the single most important para-church influence on the Catholic vote in the United States. EWTN is the closest thing to the Moral Majority or the Christian Coalition that Catholics have. Although not political, EWTN drives a message that subverts the pro-abortion positions of Catholic politicians, most of whom are Democrats.

What one research study has said about the "alternative universe" of Evangelical media really should be applied to Christian media in general: "Given their content and their reach, it's likely that Christian broadcasters have helped drive phenomena that have recently confounded much of the public and the mainstream media—including the surge in 'value voters' and the drive to sustain Terri Schiavo's life, a story that was incubated in Evangelical media three years before it hit the mainstream. Nor has Evangelical media's influence escaped the notice of those who stroll the halls of power." [21]

Conservative Jewish and Muslim groups are building subcultures as

21. Blake, "Stations of the Cross."

well, primarily through organizations and print publications, with electronic outlets to follow eventually. Grover Norquist, president of Americans for Tax Reform, who has had extensive experience in coalition building for the GOP, told me that both Orthodox Jews and mosque-attending Muslims are natural allies of the Religious Right, but "no one has yet reached out to them." Both are now small in number, but according to Norquist, Orthodox Jews soon will become the dominant group among the more than 5 million Jews in the United States, and religiously active Muslims soon will outnumber Jews altogether. Norquist, however, may be overly optimistic. Yes, traditional Christians, Jews, and Muslims agree on social issues, but September 11, 2001, and the war in Iraq intensified the Evangelical support for Israel that alienates many Muslims from the GOP base. (It goes without saying that politically active Jews and Muslims have an increasingly tenuous relationship.) Add this to the lingering belief among Evangelical Christians, and some conservative Catholics, that Jews and Muslims will not be rewarded with eternal salvation, and the prospects of growing a political coalition among all three groups is tenuous.

If a secular liberal thinks the existence of a religious subculture is appalling, he should ask himself how that is any different from living in a major city in the Northeastern United States where an ordinary citizen has practically no exposure to anything other than secular liberalism. The Evangelical churches, for example, of urban areas such as New York and Boston, operate entirely under the media radar. The readers of the *New York Times* would be shocked to read that the level of religious affiliation and activism in urban centers is not inferior to either suburban or rural areas, largely because of these unnoticed Evangelical congregations.[22]

It is no surprise that the notion of culture wars was first articulated by James Davidson Taylor, an Evangelical scholar teaching at the University of Virginia. A Southern Evangelical is more likely to be aware of the disparity of opinion on ethical and religious questions between elites in

22. Roger Finke and Rodney Starke, *The Churching of America, 1776–2005: Winners and Losers in Our Religious Economy* (New Brunswick, N.J.: Rutgers University Press, 2005), 201.

New York and Los Angeles than a secular liberal who never meets anyone who challenges his core assumptions. As L. Brent Bozell III, president of the Media Research Center, has described it, the America between the East and West Coasts is just "fly-over country" to the media and entertainment moguls. The Evangelical, like many socially conservative Catholics, has been experiencing this tension and feeling its rise for decades.

The voice of secular liberalism has long been heard throughout the country through its domination of the media and entertainment, while the voice of Evangelical Christianity and conservative Catholicism has only recently been heard outside its subculture. With the entry of conservatives and religious conservatives into radio, television, and publishing (and, to some extent, film and music), the liberal elites have been forced to acknowledge the existence of a point of view they thought had been dead and buried with the *Scopes* trial in the 1920s. As a matter of fact, religious conservatism never retreated to the sidelines; it only changed its focus issue. Shortly after losing the skirmish over evolution in Dayton, Tennessee, the precursors of the modern Religious Right set their sights on the atheistic threat of Communism, both in Russia and in China.

The issue of belief in God stands at the center of the culture wars. Critics of the Religious Right talk about policy issues, but what really troubles them is God. The debate with the Religious Right is really an argument about what they believe God has revealed to them about the truth of human life. These critics insinuate that traditional Christians should be feared. Such people are filled with moral certainties and seek to impose their certainties on people who do not share their faith.

There are, of course, *religious* critics of the Religious Right, such as *Sojourners* editor Jim Wallis; Rabbi Michael Lerner, editor of *Tikkun;* and Reverend Barry Lynn. These critics believe in God; the two Christians believe in Jesus Christ, but they claim that the Religious Right distorts both Christianity and Judaism. They assert that the Religious Right gets God wrong, interprets Scripture wrong, and misunderstands the law and the prophets. For example, they argue that the Religious Right cares only about abortion and homosexuality and ignores what the Scriptures really emphasize: caring for the poor and promoting nonviolence.

ROBERTSON AGAINST THE CRITICS

Then there are the secular critics of the Religious Right, including Salon .com writer Michelle Goldberg, scholar Frederick Clarkson, and journalist Sara Diamond. The best thing they can say about religion is that it should be kept as a private affair, so that its voice is never heard in public. They view religion as outmoded and feel it should simply disappear. What remains of religion, as taught by Nietzsche and Marx, is simple self-deception, the product of personal cowardice and/or class control and manipulation.

Those who still believe, according to the critics, should be feared. People of faith are chock full of moral absolutes, which inclines them toward despotism and fascism. Barry Lynn puts it bluntly: "I've studied the tactics of these groups [of the Religious Right] for more than thirty years. I know what they want. They want to run your life, mine, and everyone else's as much as they possibly can."[23]

I asked Pat Robertson, founder of the Christian Coalition, to comment on the kind of criticism that the Religious Right habitually receives. In his office at Regent University in Virginia Beach, Robertson was dressed comfortably in his riding clothes, clearly a remarkably fit man in his late seventies. (About half of the Regent University newsletters sitting on the coffee table were devoted to health matters.) He smiled with patience when I asked him how the movement succeeded in spite of the torrent of often vitriolic criticism. Robertson, it appeared, has not shrugged off this criticism through the years. He knows why the movement he helped to create has succeeded—he has no doubts about the reasons. But he answered with a tone that suggested he himself was a bit surprised that he should be asked to explain what should be obvious to

23. Lynn, *Piety and Politics*, 17.

everyone: "I believe we touched the heart of America. . . . The leftist movement wanted to destroy the family, certain kinds of private owner-ship of property, and the religious juncture at the heart of the move-ment. It is a spiritual struggle, not necessarily a political one. All that happened since the '70s and '80s is a reaction of religious people to the destruction of their time-honored customs. . . . The other people say this is a violation of 'separation of church and state,' which is utter non-sense."

For Robertson, the issue is not how to run everyone else's life but how to keep the state from running the lives of religious citizens who do not want it cramming the values of the secular left down their throats.

Lynn's complaint is about personal freedom in relation to the leg-islative agenda of religious conservatives. Any legislation restricting abortion, the use of fetal stem cells, and homosexual marriage is an "im-position" of religious values. Lynn and his fellow critics never make the same complaint about other forms of social legislation, such as civil rights and welfare entitlement programs. Legislators evidently are only seeking to run your life when they pass laws that you disagree with.

It's the meaning of freedom itself being disputed. Pat Buchanan told me his Houston speech was prompted by a defense of "freedom, the or-ganizing principle of this republic." If freedom is judged by the quick-ness to laugh, then Buchanan may be the freest person I have ever met. Nearly every serious comment he made was turned into some kind of jest, even at his own expense. His lightheartedness took some of the sting from his comments, such as this: "The Left does not recognize that free-dom cannot be found in the complete lack of restraint." For Buchanan, a practicing Roman Catholic, freedom cannot be conceived apart from the self-restraint of the virtues, those moral habits that incline a person toward the moral order established by God. Freedom is best exercised by obedience to the moral order rather than the enjoyment of personal preferences.

Lynn, however, would respond by saying that of course, there is a moral order; we just disagree about what it is. This is accurate only to a point. On some issues, the left asserts the value of personal preference or

choice or rights as a trump card over all else. For example, the life of
Terry Schiavo became the public battleground on which these conflicting notions of moralities met head-on. To religious conservatives, the
issue was protecting the life of a woman who was still alive; to the left,
the issue was her husband's right to remove her feeding tubes. Each side
was confident in the moral order that supported its point of view, but no
matter how much the word "morality" was used, it could not disguise
the chasm that separates the two.

The two Americas evinced by the Schiavo affair are the consequence
of the ongoing religious war. Interestingly, neither Buchanan nor Robertson sounded like a preacher when I talked to him. Both men talked in
philosophical terms about defending America, defending religious liberty, and the basic values taught in their faith tradition. When I asked
Robertson whether or not he sought to employ secular, philosophical
argument to further his cause, he was surprised, saying, "I do it all the
time." Catholics, theoretically, have the advantage of a developed philosophical tradition from which to draw their political arguments. Robertson, like the other Evangelicals I interviewed, was perfectly capable of
defending his views without recourse to quoting the Bible. This should
have come as no surprise. Robertson, after all, had run for president in
1988, and the Religious Right as a movement has been in play for thirty
years.

The religious war that drew so many Evangelical leaders into the public square had over the years equipped these leaders with the public arguments they once lacked. As a result, Evangelicals suddenly found
themselves making common cause with Catholics in more explicit ways.

3

NOT SEX, THE FAMILY

ABORTION WASN'T THE ISSUE THAT LAUNCHED THE RELIGIOUS Right. It was the realization by conservative Christians that government was no longer on their side. Critics who accuse the movement of being "obsessed with sex" miss this. Religious conservatives recognized a widening gap between their worldview and the cultural effects of successive rights movements of the '60s and '70s. The intrusive impact of these movements on families and communities created the political coalition that elected Ronald Reagan in 1980 and George H. W. Bush in 1988, turned white-hot with rage during the Bill Clinton years, and spent that rage to elect George W. Bush in 2000 and 2004.

The original skirmishes were fought by the Religious Right on three major fronts from the early to mid-'70s: in the South, over the integration of Christian schools; in the battleground states where ERA was being contested; and in places such as Dade County, Houston, and Dallas, where the demand for gay rights stirred a public debate.

The pro-life movement was in its nascent stage at this period. The Catholic bishops responded so quickly in 1973 to *Roe* v. *Wade* that abortion was considered a Catholic issue. Small state right-to-life groups immediately joined to create National Right to Life with the encouragement of the Catholic bishops. The name was owned by the bishops, but they soon allowed the organization to become independent and lay-run.

According to Paul Weyrich, Catholics were the dominant figures in the early pro-life movement because "the Evangelicals' attitude was that 'it's not our problem.' They had a ghetto mentality and didn't foresee the impact of the decision." Some Evangelicals admit that they stayed away from the abortion issue precisely because Catholics were already involved. Other prominent Evangelicals, such as Reverend W. A. Criswell of First Baptist Church of Dallas, initially approved of the *Roe* decision.

EVANGELICALS DISCOVER ABORTION

As Ralph Reed told me, and others confirmed, abortion only became a central issue for Evangelicals as a result of a book and ten-part film series in 1976, *How Should We Then Live? The Decline of Western Thought and Culture,* by Christian apologist Francis Schaeffer.[1] The film series based on *How Shall We Then Live?* was intended as a Christian version of Sir Kenneth Clark's popular *Civilization* series on public television. But this book and film series presented an overview of Western civilization, not as a celebration of the West's humanistic intelligence and imagination, as in Clark's version, but as the progressive rejection of the Judeo-Christian tradition culminating in the abortion movement. Schaeffer and his son Frank, who produced the film, took it on an eighteen-city seminar tour, effectively taking his message of cultural apologetics to the laity as well as the ministers.

If you were an Evangelical in the '70s looking for intellectual respectability outside of biblical studies but within your own tradition, Schaeffer was the man. A visit to Schaeffer's L'Abri community, which he founded in 1955, was a mark of distinction. Schaeffer gave an entire generation of ministers the permission to read philosophy and to be engaged with the culture. It was not unusual for a ministerial student to be accused of "carnal-mindedness" for reading philosophers or, even

1. Francis A. Schaeffer, *How Should We Then Live? The Decline of Western Thought and Culture* (Old Tappan, N.J.: Fleming H. Revell, 1976).

worse, novelists, in an attempt to broaden the range of Christian apologetics. Schaeffer opened the door to the study of intellectual history,
the arts, and politics. Although Schaeffer's interpretation of the philosophers and artists usually found them wanting in some serious way
from a Christian perspective, he can be credited for overcoming the monopoly of biblical studies and theology in the education of Evangelical
ministers.

Dr. Richard Land, who represents the Southern Baptist Convention
in Washington, D.C., recalls the impact of Schaeffer on him as a college
student: "As an Evangelical Princeton University undergraduate in the
late 1960s, I, like so many in my generation, was electrified and galvanized by Schaeffer's challenge to rejoin the contemporary cultural and
philosophical debate armed with what he called 'true truth.' . . . Schaeffer
gave us a cultural grid for both understanding and interacting with a
culture increasingly hostile to Christian presuppositions of truth and
moral absolutes."[2]

In 1979, Schaeffer coauthored with pediatric specialist C. Everett
Koop *Whatever Happened to the Human Race?* which also was paired
with a film series. The one-two punch of these books brought the Evangelical community into the abortion battle. Nothing could have been
more assuring to the pro-life community than Ronald Reagan's appointment of Dr. Koop as surgeon-general.

The Religious Right is a single-issue movement. That issue is the family. The family can be viewed from a variety of angles: marriage, children,
education, religious liberty, gender roles, parental prerogatives, government intrusion, social engineering, cultural influence, and, of course,
abortion. Protecting the family was what prompted the response to the
ERA and motivated the resistance to Jimmy Carter's White House Conference on Families and, most recently, the protest against homosexual
marriage in Massachusetts. Defending the traditional family always will
be a source of political motivation for conservative Christians. Even in
the 2006 election, when many pro-life legislators were swept from office

2. Richard Land, "Francis Schaeffer and C. Everett Koop's Invaluable Impact on Pro-Life Evangelism," www.nrlc.org/news/2003/NRL01/land.html.

on the tide of anti-Bush and anti-Iraq sentiment, six out of seven gay-marriage bans passed in the states.

The priority of the family provided the natural affinity between conservative Christians and the Republican Party after it was reshaped by Barry Goldwater. Parents have full authority over a child's education and upbringing, which should not be usurped by intrusive government policies. For Catholics, the family is the foundation of social teaching. As explained in the *Catechism of the Catholic Church:* "The family is the original cell of social life. It is the natural society in which husband and wife are called to give themselves in love and in the gift of life. Authority, stability, and a life of relationships within the family constitute the foundations for freedom, security, and fraternity within society. The family is the community in which, from childhood, one can learn moral values, begin to honor God, and make good use of freedom. Family life is an initiation into life in society."

The most powerful figure in the Religious Right today came to prominence with a book on child rearing. Although he founded Focus on the Family in 1977, Dr. James Dobson first attracted public attention with *Dare to Discipline,* first published in 1970. This book was controversial because it was Dobson's answer to the '60s and Dr. Spock.[3] He challenged the then-popular notion that spanking was inherently harmful to a child's self-esteem. He recognized the role reversal that was occurring, where parents were giving over their authority to the demands of children, and he challenged parents, especially fathers, to reassert their authority over their families. Spanking was recommended as a way of reasserting authority. Many having just drunk deeply from '60s Kool-Aid were aghast. But religious conservatives responded to Dobson's message with their time and their financial support. Dobson's daily radio show is now the most potent voice for the Religious Right, carried on more than 6,000 stations, reaching 200 million people in more than 160 countries.

When President Bush and Karl Rove wanted support for the nomina-

3. Dan Gilgoff, *The Jesus Machine: How James Dobson, Focus on the Family, and Evangelical America Are Winning the Culture War* (New York: St. Martin's Press, 2007), 22–23.

tion of Harriet Miers to the Supreme Court, it was Dobson who was called by Rove. When Dobson was told that Miers was a "born-again" Christian who could be relied on as a Supreme Court justice, he took Rove's word for it and spoke up in support of the nomination on the morning it was announced. It was no secret that the Evangelical coalition of the GOP was hoping for an Evangelical nominee to go alongside the Catholic justice, John Roberts. The trouble was, however, that Miers could be found nowhere on the list of nominees preapproved by groups such as the Federalist Society and Manny Miranda's Third Branch Conference, a judiciary watchdog coalition. For grassroots religious leaders and judiciary watchers, Miers being "born again" was not enough assurance. They wanted to see proof of intellectual caliber and legal expertise qualifying her for the Supreme Court. When neither was supplied by the White House, Dobson and several other White House religious coalition leaders were left all on their own. Dobson, embarrassed at not having done his homework, had to retract his endorsement and temporarily lost some of his prestige as a result.

The Religious Right will not cut anyone any slack when it comes to its core issues, especially when it comes down to where most of the damage has been done to the family: the judiciary. As the Religious Right matures, political leaders courting its clout are learning valuable lessons. Unlike other political movements, compromise is not an option. Even Dobson cannot sound reveille for a candidate with a track record in the public square that shows silence, ambiguity, flip-flopping, or opposition on core issues. The Miers kerfuffle was a clear vote of no confidence for conjecture based on recent conversions of the heart.

LIBERALS PREFER VILLAGES

It's easy to see why Hillary Clinton's mantra, "It takes a village to raise a child," raises some hackles on the backs of Christian conservatives. Why she chose to reissue her famous book before the 2008 election only serves to remind religious conservatives of her antipathy toward them. Senator Rick Santorum had the right idea when he authored a rebuttal of Clinton in *It Takes a Family*.[4] Santorum's book contained all the right ideas but was written in a militant manner that provided his enemies ammunition to caricature him. If Santorum had been writing to an Evangelical community, his style would have gained him votes rather than losing them. Religious conservatives, who feel strongly about defending the family, differ on how they want that defense couched. Some, especially Catholics, are uncomfortable with stridency.

Crisis magazine's research on the difference between Catholic and Evangelical voters showed that Evangelicals prefer a morally spiked rhetoric from their political leaders, while Catholics prefer softer edges such as the "compassionate conservatism" of Bush's 2000 campaign.[5] The different rhetorical preferences of American Catholics can be traced back to vivid memories of their Irish, Italian, and Slavic ancestors, who were viewed as virtual slave labor by a self-righteous Protestant establishment in the Northeast. Evangelicals live in a religious culture where public confession of sin and redemption are a weekly experience. Catholics, for the most part, confess only to their priests and find the Evangelical practice of "testifying" to conversion experiences hard to appreciate. An Evangelical hears the condemnation of sin, even by a politician, as the necessary prelude to a possible conversion. A Catholic sees this as an example of the ruling Protestant class using its religiosity to express its superiority over the unwashed masses.

Evangelicals thus inhabit a culture that is accustomed to moralizing and expect it of their leadership. It is integral to the revivalist, born-again mentality in which an individual becomes "saved" precisely by the public admission of sin. Evangelicals, unlike Catholics, have no central credal statement. The theological understanding of families is the same, although their articulation is "biblically" grounded in narratives such as the Christmas birth of Jesus Christ to Mary and Joseph.

Liberals on the Religious Left either ignore or ridicule this issue by reducing it to an obsession with sex or an intrusion into the bedroom.

4. Rick Santorum, *It Takes a Family: Conservatism and the Common Good* (Wilmington, Del.: Intercollegiate Studies Institute, 2003).

5. Steven Wagner, "Election 2000: A New Dawn?" *Crisis* (October 2000): 12–17.

For example, in Bill Press's diatribe against religious conservatives, *How the Republicans Stole Christmas,* he never connects Christmas to the defense of families that energizes the movement he pretends to explain.[6] His constant complaint, like that of many on the Religious Left, is against the Bush tax cuts that favored the rich over the poor. (This thesis was disproved by the growing strength of the American economy and the low unemployment rate from 2005 through 2007.) The only threats against the family that critics like Press recognize are economic. Press sees no threat in abortion, homosexual marriage, or the morass of immorality in education, all of which he sees as conforming to his Catholic faith, in spite of the *Catechism of the Catholic Church.*

Press, a regular commentator on CNN, is typical of the Religious Left. He doesn't seem to know whether he wants religion to be part of politics at all. He begins by congratulating the Democrats for their tradition of keeping "religion and politics as two separate camps" but then argues in favor of the religious values that animate his favored policy positions of the left. He urges his fellow Democrats, who, if you remember, keep religion and politics in separate camps, to profess loudly their belief in gospel morality. Whose faith and gospel morality he refers to remains a mystery to orthodox Catholics. "Our faith should motivate everything we do. Just as faith should motivate every decision a religious public official makes—on foreign policy or the budget." Which way does Press want it? The secularists and the ascendant Religious Left will have to smoke a peace pipe and pretend there is no argument between them. And, in actuality, there isn't. Like Press, the Religious Left *subsumes its religion to its politics,* placing it under the mantle of the Democratic Party.

As long as the political expression of religion is the most important aspect of religion itself, the secularists and the Religious Left will get along just fine. Both will continue to treat the notion of family values as a joke, but it will be the engine that drives the religious conservative movement from one stage to the next. If the Democratic leadership had

6. Bill Press, *How the Republicans Stole Christmas: The Republican Party's Declared Monopoly on Religion and What Democrats Can Do to Take It Back* (New York: Doubleday, 2005).

realized this, it would have moved heaven and earth to keep the Massachusetts Supreme Court from mandating gay marriage before the 2004
presidential election. That decision ensured that the Evangelical and
conservative Catholic turnout would surpass the 2000 mark, which it
did at historic levels. The state with the largest increase in Catholics
voting for the Republican nominee was Massachusetts, at 16 percent.
The Democrats' religious outreach in Pennsylvania, Ohio, Michigan,
and Kansas in 2006 represented a kind of stealth *mea culpa* to religious
voters.

The fight against gay marriage will continue to fuel the movement after
the drubbing taken in the 2006 election. Whether or not the new Democratic Party leadership recognizes this fact is yet to be seen. Certainly, the
candidates chosen to defeat Republicans in 2006, such as Bob Casey Jr. in
Pennsylvania, seemed chosen to make Democrats more appealing to religiously motivated voters. But the Democrats have decades of bad political
habits toward the Religious Right to overcome. One of those habits is un-
derestimating the staying power of religious conservatives.

Richard Viguerie is well known in Washington circles as the man who
invented direct-mail funding of political causes and candidates. Like
other founders of the Religious Right, Viguerie is a Catholic who talks
like an Evangelical. He has no lobbyist polish, no strategist finesse. Viguerie is a shoot-from-the-hip activist, writer, and businessman. I met with
him in his Manassas, Virginia, office and asked him why, for so long, the
political left didn't take religious conservatives seriously: "They don't see
us as legitimate opponents—we are just some kind of fringe group—far
extreme right. They remind me of the old segregationists who used to
say, 'Don't get me wrong, I like blacks, and some of them are my best
friends, but it is these new young radicals that make me nervous.'"
Of course, the young radicals are the pro-life movement, now three decades old.

Viguerie remembers a press meeting with the *Christian Science Moni-
tor* on the Monday after the election of Ronald Reagan. The convener
opening the meeting by asking, "Where did this come from? Nobody
saw it coming." The morning after the 2004 election, PBS journalist

Charlie Rose called Ralph Reed to ask him the identical question. The Democratic Party and its friends in the media have thus far refused to recognize the power of the Religious Right or to show any respect for the concerns that motivate it. The 2006 election was the first time, apart from some piecemeal announcement after the 2004 defeat, the Democrats showed any willingness to let the pro-life, pro-family message come under their tent. The most likely outcome will be a replay of what happened to the first generation of Catholic pro-lifers when the Bishops Conference moved to the left. They will be expected to toe the line on all the major issues of the liberal agenda or be consigned to the outer darkness as "extremists."

In my interview with Viguerie several months before the 2006 election, he said that it would take a GOP defeat in 2006 or 2008 for the Republicans to stop taking their religious conservatives for granted. "They will do it if they are faced with, as Dr. Johnson put it, 'the impending hanging which focuses one's attention.'" For the GOP, the temptation will be to listen to those who blame a loss on the influence of Christian conservatives. Richard Viguerie, Ralph Reed, and others point out that it was the influx of religious conservatives into the Republican Party that made it the majority party. Viguerie estimates that it added 10 percent to the GOP total vote nationwide. In elections that are settled by 10,000 votes in one state and 7,000 in another, that 10 percent wins or loses them.

The influx of religious conservatives into the GOP started with the grassroots opposition to the Equal Rights Amendment. The legislative attempt to provide women with explicit constitutional rights was met with a furious response from women in what are now called red states. C. S. Lewis once remarked that if his dog had bitten a neighbor's child, he would prefer to work things out with the father rather than the mother. The mother, he observed, would be the more ferocious and unforgiving of the two. Lewis would find support in the history of the Religious Right. It began with a band of women, mothers galvanized in opposition to the Equal Rights Amendment. The feminist movement, soon allied with gay-rights activists, set in motion the first stirrings of religious conservatives at the grassroots level. As will be discussed later, it was the IRS attack on supposed segregation in Christian schools that brought the pastors, the men, into the fray.

INVENTING THE PRO-FAMILY MOVEMENT

"I think we invented a pro-family movement in April 1976," Phyllis Schlafly told me in an interview at the Mayflower Hotel in Washington, D.C. I mean it as a compliment when I say that Schlafly is ageless. Attractive, overwhelmingly articulate, and perceptively intuitive, Schlafly asked me for a brief description of my book and then anticipated almost every question I wanted to ask. It's easy to misunderstand her because her grasp of questions is so facile and immediate that she can seem brusque, even rude. That's not the case. Schlafly has been a woman, a wife, and a mother on a mission since she became a public figure during the 1964 Barry Goldwater campaign.[7] Her first book, in 1964, *A Choice Not an Echo,* attacked the Northeastern Republican establishment and helped Goldwater win the presidential nomination. Schlafly, a Catholic from southern Illinois, was by that time already established as one of the nation's leading Cold War warriors, responsible for the creation of 5,000 study groups on anti-Communism.[8]

But the defeat of Goldwater had left Schlafly and fellow movement conservatives feeling as if they were a losing "remnant." "We simply didn't have enough people to get anybody elected." Schlafly felt no vindication with the election of Richard Nixon in 1968. As she says, "I can't say anything good about him." From Schlafly's perspective, Nixon's failings were legion, but his support of the Equal Rights Amendment typified him as part of the Republican establishment she despised.

In 1972, Congress began consideration of the Equal Rights Amendment. When Schlafly published a critique of the ERA in her newsletter,

7. Schlafly's latest preoccupation is no-fault divorce, which she brought up repeatedly throughout the interview: "People ask me, what's the worst thing that's happened to this country—it's no-fault divorce, not abortion. I think that is the biggest attack on our culture."

8. The original publisher of *A Choice Not an Echo* had an obviously Catholic name, Pere Marquette Press.

the *Phyllis Schlafly Report,* she was surprised by the response. "My report struck a nerve. When the feminists started out, their purpose was to make the homemaker economically impossible and socially disdained, which they did . . . it was fraud. They said they were going to put women in the Constitution, but men were not in the Constitution. It was an attack on wives. But later on, I realized that abortion and gay rights were their real agenda. It's clear that if ERA had been ratified, we would have had same-sex marriage twenty-five years ago."

In December 1972, Schlafly called a meeting of 100 women from thirty states and formed Stop ERA, renamed Eagle Forum in 1976, for the sole purpose of defeating the ERA. These women were from the group that had unsuccessfully supported her campaign for the presidency of the National Conference of Republican Women. ("They stole it from me," Schlafly recounts.) Under Schlafly's leadership, this core group of women began an organized lobbying campaign throughout the country, especially in the states where the ERA had not yet been ratified.[9]

Schlafly herself was in charge of her home state of Illinois. Once again, she was faced with the problem of numbers. How could she make an impression on the Illinois legislators without a sizable number of people? She decided to reach out to women who were most likely to be horrified by the ERA, women active in traditional churches. Schlafly did not contact the pastors first: "I called the women I knew in the churches." She asked them to recruit fellow church members for the first anti-ERA demonstration in Springfield.

"I sent the word out to every church I knew and prayed that we would get 1,000 people to the state capitol. We had people who had never been in the same room with each other: Catholics, Protestants, Mormons, and Orthodox Jews. Most of these people didn't even know where the state capitol was. I made them all work together." She got them to do this by telling them, "We've got a goal that we share, defeat ERA, which is a threat to you personally and to society. Nobody felt theologically threatened. I just wouldn't let them. But it was largely Evangelical."

9. The details of this movement are recounted in Donald T. Critchlow, *Phyllis Schlafly and Grassroots Conservatism: A Woman's Crusade* (Princeton, N.J.: Princeton University Press, 2005).

One thousand demonstrators showed up that day in Springfield. "The legislators," Schlafly recalls, "had never seen anything like this." The Illinois rally was the beginning of the grassroots religious conservative movement that would eventually undergo several permutations and take hold in the Republican Party.

"This all predates Falwell and Robertson," Schlafly remarks, "but they got the message. Falwell came to one of our later anti-ERA demonstrations when 10,000 showed up at the capitol in Springfield."

From a distance, it appears that the anti-Communist conservatives of the Goldwater era would have been allies of Schlafly in her new crusade against the ERA. After all, the fierce patriotism of the Goldwater years was shared by many prominent religious figures, such as Reverend Billy Graham, Reverend Billy James Hargis, Reverend Carl McIntyre, Cardinal Spellman, and Bishop Fulton Sheen. It would seem that implicit in the rejection of atheistic Communism, there would be strong support for the defense of the traditional family. But Schlafly insists this was not the case. "No, except for my personal supporters, none of the old Goldwater crowd supported me in this. They were a completely different group of people." She adds that most of the people she recruited from the churches in her fight against the ERA were Democrats. "We never had the numbers before; now we were finding a whole new group of people."

Schlafly credits the feminist movement for the introduction of gay rights into the mainstream of public consciousness. The turning point came at the congressionally funded National Women's Conference held in Houston in November 1977. Congress appropriated $5 million for the conference "to identify barriers that prevent women from participating fully and equally in all aspects of national life." A National Plan of Action, containing twenty-five points, was presented to the delegates for their approval. On most of the points, there was agreement among all parties, but on three—abortion rights, homosexual rights, and the ERA—there was a deep split.

The homosexual-rights statement, in fact, had not been included in the original set of points. It was added, according to Schlafly, by feminists who were concerned about losing the vote on the ERA. "Prior to the conference, people like Betty Friedan hadn't sold out to the lesbians, but they became concerned about what we were doing. They were looking for more troops, and that is when they invited the lesbians, and that is when people like Friedan made impassioned pleas to the audience to support gay rights. Since then, you can't be a member of a feminist organization without endorsing the gay-rights agenda. The feminists needed more troops, and that gave them more troops."

Gay rights elicited another one of the first salvos from the Religious Right in Dade County, Florida, the same year as the Houston conference. Former Miss America Anita Bryant was outraged by the passage of a gay-rights ordinance and succeeded in getting it repealed. A key mobilizing force for Bryant's campaign came from the national media ministry of Reverend Jerry Falwell. Following the success of the repeal effort under the "Save Our Children" banner, Falwell created the Moral Majority.[10]

William Martin, in his 1996 history of the Religious Right, comments on the importance of the National Women's Conference: "For years, and with good reason, committed feminists and zealous pro-family Christian women alike would look back on three days in Houston as a time when both their movements entered a new era."[11] Feminists embraced the larger agenda of gay rights, and Schlafly's ERA forces realized they could organize on a national scale and use the media coverage to gain support.

THE IRS STRIKES A MATCH

If Schlafly is the godmother of the Religious Right, Paul Weyrich is surely the godfather. Although he said publicly at a Washington dinner in his honor on September 15, 2006, that he "shouldn't be given credit for starting the movement," he is widely credited for doing so. Weyrich also could be described as the Saint Benedict of religious conservatives. Just

10. John C. Green, Mark J. Rozell, and Clyde Wilcox, eds., *The Christian Right in American Politics: Marching to the Millennium* (Washington, D.C.: Georgetown University Press, 2003), 85.
11. William Martin, *With God on Our Side: The Rise of the Religious Right in America* (New York: Broadway Books, 1996), 167.

as Benedict codified the monastic life in the early Middle Ages, Weyrich
provided a political playbook from which succeeding generations of Religious Right leaders got their start. Weyrich belongs to an Eastern Rite
communion of the Catholic Church. He is also an ordained deacon in
his church, a role that befits his intensity and his habit of speaking in
prophetic terms. There was an expectation that his surgery in 2005 to
remove both legs would be the end of his career. But, if anything, his
voice to religious conservatives only grew louder at a time when the lus-
ter of the Bush administration had dimmed. There was good reason for
his conference to discuss the direction of conservatism after the 2006
election to be standing-room-only.

Weyrich disagrees somewhat with his friend Phyllis Schlafly about
what issue initially brought religious conservatives into politics: "It
wasn't abortion or equal rights that started the Religious Right; it was
Carter's attempt to shut down private Christian schools. In Carter's administration, if your schools didn't reflect the ethnic diversity of the
community, they couldn't qualify for tax exemption." The number of
private Christian schools had exploded across the South in the wake of
federally mandated busing. In the period between 1970 and 1980, en-
rollment in public schools declined by 13.6 percent. The number of students in private Christian schools doubled, and by the mid-'80s, more
than 17,000 of these schools had been created.[12]

It would be a mistake to make too much of the difference of opinion
between Schlafly and Weyrich, as they are reflecting two different points
of view on events that happened almost concurrently. Schlafly is looking
from her grassroots perspective, while Weyrich is thinking of what finally activated the Evangelical ministers to get involved. What Schlafly
was doing from the ground up in Illinois and other ERA battleground
states Weyrich was doing out of Washington, D.C., through his series of
meetings with pastors both in D.C. and around the country.

The IRS story actually begins in 1969, well before the election of
Jimmy Carter. Parents of black children in Mississippi public schools

12. Godfrey Hodgson, *The World Turned Right Side Up: A History of the Conservative Ascendancy in America* (Boston: Houghton Mifflin, 1996), 171.

sued in a District of Columbia court to enjoin the Internal Revenue Service from providing tax-exempt status to private schools that discriminated against them.[13] On January 12, 1970, the three-judge District Court for the District of Columbia issued a preliminary injunction prohibiting the IRS from according tax-exempt status to private schools in Mississippi that discriminated based on race. This case—*Green* v. *Connally*—became the touchstone of subsequent judicial findings. The judges found that "discrimination on account of race is inconsistent with an educational institution's tax exempt status."

The IRS, with President Richard Nixon's reluctant approval, expanded this ruling by enforcing the court decision beyond Mississippi. In November 1970, the IRS informed Bob Jones University that its tax-exempt status would be revoked because the school refused to accept nonwhite students. BJU appealed the ruling on the grounds that it denied admission to nonwhite students based on biblical authority, which called for a separation of the races. The university's challenge to the IRS decision began a decade of litigation that would be argued twice before the Supreme Court. The second time it went before the Supreme Court, it was combined by the Fourth Circuit Court of Appeals with a similar case about school segregation involving the Goldsboro Christian school of Charlotte, North Carolina, founded in 1963. Both BJU and Goldsboro disputed the IRS decisions on the grounds of the Constitution's "free exercise" clause. Thus, it was under the Nixon administration that the first basic challenge was posed by the IRS against private Christian schools.

The IRS did relatively little to enforce this change in policy until the election of Jimmy Carter. Early in 1977, when Carter appointed Philadelphia tax lawyer Jerome Kurtz to be commissioner of the IRS, this was altered. Kurtz, a forty-five-year-old Harvard Law School graduate, had served as the chief tax legislative counsel for the Treasury Department from 1966 to 1968. An early activist of the Christian right later com-

13. I am following the chronology presented by Aaron Haberman, "Into the Wilderness: Ronald Reagan, Bob Jones University, and the Political Education of the Religious Right," *The Historian* (2005).

mented, "Jerome Kurtz has done more to bring Christians together than any man since the Apostle Paul." [14] Kurtz would become a lightning rod for criticism from conservative Christian leaders.

Kurtz soon upped the ante with private Christian schools. He required that the schools "prove their compliance with federal policy against racial discrimination." Kurtz set the bar at 20 percent of the minority school-age population in the community where the school was located. "Kurtz, like many civil rights advocates before him, believed that too many private schools had been created to avoid desegregation while still being able to enjoy a tax exemption." [15]

In August 1978, the IRS issued the following guidelines:

> A prima facie case of racial discrimination arises from evidence that the school (1) was formed or substantially expanded at or about the time of desegregation of the public schools, and (2) has an insignificant number of minority students. In each case, the school has the burden of clearly and convincingly rebutting this prima facie case of racial discrimination by showing that it has undertaken affirmative steps to secure minority students. Mere denial of a discriminatory purpose is insufficient. [16]

Kurtz's IRS stirred presidential candidate Ronald Reagan to speak out. In one of his national radio addresses (November 1978), Reagan criticized Kurtz by name, saying the IRS "threatens the destruction of religious freedom itself with this action," and claimed that "virtually all" of the schools whose tax status had been revoked were "presently desegregated." [17] The official campaign literature for Reagan highlighted the issue of religious liberty for private schools.

Congress also moved to act. In 1979, Representatives Robert Dornan (R-California) and John Ashbrook (R-Ohio) put a rider on an appro-

14. Tom Edsall and Mary Edsall, *Chain Reaction: The Impact of Race, Rights, and Taxes in American Politics*, reprint ed. (New York: W. W. Norton, 1992), 133.

15. Haberman, "Into the Wilderness," 238.

16. Hodgson, *The World Turned*, 176.

17. Haberman, "Into the Wilderness," 239.

priations bill forbidding the IRS from revoking the tax exemptions of any more schools. (Schools whose tax exemption had been revoked before August 22, 1978, were not affected.) The IRS's treatment of private Christian schools even made it into the 1980 party platform, which included a reference "to halt the unconstitutional regulatory vendetta launched by Mr. Carter's IRS commissioner against independent schools."[18] As a result, Republicans successfully used this issue in attracting religious conservatives.[19] The IRS contributed to the election results: 62 percent of conservative Christians voted for Reagan in 1980. The religious voters who had enabled Jimmy Carter to take office in 1976 deserted him in large numbers.

On this issue, however, Reagan's administration initially did nothing until Congressman Trent Lott sent a memo asking Reagan to reverse the policy. Reagan agreed and delegated the matter to Don Regan. On January 8, 1982, the Reagan administration reversed the IRS's revocation of tax exemption, including the cases of both BJU and Goldsboro. A political firestorm ensued, with most accusing Reagan of promoting racial discrimination.

So many described Reagan's actions as being racist that he quickly began to try to limit the damage with moderate white voters.[20] On January 12, 1982, Reagan submitted legislation prohibiting "tax exemptions for organizations that discriminate on the basis of race." If this signaled a break with the Religious Right, its leaders didn't show it. Most of them did not openly criticize Reagan but blamed this legislation on the influence of entrenched bureaucrats. Bob Jones III, however, did not hold back: Ronald Reagan was a "traitor to God's people."

Subsequent events took the monkey off Reagan's back. In February 1982, the U.S. Circuit Court of Appeals issued a ruling prohibiting the

18. Raymond Wolters, *Right Turn: William Bradford Reynolds, the Reagan Administration, and Black Civil Rights* (New Brunswick, N.J.: Transaction, 1996), 475.

19. Also see Don Critchlow, "Mobilizing Women: The Social Issues" in *The Reagan Presidency*, ed. W. Elliot Brownless and Hugh Davis Graham (Lawrence: University of Kansas Press, 2003), 293–326.

20. Dan T. Carter, *The Politics of Rage: George Wallace, the Origins of the New Conservatism, and the Transformation of American Politics* (New York: Simon & Schuster, 1995). Kenneth O'Reilly, *Nixon's Piano: Presidents and Racial Politics from Washington to Clinton* (New York: Free Press, 1995).

Treasury Department from reinstating the exemptions. Realizing that this action placed the spotlight on pending legislation that might anger conservative Christian leaders, the Justice Department intervened, asking the Supreme Court to hear the case of BJU and Goldsboro. In October 1982, the Court heard arguments and nine months later ruled in favor of the IRS. The Religious Right now had another reason to abhor the Supreme Court.

Evangelicals did not abandon Reagan for reversing his position on tax exemptions. The following year, 1984, conservative Christians would cast 80 percent of their votes for Reagan. That they decided to vote for him in spite of their disappointment was an important political lesson for the Religious Right. As Haberman argues, at that point in time, religious conservatives were a "captured group" which had no choice but to stick with the GOP; they realized that it was time to get involved in grassroots politics.[21] And they did.

PREACHERS GET INTO THE ACT

Weyrich's vision of fusing religiously active voters with grassroots politics started the ball rolling. It was an idea he had been thinking about since he was a teenager in Racine, Wisconsin. He came from a half-Catholic, half-Protestant family; his father was a cradle Catholic, and his mother converted. He became aware at an early age of tensions between Catholics and Protestants: "Members of my mother's family would not speak to her because of her conversion. A relative was constantly sending her Billy Graham tracts."

Weyrich remembers that he listened to both sides and heard a lot of overlap of what both sides believed in. "I knew instinctively in terms of public policy there were no differences, especially when you talked to the grassroots."

A very precocious nineteen-year-old, Weyrich called the chairman of the Wisconsin Republican Party after the 1962 Supreme Court decision

---

21. Haberman, "Into the Wilderness," 237.

outlawing school prayer. "I told him, 'This is a tremendous opportunity to get lots of people involved because a lot of people feel very strongly about this.' I told him this was a terrible ruling and had terrible implications for the country, and the party needs to come out and decry the ruling of the Supreme Court. You will get an influx of people from this important issue. He knew me because I had been active in the Young Republicans, and he had heard from me any number of times. He was always polite when I would call and tell him things I didn't think he knew. He said, 'Paul, we can't get involved in something like this, mixing church and state, it's none of our business, people would not understand.' I never forgot that, and I thought if I ever had the opportunity to change that attitude in the GOP, I would do it."

Weyrich points to a September 1977 meeting of Protestant pastors as the beginning of the Religious Right. That meeting came about totally by chance. In 1977, he met Bob Billings coming out of the cafeteria of the Dirksen Office Building and asked him what he was doing. Weyrich had supported Billings in a failed congressional race. Billings told Weyrich he was moving to Florida to take a job lobbying for Christian schools against the IRS threat to remove their tax exemption. "I asked him why he was going to Florida when all the action was here in Washington. We talked for the better part of an hour. God bless him, on my say-so he moved his family to Washington, sold his house, gave up his ministry, and started an organization called Christian School Action. He traveled the country for two years to fundamentalist churches and preached sermons in return for which the pastors agreed to take up a second collection. That is how he funded his organization until we taught him direct mail."

Billings told Weyrich he wanted to hold a meeting with pastors from around the country and asked him to be the main speaker. Weyrich reserved a large caucus room on the House side of Congress. "I was to be the main speaker. When I arrived, the room was filled with 300 ministers—they filled every seat and lined the walls. It was the first time I have ever heard 'Amen, brother' after everything I said, and they even gave me a standing ovation before I had opened my mouth. It was a culture-changing experience. That was the beginning, I think."

This historic meeting never made the newspapers, even though some members of Congress, such as Mormon Congressman Orrin Hatch, attended. Billings, at Weyrich's recommendation, would go on to become the second executive director of the Moral Majority under Falwell.

What motivated the pastors to come to Washington that day was religious liberty, specifically the right to educate their children in schools of their own choosing. This series of episodes regarding the tax-exempt status of private Christian schools, particularly across the South, represents the core of what inflamed conservative Christians. But to their critics, both in Congress and in the media, it was just another episode in Southern racism, transposing racism into a different set of issues. The religious liberty issue, for example, was just another way to perpetuate segregation. It was obvious that Jimmy Carter and his IRS saw it the same way.

THE CHARGE OF RACISM

The latest version of this charge comes from a moderate-left Evangelical, Randall Balmer, a professor of American religious history at Barnard College in New York City. As an editor-at-large for *Christianity Today* and occasional contributor to *Sojourners* and the *New Republic,* Balmer is a respected voice on the Religious Left. He recounts hearing Weyrich at a conference in 1990 making many of the same comments regarding the IRS and the beginning of the Religious Right. Balmer found Weyrich's comments "jarring" and came to the conclusion that "the Religious Right arose as a political movement for the purpose, effectively, of defending racial discrimination at Bob Jones University and at other segregated schools." [22]

Balmer uses his charge of racism to remove pro-lifers from their moral perch. He specifically rejects the comparison made by pro-lifers of their struggle with that of abolitionists. Balmer cites the hostility of religious conservatives to the IRS as proof of their supposed racism. This

22. Randall Balmer, *Thy Kingdom Come: An Evangelical's Lament* (New York: Basic Books, 2006), 14, 17.

original racism, for Balmer, compromises the intention of pro-lifers. It's a strange and forced argument that a bad deed on one day makes all the deeds that follow bad ones.

Balmer himself calls abortion a "travesty" and describes himself as a "libertarian" on the issue of government interference. He prefers that "the government have no jurisdiction whatsoever over gestation—a position, by the way, much more consistent with the Republican Party's avowed principle of less governmental interference in the lives of individuals."[23] His explanation of the difference between government interference in the cases of slavery and abortion is innovative: "Regrettable though it may be, the act of abortion is personal and episodic, whereas slavery was systematic and institutionalized."[24] He adds an argument from utility, that slavery can be effectively ended by new laws, while abortion will go on regardless of making it illegal. It's difficult for someone on the antiabortion side to accept a procedure as "personal and episodic" that is repeated approximately 1.25 million times a year, has been a central component of United States and United Nations population and health policy, and has been included in political party platforms for decades.[25]

In his complaint about laws against abortion, Balmer is ignoring the way law functions as an educating voice for public morality. A socially acceptable sense of right and wrong, even to the cynic, retards some behavior and encourages other. Is there any better example of this than the civil rights movement that Balmer praises? The aftermath of that movement, with its succession of laws opposed to racial discrimination, is historical proof that a change in laws can promote a change in behavior and underlying attitudes.

Ralph Reed's doctoral advisor at Emory University in Atlanta was Dan Carter, whose books on Southern politics also have made this accusation. Carter argued in his book on George Wallace that Wallace was the

23. Ibid., 19.
24. Ibid.
25. For statistics on legal abortions in the United States, see the reports of the Guttmacher Institute at www.guttmacher.org/pubs/fb_induced_abortion.html.

father of Reagan conservatism.[26] "Dan and I just disagree," Reed told me. "There were far more people worried about the churches' tax exempt status and defending religious liberty than any kind of racial impulse." Reed thinks it is a misunderstanding of political history to say that religious conservatives emerged from massive resistance to desegregation. "No one would deny that there were individuals and institutions with segregated pasts that came into the pro-family movement. But during that period of our history, there were racist attitudes throughout the country on both sides of the aisles—it permeated society."

Reed was chairman of the Republican Party of Georgia in 2002, when the state elected the first Republican governor since Reconstruction, Sonny Perdue. During the campaign, Perdue was critical of then-Governor Roy Barnes's decision to change the Georgia flag, which had borne the Confederate stars and bars in the corner since 1956. He was accused of "race baiting" at the time. Reed points out that no one ever accused Jimmy Carter of racism when he was governor of Georgia and did nothing to change the Georgia state flag. "Was it a moral failure? If so, why has no one mentioned it?"

Reed is correct to point out that Republicans, especially Southern Christian ones, don't get the benefit of the doubt when it comes to the race issue. He argues, "You have to ignore too much countervailing evidence to conclude the movement was motivated by racism." Reed points to the example of his former boss, Pat Robertson. "Robertson came out of the Pentecostal, charismatic movement, which was multiracial. It's no accident that Robertson was very much a liberal on race issues for his time. He spoke out on laws banning interracial dating and had a biracial couple on his staff when he founded CBN in 1963." Later, a regular co-host on Robertson's *700 Club* was Ben Kinchlow, an African-American.

"There is some truth to the charge of racism," Reed remarks, but he adds that it was the Southern Democrats who opposed the Civil Rights Act of 1964, while a majority of Republicans voted for it. He also points out that he was only four years old when the march at Selma took place.

---

26. Dan T. Carter, *From George Wallace to Newt Gingrich: Race in the Conservative Counterrevolution, 1963–1994* (Baton Rouge: Louisiana State University Press, 1996).

"It's simply not fair to accuse me, or anyone of my generation, of not being part of the civil rights movement."

Many of the leaders of the Religious Right lived through those changes that affected the South in particular. Reverend Don Wildmon, president of the American Family Association, admitted to me that racial prejudice was certainly a factor at the beginning of the movement. However, one 1979 study by a sociologist who visited Christian schools in North Carolina failed to find any racism either in the attitudes of staff and students or in what was being taught.[27] The court-ordered busing that stimulated the growth of Christian schools was the last straw in a series of perceived attacks on conservative Christian families. No doubt, there were families who did not want their children going to school with African-Americans. But where Carter and his IRS saw only racism, there was a seething discontent ready to explode into a mass movement.

27. Hodgson, *The World Turned,* 171.

4

THEOCRACY, THE MYTH

"**N**ONSENSE," SAYS JIM TOWEY WHEN I ASK HIM IF THE FAITH-based initiative of George W. Bush is an example of theocracy in action. Towey, a lifelong Democrat, was appointed by Bush in 2000 to be director of the White House Office of Faith Based and Community Initiatives. He stepped down in May 2006 to become president of St. Vincent's College in Latrobe, Pennsylvania.

Towey's road to the White House began as an encounter with Mother Teresa of Calcutta, who changed the direction of his life. He had worked ten years as senior advisor to Senator Mark Hatfield and Florida Governor Lawton Chiles, when he decided he needed a vacation far away from politics. In August 1985, Towey headed toward India, and, being an admirer of Mother Teresa, he decided to go to Calcutta to meet her. He only wanted to shake her hand, perhaps have a short conversation, and be on his way. "Well, when I got to the home for the dying, Sister Luke greeted me there as if I came to volunteer. She said, 'Great, I'm glad you came. Here's some cotton and solution, and clean this fellow in bed 46 who has scabies.'" A stunned Towey did as he was told, and, as he has said, "I met Jesus Christ in bed 46." When Towey returned home, he started doing legal work for Mother Teresa's Missionaries of Charity and worked as a volunteer in her soup kitchen in Anacostia in the southeastern section of Washington, D.C. Several years later, he lived in that home and served for a year at a mission in Mexico. In all, Towey served as Mother Teresa's legal counsel for ten years.[1]

Given his experience, Towey was one member of the Bush administration no one could accuse of not caring about the poor. He took the White House job following the resignation of the first director, Dr. John DiJulio, who had faced nonstop political attacks on the faith-based initiative. The program, a centerpiece of the Bush administration, had become a symbol of the incipient theocracy in America led by the Evangelical president.

During Bush's first term, "theocracy" replaced "Religious Right" as the label of choice to assail the political activism of religious conservatives. Over the years, "Religious Right" lost its power to alarm, becoming a descriptive phrase and leaving critics to devise a new attack language. Members of the Religious Right are now called "theocrats," their political methods are "theocratic," and their political aim is a "theocracy." Literally meaning government by God, "theocracy" is the newest pejorative employed to demonize religious conservatives.

Towey thinks the charge exposes the "fundamental disagreement of liberals with conservative Christian leaders—Christian leaders don't look for government to be their Messiah." In other words, liberals expect more from government, expect it to be more expansive than the religious conservatives they criticize.

"What the critics don't get," says Towey, "is whether this or that program is about really helping the poor. The Religious Left would speak sincerely about their concern for the poor, but what amazed me was the blind spot they had when it came to asking, on behalf of the poor, 'Does this addiction center getting all this government money actually help people to recover?'"

In our interview, Towey often came back to the liberal habit of throwing government money at social problems. "A lot of people have measured the compassion of government by how big its block grant is, but

---

1. See Deal W. Hudson, "*Crisis* Interview with Jim Towey," *Crisis* (June 2002).

after thirty years, the poor are still trapped in their poverty. If you really care about the poor, you have to ask the question whether or not such programs work."

When I asked Towey if he got results, he said, "Absolutely. The focus of the debate is now shifting toward results instead of giving to the same old groups. Two-thirds of governors have faith-based offices. The states are getting over the knee-jerk reaction about church and state and realizing if you want to help the poor, you have got to connect with the faith-based community."

Democrats and liberal critics accused Bush and Karl Rove of using the faith-based initiative for political purposes, to attract larger sections of African-American and Latino voters. Towey calls that "cynical." "Look at the voting results. The African-American vote barely budged. It's laughable, really. The idea they would sell their souls for a government grant and become obedient Republicans is insane. They weren't going to vote for Bush in a million years—they really didn't like him."

On the eve of the 2006 election, one of Towey's former employees, David Kuo, published a book calling the faith-based initiative part of a vast "seduction" of religious conservatives by the Bush White House.[2] "That's a very naïve read of what Bush was doing," says Towey. "Religious leaders know that political leaders have an agenda. They're not blind, and religious leaders have their own agenda, too. That's the nature of meetings in Washington, D.C." If Towey is right, then religious conservatives have come a long way since the days when Chuck Colson and Pat Buchanan were running religious outreach out of the Nixon White House. Colson told me that religious leaders were the "first to compromise" their core beliefs in order to keep their access to the White House.[3]

2. David Kuo, *Tempting Faith: The Inside Story of a Political Seduction* (New York: Free Press, 2006).

3. For Colson's role in the Nixon White House, see Jonathan Aitken, *Charles W. Colson: A Life Redeemed* (Colorado Springs, Colo.: Waterbrook Press, 2005), chapter 7. One of the most interesting stories in the book is Nixon's comment to Colson that he was considering a conversion to Catholicism. Colson quotes Nixon as saying, "What I like about Catholicism is that it is unswerving, stable, and solid in its teachings of traditional morality. Catholics don't go off preaching all these half-cocked social issues. They stay with the fundamentals of man's obedience to God" (163).

Towey thinks those days are past: "The idea that religious leaders come in and swoon at the sight of the Oval Office is selling religious leaders short."

As for the charge by Kuo that he often heard jibes toward religious conservatives at the White House, Towey says, "Baloney. He may have heard something at the lower levels in the White House. It wasn't uncommon to see a staffer show some frustration at a religious leader saying something that would inflame Muslims or put social conservatives in a bad light, but that's all."

I asked Towey how important the faith-based grants were in keeping religious conservatives in the coalition. "Most of the Evangelicals weren't interested in getting government money. Reverend Eugene Rivers never got a grant; neither did Tony Perkins or James Dobson. These leaders were there because they shared the president's belief that the government cannot love, cannot give compassion."

Kuo, interviewed by Bill Maher on his HBO show (October 20, 2006), accused President Bush of "deception" in the faith-based initiative. Interestingly, Kuo is able to recount in his book the exact details of conversations during the entire time of his employment in the faith-based office. No one I talked with from the White House, including Towey, knew that Kuo was taking notes for a book while he worked there.

In the *60 Minutes* segment (October 15, 2006) devoted to Kuo's story, Lesley Stahl is shown interviewing Kuo in front of a literature table at the Family Research Council Action's Values Voter Summit. In Kuo's and Stahl's comments, Towey points out there's "no mention of the poor, only abortion." But clearly pictured on camera were nearby tables of literature about precisely what Kuo said was missing—the need to address problems of poverty. No one at *60 Minutes* thought to edit Kuo's comments on the broadcast.

The veritable celebration in the media of the Kuo book on the eve of the 2006 election was a well-timed attempt to drive a wedge between the GOP and Evangelicals, but it had no noticeable effect (unless, of course, Kuo wants to take credit for the lower number of Evangelical voters—the percentage voting for the GOP changed only slightly).

Evangelicals were hardly going to believe the stories of a staffer who had only been in the Oval Office once, who was hardly the insider his book touted, and who was asked to resign after a long period of poor performance both before and after a difficult period of illness. Evangelicals had been in politics far too long to believe Kuo's stories. The only part of Kuo's argument with any staying power is a warning heard before from Cal Thomas and Ed Dobson[4] that Evangelicals have been co-opted by politics and need to get back to spiritual basics. Kuo's book is nothing more than another arrow in the quiver of critics who want to accuse the Republicans of manipulating religious conservatives.

THE THREAT OF DOMINION

The Religious Right has continued to prosper even in the face of many defections and several obituaries. After the 1996 reelection of Bill Clinton, the media announced the funeral of the Religious Right, only to watch it reemerge stronger than ever in the elections of 2000 and 2004. As Ralph Reed put it, "We owe a great deal to Bill Clinton. His contribution to the explosive growth of religious conservatives in the 1990s cannot be exaggerated; it was like a booster rocket." Ten years later, Alan Wolfe announced the "Religious Right's last rites" after the 2006 election. Wolfe projected his own personal wishes into his political commentary, because 2006, more than a defeat for the Religious Right, was proof that the Democratic Party had finally realized it could no longer ignore and alienate the religiously active voter.[5]

Democrats stood by and ignored the growing concern among religious conservatives about the relation of God to government. If the '70s witnessed the organization and active protest of religious conservatives, it was the Supreme Court school-prayer decisions of the early '60s that alerted conservative Christians that the government was no longer on

4. Cal Thomas and Ed Dobson, *Blinded by Might: Can the Religious Right Save America?* (Grand Rapids, Mich.: Zondervan, 1999).

5. Alan Wolfe, "The Religious Right's Last Rites," http://commentisfree.guardian.co.uk/alan_wolfe/2006/11/alan_wolfe_1.html.

their side. In *Engel* v. *Vitale* (1962), *Murray* v. *Curlett* (1963), and *Abington Township School District* v. *Schempp* (1963), the Court removed prayer and Bible reading from U.S. public schools. The overwhelming reaction in the Christian grassroots community was that the federal government was depriving their children of God. By forcibly taking God out of an important aspect of their children's lives, the government was, in effect, promoting secularism, if not atheism. In the midst of the Cold War with the godless Soviet Union, the Supreme Court was divesting American children of the very thing that was officially forbidden under Communism.

Until these Supreme Court decisions, and the ones to follow, Christianity had enjoyed a privileged place in American culture and institutions. To the ordinary Christian, the Court was doing the dirty work of a few militant atheists, such as Madalyn Murray O'Hair, and the ensuing cultural disarray of the '60s was the result.

When religious conservatives began to fight the imposition of secularism, they sought to reclaim a cultural space for public witness to and belief in God. With the exception of a group called Christian Reconstructionists, none of the leaders of the Religious Right promoted theocracy either in theory or in practice. Rousas John Rushdoony, a Calvinist theologian who died in 2001, wrote the three-volume *Institutes of Biblical Law,* published in 1973, considered the central statement of Christian Reconstructionism. Rushdoony's occasional contact with the Religious Right leadership is used to prove that the entire movement has theocratic intentions.[6] The fact that Rushdoony was invited to sit on a panel at a conference is considered irrefutable evidence that everyone who knew him secretly shared his theocratic aspirations.

Rushdoony proposed what became known as a "dominion theology," calling for Christians to exercise dominion over the earth, subjecting it to the only true laws, those being the laws found in the Old and New Testaments. His most infamous moment was recorded on videotape in 1987 as part of Bill Moyers's *God and Politics* series for PBS. During the inter-

---

6. Frederick Clarkson, *Eternal Hostility: The Struggle between Theocracy and Democracy* (Monroe, Maine: Common Courage Press, 1997), 79–123.

view, Rushdoony argued for a new justice system based on biblical laws. Rushdoony added that this would mean capital punishment for anyone found guilty of adultery, sodomy, or homosexuality. "This is what God requires," he said.

Howard Phillips, a close friend and associate of Paul Weyrich in the '70s, helped to found the Moral Majority and other early organizations of the Religious Right. Phillips converted from Judaism to Christianity and came under the influence of Rushdoony. After leaving the Republican Party, he eventually created the U.S. Taxpayers Party in 1992 (renamed the Constitution Party in 1999) to formalize the tenets of Christian Reconstructionism. In a 1998 interview, Phillips described his gradual disillusionment with the Republican Party, beginning with Reagan, whom he helped to elect, and finally with George H. W. Bush. He came to the conclusion that it was no longer "morally permissible" for him to work for the president or the party or to ask anyone else to do so.

"I decided I had two choices. I had the one choice of withdrawing entirely from politics—because I could not in good conscience rally people to the banner of 'losing as slowly as possible.' On the other hand, I had to define and articulate a vision of victory. So I had to spend a lot of time thinking about what victory in political terms meant. And in a nutshell, I concluded that it meant biblical justice, biblical jurisprudence . . . that we are one nation under God, a nation which must live by the rules that He makes."[7]

The defection of Howard Phillips from the mainstream movement of the religious conservatives into Christian Reconstructionism is more significant than the story lines presented by movement critics. But the story also demonstrates that Rushdoony's influence is minimal. Phillips, once hailed as a founder alongside Weyrich, Schlafly, and Falwell, has no visibility or influence today, though he is spoken of with great affection.

Rushdoony created the Chalcedon Foundation in 1965, which carries on his work. The statement of belief on the Web site of the foundation

---

7. Craige McMillan, "The Last Honorable Politician?" October 29, 1998, www.worldnetdaily .com/news/article.asp?ARTICLE_ID=19259.

specifically denies the charges understandably made against Rushdoony and Christian Reconstructionism:

> [I]t is sometimes assumed that we believe that capturing state apparatus and enforcing Biblical law on a pervasively unbelieving populace is one of our hidden objectives. Our critics sometimes imply or state outright that we are engaged in a subtle, covert attempt to capture conservative, right-wing politics in order to gain political power, which we will then use to "spring" Biblical law on our nation. This is flatly false. We do not believe that politics or the state are a chief sphere of dominion.[8]

This may well be an overly nuanced defense, but the fact remains that Rushdoony's followers have dissociated themselves from his theocratic tendencies. When I asked Reverend Don Wildmon of the American Family Association about whether he was influenced by Rushdoony, he answered, "Well, that's a name I haven't heard in a very long time. Yes, he was around for a short time, and then he disappeared. He never had any major influence that I am aware of." No one I interviewed considered Rushdoony a major figure, and most laughed at the level of attention devoted to his supposed "influence." Patrick Hynes, author of *In Defense of the Religious Right*, gave the same chuckle when he was asked this question.[9] Rushdoony had nothing like the influence of Evangelical figures such as Francis Schaeffer, Carl F. H. Henry, John Warwick Montgomery, R. C. Sproul, J. I. Packer, and John Stott, to name only a few.

"The biggest misunderstanding was that the Religious Right was trying to legislate its religious beliefs," says Ralph Reed, former head of the Christian Coalition. He told me that there were individuals, such as Rushdoony, who made it sound as if they wanted to legislate beliefs. But that was definitely not what he and most religious conservatives were

---

8. "What Chalcedon Believes," <http://www.chalcedon.edu/credo.php>.

9. Patrick Hynes, *In Defense of the Religious Right: Why Conservative Christians Are the Lifeblood of the Republican Party and Why That Terrifies the Democrats* (Nashville, Tenn.: Nelson Current, 2006), 198–99.

trying to do. "My religious belief teaches me that God hates divorce, but I've never heard anyone suggest that we outlaw divorce."

The word that kept coming up in my conversation with Reed was "prudence." The relationship between his religious beliefs and politics, he explained, was mediated by many prudential considerations, only one of which was the content of his faith. "My faith informs what I determine to be right and wrong, especially in the context of my personal life. How I choose to legislate that is informed by other things as well—the American civic tradition, the founders, and what is enforceable." Prohibition is a good example of such overreaching, even though it passed both houses of Congress with a two-thirds vote and was passed in three-quarters of all the states. "Prohibition was a failed experiment. For some, it was legislating a religious belief; for some, anti-Catholicism and anti-immigrant; but for others, it came from a progressive impulse, more like laws against drugs today." The importance of prudence to Reed is crucial. If a law is not enforceable and people won't do it, "then it's a failure."

For Ralph Reed, an Evangelical and a highly prized strategist of religious conservatism, the relationship between the content of faith and public policy is not immediate. The moral content of faith must be scrutinized intellectually before it can be applied to the public square.

Reed pointed out the lessons to be learned from the mistakes of the secular left. "*Roe* v. *Wade* has been a total disaster for them—they tried to impose their view by judicial fiat on the whole of nature, and it's a total failure. Religious conservatives," he counsels, "have to be cautious, skeptical, and willing to take incremental measures." Reed says this attitude was developed in his early years as a political strategist whose bottom line was "to win." He thinks it was fortunate that Pope John Paul II supported an incremental approach to political action in his encyclical *Evangelium Vitae,* which was published while Reed was still at the Christian Coalition. (Reed and his wife, Jo Anne, met John Paul II shortly before he died, and pictures of their meeting are on the walls of their respective offices.)

Reed was often criticized for this approach while he was at the Christian Coalition. He was routinely accused of "compromising," "selling out," being "more Republican than Christian," but he argues that the key is clear about the "final goal." "When I was at the Christian Coalition, I believed in bold incrementalism—you hold out the final goal, but as you seek to pass laws incrementally, you can change the culture while you are doing that." Thus, Reed was attacked from the right for compromising and from the left for being a theocrat, when in fact he deliberately sought a reasoned middle ground.

There is a certain irony, by the way, in the use of theocracy to vilify the largely Evangelical Religious Right. Theocracy is an old anti-Catholic smear, used against Governor Al Smith in 1928 and Senator John F. Kennedy in 1960. The irony is found in the fact that the people making those charges forty-eight years ago were largely the kind of earnest Evangelicals now leading the Religious Right. Now the Evangelicals share the brunt of the attack with Catholics.

Former Senator Gary Hart is one commentator who has made the charge of theocracy his drumbeat against religious conservatives. A former seminarian, Hart is aware that the old complaint against Catholic influence can now be made toward Evangelicals. In a recent interview regarding his book *Religious Right: God and Caesar in America: An Essay on Religion and Politics,* he warned against the coming theocracy. He decried the influence of Evangelicals on the withdrawal of the Harriet Miers Supreme Court nomination. He ponders what might have happened if Kennedy had sought the pope's advice. "The country veers toward theocracy," Hart said, "when religious interest groups hold so much influence." [10]

Religious influence, as we shall see, is the crux of the complaint against religious conservatives. Calling this influence "theocratic" ignores all previous accepted usages of the term.

10. *Denver Post,* November 4, 2005, B4.

THEOCRACY GOES PUBLIC

On July 18, 2006, in the midst of the debate over nominations to the Supreme Court, Senator Chuck Schumer (D-New York) gave what was up
to that time the most public airing of the theocracy charge: "There is a
group of people of deep faith. I respect that faith. I've been in enough
inner-city black churches, working-class Catholic parishes, rural Methodist houses of worship, and small Jewish synagogues to understand that
faith is a gift. The trouble with this group, which I call theocrats, is they
want their faith to dictate what the government does. That, in a word, is
un-American. That is exactly what the Founding Fathers put down their
plows and took up their muskets to fight." Religious leaders across the
nation exploded with indignation.[11]

Schumer's rant was remarkable, not only for the charge of theocracy
but also for the notion that the American Revolution itself was elicited
by oppression of British theocracy, not taxes and the myriad other reasons behind the colonial revolt. As we will see, those who try to make the
charge of theocracy stick also have been busy concocting an entire mythology of the American founding to ground their position in an ongoing struggle between religious zealotry and constitutional restraints
throughout U.S. history. It wasn't Anglican prayer books the Americans
threw into Boston Harbor.

Democrats, by the way, aren't the only politicos repeating the charge.
Republican Congressman Christopher Shays of Connecticut remarked
during the Terri Schiavo ordeal, "The Republican Party of Lincoln has
become the party of theocracy. . . . There are a number of people who
feel that government is getting involved in their personal lives in a way
that scares them."[12] It was also a former Republican operative and strategist, Kevin Phillips, who published a best-selling book in 2006 entitled
American Theocracy. Phillips is perhaps the first political strategist who
recognized how the influence of religious conservatives—Southern

---

11. "National Church Leaders Demand Schumer Apologize," *Christian Newswire,* July 19,
2006.

12. Interview with Alex Chadwick, National Public Radio, March 24, 2005.

Evangelicals and ethnic Catholics—was going to reshape American politics in favor of the GOP.[13] Now, the political realignment he once foresaw is scaring the hell out of him.

"Religious Right," at least, had the advantage of being a plausibly fair description of Christians and other religious conservatives, but the attempt to replace that label with a more explicitly negative one is problematic. To make the charge of "theocracy" credible requires an enormous stretching of the common sense of the term. But expanding the accepted meaning is precisely what the critics are doing. Critics of the Religious Right have rolled the dice, believing the charge of theocracy will steer voters away from religious conservatives in future elections. But the attempt itself also provides further evidence that the heart of the controversy of religious conservatives in politics is not about policy per se but, as I have said, is about religion.

The critics have construed theocracy in such a broad way that their intention to keep all expressions of religious faith from having any influence in the sphere of public policy and legislation is revealed. The very act or intention of influencing politics with a morality derived from the content of faith is defined as theocratic. It makes no difference whether that influence is expressed through the democratic process. The fact that the moral perspective is informed by faith qualifies it as theocratic.

The history of politics abounds in various forms of theocracies, including familiar ones, from the history of medieval Europe and the Puritan colonies of America, to the ayatollahs of the Middle East, to emperor cults of the Far East and the ancient world. The first use of the term "theocracy" is found in the Jewish historian Josephus, who used it to describe the way Jews viewed themselves as being under the direct government of God.

The characteristics of theocracies are somewhat varied but fall within a general outline, beginning with Josephus's notion of direct government under God. In each case, the government and the dominant religion are intertwined under the leadership of a divinely ordained ruler.

13. Kevin Phillips, *The Emerging Republican Majority* (New York: Arlington House, 1969).

The authority of the ruler and the entire government is derived from the supernatural, and the structure of law and justice is based directly on religious morality, with no attempt to distinguish between obligations toward the state and those toward religion. Because both secular and sacred authorities are united in the ruler, his power is absolute and unassailable.

This may sound wonderfully efficient, but as a matter of fact, theocracies in the Christian West are difficult to maintain because of differences that arise between the authority of the ruler and the religious tradition itself, whether it is vested in the Vatican or in the inspired interpretation of sacred Scripture. Religious authority is not limited to the divinely inspired pastor or an emperor as the unique human embodiment of the divine. In the case of theocracies of medieval Europe, tension often developed between the authority of the Vatican, as the head of the universal Church, and the divine-right king, as head of an empire or a nation.

One of the many things about religious conservatives that their critics do not understand is the impossibility of controlling them. Left-wing commentators are used to dealing with religionists who view everything through the lens of Democratic Party politics and are therefore docile before party leadership. Critics seem to think that religious conservatives have some kind of master plan spelling out where and when the Religious Right is going to weigh in on particular issues in order to influence electoral outcomes. Leaders among religious conservatives and the GOP often wish they had a master switch to activate the grassroots, but it just isn't so.

WHITE HOUSE EXORCIST

This misunderstanding is the central assumption of the book about Karl Rove coauthored by James Moore and Wayne Slater and titled *The Architect*.[14] The story line of the book portrays Rove, traumatized as a young man by the desertion of his homosexual father, later devising a strategy

14. James Moore and Wayne Slater, *The Architect: Karl Rove and the Master Plan for Absolute Power* (New York: Crown, 2006).

for the 2004 presidential election focused on the gay-marriage issue. In actual fact, as Ralph Reed explained to me, "The gay marriage issue was not on anybody's radar screen until eight members of the Massachusetts Supreme Court decided to redefine marriage."

Critics are always attributing more cunning to the Religious Right leadership than exists. But they ignore how left-wing activists alienate mainstream America with their radical social engineering. The marriage issue was not one that the Bush White House wanted to embrace prior to the Massachusetts decision—it didn't think it was necessary because of the Defense of Marriage Act passed during the Clinton administration. Marriage activists such as Matt Daniels of the Alliance for Marriage had been pressing the White House for several years, arguing that the only solution was support for a federal marriage amendment. It was the Massachusetts Supreme Court, not Bush and Rove, that elevated this into the front rank of issues for the White House and the 2004 election.

The use of "theocracy" to describe the activities of the Religious Right was made popular more than a decade ago by Frederick Clarkson. His writings were gathered in a book titled *Eternal Hostility: The Struggle between Theocracy and Democracy* and published in 1997. (In the acknowledgments, Clarkson thanks his "former colleagues at Planned Parenthood Federation of America.")[15]

Clarkson uses the entirety of American history as the background for his discussion:

> From the persecution of Quakers, Jesuits, and "witches" in the Massachusetts Bay Colony during the 1600s through the bitter presidential election campaign of 1800, and the advent of the Christian Right in the 1980s, an animating, underlying theme of the American experience has been the struggle between democratic and theocratic values. The descendants of the losing side have not forgotten. Self-proclaimed "orthodox" Christians have opposed democracy, pluralism, and religious freedom for hundreds of years. Having re-

15. Frederick Clarkson, *Eternal Hostility: The Struggle between Theocracy and Democracy* (Monroe, Maine: Common Courage Press, 1997), viii.

grouped after losing most of the major battles since the ratification of the Constitution, they are attempting a comeback.[16]

What is evident here is that Clarkson is not attempting a serious head-on discussion of the merits and demerits of religious conservatives. He is constructing a mythology. Just as he finds David Barton and Pat Robertson guilty of touting a "Christian Nation," Clarkson creates a caricature of the secularism that informs the Constitution and especially the First Amendment. It is quite one thing for the Founders to have created a state without an established religion; it is quite another thing to regard religion as the perennial enemy of that state.

The essentials of Clarkson's mythology are contained in the quote above; namely, that before the American founding, theocrats enjoyed a free hand in ruling their communities. Then the Constitution came along, taking away their power by establishing a democracy, human rights, and religious liberty. These same theocrats have been scheming ever since to overthrow the Constitution and reestablish their lost theocratic communities.

If Clarkson is right, Falwell, Robertson, Reed, and Dobson evidently spent their early lives seething inwardly over the U.S. Constitution and the barrier it presented to establishing the New Jerusalem ruled entirely by law derived solely from the Bible. Once again, a critic of the Religious Right refuses to address the actual issues that rallied religious conservatives into the political process: judicial decisions and federal laws hostile to religious families, institutions, and communities, particularly laws that contained egregious challenges to the fundamental sense of right and wrong found in those communities.

IT'S ALL JUST NONSENSE

When I asked Reverend Don Wildmon of the American Family Association about the charge of theocracy, his one-word answer was identical to

16. Ibid., 4–5.

Jim Towey's: "Nonsense." Similar answers were given to me by every leader of the Religious Right I interviewed. Like Wildmon, they find the description so far-fetched as to be laughable. When I asked Pat Robertson if he was a theocrat, he answered, "Absolutely untrue. I am a Jeffersonian conservative brought up in traditions of the early founders of this nation. The last thing I want to see is a theocracy in America. It is a secular state that acknowledges the presence of God."

I asked Robertson why he thought he was accused of supporting theocracy. He offered that those on the left were merely accusing him of what they would do if they had the opportunity. "It's easier to set up a straw man and knock him down and vilify him. If you let somebody be who he is, then of course it's impossible to have the thirty-second sound bite in a political campaign. This is all political. These people are power-hungry. In addition, the left attributes to somebody like me what they would do if they were in my position. I don't share their desires, their motives, or operations, so as a result, they are attributing theirs to me. Transference is the psychological name of what they do."

While religious conservatives have not usurped the Constitution, they have used its democratic process to secure political change. Clarkson himself understands this very well; his narrative detailing the alliance of religious conservatives with the Republican Party is thorough and insightful. Why does Clarkson, like so many others, ignore the fact that religious conservatives play by the rules? They employ the democratic process. Theocracy is indeed the enemy of democracy *if* the authority to rule and make laws is put into the hands of an unelected religious elite. But as long as the influence of religious conservatives is being expressed through democratic means, why are they still charged with being theocrats?

Sometimes answers to such questions are deceptively simple. The reason such an answer can be overlooked is that it appears too preposterous to be true. But what appears ridiculous to one group can appear perfectly reasonable to another, and that, unfortunately, is where this debate stands. Critics regard any action of religious conservatives as theocratic precisely because they are religious first and political second. The critics regard any political aim as theocratic if it is motivated by a religious impulse or measured by a religious standard.

Kevin Phillips is one critic of the Religious Right who has been honest about this. He admits that the theocracy he sees in the George W. Bush administration is nothing compared with the theocracy of premodern times—it is rather defined as "some degree of rule by religion." [17] Neither Phillips nor Clarkson gets upset over religiously motivated support in the twentieth century for civil rights, environmental protection, poverty assistance, health-care reform, and so on. They are alarmed solely by religious motivations behind proposed strictures on abortion, fetal stem-cell research, euthanasia, and homosexual rights.

They also take no note of Religious Left writers such as Reverend Jim Wallis, Rabbi Michael Lerner, and Tony Campolo, who offer religious justification for the agenda of the Democratic Party (and the "Greens"). Are these examples of theocracy to Phillips and Clarkson? Indeed, they must be: "some degree of rule by religion"; the definition fits.

This view of theocracy is obviously very different from the one we learned in school, but it is important to try to make sense of the charge. It will help to reveal more about the gap that exists between the two sides of the debate. In Clarkson's mythology, the Religious Right, in addition to being theocratic, is "anti-democratic." He defends this by claiming that religious conservatives don't represent the "mainstream" values of the American people. Religious conservatives are thus "anti-democratic" for actively opposing beliefs that, according to Clarkson, are held by a majority of Americans. As a result, groups who oppose religious conservatives can be termed "pro-democracy" rather than pro-abortion, pro-euthanasia, or pro-gay marriage.

Nowhere, by the way, does Clarkson pause to consider that religious conservatives don't settle these issues by taking a head count. Clarkson implies that if a majority of people consider abortion ethically acceptable, then no one should attempt to overturn the laws permitting it. There seems to be something intrinsically wrong, according to Clarkson, in opposing someone else's values already embedded in the political

17. Kevin Phillips, *American Theocracy: The Peril and Politics of Radical Religion, Oil, and Borrowed Money in the 21st Century* (New York: Viking, 2006), 208.

sphere. But isn't that what the political process is all about, airing opposing points of view, making public arguments for and against, and letting
the people vote for the agenda they support?

Clarkson, like so many Religious Right critics, wants to baptize the
secular status quo. He treats the '60s the way a conservative Republican
is accused of treating the '50s: as a utopian era that should be frozen in
time. Religious conservatives are anti-democratic for trying to change
laws that they view as morally repugnant. One wonders if Clarkson
would label any and all social movements anti-democratic if they sought
to change laws supported by majority opinion. What would he think of
the gay-marriage movement, for example? Would Clarkson consider it
anti-democratic? The majority of Americans, after all, are opposed to
gay marriage by a large margin.

Critics of the Religious Right are constantly leveling charges that
could just as easily be applied to the civil rights movement of the '60s
and other religiously inspired social movements such as the abolition of
slavery. Don't bother looking for consistency in their criticism. It can't
be found, and this comes from the crowd that bears the standard of Enlightenment rationality.

What evidence does Clarkson produce that millions of Evangelicals
and Catholics hanker for the good old days of witch burning and the
thumbscrews of the Inquisition? Rushdoony's Christian Reconstructionists are all he can produce. Sure, Rushdoony types exist, but they are
few and far between, and he knows it. So, using random comments of
Falwell and Robertson, Clarkson accuses the Religious Right of harbor-
ing deep prejudice against women, Jews, and homosexuals.

These arguments may stir those already disposed to dismissing the
Religious Right, but members of the movement themselves are not
moved by them. My interviews with grassroots members of the Moral
Majority and the Christian Coalition found no weakening for their support of Falwell and Robertson, even when they made disagreeable statements. As one longtime supporter, Lois Davis of Houston, told me, "My
confidence is not in the men but in the message, in the truth. And that
truth is the one person that I believe in, Jesus Christ."

Regarding their supposed hatred of and prejudice against gays, women, and Jews, religious conservatives reject the line of argument that transposes opposition to abortion and gay marriage into hate crimes. They also reject the charge of anti-Semitism based on their belief that faith in Jesus Christ is the sole means of achieving eternal life.

Religious conservatives also refuse to recognize anything as a "right" that is at odds with the moral order. How can anyone have a "right" to kill an unborn child? There is no such thing as a "right" to do something bad. They understand that the courts and the government have recognized such "rights," but their political aim is to overthrow these false rights just as Lincoln's Emancipation Proclamation declared that no one has a "right" to own another person as a piece of property. As I said earlier, the kind of moral discontent born out of religious commitment cannot be controlled by talk about majority opinion, public consensus, or Supreme Court interpretations.

One wonders how successful the theocracy strategy will be in demonizing the Religious Right when it takes such a reach to view religious conservatives as seeking to overthrow the Constitution, destroy the democratic process, and place the U.S. government, using Josephus's words, directly under God? It will be especially difficult, after the much-touted success of the Democrats in 2006, to reach out to religious voters by encouraging candidates to talk publicly about their faith.

Those in the media and the academy who report on our past to us via interpretations of current events in print and electronic media have missed an important part of the story. The '60s did not overthrow the dominance of traditional religion in the heartland of this country. Yes, there are obvious differences. There seems to be as much difference between the '50s and '60s as a black-and-white photograph differs from one in full color.

The emergence of the Religious Right suggests more of a subterranean continuity with the postwar years than is usually acknowledged. It's commonplace for cultural historians to proclaim the '60s and the decades following as a period of rapid cultural changes, a revolution in mores and morals.

But something important is missing from that characterization: the way groups with deeply rooted allegiances to traditional religion and values resisted the revolution and eventually struck back.

Conservative Evangelicals and Catholics were not insulated from the tumult—they processed the succession of '60s and '70s social experimentation as everyone else did. But within these communities, there always hangs a lifeline to the past. Recall, however, that three generations will experience social change at any given time: children, parents, and grandparents. The meaning and impact of the change will be thought and felt differently by the generations. In families with a history of religious practice, the generational responses, that is, the reaction of the grandparents, will not be unfelt by their children, their children's children, and their grandchildren.

The grandparents will despair over the too-long hair, beards, body piercing, and tattoos of the grandchildren, as well as the divorces, drug use, and depression of their own children. Such generational interdependence is common to religious groups, especially those who consider prayer and faith necessary to a happy life and eternal reward.

A grandparent who sees a child breaking one of the Ten Commandments without remorse or a grandchild who is not attending church on Sunday will not sit idly by. Catholic grandparents will send their grandchildren books and tapes by Bishop Fulton Sheen and Pope John Paul II; Evangelicals will send Billy Graham, Jerry Falwell, or the apocalyptic novels of Tim and Beverly LaHaye. How many college students in the '60s found the *National Review* arriving in the mailbox, as I did, because a relative was afraid of liberal, perhaps even socialist or communist, teachers? The '60s brought change, no doubt, but in doing so heightened the generational struggle, which has yet to end.

The continuity in worldview and belief does not survive only because of external pressure from previous generations. Children who are raised to attend church or parish on Sunday, who attend Sunday school or say the rosary, who see pictures of Jesus and the pope on the wall, will carry these experiences inside them. These will be the internal pressure or memory of life before the revolution.

The stories of "reverts," those who lost their faith or stopped their practice and then resumed again, are commonplace among the Evangelical members of the Religious Right and socially conservative Catholics. These movements receive repeated injections of new enthusiasm and new adherence from people who have the experience of rediscovering the lost faith of their parents and grandparents.

Alongside the reverts are the converts, those who "find Jesus" in an evangelist's megachurch, such as Houston's Reverend Joel Osteen, or those who take the "path to Rome," such as popular writer Scott Hahn, responding to the remarkable vitality and charisma of John Paul II. The conversion to Catholicism of Lutheran pastor Reverend Richard John Neuhaus in September 1990 is considered a milestone marking the influence of John Paul II on the U.S. Church.

This phenomenon occurs rarely in "old Europe," where Christianity is centuries older than in the United States. This is not to say that a religious revival will not one day occur in Europe—it is highly probable given the cultural meltdown and the population crisis. But obviously, the living roots of religious belief create more offshoots in this country than in the countries of those who settled here. Yes, the United States always has enjoyed a high degree of religious practice and affiliation, and its democracy developed with full support from people of faith.

Pat Robertson told me, "It is amazing how the left has been able to convince people that religious conservatives are not respectful of the secular nature of democracy. The only reason some things are allowed is because the Supreme Court has seized power it was never given under the Constitution. Consequently, people are frustrated, they feel helpless, and they are fighting a system where the ultimate arbitrator consists of nine old men in black robes. What happened was, with the stroke of a pen, the laws of most of the states and the traditions of America for hundreds of years have been wiped out by *Roe* v. *Wade.* It was an imposition of the imperial court over democratic process."

Kevin Phillips has no sympathy for the judicial activism that riles Robertson and the rest of the Religious Right. He views the influence of religious conservatives (his radical religion) in the Republican Party as the moral equivalent of the ayatollahs who celebrated the carnage of

September 11, 2001. But, like Pat Robertson, Phillips makes no attempt to moderate his rhetoric. "The rapture, end-times, and Armageddon hucksters rank with any Shiite ayatollahs, and the last two presidential elections mark the transformation of the GOP into the first religious party in U.S. history."[18] This, he argues, is a result of the migration of observantly religious voters into the Republican Party since 1980. As a result, a large minority of Republican voters identify themselves as not merely observant but "born again."

This sort of reckless comment is not something one would expect from the man who was once considered the most thoughtful and cutting-edge of Republican strategists. His 1969 book, *The Emerging Republican Majority,* is still widely quoted for foreseeing precisely the kind of alliance between religious conservatives and the GOP that he now detests.

Does Phillips realize how his definition casts a theocratic shadow over any institution whose communities seek to direct its activities, however mildly, according to religious principles? Surely he does not think of religious schools and colleges, faith-based social services, or organizations such as the Knights of Columbus as theocratic.

THE DEMOCRATS ARE "LEFT BEHIND"

Let's grant Phillips, however, the benefit of the doubt and recast his question. Do the Republican Party and the Bush administration admit more religious display and more religious influence than is appropriate to our form of government?

Religious conservatives have become a powerful voice within the GOP. But it's laughable to claim that the GOP now exists solely to serve its religious concerns. In fact, it has become something of an old saw around Washington that for all the support given by the Religious Right to Jimmy Carter, Ronald Reagan, and George H. W. Bush, they had little

18. Ibid., vii.

to show for their efforts. It was only with George W. Bush that the religious coalition began to see substantial results.

Far from giving them just a "seat at the table," Phillips considers the Bush White House and the GOP completely dominated by its religious constituency and its "radical" program of opposing abortion, fetal stem-cell research, homosexual marriage, and euthanasia, and creating the faith-based initiative. That Phillips would call such concerns evidence of "radical religion" reveals that at some level, his book is just another East Coast protest against the encroachment of the pro-life conservatives into the Republican Party.

The regional chauvinism at play in *American Theocracy* is corroborated by Phillips's description of the "Southernization" of the GOP. He also grasps the central importance of the Southern Baptist Convention, the denominational engine of Evangelical fundamentalism, in bringing Southern Evangelical culture to regions well outside the South. In doing so, the power base of the Christian Right spread and created outposts nationwide, from western Pennsylvania through the Midwest and the West to its historic point of origin, Orange County, California.

The alliance of Bush's Republican Party, according to Phillips, with "radical religion" has engendered a "national hubris" that has infected both domestic and foreign policy. A flawed policy in Israel, the war in Iraq, overdependence on foreign oil, and the dramatic increase in borrowing by the federal government are its principal examples.

For Phillips, this last group of issues is linked by the preoccupation of Evangelicals with the end of the world and the second coming of Christ. Phillips's argument runs as follows. Because the Book of Revelations teaches that the Jews must be in the Holy Land when Christ returns, Israel must be defended against external threats such as Iraq. Since the world is going to end, probably sooner rather than later, why worry about oil consumption or the national debt?

Phillips has made no attempt to distinguish between the religious conservatives who are motivated by millennial concerns and those who are not: "[T]he Republican coalition and administration of George W. Bush is heavily weighted toward the 30 to 40 percent of the electorate caught up in Scripture and the prospect of being suddenly transported to God's side."[19] The active Catholics who voted for Bush in 2004—56 percent—can hardly be characterized in this way. Anyone familiar with the various strains of Evangelicalism knows that millennialism is not the common element that keeps them politically united.

Phillips seeks to demonstrate the millennial ardor of the GOP by the popularity of the *Left Behind* series of novels by Beverly and Tim LaHaye. The *Left Behind* phenomenon evidently expresses both the core concern of the Christian Right and the biblical worldview that dominates White House policy making. The argument is hardly compelling. If Phillips is so convinced that best-selling religious novels reveal the political intentions of 30 million voters, then why did he fail to comment on the parallel phenomenon of *The Da Vinci Code*? If the readers of *Left Behind* are determined to prepare for Armageddon through support of Israel and the invasion of Iraq, what do the readers of Dan Brown intend to do? Are they intent on subverting the Christian faith? Destroying Opus Dei?

The truth is that readers of novels are hardly uniform in their responses. Phillips assumes that the Evangelical readers of the *Left Behind* novels all came to the same conclusion. Does he also assume that all readers of *The Da Vinci Code* came to the firm conclusion that Jesus was married and there was a huge cover-up in the history of the Church? If so, we could ask Phillips if they were more likely to support the Democratic Party. (Of course, it's a silly question.)

At various points in his book, Phillips's concern regarding the presence of believing Christians in the White House reaches absurd heights. For example, he cites David Domke, a critic of Bush's religiosity, who counted the number of times the president used the words "freedom" and "liberty" in his 2005 State of the Union and second inaugural addresses. Thirty-nine and forty-nine, respectively. Domke concluded that such diction is "indicative of how central an Evangelical worldview is to Bush's conception of the United States' role in the post 9/11 world."[20]

19. Ibid., 103.
20. Ibid., 207.

Evangelicals hardly have a monopoly on words such as "freedom" and "liberty." There were quite a few Enlightenment philosophers—Locke, Voltaire, and Rousseau—who used those words quite a bit, probably as much as George W. Bush. As I will discuss later, the Evangelical meaning of "freedom" is precisely what has created the divide between religious conservatives and those who accuse them of theocracy.

5

THE LAND OF CIVIL RELIGION

I s the United States a Christian nation? Religious conservatives are divided on this question. The lack of uniformity is surprising. Most commentators treat "America as a Christian nation" as
something of a rallying cry for the Religious Right itself.

In June 2004, the Republican Party of Texas approved a plank in its
platform stating that the United States was a "Christian nation." The
exact language reads: "The Republican Party affirms that the United
States of America is a Christian nation, and the public acknowledgement
of God is undeniable in our history. Our nation was founded on Judeo-
Christian principles based on the Holy Bible."

The platform goes on to affirm the Ten Commandments as "the basis
of our basic freedoms and the cornerstone of our Western legal tradition." It also adds a pledge "to exert its influence to restore the original
intent of the First Amendment of the United States Constitution and
dispel the myth of the separation of Church and State."

Although it's hard to see how the Ten Commandments can be the
basis of "basic freedoms" since each of them *forbids* a form of conduct,
the point about the legal tradition is well taken. The "myth of separation" propounded by the Supreme Court since the *Everson* decision in

1947 forbids the federal government from supporting or aiding religion in any way—a far cry from the *establishment* of a state religion.

When asked why they agree that the United States is a Christian nation, most religious conservatives answer, "Our nation was founded upon Judeo-Christian principles."[1] Almost every religious conservative I interviewed said this, even those who reject the idea of the "Christian nation" argument. The latter said that the founding principles were not as important as what the nation believes *now* and how it behaves *now*. Consequently, there is no way they would *describe* America as a Christian nation. But if the Judeo-Christian principles were understood in a *prescriptive* way, as seen in the Republican platform of Texas, most emphatically agree that America is a Christian nation. These principles act as moral measures of the nation's policies and practices. They remind us of the worldview that inspired the Founding Fathers to create a democratic government in an age of monarchy.

"America is a Christian nation" represents an Evangelical altar call to bring Americans back to the principles that religious conservatives believe animated the nation from the beginning. What better maxim to capture the intent of a movement designed to protect Christian families and communities from a hostile secular culture and federal government?

DON'T MESS WITH TEXAS

The person most associated with this rallying call is David Barton. Barton was vice president of the Texas Republican Party at the time its platform was changed. (As of 2006, the platform has not been changed, although some significant challenges to the wording are beginning to be heard.) Appointed to the post in 1997 by then-GOP-chair Susan Weddington, Barton is not the kind of well-connected political figure normally associated with such a position on the state level in party politics.

David Barton is the president of a nonprofit religious organization he

1. The kind of principles I have in mind are monotheism, an intelligible moral order, law as an external measure, human freedom and responsibility, human dignity, and human equality.

founded in 1997 in Aledo, Texas, a suburb of Fort Worth, named Wall-Builders. Over the past decade, Barton has become the nation's leading Evangelical on the topic of the American founding and the Christian faith. If any one person is responsible for the resurgence among the Religious Right of the notion that the United States is a Christian nation, it is Barton.

Through his videos, tapes, and books, which have saturated conservative Christian communities, Barton has become the champion of conservative Christians who want to make "Christian nation" their battle cry. He has become a staple of Evangelical radio and TV and the convention circuit. His work has been touted by Newt Gingrich and Bill Frist. He has emerged as the main conduit between the Republican Party and the Evangelical churches in Texas. As a recent watchdog report put it, "Barton provides the secular justification for why Evangelicals should make their religious beliefs the basis for government policy. After all, he argues, that is what the nation's Founders wanted."[2] The secular justification Barton offers is an impressive array of not only the Founders' writings, including personal correspondence, but the history of U.S. jurisprudence pertaining to the question of the "Christian nation."

The power of the Religious Right in Texas Republican caucuses enabled Barton to insert the "Christian nation" plank into the party platform. Not all but perhaps most members of the Religious Right would agree entirely with Barton on this point. Religious Right members cannot view the United States in purely secular terms. They cannot separate their faith from their patriotism, nor, when challenged, do they think it necessary. The belief is that in *some sense,* the United States is a Christian nation.

Critics have made this issue a central topic in their attempt to describe religious conservatives as intolerant and opposed to pluralism.[3] Making the "Christian nation" argument the core of the movement may be a tactical mistake. The assertion, at least in its literal meaning, can give a

2. Texas Freedom Network, "The Anatomy of Power: Texas and the Religious Right in 2006," www.tfn.org/files/fck/SORR%2006%20ReportWEB.pdf, 18.

3. Sam Harris, *Letter to a Christian Nation* (New York: Alfred A. Knopf, 2006).

militant and exclusivist impression. It lends credibility to the charge that the Religious Right is opposed to pluralism. A non-Christian can be made to feel that only Christians should live in America.

David Barton is aware of this criticism but explains, "We are talking about a Christian nation that has a republican form of government and a completely noncoercive attitude toward non-Christians. Everyone, including Christians, competes in the free market of ideas." To Barton, it's an issue of historical fact, established by his years of combing through the historical records of quite often arcane letters and documents.

I asked him how he made his argument with someone who doesn't believe in the authority of Scripture. "I become populist at this point." To illustrate, he told me the story of a recent debate with a professor at the University of Iowa. "I took with me some original documents, handwritten letters from the Founders. The professor finally conceded that the so-called separation of church and state is not what it is claimed to be. Then he argued that our opinions should reflect what most people believe now, not in the past. I said to him, 'I'm so glad to hear that,' and started quoting the polls showing a majority of Americans want prayer back in schools, an end to abortion on demand, etc. The professor interrupted me and said, 'But all that is a violation of church and state.' He had forgotten that he had already admitted his strict separationist view was wrong."

It's very unlikely that most people offended by the "Christian nation" mantra have heard any good reasons that a Christian nation would be hospitable to non-Christians. Those reasons exist, as Barton can explain, but they are rarely mentioned in public debate. Meanwhile, the "Christian nation" claim has specifically caused alarm in the Jewish community and is the source of pressure being placed on the Texas GOP to change its platform. "Christian nation" has the appearance of a dominant religious group simply claiming all the territory for itself.

When religious conservatives claim that the United States is a Christian nation, they can mean different things. Arguments are tossed aside in favor of bald assertions of dubious inferences and unsupported causal connections. But there appear to be some basic approaches that keep recurring: the numbers and habits of religious adherents, American exceptionalism, the historical influence of Christianity, and the intentions of the American Founders.

The simplest approach to this question is numerical. Just take a head count of Christians in the United States versus non-Christians, and you will come to the conclusion that the United States is a Christian nation, without doubt. No one disputes that a majority of U.S. citizens belong to, or profess to belong to, Christian denominations (76.5 percent).[4] If Israel is a Jewish nation and Egypt a Muslim nation, then the United States can be labeled for the religious preference of the majority: Christian. Fair enough. The problem with relying on this argument is obvious. If ever the moment comes when the number of Christians falls below 50 percent, is the country no longer considered Christian? Anyone who relies on this argument for legitimizing the public work of the Religious Right loses the rationale for its political involvement.

This perspective also appeals to those who do not want to count practitioners (a much higher standard) rather than adherents. Self-identification—of those who adhere to a faith tradition—is one thing; people practicing what they preach is another. This way of answering the question led some of the religious conservatives I interviewed to answer, "No. How can a nation be Christian when it aborts more than a million babies a year?"

The notion of Christian exceptionalism already has been discussed, but it can also buttress the "Christian nation" argument. What else would the United States be, if since its founding it has been given a special status by God, analogous to that of Israel in working out God's providence through history? That special status, that exceptional status of the United States before God, is something that some members of the Religious Right see prophesied by Scripture and corroborated by the historical record. Obviously, only those who read Scripture and history in a certain way are going to hold this view. This kind of exceptionalism is not the same thing as garden-variety patriotism, which is more common among

4. See the American Religious Identity Survey from 2001, www.gc.cuny.edu/faculty/research_briefs/aris/aris_index.htm.

religious conservatives in general than among self-acknowledged members of the Religious Right.

No one would deny that the United States has been, and continues to be, deeply influenced by the Christian tradition. Of the 204 Founding Fathers, eighty-eight were Episcopalian or Anglican, thirty Presbyterian, twenty-seven Congregationalist, seven Quaker, six Dutch or German Reformed, five Lutheran, three Catholic, three Huguenot, three Unitarian, two Methodist, and one Calvinist. The line of influence from these Christian Founders, some of whom were not exactly orthodox, to be sure, is often referred to as Judeo-Christian, not so much because of the direct influence of Judaism but because Christianity views itself as Judaism's extension and fulfillment. Garry Wills has taken issue with this phrase, calling it the declaration of a "mythical amity" between Jew and Christian.[5]

Historians agree that the United States of America has been influenced throughout its history by the presence of Christian thought, piety, and doctrine. The use of this phrase probably has as much to do with seeking to appear ecumenical than affirming an actual historical continuity. And the actual content of that continuity can be stretched too far. Yet at the level of basic themes such as God, creation, image of God, and moral law, a Judeo-Christian tradition no doubt exists, especially when compared with modern secularism. Even commentators hostile to Christianity would agree that this country has been influenced by the Western religious tradition, even if they would shake their heads with regret at the admission. Whether that influence is to so great an extent that it would be impossible to imagine the United States without it is the further, and crucial, question. In other words, if we subtract the Christian influence, would the United States be a very different kind of nation?

Another way of looking at the question is to acknowledge the historical influence of Christianity but underline the decisions of the Founders to create a state without an established religion and a Constitution de-

---

5. Garry Wills, *Under God: Religion and American Politics* (New York: Simon & Schuster/Touchstone, 1990), 382.

void of any religious references. The Founders consciously rejected the model of a European theocracy that was the product of Christian Europe. They were determined to avoid the kinds of religious oppression and violence that had dominated Great Britain and Europe for centuries. These men recognized that the disestablishment of religion would help remove the cause of violence between sects and possibly be an aid to religion itself. In this regard, the United States represents an important stage in the development of modern secular society. The invariable mistake made by secularists, however, is their interpretation that disestablishment implies hostility to religion, an intention of the Founders to discourage faith and its practice among American citizens.

Religious conservatives would never accept the secularist argument. They view the Founders as having allowed Christianity to make a permanent impression on the ethos of this country at the level of its basic principles and core values. In other words, the principles and values underlying the concepts stated in the founding documents—the Declaration, the Constitution, and the Bill of Rights—are a product of the Christian tradition as it passes out of seventeenth- and eighteenth-century Europe and took root in the colonies of North America. These Judeo-Christian principles govern the meanings of words such as "liberty" and "rights" and reveal the original intent of the Founders who uttered them. It comes as no surprise that a dispute would one day arise over the meanings of these terms. Stripped of their relationship to a Christian worldview, concepts such as liberty and rights can take on very different meanings. The cry of "Christian nation" can mean, in this context, merely a return to the original meaning of the values on which this country was founded.

David Barton takes this a step further; he amasses quotations from the Founders to prove that their intention was to create not only a nation founded on Judeo-Christian principles but one that was also Christian in its identity. Some claim that Barton's published research contains inaccuracies.[6] On the *700 Club,* Pat Robertson asked Barton for "proof" America was "founded" as a Christian nation. Barton answered, "There

---

6. Baptist Joint Committee on Public Affairs, "Critique of David Barton's 'America's Godly Heritage,'" http://candst.tripod.com/bjcpa1.htm.

is a lot of proof." He then cited a July 4, 1837, speech by John Quincy Adams, "one of the guys who fought in the Revolution." [7]

Barton stretches the point. John Quincy Adams was not a Founder. It was his father, John Adams, the second president of the United States. Second, the son was seven years old when his mother took him to the top of Penn Hill on the Adamses' farm to watch the Battle of Bunker Hill. He was scarcely in his teens when the war ended. But most important, the complete text of the speech cited by Barton does not really support his argument. Adams said:

> Why is it that, next to the birthday of the Savior of the world, your most joyous and most venerated festival returns on this day [the Fourth of July]? Is it not that, in the chain of human events, the birthday of the nation is *indissolubly linked* with the birthday of the Savior? That it forms a leading event in the progress of the Gospel dispensation? Is it not that the Declaration of Independence first organized the social compact on the foundation of the Redeemer's mission upon earth? *That it laid the cornerstone of human government upon the first precepts of Christianity?* [8]

Adams's words do not support the claim that the Founders themselves *believed and intended* the new nation to be Christian. The phrase "laid the corner of human government upon the first precepts of Christianity" is exactly what is meant by those who hold the broader view that America was founded on Judeo-Christian principles. Much of the disagreement results from making a stronger claim than the historical record supports. In addition, Barton must overcome powerful evidence to the contrary. A prime example is the Treaty of Peace and Friendship with Tripoli drafted in Washington's administration, ratified by the Senate on June 7, 1797, and signed by John Adams. The treaty states explicitly, "As

7. "David Barton on the Foundation of American Freedom," *The 700 Club*, www.cbn.com/spirituallife/ChurchAndMinistry/ChurchHistory/David_Barton_Foundations0207.aspx.

8. John Quincy Adams, July 4, 1837, speech at Newburyport, Mass., www.eadshome.com/QuotesoftheFounders.htm. Emphasis added.

the government of the United States of America is not *in any sense* founded on the Christian religion . . ." (emphasis added).

JOHN LOCKE, NOT JESUS

Brooke Allen is at the opposite pole from Barton. She asserts categorically that the United States is not a Christian nation, not even in the weaker sense of being founded on Judeo-Christian principles.[9] She then goes on to say, "The man who had the greatest single influence on the United States Constitution was not Jesus Christ but John Locke."[10] Allen's version of Locke is of an Enlightenment secularist whose ideas pervaded the collective mind of the Founders and the founding documents themselves.

Allen's book, surprisingly, contains very little about John Locke except for three pages (165–68) where she points out that Locke's preference for an officially secular nation was influential in the minds of the American Founders. "A nation should not," Locke argued, "impose any form of religion, but should tolerate all religious belief as a matter of individual conscience and personal practice." In other words, the state should limit itself to governing its citizens to specific "civil interests" and leave religion to the individual's choice. For Allen, this Lockean influence is responsible for the secular nature of the Constitution, its lack of any reference to God, and so forth.

But is this enough of an argument to prove her point? I think not. Allen assumes that if the United States were founded on Judeo-Christian principles, then the nation would be obliged to establish that religious tradition as an enforceable standard to govern its laws and public policy. The elected members of our nation feel no such compunction, and the Constitution ensures that even elected officials and judges are free to advocate varying interpretations of founding principles, whatever they may be.

9. Brooke Allen, *Moral Minority: Our Skeptical Founding Fathers* (Chicago: Ivan R. Dee, 2006), xi.

10. Ibid., xv.

Those who believe the nation was founded on Judeo-Christian principles are trying to reassert the idea of human existence that inspired the
Founders, a view that led them to affirm inalienable rights, divide the
church from the state, and reject monarchical rule. The problem with
Allen's argument is that she does not see how these decisions are connected. So exclusive is her focus on Locke's view of the separation between religion and the state that she ignores his larger religious view of
human nature, which undergirds the words of the Declaration of Independence. The Declaration, it can be noted, is passed over with hardly a
comment in Allen's book.

This is especially surprising when you look at the list of Locke's "civil
interests" quoted by Allen. They echo the Declaration so loudly that the
problem with Allen's argument is evident. To quote Locke in full:

> Civil interests I call life, liberty, health, and indolence of body; pos-
> session of outward things, such as money, lands, houses, furniture,
> and the like. It is the duty of the civil magistrate, by the impartial
> executive of equal laws, to secure unto all the people in general, and
> to every one of his subjects in particular the just possession of these
> things belonging to this life." [11]

These civil interests are no small matters; two of them are identical
with the three inalienable rights of the Declaration. And the others, as I
have shown in a previous work, are directly connected to Jefferson's inalienable right to the "pursuit of happiness." [12] For Jefferson, the ability
to pursue worldly goods and success, though not in a morally unfettered
way, was integral to the pursuit of happiness.

Locke, although an Enlightenment philosopher, considered himself a
Christian and described the nature of man and his search for happiness
very much as man's desire to enjoy God in eternity. His utilitarianism
was based on his belief in the Christian cosmos of earthly life bounded

---

11. Ibid., 166.

12. Deal W. Hudson, *Happiness and the Limits of Satisfaction* (Lanham, Md.: Rowman & Littlefield, 1996), chapter 5.

by heaven and hell: "The Rewards and Punishments of another Life, which the Almighty has established, as the Enforcements of his Law, are weight enough to determine the Choice, against whatever Pleasure or Pain this life can shew, when the eternal State is considered but in its bare possibility, which no Body can make any doubt of."[13] Locke's work abounds with such comments, which are integral to his worldview and philosophy. It's hard to believe someone is a secularist who wrote books with titles such as *The Reasonableness of Christianity, as Delivered in the Scriptures; A Vindication of the Reasonableness of Christianity; A Second Vindication of the Reasonableness of Christianity; A Discourse of Miracles;* and *An Essay for the Understanding of St. Paul's Epistles, by Consulting St. Paul himself.* Allen, in her book, makes no mention of these works.

For Locke, the fact that man is a creature of God, destined for God, is what gives man his inalienable rights and basic dignity. The respect for human rights and the freedom of self-determination at the core of human dignity are what led the colonists to revolt against the tyranny of Great Britain and its established church and create a new kind of nation. Allen is correct to point out Locke's insistence on a state without religious compunction. What she does not recognize is that the Judeo-Christian principles she dismisses are still implicit in every understanding of man that demands the state not only respect religion but avoid imposing one.

This argument was made by James Madison in his famous essay "Memorial and Remonstrance," published in 1785. He wrote this essay in opposition to a proposal made by Patrick Henry that the citizens of Virginia be taxed in order to support "Teachers of the Christian Religion." The first paragraph contains a remarkable explanation of why legislators must recognize themselves as subject to the "Governour of the Universe," who obligates government not to impose any kind of legal requirement regarding religion on citizens. Madison recognizes that the very nature

---

13. John Locke, *An Essay concerning Human Understanding,* ed. Peter H. Nidditch (New York: Oxford University Press, 1975), 281.

of being religious requires that a person freely assent to the dictates of faith:

> The Religion then of every man must be left to the conviction and conscience of every man; and it is the right of every man to exercise it as these may dictate. This right is in its nature an unalienable right. It is unalienable, because the opinions of men, depending only on the evidence contemplated by their own minds cannot follow the dictates of other men: It is unalienable also, because what is here a right towards men, is a duty towards the Creator. It is the duty of every man to render to the Creator such homage and such only as he believes to be acceptable to him. This duty is precedent, both in order of time and in degree of obligation, to the claims of Civil Society. Before any man can be considerd as a member of Civil Society, he must be considered as a subject of the Governour of the Universe: And if a member of Civil Society, do it with a saving of his allegiance to the Universal Sovereign. We maintain therefore that in matters of Religion, no man's right is abridged by the institution of Civil Society and that Religion is wholly exempt from its cognizance. True it is, that no other rule exists, by which any question which may divide a Society, can be ultimately determined, but the will of the majority; but it is also true that the majority may trespass on the rights of the minority.[14]

This conception of the foundation of religious liberty was understood not just by Madison but by the other Founders as well and was included in the Constitution as the "establishment clause" of the First Amendment. Their aim was to protect the individual conscience against not only coercion but also religious institutions themselves.[15] The rejection of an established church was aimed directly at Europe and Great Britain,

14. James Madison, "Memorial and Remonstrance against Religious Assessments," *James Madison: Writings,* ed. Jack N. Rakone (New York: Penguin Putnam, 1999), 30.

15. Patrick M. Garry, *Wrestling with God: The Courts' Tortuous Treatment of Religion* (Washington, D.C.: Catholic University of America Press, 2006), 29.

where the institutional church and the mechanisms of state remained, often tragically, entangled.

The Catholic Church eventually affirmed the necessity to protect the freedom of the individual to believe without state coercion. The Vatican II "Declaration on Religious Liberty" in 1965 stated that the dignity of the human person as found in divine revelation means that matters of truth and religious belief should never be imposed by force. Governments should protect the right to religious liberty. "It is in accordance with their dignity that all men, because they are persons, that is, beings endowed with reason and free will and, therefore, bearing personal responsibility, are both impelled by their nature and bound by a moral obligation to seek the truth, especially religious truth." [16]

The main author of those words was a professor from Georgetown University, Father John Courtney Murray, S.J. Murray is often credited for laying out the framework for the contemporary rapprochement between Catholicism and democratic government. He famously wrote in his memo to Cardinal Cushing in opposition to the criminalizing of selling contraceptives: "It is not the function of civil law to prescribe everything that is morally right and to forbid everything that is morally wrong. By reason of its nature and purpose, as the instrument of order in society, the scope of law is limited to the maintenance and protection of public morality. Matters of private morality lie beyond the scope of law; they are left to the personal conscience." [17]

In this statement, Murray laid bare the most sensitive issue for those on both sides of the "Christian nation" debate. How do those who believe that Judeo-Christian principles are the foundation of the country decide which moral teachings should be inscribed into law for the "maintenance and protection of public morality"? Obviously, the right to life for unborn children is one the Religious Right would like to see back in the law. Another is affirmation that marriage is only between a man and

16. "Dignitatis Humane" I.2., Austin Flannery, ed., *Vatican Council II: Constitutions, Decrees, Declarations* (New York: Costello, 1996).

17. John Courtney Murray, "Memo to Cushing on Contraception Legislation," Murray Archives, Woodstock Theological Seminary Library, Woodstock Theological Center, Georgetown University, Washington, D.C.

a woman. One man's determination to protect public morality, however, has led to another man's protest against the imposition of religious values.

ONE NATION UNDER DEITY

The contemporary rallying cry of the Christian nation has been heard many times before. Constitutional amendments declaring America a Christian nation have been repeatedly introduced and always rejected. The present debate can be traced back to the work of the National Reform Association, founded in 1864, an organization still functioning in Pittsburgh. This association grew out of an 1863 conference of Covenanters, a schismatic sect of the Presbyterian Church from western Pennsylvania. There, a proposed constitutional amendment was read by an attorney, John Alexander, in an attempt to address, at a national level, the sins that led to the Civil War and the need for national repentance:

> We, the People of the United States *[recognizing the being and attributes of Almighty God, the Divine Authority of the Holy Scriptures, the law of God as the paramount rule, and Jesus, the Messiah, the Savior and Lord of all]*, in order to form a more perfect union, establish justice, insure domestic tranquility, provide for the general welfare, and secure the blessings of liberty to ourselves and to our posterity, do ordain and establish this Constitution for the United States of America." [18]

The Covenanters elected Alexander as the president of the National Reform Association and wrote Congress requesting consideration of a constitutional amendment:

> We, the people of the United States, humbly acknowledging Almighty God as the source of all authority and power in civil gov-

18. Jim Allison, "The NRA (National Reform Association) and the Christian Amendment," www.candst.tripod.com/nra.htm.

ernment, the Lord Jesus Christ as the Ruler among the nations, his revealed will as the supreme law of the land, in order to constitute a Christian government, and in order to form a more perfect union, establish justice, insure domestic tranquility, provide for the common defense, promote the general welfare, and secure the inalienable rights and the blessings of life, liberty, and the pursuit of happiness to ourselves, our posterity, and all the people, do ordain and establish this Constitution for the United States of America." [19]

It gained some support among senators, was sent to committee, and was rejected on March 2, 1865, as "unnecessary and injudicious." Having been rebuffed by Congress, the NRA regrouped and began publishing *The Christian Statesmen*.[20] Its new president, Judge William Strong from the Pennsylvania Supreme Court, continued the effort. (Strong became a justice on the U.S. Supreme Court while he was still president of the NRA.) The NRA, like the Religious Right groups of today, sponsored meetings to urge ministers and laypersons to support the amendment and send petitions to Congress. Their petitions led to a great deal of debate on the floor of Congress, but Congress took no action in 1869, 1870, or 1871. In March 1873, a constitutional convention was held in Pennsylvania to consider changes about God in its state constitution. The preamble was rewritten, giving only thanks to God and requesting guidance. The NRA used this change to put more pressure on Congress.

The constitutional amendment declaring the United States a Christian nation went to the judiciary committee again in 1874, but the committee decided that no religious creed of any kind belonged in the Constitution. There has been an ongoing effort to pass Christian nation amendments, but all have failed. The contemporary attempts all refer to the 1897 Supreme Court decision *Church of the Holy Trinity* v. *United States*, in which Justice David J. Brewer concluded, "This is a Christian

---

19. Ibid.

20. The Free Religious Association was founded in 1867 by Octavius Frothingham to oppose the Christian amendment. He and Francis E. Abbot created *The Index* to counter the influence of *The Christian Statesmen*. They also adopted the organizing tactics of the NRA. See Allison, ibid.

nation." At issue was whether or not a minister invited from Great Britain to be pastor at Holy Trinity was in violation of a law prohibiting the "importation and migration of foreigners and aliens ... to perform labor in the United States." The Supreme Court ruled that a minister was not a manual laborer and was, therefore, not in violation of the law. Justice Brewer added a lengthy section to his decision that chronicled evidence that the United States was a "religious" and specifically "Christian nation."[21]

I asked David Barton why Brewer devoted half of his decision to an argument that appeared to have no necessary connection to the findings. "Brewer wanted to make it clear that the government has no power to restrict Christianity. Even if the minister was in violation of the statute, it was important to establish that the government could not interfere with the decision of the Holy Trinity Church." Barton noted that Brewer cited the "free exercise clause" of the Constitution, which "should have been sufficient," except for the threat posed by the secularist movement led by Robert Ingersoll and the National Liberal League. Ingersoll, a popular speaker and free thinker of the late nineteenth century, was having significant influence on public opinion at the time.[22] "The NLL was seeking to get the Supreme Court to attach strict separation of church and state to the establishment clause, a position the Court rejected up until Hugo Black made it the majority position."

Between Barton and Allen is another position that, at first glance, is appealing. In *American Gospel: God, the Founding Fathers, and the Making of a Nation*, Jon Meacham offers an intriguing argument that the Founders intended to create a nondenominational civic religion that would serve the important role of providing a metaphysical foundation for the Constitution. For Meacham, the reassertion of American civic religion was an opportunity to register the protest of a mainstream Prot-

21. Jim Allison, "The 'Christian Nation' Decision and Rebuttal," http://members.tripod.com/~candst/holytrin.htm.

22. Robert Ingersoll (1833–1899) is the precursor to modern champions of secularism such as Madalyn Murray O'Hair, Sam Harris, Daniel Dennett, Richard Dawkins, and, most recently, Christopher Hitchens.

estant against the influence of the Evangelical right in understanding the religious character of the Founders.[23]

Meacham's research is impressive, his conclusions convincing, but his application of those conclusions to the Religious Right misses the mark. Meacham writes, "The Right's contention that we are a 'Christian nation' that has fallen from pure origins and can achieve redemption by some kind of return to Christian values is based upon wishful thinking, not convincing historical argument."[24] This is too dismissive of a position that may be wrong but can be made at least plausible by a willing historian.

According to Meacham, what the Founders intended to do was keep any sectarian point of view, particularly Christianity, from becoming part of the founding documents. What they did allow was precisely what most of them believed in, a kind of "public" or "civic" religion that had been the product of Deistic thinking for a century. For Meacham, the Founders "consciously allowed a form of what Benjamin Franklin called 'public religion' to take root and flower."[25]

The notion of a public religion is hard to understand today, especially for Evangelicals who measure faith by the intensity of their personal relationship with Christ. The public religion created by the seventeenth- and eighteenth-century philosophers stripped sectarian religion of all its particularities, leaving only what was considered essential by "men of reason." Public religion was rational religion and, because of that, promoted complacence, not passion.

Deism is, like most philosophical movements, a bulky, multifaceted phenomenon resistant to simplification. But, for our purposes, to characterize the attitude toward religion expressed by the majority of its key founders, certain generalizations can be safely made. The first and most important is that Deists sought a form of religion that required no historical revelation, no miracles, no ancient prophets or lawgivers, no John

23. John Meacham, *American Gospel: God, the Founding Fathers, and the Making of a Nation* (New York: Random House, 2006).

24. Ibid., 18.

25. Ibid., 20.

the Baptist, no Jesus Christ, and no apostles. The Deists transposed traditional religion into purely philosophical terms and rejected religion based on God's action in history. Deists thus created the possibility of a so-called public religion, a religion that didn't require a leap of faith, even if it required a considerable effort of reason.

Meacham's description of America's public religion is a good one. I paraphrase him as follows. There is a God such as the one Jefferson referred to in the Declaration as the "Creator" and "Nature's God." This God as the Creator made human beings in his image and endowed them with sacred (natural) rights to life, liberty, and the pursuit of happiness. Since God has given these rights, no government or law can remove them. The God of public religion is interested in the affairs of this world. The God of public religion may be seen as capable of rewarding or punishing individuals or the nation here and now or later, beyond time. And the God of public religion is sometimes spoken of as a God who founded the American nation, in Jefferson's words, "as Israel of old." [26]

This list contains quite of bit of what most people think of as traditional religious beliefs. Deism, after all, is a theological viewpoint that often gets dismissed for being at odds with traditional Christianity. But here you get the existence of one God (monotheism), you get God as Creator, human beings made in the image and likeness of God with natural rights, and a God who is involved in human history, at least to the extent that the United States has been given a special divine mission.

DEISM AND DYING CHURCHES

For all the substance of this description of the American Deist, this is the kind of religious credo that immediately provokes objections in the Evangelical mind. The Great Awakening of the 1730s associated with the preaching of Jonathan Edwards and the Methodism of John Wesley kept grassroots religion inoculated from the influence of Deism.

The intent of the Deist, as is made clear in the work of its first system-

26. Ibid., 22.

atic figure, Edward Herbert (1582–1648), is the subordination of the specific revealed religion of Christianity to a natural religion governed by reason alone. The rituals and doctrines of historical Christianity are left behind, replaced by a discreet and efficient list of ideas, such as that provided by Meacham, upon which all men of reason can agree.

By reducing revealed religion to its rational essence, the Deist creates a religion that can subsume all particular religions within its parameters, eliminating the need for any future religious conflict. Thus, the Deist solves not only the theological problems associated with faith but the political ones generated by conflicting claims between, for example, Protestants and Catholics.

Deism is antisupernaturalism, a form of natural reason opposed to revealed religion, especially Christianity.[27] It creates agreement by eliminating the distinguishing marks of specific religions, those demands of a revealed faith that create disagreements. Deists look to natural morality as a way of forging agreement—the essence of religion is captured when a consensus on morality is reached. It is no surprise that Deism created the "principle of tolerance," intended to end all wars of religion.

Deism, historically, was a major step toward modern atheism. Catholic philosopher Cornelio Fabro points to its elimination of any personal relationship with God and, consequently, of any obligation toward God as the personal, supreme being.[28] This extracts the *practice of religion*, of worship and personal devotion, from belief in God. Deism's purely natural morality, with man as the source of truth and human values, eliminated supernaturalism. As a result, ethics became the core of Deism, replacing revealed doctrine and the systematic theology based on that revelation.

Meacham does not mention any of the theological downsides of Deism as a public religion. In his view, Jefferson's public religion "staked out an American middle ground between the ferocity of evangelizing Christians on the one hand and contempt for religion of secular

27. Cornelio Fabro, *God in Exile: Modern Atheism,* trans. Arthur Gibson (Westminster, Md.: Newman Press, 1968), 223.

28. Ibid., 224.

philosophes on the other. The Right would like Jefferson to be a soldier of faith, the Left an American Voltaire. He was, depending on the moment, both and neither: he was, in other words, a lot like many of us." [29]

The "many of us" that Meacham invokes sounds like those in the mainstream of Protestantism. Meacham continues in that vein on and off throughout his book, praising the public religion where "religion shapes the life of the nation without strangling it . . . faith is a matter of choice, not coercion, and the legacy of the Founding Fathers is that the sensible center holds." [30] Indeed, and perhaps this is the most telling remark, "The Founding Fathers struggled to assign religion its proper place in civil society—and they succeeded." [31]

The idea that religion can be assigned a "proper place" would never come forth from the mind or mouth of an Evangelical Christian. But it would, in fact, sound reasonable to many members of the mainstream Protestant denominations that have been losing members steadily over the years. To attempt to afford religion a proper place is to misunderstand the nature of religion, at least if you are talking about Evangelical Christianity.

In *The Churching of America, 1776–2005*, Roger Finke and Rodney Stark explain the gradual demise of the mainstream groups and the rise of the Evangelical sects. They call it "The Rewards of a Costly Faith." [32] "Those denominations decline that ask too little of their members. Those who ask for much, and require the belief in a doctrine that motivates that sacrifice have steadily grown. Those who have replaced a supernatural worldview with nothing more than political policy positions have removed the very reasons that motivate people to participate avidly in a religious community." [33]

Notice that the very form of religion that Meacham recommends may

29. Meacham, *American Gospel*, 4.

30. Ibid., 5.

31. Ibid., 6.

32. Roger Finke and Rodney Stark, *The Churching of America, 1776–2005: Winners and Losers in Our Religious Economy* (New Brunswick, N.J.: Rutgers University Press, 2005), 249.

33. Finke and Stark's findings have been reconfirmed by Dave Shiflett, *Exodus: Why Americans Are Fleeing Liberal Churches for Conservative Christianity* (New York: Penguin, 2005).

satisfy intellectuals, but it turns away and turns off the adherents. If it can be said that the spirit of public religion is what gradually infiltrated mainstream Protestantism to the point of almost killing it, then Meacham's admiration is odd, to say the least.

Nowhere in his book does Meacham indicate anything other than distaste for Evangelicalism. For example, he criticizes Falwell for calling for "an old-fashioned, God-honoring, Christ-exalting revival to turn America back to God."[34] That Meacham can find fault with this demonstrates his tin ear to the movement he is criticizing.

And nowhere does Meacham examine the steady decline of adherents to the religious tradition he admires. He merely extols the balance, restraint, and "supple" wit of the religious views of his beloved Founders and expects the rest of us to fall at their feet. But why would we want to emulate men whom Meacham describes as "devoted to the general idea of religion as a force for stability"?[35]

Individual salvation, rather than social stability, is the end being sought by those who identify themselves with an Evangelical faith. That salvation actually may require the experience of social instability is a fact Evangelicals clearly acknowledge. The Christian faith, in short, is not something that an Evangelical can assign to its "proper place."

To some extent, whether or not public religion leads to the decline of a Christian nation is not relevant to this question. The issue of whether a group of beliefs can successfully sustain a community is different from whether it provides an intellectual foundation for understanding, say, fundamental human rights.

There is no doubt that the Founders, however, intended to use their Deistic conception of God to provide an irrefutable rationale for basic human rights guaranteed in the Declaration and again in the Constitution and the Bill of Rights. The individual human being was deemed worthy of having natural rights because he was a creature of God and bore God's imprint. This relationship to God is the source of their "inalienability."

34. Meacham, *American Gospel*, 219.
35. Ibid., 11.

MAYBE IT'S JUST PHILOSOPHY

There's another way of looking at the theological elements of the founding documents, according to Matt Spalding, director of the B. Kenneth Simon Center for American Studies at the Heritage Foundation. Spalding is a Catholic who has published extensively on the Founders, especially George Washington. In discussing the Meacham book, Spalding says, "Yes, there is an effort to speak in nonsectarian terms, but the Founders did not see the radical break between revealed religion and public religion." He argues that the Founders were not trying to put a civil religion in the place of a revealed one. For Spalding, the Declaration should be read philosophically as a "natural theology." It should be recalled that in the eighteenth century, arguments for the existence of God were still widely accepted in spite of David Hume's skepticism on this issue. American college students read books of natural theology until the middle of the nineteenth century.

The difference between a natural theology and a civil religion turns on the issue of piety and ritual. The God of civil religion is the object of worship, even if that means using the Bible at a swearing-in ceremony or a prayer day when Congress is in session. But the divinity of natural theology, as Spalding says, "grounds the moral life." This is a decidedly Catholic point of view, as Spalding admits. Evangelicals "don't understand natural theology and end up skipping around in the writings of the Founders trying to bolster their religion. They don't need to." Whereas Evangelicals want to beef up their arguments for their faith, the attraction of Deism to critics of the Religious Right is "the lack of moral issues—moral issues grow out of natural theology."

The Founders, in Spalding's view, regarded morality as grounded in nature and "nature's God," and he cites the antisodomy statute that Jefferson included in the state law of Virginia, as well as his view that slaves had some rights. He also notes the intervention of John Quincy Adams in the *Amistad* episode. In 1840, Adams was a congressman; he intervened to defend thirty-six African men being held outside New Haven, Connecticut. They were being tried for murder and piracy, having mutinied on a Spanish slave ship. Adams began the case by gesturing toward the Declaration of Independence on the wall of the room where the Supreme Court met. He said, "I know of no other law that reaches the case of my clients, but the law of Nature and of Nature's God on which our fathers placed our own national existence. The circumstances are so peculiar, that no code or treaty has provided for such a case. That law, in its application to my clients, I trust will be the law on which the case will be decided by this Court."

Spalding points out that liberals can't really make Adams's argument anymore, because they don't believe that morality is grounded in nature. "The whole modern progressive movement is a rejection of arguments from nature." This loss of nature and natural theology is the cultural vacuum into which Evangelicals entered. "They don't make arguments from nature, either; they use Jesus Christ as their moral norm." Spalding, though disagreeing with both Meacham and Evangelicals, still thinks the United States is a Christian nation but only in the sense that its moral teachings are founded on natural law.

The United States is a product of the Christian West. It has been argued that there are nonreligious, non-Christian traditions in ancient philosophy that supplied the rationale for natural human rights, but the fact is that they didn't. Those traditions were all refracted to the eighteenth century through the Christian culture of medieval and Renaissance Europe. It's wishful thinking to claim that the influence of Stoicism or pre-Christian Anglo-Saxons superseded the Christian tradition in the minds of the American Founders.

The United States is "indissolubly linked," to use the phrase of John Quincy Adams, to Judeo-Christian principles, such as the nature and dignity of the human person created by God. This statement, however, doesn't justify the conclusion that America *is* a Christian nation. To claim an ongoing *identity* where there is only an indigenous *inclination* goes too far. Yet those who espouse that America is founded on Judeo-Christian principles are much closer to David Barton than they are to Brook Allen's extreme secularism or Jon Meacham's Deism.

The deposit of Christianity found in the Declaration is just that, a deposit in the form of metaphysics and natural law, which needs to be resuscitated to its full meaning. Evangelicals in politics insist on a maximal understanding of that meaning. For them, public religion—religion according to reason—may be a "religion" of some sort, but it's not Christianity. In recalling this nation's Christian past, the Religious Right has helped remind us that the founding was not the product of atheists and certainly not the product of men who intended to put religion out of business.

6

IS THERE A CATHOLIC
RELIGIOUS RIGHT?

I F YOU WERE TO ASK A PRO-LIFE, PRO-FAMILY CATHOLIC WHO VOTES Republican if he or she belongs to the Religious Right, the answer will usually be no. Having done this a number of times with various groups and in different parts of the country, I can attest to the reaction. Conservative Catholics, even if they identify with the pro-life efforts of the Republican Party, do not identify with the leadership of the Religious Right. Catholics, especially those from the Midwest and the Northeast, are reluctant to be associated with Southern Evangelicals whom they don't understand and regard with suspicion.

Given this disconnection, it's predictable that Catholics don't recognize their own contribution to the Religious Right. Even scholars have failed to notice it. One of the most cited books on religion and politics in the United States contains the following: "Despite the heavy emphasis on abortion, the Christian Right has done poorly among Roman Catholics."[1] The claim, although commonly accepted, sounds a false note in an otherwise excellent survey of the role of religion in American politics.

Religious and political historians usually will phrase their description of the Religious Right as "made up of thirty million Evangelicals and a

1. Kenneth D. Wald, *Religion and Politics in the United States*, 4th ed. (Lanham, Md.: Rowman & Littlefield, 2003), 227.

few conservative Roman Catholics." In the midst of the careful parsing of the difference between fundamentalists and Pentecostals among Evangelicals, Catholics rate only a passing reference. The historical and analytical accounts of the Religious Right, with a few exceptions, treat the Catholic element as a small cog in an overwhelmingly Evangelical political machine. Yet the original political strategists of the Religious Right were mostly Catholic, as were a substantial number of the original grassroots activists.

IN THE BEGINNING, THERE WERE CATHOLICS

It's easy to understand why Catholic participation in the movement is overlooked. Robertson, Falwell, Reed, and Dobson have been the most visible spokesmen for the Religious Right. Catholic leaders in the early part of the movement—Paul Weyrich, Phyllis Schlafly, Richard Viguerie, and Terry Dolan—did not go out of their way to advertise their Catholic faith, knowing it was going to be an impediment to working with Evangelicals. Schlafly admitted that many of the people who worked with her to defeat the ERA didn't know she was Catholic, and she avoided telling them unless pressed to do so.

However, Catholic strategists, grassroots leaders, and the Catholic bishops were a key element in the preparation for the Religious Right. Viguerie told me that the strategy of bringing religiously active voters into the conservative movement came out of a series of weekly breakfast meetings that started in 1973. These meetings included Weyrich, Ed Feulner, Dolan, Howard Phillips (the latter being Jewish at the time and the only non-Catholic), and himself. Conversely, Schlafly claims she founded the "pro-family" movement when she started organizing church members to rally at the state capitol in Indiana to defeat the ERA as early as 1972.

In fact, Catholic activism in the pre-Religious Right period goes back even farther, to the late 1960s. In *Suburban Warriors: The Origins of the New American Right*, Lisa McGirr looks at the origins of socially conservative activism in Orange County, California, in the mid- to late '60s.[2] The activism described by McGirr possesses the same dynamism seen in the religious-political activism of the early '70s: Anita Bryant's protest against gay rights in Dade County; Phyllis Schlafly taking up arms against the ERA; the Kanawha County, West Virginia, textbook controversy led by Alice Moore. In each case, religiously motivated parents took up arms to defend their families against social change.

McGirr describes an early antiabortion organization, the Citizens Action Committee, founded in 1969 by Cathy Sullivan at the request of two local Catholic priests. McGirr writes that Sullivan's organization "symbolized the new alliance struck between Catholics and Protestant Evangelicals. This alliance was focused at the grassroots level around abortion, as well as the early politicization of some churches around the issue."[3] This comment suggests that McGirr is not aware that Evangelicals were not yet activated by the issue of abortion and ends up subsuming the distinctive Catholic element in an Evangelical movement that did not yet exist. McGirr never comments on how Sullivan's Catholicism provided the motivating factor for her becoming an activist.

To her credit, McGirr is meticulous in showing the overlap between the concerns of the old and new Christian Right. Cathy Sullivan, for example, had been a Goldwater supporter and a John Birch Society member. Phyllis Schlafly herself had been a major player in the Goldwater campaign before starting an organization to defeat the Equal Rights Amendment. One scholar has even argued that the Republican Party apparatus of South Carolina was fundamentally changed by the incursion of religious fundamentalists associated with Bob Jones University who became politically active during the Goldwater campaign.[4]

In what is easily the most comprehensive history of the Religious Right written thus far, *With God on Our Side*, William Martin tells the story of another conservative Catholic in Southern California, Eleanor

2. Lisa McGirr, *Suburban Warriors: The Origins of the New American Right* (Princeton, N.J.: Princeton University Press, 2001).

3. Ibid., 233.

4. John C. Green, Mark J. Rozell, and Clyde Wilcox, eds, *The Christian Right in American Politics: Marching to the Millennium* (Washington, D.C.: Georgetown University Press, 2003), 22–23.

Howe, who started the "Battle of Anaheim" in 1968 over sex education being taught to her sons in public school.[5] Her activism led to the reactivation of the California Citizens Committee, originally formed to help Goldwater in 1964 and Reagan for governor in 1968 and renamed as California Families United. The Howe story is just another instance of the way Catholic anti-Communists merged into the New Christian Right through the lives of the activists on the ground.

CATHOLICS ON THE CONSERVATIVE SPECTRUM

Clarence Manion, like Schlafly, is a pivotal figure in the creation of a conservative Catholic subculture that supported the Republican Party, fought Communism, resisted Catholic post-Vatican II liberalism, and helped instigate the pro-family, antiabortion cause. Manion is perhaps best known for his effort to persuade Barry Goldwater to run for president, another indication of how the Goldwater campaign became a launching platform for religious conservatives.[6] His radio show, *Manion's Forum of Opinion,* broadcast for twenty-five years from October 1954 to July 1979, was the leading conservative voice on radio at the time. He recorded his last program two weeks before he died, just as the Moral Majority was being founded.

Manion started his radio show after retiring as dean of the University of Notre Dame Law School in 1952 and after an abbreviated stint in the Eisenhower administration. His son, Chris Manion, tells the story of why he left the administration: "I call it a Catholic moment. Eisenhower asked Dad, in front of Sherman Adams, to get off the issue of the Bricker Amendment. Ike said, 'Look, you were against FDR, but I am president now. If you will just go neutral, I'll put you on the Supreme Court.'"

The Bricker Amendment, named after its sponsor, Senator John

5. William Martin, *With God on Our Side: The Rise of the Religious Right in America* (New York: Broadway Books, 1996).

6. Rick Perlstein, *Before the Storm: Barry Goldwater and the Unmaking of the American Consensus* (New York: Hill & Wang, 2001).

Bricker (R-Ohio), sought to protect the prerogatives of Congress in determining foreign policy by limiting the scope of U.S. treaties and executive agreements. Eisenhower opposed the Bricker Amendment as an unnecessary and dangerous restraint on presidential leadership in world affairs and wanted Manion on his side. "My dad said, 'No soap.' A couple of years went by, and a Supreme Court seat came open, and another Irish Democrat named Brennan got the job.'"

Clarence Manion is closely connected with L. Brent Bozell Jr., another conservative Catholic and anti-Communist leader who took up the pro-life cause well in advance of the Evangelicals. (His son L. Brent Bozell III now runs the Media Research Center in Alexandria, Virginia.) Bozell, along with William F. Buckley, his roommate at Yale University, had published *McCarthy and His Enemies* in 1953. In 1970, Bozell led the first abortion protest in the nation's capital.

Bozell had become an editor of *National Review* at its founding in 1955 but left the magazine in 1962 in a dispute over the importance of Catholic principles in relation to the conservative movement. Like Manion, Bozell experienced a "Catholic moment" that defined the remainder of his career. While at *National Review*, he wrote speeches for Senator Joseph McCarthy, including the speech that led to his first censure.[7] He ran for the Senate in Maryland and lost before founding *Triumph Magazine* in 1967. Bozell intended *Triumph* to be a truly Catholic *National Review*, according to Michael Lawrence, who worked at *Triumph* from the beginning. As his wife, Trish, a sister to Bill Buckley, told me in an interview, the split between her husband and her brother was a matter of whether Bozell was going to be a "Catholic conservative or a conservative Catholic."

7. L. Brent Bozell Jr. and his wife, Trish, had a high regard for McCarthy, whom Trish referred to in our interview as "a very good man and not vindictive in the slightest." She told the following story to illustrate: "Mamie Eisenhower at the time was asking several senators' wives to have lunch with her. Jeannie [McCarthy] came storming in one day to our house in a rage because Mamie had invited her. Only Brent and I were there at the time, not Joe." She said, "How dare she invite me knowing what her husband had done to my husband!" Joe appeared about that time and after hearing his wife's indignation, said, "Oh, Jeannie, do go, that poor woman. She had nothing to do with the other thing." And he meant it.

On June 6, 1970, after two court decisions in the District of Columbia allowed abortion to protect the mental health of the mother, Bozell, his *Triumph* staff members, and supporters held the first "Operation Rescue" at George Washington University Hospital. They were beaten, arrested, and put on probation.[8]

Three hundred fifty people rallied, calling themselves "Action for Life." The group met at St. Stephen Martyr Church for mass. It included "The Sons of Thunder," who dressed in khaki and red berets, wore rosaries around their necks, and carried papal flags. The founder was a University of Dallas student named Michael Schwartz, who went on to become one of the leading pro-life Democrats in the nation. (Schwartz is now chief of staff to Republican Senator Tom Coburn.)

They walked a few blocks to the hospital from the church, and Bozell put on his red beret, took hold of a wooden cross, and walked toward the clinic entrance. Along with others, he was met by police and was clubbed on the head. A police officer grabbed his cross and broke it in half. He was thrown down and handcuffed. Trish Bozell, who had been standing to the side saying the rosary, ended up joining in the screaming. Five of the demonstrators were taken to the police station and booked.

The next day's headlines in the *Baltimore Sun* were predictable: "Foes of Abortion Turn to Violence." Obviously, nothing has changed regarding media coverage of the pro-life movement since 1970. Bozell and the staff at *Triumph* were undeterred and remained active in early pro-life work, including the organization of the first March for Life demonstration in 1974 led by Catholic activist Nellie Gray.

L. Brent Bozell is another example, and perhaps the most important, of how many religiously motivated anti-Communists later embraced the pro-life issue as their greatest political cause. After cowriting the book on McCarthy with his future brother-in-law Buckley, Bozell served a short stint as a lawyer before taking a job writing speeches for another Catholic anti-Communist, Senator Joseph McCarthy. Clarence Manion got Bozell the job of ghostwriting *The Conscience of a Conservative* in

---

8. Michael Lawrence, ed., *The Best of Triumph* (Front Royal, Va.: Christendom Press, 2001), 19.

1960 for Barry Goldwater. (Manion, by the way, spent his own money publishing the book under the imprint of Victory Publishing.) This explains the echo of Catholic social teaching resounding throughout the pages of a book whose "author" was Episcopalian. Only someone schooled in the natural law tradition would posit "the enhancement of man's spiritual nature as the primary concern of political philosophy."[9] After reading Lee Edwards's treatment of Bozell's infusion of the Catholic natural-law tradition into the Goldwater credo, it's difficult to avoid the conclusion that Bozell helped lay the groundwork for the influx of religious conservatives into the GOP after Goldwater's defeat.[10] Without Bozell, Goldwater might well have sent conservatism in a different direction.

Bozell and Buckley remained friends until Bozell's death in 1997. But their disagreement over the relationship between Catholicism and conservatism foreshadowed the rise of religious conservatism and the Religious Right. That Buckley is a serious Catholic cannot be questioned, but *National Review*'s offhanded dissent from Pope John XXIII's encyclical *Mater et Magistra* (1961) as a "venture in triviality" created a kind of dividing line between the conservatism that Buckley was developing and the conservative Catholicism that would arise in response to the leftward drift of American Catholics and their bishops after Vatican II. The mocking phrase "Mater, si; Magistra, no" (Mother, yes; Teacher, no) was not coined by Buckley but did, in fact, catch the difference between Buckley and the Catholic conservatives—the so-called theocons—who remained obedient to the Magisterium of the Church. Though "theocons" was a term invented by a left-wing critic, it does accurately describe the kind of public philosophy being written by Catholics such as Father Richard Neuhaus, publisher of *First Things;* writer George Weigel; and Robert George of Princeton University.

In the context of the '60s, by publishing dissenting pieces on contraception, Buckley had placed himself and *National Review* outside the

9. Barry Goldwater, *The Conscience of a Conservative,* quoted in Lee Edwards, *Goldwater: The Man Who Made a Revolution* (Washington, D.C.: Regnery, 1995), 121.

10. Edwards, *Goldwater,* 120–24.

rising tide of pro-life, pro-family concern that could be seen at the grass-roots in Southern California and elsewhere. *National Review,* as Phyllis Schlafly told me, offered no support at all in her fight against the ERA. Likewise, Paul Weyrich, in our interview, expressed his admiration for Buckley and *National Review* but reported that little or no help came from that quarter in political organizing.[11]

Regardless of whether or not Buckley or *National Review* provided direct support to political and grassroots organizers, there is no doubt that he gave the early conservative movement a strong Catholic flavor. Buckley, after all, first came to public attention at age twenty-five with his book *God and Man at Yale* (1951), accusing Yale professors of seeking to deprive students of their religious beliefs. Like other traditional con-servatives such as Russell Kirk, Buckley always recognized the impor-tance of religion to the conservative account of human nature. His spiritual memoir, *Nearer My God,* a masterpiece of confessional indirec-tion, is the culmination, in my opinion, of his long struggle to reconcile his differences with his late brother-in-law.[12]

Unlike Weyrich and others, Buckley and several of his major contrib-utors were known to be Catholic by his readers. Buckley's influence on generations of conservative thinkers, leaders, and activists made them aware that the Catholic faith was somehow compatible with the basic tenets of conservatism. Indeed, as Buckley and *National Review* grew in importance, the Catholic Church in the United States was moving to-ward the political left. There was a period in the late '60s and early '70s, before the rise of the Catholic theocons, when Buckley was the most im-portant Catholic public intellectual in the country, in spite of his low-grade dissent on *Mater et Magistra* (1961), *Pacem in Terris* (1963), and *Humane Vitae* (1968).

Lee Edwards, a respected historian of the conservative movement, ex-plained to me the Catholic influence on conservatism in its early years,

---

11. For Buckley's position on abortion at the time, see "The Catholic Church and Abortion," *National Review,* April 5, 1966, 308.

12. William F. Buckley Jr., *Nearer My God: An Autobiography of Faith* (New York: Doubleday, 1997).

implicitly through figures such as Bishop Sheen and explicitly in Buckley's public persona and *National Review*. "The Catholic character of the *National Review* in the beginning was very apparent, and it was very attractive to young conservatives like myself. We saw it as conservative and Catholic—I'd be careful about that, conservative first, but definitely with a Catholic underpinning to it. I recall very well that other Catholics and I who were active in the early conservative movement, Young Americans for Freedom, and so forth, very much looked forward to seeing what *National Review* was saying. Now, we were upset sometimes when Bill or Gary Wills would go off in certain directions, like that famous wisecrack about 'Mater, si; Magistra, no.' So, you know, we did not look at it as *ex cathedra*, but at the same time, *National Review* did reinforce our Catholic understanding and approach to issues such as anti-Communism, which was always very strong. Senator Joe McCarthy, who was very close to my father, was a frequent guest in our home," said Edwards.

George Nash, along with Edwards a leading historian of the conservative movement, makes it clear that Catholics were very much part of the founding through their association with *National Review*. "One of the most remarkable features of this movement was that, in a country still substantially Protestant, its leadership was heavily Roman Catholic, Anglo-Catholic, or critical of Protestant Christianity. Erik von Kuehnelt-Leddihn, Thomas Molnar, Francis Wilson, Frederick Wilhelmsen, and William F. Buckley Jr. were all Catholics. Eric Voegelein called himself a 'pre-Reformation Christian.' Bernard Iddings Bell was an Episcopalian clergyman; John Hallowell and Anthony Harrigan were Episcopalians. Although he was once an atheist, Russell Kirk, by 1953, was on the road to Roman Catholicism. While remaining Protestant, Peter Viereck wrote to Francis Wilson that he considered himself 'in many ways [but not all] a fellow-traveler of the Catholic Church.' In a famous aphorism, Viereck remarked, 'Catholic-baiting is the anti-Semitism of the liberals.' "[13]

Buckley made it respectable to be a Catholic and a conservative.

13. George H. Nash, *The Conservative Intellectual Movement in America since 1945*, (Wilmington, Del.: Intercollegiate Studies Institute, 2006), 119–20.

Catholics could read *National Review* and take solace in its "fusion-ism" of traditional conservatism, with its emphasis on tradition, char-acter, and moral virtue, with the economic conservatism derived from F. A. Hayek.[14] And as Trish Bozell reminded me, "*National Review* came around." But, for a time, some Catholic conservatives did not want to identify too closely with a magazine that made light of Church authority. One of those was L. Brent Bozell; another was Lyman Stebbins.

Stebbins founded Catholics United for the Faith in 1968. CUF, along with Bozell's *Triumph Magazine,* represented the orthodox Catholic protest against the leftward charge of the U.S. Church in the late '60s. Bozell helped Stebbins get media attention for the launch of CUF in September 1968 at the Mayflower Hotel in Washington, D.C. CUF founded state chapters throughout the country and became one of the first Catholic networks to oppose publicly the influence of dissent among bishops, priests, and laity. Bozell and Stebbins were the true precursors of the Catholic revival that John Paul II would stimulate in the '80s. Stebbins is significant also for the respect he continued to show the bishops. This tone of obedience put him at odds with his friend Bozell, according to his widow, Madeleine Stebbins. At a time when some con-servative Catholics were leaving the Church to create "pure" commu-nions, "CUF was inviting them to stay and fight liberalization from within."[15]

In addition to the leadership of Catholics at the public and grassroots level, there are at least three other issues central to giving an account of the Catholic Religious Right: the nature and chronology of the pro-life movement and the U.S. Bishops Conference, the influence of Catholic social teaching and the papacy of John Paul II, and the background of Catholic vehemence against Communism, both in the Soviet Union and at home.

This anti-Communist period of Christian political fervor can be

14. The term "fusionism" was coined by *National Review* editor Frank Meyer in 1956.
15. Michael W. Cuneo, *The Smoke of Satan: Conservative and Traditionalist Dissent in Contem-porary American Catholicism* (Baltimore: Johns Hopkins University Press, 1997), 23.

called, as it is by other commentators, the Old Christian Right, as opposed to the Religious Right or the New Christian Right.[16] Admittedly, the last of these issues, Christian anti-Communism, raises a question that shadows the entire historical narrative of the Religious Right. When did it start? What distinguishes it? Did it begin as far back as the Goldwater campaign of 1964? Was it the campaign to defeat the ERA started by Phyllis Schlafly in 1972?[17] Did it begin, as *Sojourners Magazine* claimed, with the secret meeting of prominent Evangelicals in 1974 to create New Century Publishing Company to support and fund Evangelical political action?[18] Or did it begin with the draft Reagan movement at the 1976 Republican National Convention? Did it start with the famous 1974 textbook controversy in Kanawha County, West Virginia, or the 1977 grassroots outburst in Dade County, Florida, over gay rights? Or, as is most commonly thought, was its origin the creation of the Moral Majority in 1979?

The New Christian Right can be traced back to the Christian Cold Warriors who saw how postwar Communism was infusing atheism into the heart of Europe and directly threatening the United States. Historian George Marsden argues that prominent anti-Communist Evangelicals such as Fred Schwarz, Carl McIntyre, and Billy James Hargis "paved the way for the Religious Right."[19] Marsden implies, I think correctly, that an intense patriotism is the common thread through every generation of conservative Christian activism since World War II.

It's hard to believe, given the Los Angeles Archdiocese of today, but in the 1950s, James Francis Cardinal McIntyre sent his priests to right-wing political meetings, including those of the John Birch Society. McIntyre was the most conservative of the U.S. cardinals from 1953 until his retirement in 1970. He opposed, for example, the liturgical changes man-

16. Leo P. Ribuffo, *The Old Christian Right: The Protestant Far Right from the Great Depression to the Cold War* (Philadelphia: Temple University Press, 1983).

17. Schlafly's organization Stop ERA was renamed the Eagle Forum in 1975.

18. *Sojourners,* April 1976; cited in Sara Diamond, *Spiritual Warfare: The Politics of the Christian Right* (Boston: South End Press, 1989), 49.

19. George M. Marsden, *Fundamentalism and American Culture,* 2nd ed. (New York: Oxford University Press, 2006), 232.

dated by the Second Vatican Council in the early '60s. His archdiocesan newspaper, *The Tidings,* resonated with a pro-Birch message. One of his priests, Paul Peterson, pastor of St. Boniface Parish in Orange County, used his bulletin for anti-Communist messages. As one historian put it, "McIntyre provided fodder for Catholic participation in conservative activism." [20]

The Catholic anti-Communism effort is well documented: Father Charles Coughlin's radio broadcasts of 1926 to 1939; Cardinal Spellman and Bishop Fulton Sheen; the Cardinal Mindszenty Foundation; the Blue Army of Fatima formed by Monsignor Harold V. Colgan in 1947 to end the Red Army and Communism and to pray for the conversion of Russia; the Knights of Columbus, who played a major role in the campaign to include "under God" in the Pledge of Allegiance in 1954. And at the extreme, there was significant Catholic participation in the John Birch Society, founded in 1958 by a fundamentalist Baptist, Robert Welch. The John Birch Society was denounced by the Catholic bishops as early as 1961 for its anti-Semitism. One surprising aspect of this Catholic anti-Communist crusade was the way some of its leaders accused Protestants of turning "pink" with sympathy for the Communist cause. [21] It appears that in this moment of Catholic visibility following World War II, some Catholics gave in to the temptation to give Protestants a taste of the bigotry they had suffered since colonial times.

ALL ROADS LEAD TO BUCKLEY

Lee Edwards agrees that anti-Communism was the theme that launched the marriage between Catholicism and conservatism: "It certainly wasn't the demand for social justice—that was something which conservatives were uncomfortable with because it required the federal government to be in welfare and so forth. But did anti-Communism lead to conservatism—absolutely. I remember there were all kinds of meetings held in

20. McGirr, *Suburban Warriors,* 107.

21. Mark S. Massa, *Catholics & American Culture: Fulton Sheen, Dorothy Day, and the Notre Dame Football Team* (New York: Crossroad, 1999), 74.

New York City by anti-Communist groups strongly Catholic for McCarthy, and for Bill Buckley."

When I pressed Edwards on why Catholic anti-Communism would connect with conservatism, he answered, "I think it was good versus evil. We young conservatives saw Communism as evil. That was *the* motivating force as young conservatives. We saw it as evil—we saw it as almost satanic. We may not have used that word (maybe we did use it), but the Catholic approach of believing in the devil, believing in good and evil, helped us to be able to make that judgment." (Note the Manichaean inspiration in Edwards's story.) Mark S. Massa, in his account of McCarthy's anti-Communist crusade, comes to a similar conclusion but without the approving tone: "McCarthy offered a clear-cut model to comprehend the evil in the world as well as the solution to that evil." [22]

The challenge of Communism and the Soviet Union ran smack into the Catholic sense of "American exceptionalism." The United States, in their view, was uniquely positioned to overcome the threat of the Soviet Union to democracy and religious freedom. The root of American exceptionalism is partially religious—in the belief that God had set this country apart to have a special role in world history. As a result, hyperpatriotism is found throughout the politics of the Christian Right.

In fact, when Steve Wagner and I did the original Catholic vote research for *Crisis* in 1998, we discovered that a belief in American exceptionalism was one of the five top issues that led Catholic voters to migrate steadily toward the Republican Party since 1960. Thus, it comes as no surprise that all the recent critiques of the Religious Right take dead aim at the issue of exceptionalism and the associated claim that America is a Christian nation.

Catholics donated money to Religious Right organizations, not simply because they fought abortion but because they espoused an unambiguous patriotism, which included a pride in the military and traditional values. Since World War II, a disproportionate number of Catholics have made careers in the military. These patriotic Catholics with a deep re-

22. Ibid., 79.

spect for the military were not deprived of their national pride by the one-two punch of Vietnam and Watergate. As Ralph Reed told me, out of 2 million members of the Christian Coalition, somewhere between 15 to 20 percent were Catholics. The same was true for the Falwell Moral Majority, which boasted 7 million members at its zenith. This ad hoc coalition of Catholics and Evangelicals continued through Don Wildmon's American Family Association and James Dobson's Focus on the Family. Wildmon and Dobson have a significant Catholic membership, though they did not supply precise figures.

WHY CATHOLICS RESPONDED

On the beginning of the actual pro-life movement, all commentators agree: the earlier response to *Roe* v. *Wade* came from Roman Catholics, not from the Evangelical leadership that eventually came to the forefront in the late '70s and the '80s. As William Martin writes, "Evangelical and fundamentalist Protestants, many of whom now consider abortion a litmus test of extraordinary importance, had little to say about it one way or the other."[23] Martin notes that anti-Catholic bias may have been involved, and he cites leading Evangelical theologian Harold O. J. Brown, saying, "At that point a lot of Protestants reacted almost automatically— 'If Catholics are for it, we should be against it.'"[24]

The earliest responses came from lay Catholics such as Cathy Sullivan, Eleanor Howe, and those who started the original state Right to Life organizations, which were eventually merged into National Right to Life. One of those is Dr. Jack Willke, a Catholic obstetrician from Cincinnati. He refers to himself as the "educator of the movement," and indeed he is. Written with his wife, Barbara, and self-published in 1971, *Handbook on Abortion* was the first scientific training guide for pro-life activists. Willke, one of the founders of National Right to Life, served as its president for more than ten years.

The Willkes were deeply involved in wedding preparations and sex

23. Martin, *With God on Our Side*, 193.
24. Ibid.

education when they were challenged in 1970 by Father Paul Marx, founder of Human Life International, to take on abortion. They were reluctant, since they were already lecturing nationally, he was in practice by himself, and they were raising six children. At Christmas, Willke's two college-age daughters came home from Notre Dame and asked him about abortion. The girls urged their mother and father to write a book on abortion. Still, the parents demurred. Then the daughters offered to type and edit the book if their parents would put it on a dictating machine. In February, the Willkes started dictating, and by June, the book was printed. Willke says, "It went like wildfire because there was nothing out there." In the next three years, the *Handbook on Abortion* sold more than a million copies, and it eventually grew from 100 pages to 400 pages and was translated into twenty-three languages. It became the "the Bible of the pro-life movement."

"Nothing was organized in the early '70s. Barbara and I just went from town to town lecturing and trying to start small groups." Willke says the earliest attempt to bring pro-life leaders together was organized by Monsignor Jim McHugh at the U.S. Bishops Conference. Starting in 1968, he held ad hoc meetings once a year under the name National Right to Life. The Willkes attended their first McHugh meeting in 1971.

Willke recalls that before any pro-life organizations were created, the Knights of Columbus was the most important national group to support the cause. With Knights in every parish in the United States, they "had the message" before anyone else, and they published it in their magazine, *Columbia*. "It was with volunteers from Catholics like the Knights that we were able to place the pro-life pamphlet on the doorstep of every home in Michigan and North Dakota for the 1972 abortion referendums." Abortion was defeated in both states that year.

But in January 1973, the Supreme Court handed down *Roe* v. *Wade*. Willke says the furor led to a meeting that summer in Detroit of leaders from 300 small pro-life groups scattered around the country. Many of these, some called "kitchen-table" groups, were started by the Willkes on their lecture tours. With the permission of the bishops, they took the name of National Right to Life and created the first national pro-life organization. "We had no money, but it did not stop us." Willke remembers the group was "heavily Catholic," with a sprinkling of Protestants.

This first generation of pro-lifers was able to pass through Congress in 1976 what is still the most important piece of antiabortion legislation. The Hyde Amendment prohibits the government from paying for abortions except when the life of the mother is endangered. The next major victory came in 1984, when Ronald Reagan extended the principle of the Hyde Amendment to foreign policy by declaring the Mexico City Policy. Named after the place where it was announced, the policy stipulated that "nongovernmental organizations agree as a condition of their receipt of Federal funds that such organizations would neither perform nor actively promote abortion as a method of family planning in other nations." Bill Clinton rescinded it on the first day of his presidency in 1993, and George W. Bush reinstated it on the first day of his 2001 term.

THE BISHOPS AND THE ABORTION BATTLES

Ardent Catholic pro-lifers usually speak with great disappointment about the role of the bishops in battling abortion. They accuse them of not having done enough in overturning *Roe* v. *Wade* or challenging pro-abortion Catholic politicians. But that was certainly not true in the early days of the U.S. Bishops Conference after its founding in 1966. Its first great and consuming cause was the pro-life issue. It was their pro-life effort that brought the bishops into the political arena, and it was the unforeseen outcome of their pro-life advocacy that led them gradually away from the issue. The U.S. bishops published *Human Life in Our Day* in 1968, two years after the creation of the Conference and five years before *Roe*. That the bishops were deeply committed to the abortion cause is evidenced by this document and the three others published before *Roe*. One commentator notes the "increasingly aggressive tone of their statements."[25]

Before 1973, their efforts were localized because abortion was a state

25. Timothy A. Byrnes, *Catholic Bishops in American Politics* (Princeton, N.J.: Princeton University Press, 1991), 56.

issue, but when *Roe* v. *Wade* overturned state laws restricting abortion, the bishops' effort became a national one. The Bishops Conference reacted quickly. Its ad hoc committee on pro-life activity met for the first time the day after *Roe* was handed down. The same year, the bishops decided on a strategy for amending the Constitution and created the National Committee for a Human Life Amendment. The next year, four Catholic cardinals—Krol of Philadelphia, Cody of Chicago, Medeiros of Boston, and Manning of Los Angeles—testified before the Senate Judiciary Committee in support of the many amendments that were offered to offset *Roe.*

The bishops' post-*Roe* effort culminated in 1975 with a comprehensive "Pastoral Plan for Pro-Life Activities." The plan called for "the development in each congressional district of an identifiable, tightly knit and well organized pro-life unit. This unit can be described as a public interest group or a citizen's lobby." [26] The bishops were well aware of the dangers such a national organizing effort would present to their Conference, such as an IRS challenge to their tax-exempt status. They included language in the plan that specified that these pro-life groups were not "an agency of the church, nor operated, controlled or financed by the church." [27] This qualifying language doomed the enterprise to failure, no matter how well intentioned the effort. Given the hierarchical nature of the Church, there is no way the bishops could actually start an organization and allow it to operate a national campaign without any ecclesial oversight.

The Pastoral Plan for Pro-Life Activities, in retrospect, looks as though it could have served as the blueprint used by the Moral Majority and the Christian Coalition to organize Evangelical churchgoers for a political uprising. What the U.S. bishops conceived of doing on a national scale is precisely what the Evangelicals were bold enough to do. Indeed, the Evangelical organizations ran into challenges from the IRS and the Federal Election Commission but never suffered even a near-fatal blow. The

26. Ibid., 59.
27. Ibid.

Bishops Conference, ever since, has increasingly used the fear of losing its tax-exempt status to etch a boundary line around its pro-life activity.

Liberal Catholics, who want to downplay or dispose of the abortion issue, point to polling indicating that most Catholics don't feel as strongly about this issue as those in the pro-life movement. I asked one of the nation's best-known priests why many Catholics are lukewarm on this issue. "The shanty Irish emerged from their ghettos and embraced fashionable ideas," says Father Benedict Groeschel. Groeschel is a life-long New Yorker and earned his doctorate in psychology from Columbia University in 1971. He is now director of spiritual development for the Archdiocese of New York, and in 1987, he helped to found the Franciscan Friars of the Renewal, which runs a retreat center in Larchmont, New York, and a shelter for the homeless in the South Bronx and Harlem.

Groeschel sees the problem as assimilation. The Kennedy election of 1960 multiplied the problem—"they left the ghetto and moved up too fast—they weren't ready to grapple with the culture." The ethnic Catholics, having just entered the cultural mainstream, "started reading existential philosophers and humanistic psychologists like Carl Rodgers—and the nuns started reading it, too." Groeschel describes successive generations of Catholics who just stopped being "religious." This radical change among much of the laity is what made it possible for the bishops to make their turn to the political left in the late '70s.

BERNARDIN GETS BURNED

But the early antiabortion efforts of the bishops in the years before and after *Roe* helped to make abortion an important political issue, one that favored conservatives and Republicans, rather than Democrats who were favored by most American bishops and certainly by the staff at the U.S. Catholic Conferences.[28] Since the death of FDR, Catholic voters, with the exception of the 1960 election, had been showing more inclina-

---

28. Richard J. Gelm, *Politics and Religious Authority: American Catholics since the Second Vatican Council* (Westport, Conn.: Greenwood Press, 1994), 113.

tion to vote for the GOP presidential candidate, most notably in an over-whelming rejection of McGovern in favor of Nixon in 1972 (61 percent of self-identified Catholics). For the bishops to be promoting an issue that further alienated Catholic voters from Democrats was creating a great deal of tension within the Conference, a tension that was bound to explode, as it did in the presidential campaign of 1976. It was this explosion that led the bishops to change fundamentally their approach to the abortion battle to one that placed abortion among a broad spectrum of other issues.

The Pastoral Plan did not signal the retreat of the bishops from the abortion fight. It may have revealed the differences within the Conference that undermined the effort, but the bishops remained publicly opposed to abortion. Their determination led to an incident in 1976 involving Archbishop Joseph Bernardin, then president of the National Conference of Catholic Bishops; President Gerald Ford; and presidential candidate Governor Jimmy Carter. It began with the pro-abortion plank of the platform adopted at the Democratic National Convention. Bernardin didn't like it and said so publicly. Carter, anxious to win back some of the Catholic vote, tried to conciliate Bernardin through an interview with the Catholic News Service. That strategy only succeeded in provoking Bernardin to speak out against the Democratic platform for the second time. This was followed by another statement in which Bernardin praised the Republicans for their support of a constitutional amendment banning abortion.

The Democrats inside the Conference realized they had to do some damage control, so they arranged a meeting between the Conference secretary, James Rausch, and Andrew Young, who was working for the Carter campaign. Rausch represented those in the Conference who thought too much priority was put on abortion as a single issue and thought it best placed within a variety of other issues important in Catholic social teaching. In short, Bernardin and Rausch, the Conference president and its secretary, were not on the same page. In subsequent weeks, Rausch became very close to the Carter campaign (he was already a friend of vice-presidential candidate Walter Mondale) and even sent someone from the Conference to sit in on a Carter campaign meeting in Plains, Georgia. Out of these discussions came the decision that Carter should meet personally with Bernardin and the NCCB executive committee.

Carter had assurances that some accommodation would be achieved at the meeting, but Bernardin did not budge from his demand that Carter repudiate the Democratic platform and endorse the Human Life Amendment. Carter tried to suggest some kind of middle ground on a constitutional amendment but got nowhere. When Bernardin emerged from the meeting to the waiting press, he announced that he was "disappointed" with Carter's stance on abortion.

President Ford acted quickly and invited Bernardin and the other bishops to the White House. Ford did not support the broad Human Life Amendment but told them he supported a constitutional amendment that would reverse *Roe* by returning the legality of abortion to state legislatures. Bernardin met with the press outside the White House and said, "We are encouraged that the president agrees on the need for a constitutional amendment."

When the mainstream media treated Bernardin's statement as an implied endorsement of the Republican ticket, an uproar ensued at the NCCB. Obviously, the strategy engineered by Rausch had backfired—the Catholic Church seemed more aligned with the Republican Party than ever. Russell Shaw was director of the bishops' office of public affairs at the time. He remembered that Bernardin faced a near walkout at the Conference amid the charge that he had acted in such a partisan way that the NCCB was in danger of losing its tax-exempt status. Bernardin, in the midst of a chorus of criticism, "received no support from conservatives, and he never forgot it," Shaw told me.

After 1976, the National Conference of Catholic Bishops moved in a different direction on the abortion issue. No longer would abortion be singled out by the Conference as the single most important evil to be opposed in America. It would be put on equal footing with a myriad other issues—poverty, health care, war, nuclear disarmament, education—and woven into "the seamless garment," or what is also called "the consistent ethic of life." That Bernardin himself would become the author and spokesman of the "seamless garment" gives rise to a variety of speculation about whether he had compromised in the face of opposition from within the Conference. The fact that Cardinal Bernardin went to the Oval Office to receive the Medal of Freedom from President Clinton on the same day that his fellow bishops gathered on the steps of Congress to protest Clinton's veto of the ban on partial-birth abortion does not do him credit.

What is clear, however, is that other bishops, namely Bernard Cardinal Law and John Cardinal O'Connor, did not agree with the direction taken by Bernardin and the Conference in the wake of the 1976 controversy. Since then, the Catholic bishops of the United States have been deeply divided on the best political and spiritual strategy to oppose abortion. These divisions continue to flare up, as they did when O'Connor admonished vice-presidential candidate Geraldine Ferraro in 1984, but perhaps no more brightly than in 2004, when Bishop Raymond Burke sparked a prolonged debate on whether Senator John Kerry should be denied communion.

Further proof of the forces at work inside the NCCB in 1976 was witnessed at a Call to Action conference held in Detroit in October of that year. The first president of the NCCB, Cardinal John Dearden of Detroit, was host and chairman of the event, while USCC secretary Bishop Rausch was the organizer. If there was any doubt about where Dearden and Rausch wanted to lead the U.S. Catholic Church, it was dispelled by Call to Action. The three-day conference became a veritable melee of dissident proposals—183 resolutions in all, from the open election of bishops and priests, married priests, acceptance of divorce, ending the celibacy requirement, allowing female priests, and ending the ban on birth control, to changing the teaching on homosexuality.[29] The bishops, realizing that the conference had gotten completely out of control, referred the resolutions to committees, where they eventually died. But the dissident genie had been let out of the box, and a certain form of dissent

29. George A. Kelly, *The Battle for the American Church* (Garden City, N.Y.: Image Books, 1981), 379–87.

from Church teaching became acceptable in the Catholic establishment. The leftward turn of the hierarchy, the Conferences, and the colleges and universities created a deep division among the laity out of which a conservative reaction was bound to appear. When the reaction surfaced, it was just in time to create more Catholic support for the Moral Majority.

There have been several attempts by Catholics to copy the success of Evangelical groups such as the Moral Majority and the Christian Coalition. The Catholic Campaign for America, founded in 1989 by Thomas Wykes, flourished for a few years, hosting dinners and conferences featuring Catholic celebrities such as William Bennett, Tom Monaghan, Alan Keyes, and Rick Santorum. The Campaign was forced to go out of business after suffering a financial setback from mounting a major rally that attracted an embarrassingly small crowd. On the heels of the Catholic Campaign for America came the Catholic Alliance, created in 1995 by the Christian Coalition. Ralph Reed invited a board of Catholic leaders who wanted to emulate the success of the Coalition among pro-life Catholic activists. Under its second director, Deacon Keith Fournier, the Alliance came under fire from bishops who objected to a lay-run organization using the name "Catholic" for political purposes. Bishop Howard Hubbard of Albany, New York, argued that the Alliance "will create massive confusion" among politicians and the Catholic faithful because it "purport[s] to represent the position of the Catholic Church."[30] The outrage was predictable. The bishops were not going to countenance a Catholic organization being founded and funded by Republican Evangelicals Ralph Reed and Pat Robertson. After Reed left the Christian Coalition in 1997, the Catholic Alliance soon lost its funding and went under.

The Catholic Alliance and the Catholic Campaign for America, to a lesser extent, struggled to apply the Evangelical model to organize Catholics anxious to preserve their own identity in the political and cultural struggles being led by Reed and others. But they ran up against the basic difference between Catholic and Protestant church structure: the func-

30. Richard Neuhaus, "Truths and Untruths about the Catholic Alliance," *First Things* (February 1996), 7.

tion and authority of priests and bishops. The lesson of these failed attempts is that any political organizing of Catholics *as Catholics* is going to meet the resistance of bishops who either want to preserve their authority as teachers of faith and morals or simply don't like the agenda of the lay movement and want to shut it down. This ecclesial factor encourages socially conservative Catholics to get involved either in Evangelical organizations or in the Republican Party itself, as they did in 2000 and 2004.

Thus, it is no accident that the most successful Catholic political advocacy group in the nation is an organization of priests. Priests for Life was founded by a San Francisco priest, Lee Kaylor, in 1990. Kaylor wanted to use the pulpit to speak out on pro-life legislation. Since 1993, the organization has been led by Father Frank Pavone, who took over with the permission of Cardinal O'Connor of New York.

Pavone epitomizes the new generation of what I call "John Paul II priests," who have no qualms about addressing pro-life issues. Frank Pavone grew up in Port Chester, New York, a suburb in Westchester County just north of New York City. He was ordained a Catholic priest in 1988 as part of the first group of seminarians who attended Dunwoody Seminary entirely under the leadership of Cardinal O'Connor. O'Connor would have them come to St. Patrick's Cathedral at least once a month. Pavone says that it was from O'Connor that he "learned how to preach on the issue of pro-life with conviction and compassion. He taught us that the compassion we have for these women does not require us to be less convicted."

Pavone credits the success of Priests for Life, in part, to the fact that he is a priest and relies on the help of other priests. "The newer priests who have come along under John Paul II are comfortable with the fight—they know how to deal with the enemy and are not surprised by the attacks launched against them."

As is the case for many conservative Catholic leaders, the Catholic television network EWTN played a decisive role in helping Pavone grow his organization. He made his first appearance on *Mother Angelica Live* in 1994 and was so impressive that he was invited back to start his own

show, *Defending Life,* which continues to this day. His appearances on
EWTN and the speaking engagements that followed made him a national figure. The growth of Priests for Life has enabled Pavone to found
a new order of priests dedicated to pro-life work, the Missionaries of the
Gospel of Life, in Amarillo, Texas.

Pavone, not surprisingly, has been criticized by staff at the Bishops
Conference and by some bishops themselves for being perceived as the
official voice of the Church. "The sense I have gotten over the years is
'Well, you know this is our turf, why are you getting messed up in it?'"
When he hears this, Pavone simply says, "You need to talk a little louder
yourselves and not worry about Father Pavone." He hopes that more
priests and bishops will get behind groups such as Priests for Life or risk
"becoming irrelevant."

He also has been accused by bishops of exclusively supporting Republican candidates. He tells them, "All I have been doing is quoting your
documents, in particular 'Living the Gospel of Life.' If tomorrow the
parties swapped positions on abortion, our message would not change
a bit."

Pavone has caused some controversy by arguing that Catholic voters
should factor in the position of the political parties when they cast their
votes. "Why should you vote for a pro-life Democrat when the Democrats will never introduce pro-life legislation? And there is nothing
wrong with voting for a pro-abortion Republican, as long the Republicans keep introducing the right kind of legislation and nominating good
judges."

Pavone has met with many frustrated laymen who are getting the
doors shut in their faces by their pastors, so they are starting their own
movements. "The people themselves have connected the dots, and they
want to do something, but it is frustrating that the institutional Church
is saying no. It is summed up in one word, *attorneys,* even if it is issue
advocacy. The attorneys and the bishops who listen to them are making
the Church irrelevant."

Pavone has always cultivated relationships with non-Catholics. When
he was in seminary, he attended a Protestant church every Sunday after

mass. "I wanted to know what it was like to worship and pray with other Christians." His strong bond to Evangelicals is attested to by his selection as the first Catholic priest to be president of the National Pro-Life Religious Council.

To those who say Priests for Life has become too political, Pavone says, "Catholic political involvement has strengthened the faith because it has encouraged people to defend the faith." This message had to come from a priest or a bishop before it was going to be accepted by many Catholics and by the clergy themselves. Pavone's work provides the kind of spiritual confidence that conservative Catholics need to remain politically active. They want to work in "obedience" to the Church, and Pavone's example, like that of Cardinal O'Connor before him, provides them that assurance.

Is there a Catholic Religious Right? Yes. For the past thirty years, Catholics have been integral to its strategic, political, and grassroots leadership. Catholic anti-Communists created a group of intellectual leaders and an army of activists that would form the basis for the new conservative movement and the specifically religious conservatism that would arise a generation later. Even the Catholic bishops provided some impetus in the early years by responding early and vigorously to *Roe* v. *Wade*, long before it was an issue to Evangelical leaders. And after several misfires, socially conservative Catholics created their own identity in the Republican Party through the Catholic outreach efforts of 2000 and 2004. Most important, Catholic leaders have arisen who are no longer dependent on the U.S. Conference of Catholic Bishops, Evangelical organizations, or the Republican Party for their influence.

7

RELIGIOUS LEFT, RIGHT, AND CENTER

I T'S EASY TO IGNORE THE OBVIOUS. WHAT IS OBVIOUS ABOUT THE Religious Left and the Religious Right is their distinctively different views about religion. Evangelical Christians and conservative Catholics identify salvation with repentance, God's forgiveness in this life, and the promise of eternal life. Mainline Protestants and liberal Catholics think in different terms. The mixture of liberal politics and religion creates a passion for social transformation fueled by the certainties of faith. The Religious Right came to life as a defensive movement—against the attack on patriotism, the family, traditional gender roles, and the unborn. The Religious Left of mainstream Protestants and "social justice" Catholics insists on a broad restructuring of society based on its principles of equality and civil rights.

The Religious Left identifies its religion with its politics. Religion becomes a subspecies of the political left itself which treats all politics with an "ultimate concern" that is the mark of a religious commitment.[1] Jim Bopp, chief counsel of National Right to Life, sums it up this way: "There

---

1. This description of religious faith was made popular by Paul Tillich in *The Dynamics of Faith* (New York: Harper & Row, 1957). Tillich, a Lutheran theologian, used the notion of "ultimate concern" to convince would-be atheists that they believed in something ultimate, whether "God" or not.

is always an element in the thinking of religious conservatives that they want to be seeking their own salvation, but they have to be politically involved. *It is a diversion* but a necessary diversion. For the left, politics is *never* a diversion; they relish it. But for them to be successful, they have to have government to do things; it is an essential means to an end, it is their religion. That is why they get so upset when other religious folks have a say."

To Bopp, this explains why the Democratic Party and the Religious Left fought so hard against President Bush's judicial nominations to the Supreme Court: "It is Armageddon. They are not going to get their social policies implemented by the judges; the most liberal legislators are unlikely to do this. They have to have the judges. That is why it is so important to them. They are perfectly willing to tear down the democracy in order to have liberal judges."

After the 2004 election, Democratic strategists began a long-overdue reexamination of their relationship with religiously active voters. John Kerry and Howard Dean called for their party to reconsider its position on abortion. James Carville and Paul Begala, both Catholics, wrote, "If Democrats had the flexibility to give a little on the margins, they could win the abortion debate in the mainstream."[2] Senator Hillary Rodham Clinton made a remarkable speech to pro-abortion activists calling for accommodation with pro-lifers in the Democratic Party. Clinton reiterated her position, through an advisor, on the heels of the 2006 election and the victory of socially conservative Democratic candidates over GOP members of Congress.

Senator Barack Obama, however, seems more religion-friendly than the former first lady. In a June 2006 speech about religion and politics at a Call to Renewal Conference, he talked about his senatorial campaign against conservative Catholic Alan Keyes. He admitted that he was put on the defensive by Keyes's attacks and did not "adequately express the role faith has in guiding my own values and my own

---

2. Paul Begala and James Carville, *Take It Back: A Battle Plan for Democratic Victory* (New York: Simon & Schuster, 2006), 42.

beliefs."[3] (Does that mean Alan Keyes will be able to claim credit for an Obama presidency?)

Amy Sullivan, a writer and proponent of the Religious Left, called Obama's confession "The first time in modern memory, an affirmative statement came from a Democrat about 'how to reconcile faith with our modern, pluralistic democracy.'" She compared his speech with that of JFK to the Houston ministers in 1960 and that of Mario Cuomo at Notre Dame in 1984. She praises Obama's "easy-going confidence" in addressing faith and politics. Sullivan takes special note of how comfortable Obama is in talking about his faith. It's a quality notably absent from the last two Democratic presidential candidates.[4] His invitation to speak at Rick Warren's megachurch, Saddleback Church in Southern California, at a conference on the AIDS epidemic in Africa highlighted the possibilities of crossover support from socially concerned Evangelicals. Warren, by the way, refused to uninvite Obama after protests from Evangelical leaders across the country.

Politics is *a religious act* to the Religious Left, but when the Religious Right loses an election, it doesn't feel religion has been thwarted. The Religious Left is more agitated by election results. Who controls Congress and who sits in the White House determine the ability to implement a plan for the nation's salvation. (Recall Reinhold Niebuhr's call to "establish justice in a sinful world.") In the 1920s and '30s, this plan was referred to as the "social gospel." In the '70s and '80s, it was called the "theology of liberation." Now it is the concern for "social justice," as distinguished from the "social issues" of the Religious Right.

Critics of the theocratic Religious Right have forgotten that in previous generations other religious groups had a direct impact on politics. Cal Thomas has covered religion and politics as a journalist for nearly forty years. His weekly column is published in 600 newspapers, and he is a regular contributor to Fox News and *USA Today*. In our interview, he

---

3. Amy Sullivan, "In Good Faith: The Real Meaning of Barack Obama's Speech on Religion and Politics," *Slate*, July 3, 2006.

4. John Kerry's September 18, 2006, speech at Pepperdine University on "godly tasks" seems to have gone much better than his attempts to talk about religion in the 2004 campaign.

reminded me that what the Religious Right has been doing for the past thirty years the mainline Protestant denominations have done for the thirty years, or more, before that.

"The World Council of Churches used to have a slogan: 'The world sets the agenda for the Church.' That says a lot. This is the great secret: The left did all of this stuff before the right came along—we have the evidence. They were hands-on in preaching the social gospel even more than the right. All of that evidence is on the record, and they compromise their central message in exchange for political involvement, power, and 'a place at the table.'"

Former presidents Bill Clinton and Jimmy Carter have announced an initiative to create a new Baptist coalition of thirty moderate Baptist groups that are no longer connected to the Southern Baptist Convention. The focus will be on social problems such as poverty, pollution, health care, and racial and religious conflicts.[5] If successful, such an initiative would provide the Religious Left with a national infrastructure of ministers, churches, and laity, something that groups such as Call to Renewal, Interfaith Alliance, and the Tikkun Community cannot supply. This new coalition could become the launching pad for a revival of the social gospel.

The phrase "social gospel" is most often identified with a German Baptist pastor from New York City, Walter Rauschenbusch. He published *Theology of the Social Gospel* in 1917 while leading a group of Protestant clergy and laity who were seeking to help the poor who suffered in the days of the "robber barons," many of whom were prominent members of mainline denominations. Among Catholics, the social gospel has had its champion as well, principally Monsignor John A. Ryan, a professor of moral theology and economics at the Catholic University of America. He is also the Social Action Division director of the National Catholic Welfare Conference (the precursor to the USCCB). Ryan applied the social encyclicals of the popes—beginning with Leo XIII (1810–1903), particularly *Rerum Novarum* (1891)—to American politics, resulting in

5. Daniel Yee, "Clinton, Carter Back Moderate Baptists," Associated Press, January 9, 2007.

many influential policies, including the "living wage." Ryan played a major role in providing Catholic input for policies for the FDR administration and bringing Catholics into the Democratic coalition. At Roosevelt's request, Ryan served on the Industrial Appeals Board of the National Recovery Administration.

Ryan and Rauschenbusch are the forgotten precursors of luminaries such as Martin Luther King, Dorothy Day, and William Sloane Coffin. Cofounder of the Catholic Worker Movement in 1933, Dorothy Day is, along with Ryan, the most revered figure in the social-gospel–social-justice wing of the Catholic Church. Members of the Catholic Worker Movement, organized by houses around the world, seek social justice through pacifism and redistribution of wealth. Day, a convert to Catholicism, had an abortion as a young woman, and, according to John Cardinal O'Connor, "She regretted it every day of her life." O'Connor made this comment in a letter to the Vatican on February 7, 1998, initiating her canonization process.

Before Dorothy Day died in 1980, she witnessed the introduction of the issues of abortion and feminism into the social-justice movement. In spite of her progressive political views, she rejected the argument connecting civil rights to a woman's choice over her body and her child. The movement Day had led in the Catholic Church was already in the process of being married to the abortion-rights movement.[6]

A JESUIT INVENTS THE PRO-ABORTION CATHOLIC POLITICIAN

The best-known pro-abortion Catholics in the Democratic Party are Senator Ted Kennedy, Senator John Kerry, and Speaker Nancy Pelosi. Some would say that Mario Cuomo, specifically through his 1984 Notre Dame speech, was the architect of their strategy of marginalizing the abortion issue while claiming to be Catholic. Yet years before Cuomo

6. Ryan was also a social conservative on these questions, having testified before Congress against contraception. See John T. McGreevy, *Catholicism and American Freedom* (New York: W. W. Norton, 2003), 233.

made his speech and carried on his public dispute with Cardinal O'Connor, there was Father Robert Drinan, an attorney, law professor, and member of Congress from 1971 to 1981. Father Drinan deserves the credit for making it acceptable to be Catholic, support abortion, and hold public office. Drinan actually described himself as "a moral architect," a comment that could only elicit dropped jaws among pro-life Catholics.[7] He ran for a congressional seat from Massachusetts while he was dean of the Boston College Law School, in spite of the fact that the Society of Jesus forbid their priests to hold public office. Drinan campaigned on his opposition to the Vietnam War, his support for George McGovern, and his opponent's support for the Nixon administration. According to an article in the Harvard *Crimson* after the primary, "Drinan produced one of the most startling upsets in Massachusetts political history."

While in Congress and afterward, Drinan was a leading proponent of abortion, writing in defense of *Roe* v. *Wade* and Clinton's veto of the ban against partial-birth abortion. During his ten years in the House, "Drinan was developing in practice the 'personally opposed but pro-choice' position that was later to be defended formally in a famous speech by New York Governor Mario Cuomo at Notre Dame University."[8] In 2006, a Jesuit institution, Georgetown University Law School, announced the creation of an endowed chair in his name.

Drinan gave the authority of his collar and the Jesuit order to pro-abortion politics. At his 1964 and 1968 meetings at the Kennedy compound in Hyannisport, he helped to script a young Ted Kennedy to spin the abortion issue so he could follow the Democratic Party's descent into secular liberalism. As a congressman, he effectively became the poster priest and "spiritual director" of the pro-abortion movement. One historian of contemporary American Catholicism points out that Drinan's late-'60s laissez-faire attitude on abortion met with protest from Catholic activists of the time who saw this issue as another "injustice" that

7. Mark Feeney, "Congressman-Priest Dies," *Boston Globe,* January 29, 2007.
8. Robert George and William Saunders, "The Failure of Catholic Political Leadership," *Crisis* (April 2000).

needed to be addressed along with poverty, racism, and war.[9] If Drinan had not been the agent to strip the abortion issue away from the demands of social justice and had he not counseled Ted Kennedy to jettison his pro-life beliefs, the subsequent history of American politics and, especially, the Democratic Party as we know it would be completely different. Drinan, among Catholic activists, was the most responsible for ensuring that the Catholic left would be predominantly pro-abortion. His fingerprints are everywhere.

The superior general of the Jesuits, Father Pedro Arrupe, made multiple efforts to keep Drinan from running for office and from seeking reelection. But at every turn, he was thwarted by the head (called a provincial) of the New England Province, Father William G. Guindon. Guindon told Arrupe that as a "matter of conscience," he could not keep Drinan from running. He added that by forbidding Drinan from running for office, the Jesuits would be interfering in the democratic process. The American Civil Liberties Union, which has a long history of protesting against religious influence in politics, raised no complaint. Drinan already had sought their support and obtained their go-ahead.[10]

Guindon, interestingly, forbade Father John McLaughlin from running for the Senate in Rhode Island as a Republican. McLaughlin, denied the chance to be a senator, served instead on Nixon's staff while still a Jesuit priest. Guindon's successor, Father Richard T. Cleary, objected to the Jesuit's presence in the White House and called a press conference in May 1974 to say that McLaughlin was being ordered to leave the White House for fear that his comments would be perceived as a Jesuit position. McLaughlin chose to leave the priesthood rather than leave the administration. He eventually married and became a well-known television commentator.

Cleary was asked at a news conference why Drinan was not being recalled as well, especially when he was advocating abortion. Cleary responded by saying that as a lawyer, Drinan was free to advocate legal

9. McGreevy, *Catholicism*, 270.

10. James Hitchcock, "The Strange Political Career of Father Drinan," *Catholic World Report* (July 1996).

abortion if as a priest, he continued to oppose the practice on moral grounds. He did not apply the same objection to Drinan's political positions as he did to the Republican McLaughlin's.

The inside story of all the Jesuit machinations and deceptions that were used to protect Drinan from the superior general in the Vatican and other hostile bishops, is illustrative of why the word "Jesuitical" exists. The inability of Arrupe to enforce his policy forbidding Jesuit priests to hold public office was disastrous for the Church in the United States.

Drinan was duplicitous. In his private letters to pro-lifers, he cited his support for the Church's teaching on abortion. For example, he wrote to one constituent, "I do hope that everything that is feasible can be done to protect the sanctity and inviolability of unborn life." In letters to supporters of abortion, he wrote the opposite message: "It is not very pleasant to have to suggest that . . . it appears that a certain small element within the Catholic Church is seeking to impose its views on the rest of the nation." He urged pro-life groups to do all they could to overthrow abortion on demand, while personally supporting the work of abortion-rights groups.[11]

The New England Jesuits themselves never sought to alter Drinan's pro-abortion position, and finally, after less than a year in office, John Paul II intervened. After a decade of hemming and hawing by Drinan's Jesuit superiors, the Vatican had had enough and ordered Drinan to resign from Congress. He was not the first Catholic priest to serve in Congress, only the first Jesuit priest. Drinan left a legacy that other pro-abortion "Catholics" continue to emulate. Along with Drinan, another priest was also forced to leave office: Robert J. Cornell, a Norbertine priest from Wisconsin, who had been elected in 1974 and 1976. Cornell lost the election of 1978 and had been preparing a third run for office. By making a public example of Drinan, John Paul II made it clear that he intended to put the brakes on Catholic dissent in the United States.

After being forced to give up his seat in the House, Drinan still did not change his tune. He became president of the liberal lobbying organiza-

11. Mary Meehan, "Robert Drinan under Siege," *Our Sunday Visitor,* September 8, 1996.

tion Americans for Democratic Action. Additionally, he remained very much a player within Democratic Party ranks. In a *New York Times* op-ed in 1996, he defended Clinton's veto of the ban on partial-birth abortion. Drinan commented, "It would allow federal power to intrude into the practice of medicine." Cardinal O'Connor responded that Drinan could have raised a voice for life but instead had "raised it for death." To his credit, Drinan eventually retracted his statement, saying he had relied on false information. This was the first and last time he qualified his support for abortion.

Drinan was an advisor to Senator John Kerry's presidential campaign in 2004. That fact, by itself, was enough to know what kind of Catholic message the Kerry campaign was going to broadcast. Drinan had recently tangled with Cardinal Ratzinger over the issue of abortion when he publicly objected to Ratzinger's "Doctrinal Note" on some questions regarding the participation of Catholics in political life (November 24, 2002). Ratzinger formalized once again the priority that life issues should receive when deciding how to vote. He stated that Catholic politicians have a "grave and clear obligation to oppose any law that attacks human life" and that for any Catholic, "it is impossible to promote such laws or to vote for them." Drinan called it "Inquisition stuff." Thus, it comes as no surprise that during the 2004 campaign, he described Kerry as "a very good Catholic." [12]

It was fitting that shortly before his death in late January 2007, Drinan was the homilist at a mass in Washington, D.C., celebrating the election of Nancy Pelosi to speaker of the House of Representatives. Pelosi represents the third generation of pro-abortion Catholic politicians schooled by Drinan. He began with young Ted Kennedy in the '70s, Mario Cuomo and Geraldine Ferraro in the '80s, and now Pelosi and the even more ag-

12. Regarding dissident Catholics in politics, Archbishop Edmund Szoka (Detroit) showed leadership in 1983 when he objected to Sister Agnes Mary Mansour being appointed as director of the Department of Social Services in Michigan by Governor James Blanchard. When Szoka asked her to denounce public funding of abortions for poor women, she refused, saying she was personally opposed but could not deny poor women these services. Mansour had to leave the Sisters of Mercy to stay in the job. Eric O. Hanson, *The Catholic Church in World Politics* (Princeton, N.J.: Princeton University Press, 1987), 180.

gressively pro-abortion Rosa DeLauro (D-Connecticut), a former executive director of Emily's List.

The contrast of Drinan and his progeny with earlier proponents of social justice, especially Dorothy Day, explains why so many Catholic Democrats remark that the Democratic Party "left them." Mike Schwartz, chief of staff for Senator Tom Coburn of Oklahoma, describes it well: "If Ted Kennedy had maintained his pro-life posture, I don't think American liberalism would have said that it is a good thing to butcher the unborn." Pro-lifers were alienated, and out of this alienation came the Nixon Democrats, the Reagan Democrats, a realignment of party loyalties, and the creation of a large independent "swing" Catholic vote. This migration out of the Democratic Party did not happen quickly. The McGovern campaign that brought Drinan into politics also brought many young Catholic activists who did not realize at the time where the McGovern revolution was going.

LOSING CATHOLIC SONS AND DAUGHTERS

Growing up Catholic and Democrat in Rhode Island, David Carlin was part of the generation of young men and women who became political activists during the McGovern campaign. Evidently, Carlin did not see the future trajectory of the McGovern revolution, and who can blame him? Who could have known that by 1988, the Democratic Party would insert an overtly pro-abortion plank into its party platform? Who would have known that for thirty years, the pro-life voice would virtually be silenced within the Democratic Party? Carlin, like Dorothy Day, wanted a progressive politics without abortion and its corollaries. As Carlin writes, "With the completion of its second great transformation, in which secularist and moral liberal ideologies first joined labor and civil-rights groups in a tripartite coalition, then rose past them to a position of dominance, the Democratic Party became the thing it is today . . . the thing that today I can no longer love. It became the anti-Christian party." [13]

13. David Carlin, *Can a Catholic Be a Democrat? How the Party I Love Became the Enemy of My Religion* (Manchester, N.H.: Sophia Institute Press, 2006), 55.

Representative Henry Hyde served in the House from 1975 to 2006. He grew up Catholic, Irish, and Democrat in Illinois but switched to the Republican Party in 1952 to support Dwight D. Eisenhower. The most important piece of pro-life legislation ever passed in the U.S. Congress bears his name: the Hyde Amendment, which ended government funding of abortion. Sitting in his office only a few months before his retirement, we discussed the communion controversy that arose during the Kerry campaign: "I think one of the saddest things about this controversy is the Catholic senators and House members who are willing to support abortion even after being told repeatedly by the highest authorities in the Church that it is a mortal sin, yet still be willing to ignore the requirement that you be in a state of grace when you receive Holy Communion.

"It's tragic," Hyde muttered as he shook his head with sadness, "that Democrats were united against a Supreme Court nominee because he was a Catholic" (John Roberts was being considered at the time). He added, "You just can't survive in their party when you are against abortion. Someday I'd like to go up to one of these pseudo-Catholics and ask about the state of his soul, and whether he thinks the ACLU has more superior knowledge than the Holy Father."

Hyde tired quickly as we talked and even grew short of breath. His thirty-one years in the House are wearing on him. Before leaving, I asked him what his greatest regret was from his years of service. Hyde responded, "When we reached a stage where something that is a mortal sin is now a constitutional right."

Hyde left the Democratic Party for good, but David Carlin and many like him await the day the Democrats admit pro-lifers back into the party, and not on a cosmetic basis. But on the question of religion, the Democrats remain seriously divided. Some of their leadership, such as Senator Chuck Schumer, loudly accuse the pro-life Catholic nominees for the Supreme Court of being secretly theocratic. Others, such as Representative Rahm Emanuel, recruit Democratic candidates who would be attractive to the religious conservatives who want to come back to the Democratic Party of their youth, the party of their parents and grandparents. And others, such as Senator Hillary Clinton, seek to distance themselves from their former associations with such radical leftists as former U.S. surgeon general Dr. Joycelyn Elders under President Clinton and Clinton's nominee for assistant attorney general, Harvard law professor Lani Guinier.

Drinan ripped the U.S. Catholic Church in half by teaching that social justice is incompatible with the constitutional right to life for unborn children. He deliberately characterized the Religious Right as inattentive to the needs of the poor. It was another tactic to convert Catholics who couldn't separate caring for the poor from caring for the unborn to a pro-abortion position.

The hard-core supporters of the Democratic Party are going to find it hard to make room for politicians who are pro-life, opposed to gay marriage, and against fetal stem-cell research. Take, for example, Democratic Party faithful who attend gatherings such as the famed Renaissance meeting each year since 1980 between Christmas and New Year's at Kiawah Island, South Carolina. Founders of the weekend are Linda and Philip Lader, who were major donors to Bill Clinton's first campaign for the presidency. The Renaissance Weekend Web site describes the years of meetings as "a cross-generational 'continuing conversation' of accomplished individuals with broadly divergent perspectives, no political agenda, but a legacy of ideas and friendships that have fostered significant projects, ventures and public service." Most of the panelists and presenters are well-known figures on the left, but they always invite a handful of conservatives to sit on the panel and represent the "other point of view." The Web site also states, "Civility prevails," and "Partisanship is frowned upon." As proof of how difficult it is for some Democrats to be "civil" to social conservatives, take the example of Alliance for Marriage founder and president Matt Daniels, who was asked to sit on a panel discussing marriage at a plenary session of 3,000 people at the 2004 weekend.

"I told them that if one of the parties moves away from the center on an important issue, one of two things will happen. Either that party will reorganize itself, or it will be replaced. The political equilibrium will re-

store itself. That is an iron law. I argued that the results for the Democratic Party from the last election were directly connected to their
move away from the center on marriage. . . . I urged them on behalf of
the Alliance for Marriage coalition who are heavily Democratic—
Afro-American, Latino, Catholic—that they get back in touch with the
values of the base, move toward the center, and begin to become a mainstream party."

Daniels expected some tough questions from the audience, but what
happened next was certainly not expected. "During the Q&A session, an
individual who is on the board of trustees of one of our nation's top five
universities, who represented himself as a gay activist and professor,
stepped up to the mike and, after lavishly praising a couple of the other
speakers, looked at me and said, 'In response to your presentation, I really have one thing to say and that is f— y—' "

This rudeness suffered by Daniels shows that the Democrats, at least
at the leadership level, have some distance to travel before they can collaborate with leaders who view marriage as a union between a man and a
woman. Others at the conference later apologized to Daniels for the way
he was treated. There are still those in the Democratic Party who will
allow an honest dialogue with religious conservatives.

Such an experience is not without irony. Most critiques of the Religious Right contain some comments on the rudeness of religious conservatives. Authors often include some vignette, usually in the opening
chapter, of how scared they felt attending a convention or rally of religious conservatives. Jennifer S. Butler, for example, was asked by a friend
whether she thought she was going to be killed while pursuing her research.[14] Reviewing a book by *New York Times* foreign correspondent
Chris Hedges, *Christian Fascists: The Christian Right and the War on
America*,[15] Ron Perlstein found it odd that Hedges characterized the Re-

14. Jennifer S. Butler, *Born Again: The Christian Right Globalized* (Ann Arbor, Mich.: Pluto
Press, 2006), 3.
15. Chris Hedges, *Christian Fascists: The Christian Right and the War on America* (New York:
Free Press, 2007).

ligious Right as violent without providing a single example of violence from the movement itself.[16]

SEGMENTING THE EVANGELICALS

The Religious Left is predicted to grow as a result of an unappreciated political diversity among Evangelicals.[17] George Marsden, one of the nation's recognized authorities on Evangelicals and Fundamentalists, writes on the division of political vision among Evangelicals, "Dispro-portionate numbers of white Evangelicals have adopted the conservative exclusivist vision; but the vision more critical of nation and self-interest is an equally venerable part of a heritage that goes back at least to Roger Williams. Jimmy Carter, who held something like this view, was the only Evangelical to be president during the 1980s, a simple fact to take into account when considering why most Evangelicals did not vote for Pat Robertson."[18]

At first glance, there is a reasonable amount of evidence suggesting that Marsden is correct. In the 2004 election, only 12 percent of affluent white Evangelicals voted for Kerry, but among poor white Evangelicals in the South, 52 percent did. *Christianity Today,* the highly influential Evangelical magazine founded by Billy Graham in 1955, has a large audi-ence and a popular Web site that represents a strain of Evangelicalism not so closely wed to the issues of pro-life and anti–gay marriage. Until his resignation, Reverend Ted Haggard was leading the National Associ-ation of Evangelicals toward the political middle on issues such as the environment. Additionally, Rick Warren, author of the best-selling *The Purpose Driven Life* and pastor of the Saddleback megachurch in San Diego, has mounted a huge relief effort for HIV/AIDS in Rwanda. Warren's invitation to Senator Barack Obama to speak at a conference at

16. Ron Perlstein, "American Fascists," *New York Times,* January 7, 2007.

17. Michael Hout and Andrew M. Greeley, "A Hidden Swing Vote: Evangelicals," *New York Times,* September 4, 2004.

18. George Marsden, "The Modern Period," in *Religion & American Politics: From the Colonial Period to the 1980s,* Mark Noll, ed. (New York: Oxford University Press, 1990), 389.

his church in December 2006 sparked a protest from conservative stalwarts such as Phyllis Schlafly.

The question remains of how many actual voters belong to the "venerable" Evangelical tradition represented by Roger Williams, Jimmy Carter, and now Jim Wallis and others. But it may only be a matter of successfully slicing a small percentage of voters, say 3 to 5 percent, from those who have been voting GOP in the last few national elections.

The challenge of the Religious Left is to go beyond being a movement reacting to the Religious Right. The Religious Left, to be successful, must reconnect the venerable tradition of liberal politics to religiously convicted leadership. From the time of the *Scopes* trial, in which Southern fundamentalism was publicly humiliated, to the late 1970s, the voice of mainline Protestantism in the United States was dominant and liberal. The Evangelical voice, with the exception of Billy Graham, was rarely heard. Graham did tackle the issue of Communism and, except for a brief flirtation with the Nixon White House, steered clear of most political issues. The National Council of Churches, which claimed a membership totaling 50 million, virtually represented all of the mainline Protestant denominations to the media and Washington during that period. As Jennifer S. Butler explains, "Mainline Protestants during their period of ascendancy never created a large infrastructure, perhaps because they remained at home and confident with their national church leadership and felt little impetus to build alternative organizations to represent them." [19] The Religious Left leaders of today are working hard to create that infrastructure, thus creating external support for the Democratic Party.

The Religious Right has played a notable role in the election victories of 1976, 1984, 1988, 1994, 2000, and 2004. So closely aligned were Religious Right leaders and organizations to the Republican Party that it was inevitable some sort of liberal religious coalition would form around the Democratic Party to offset their losses with religiously active voters. The success of the Religious Right, in other words, made the Religious Left

19. Butler, *Born Again*, 36.

inevitable. The Religious Left, through leaders such as Jim Wallis, Tony Campolo, Ron Sider, and Rabbi Michael Lerner, seek to prove two things: first, that religion does not really support the central concerns of the Religious Right; and second, that the Democratic Party is not hostile to religion. For religious conservatives, however, to see it that way, they have to view religion as primarily a matter of enacting social justice, and, as we shall see, that is the difficulty.

The Religious Left has a different relation to Democrats from what the Religious Right has to the GOP. The Religious Right fought within the party to establish policy positions, such as the antiabortion plank, that were antithetical to the interests of the Northeastern Republican establishment and libertarians. Although it is accused of being the "tail that wags the dog," the Religious Right is still not comfortably situated in the GOP to this day, despite its present influence. The specter of an Election Day walkout on GOP candidates is always a possibility. The Religious Right fought its way into the GOP and fights to stay there, well aware of the Republican tendency to default to economic conservatism and avoid social issues. Thus, the Religious Right—and here I am thinking of figures such as Paul Weyrich, Phyllis Schlafly, Ralph Reed, Richard Land, Jay Sekulow, and James Dobson—function as a minority voice within the party coalition. From a religious perspective, they are a prophetic voice that constantly reminds the GOP of the cost of abandoning the principles that have brought them so much electoral success over the last forty years.

The Religious Left, by contrast, provides religious packaging for the existing policies of the Democratic Party. The Religious Left may urge Democrats to be more accepting of religion, but the policies they propose are materially the same as those already proposed by the Democrats for many years. Their activism does not mobilize anyone who is not already mobilized. It taps no strata of unexpressed political concern and unrest.

Just as the Religious Right has its extreme voices, so does the Religious Left. Jim Wallis, editor of *Sojourners* and author of *God's Politics,* is an example of the Religious Left; indeed, he is the person most identified with it and responsible for putting it on the map. Rabbi Michael Lerner, editor of *Tikkun* and author of *The Left Hand of God*, is the best example of the extreme side of the Religious Left. Lerner enjoyed a brief moment of public fame when his notion of the "politics of meaning" was adopted by the Clintons during their first term in the White House. His description of his period of courtship, which ended in bitter disappointment for Lerner, is a fascinating and honest account of what can happen when religious leaders get too caught up in the shifting tides of presidential attention spans.

Lerner's position doesn't differ from the radical politics of the late '60s, except that it's updated and placed in a more religious, spiritual context. I'm not imposing this view on Lerner; he says it himself: "In the 1960's there was a moment of spiritual awakening . . . drug assisted poetry and music gatherings."[20] Lerner, for example, is always careful to include the "Greens" along with the Democrats and espouses pacifism, pure and simple.

"Citizen Lerner" would be an ideal title for a review of his book. One of the major policy proposals of *The Left Hand of God* is that every corporation that makes more than $50 million should be required to get a charter issued, not by the state or federal government but by a panel of ordinary citizens.[21] Each individual, while doing this work, should be paid the same as a corporate CEO. The panel would judge the ethical responsibility of each corporation and decide whether it should be allowed to keep its charter and stay in business. This would be enforced by adding a "Social Responsibility Amendment to the Constitution requiring each corporation to reapply for a charter every ten years"[22] Remarkably, Lerner offers that little or no bureaucracy would be needed to administer this program. I wonder how you could avoid having a bureaucracy to evaluate ethically the work of the thousands of corporations that are currently over the $50 million mark. And even more to the point, who

---

20. Michael Lerner, *The Left Hand of God: Taking Back Our Country from the Religious Right* (San Francisco: HarperCollins, 2006), 171.

21. Ibid., 285.

22. Ibid., 233.

would select the individuals who sit on these panels and make hundreds of thousands of dollars a year? I guess you wouldn't need a bureaucracy; just let Citizen Lerner decide.

Lerner also proposes that the federal government should provide free college education and affordable health care to everyone, eliminate all multilateral debt, implement a global Marshall Plan, provide free media time and access for all candidates, create a "nonviolent" police force (whatever that is), and abolish the electoral college and elect the president by a simple plurality (need to get rid of those pesky red states).

Jim Wallis, at times, sounds like Lerner. But the policies he proposes are more those of the mainstream left with spiritual justifications. Wallis also takes more care than Lerner in clearly establishing just what he means by religion and how his view of religion is different from those on the political right.

ALL ISSUES ARE CREATED EQUAL

The key to understanding the programs of the Religious Left is *equivalence.* The elephant in the room in the midst of all the arguments against the Religious Right is the question of abortion and now, but to a lesser extent, gay marriage. Wallis, Lerner, and others want to convince religious voters that their "broader" social program is as spiritually and morally equivalent *in importance* as the fight against abortion and related life issues such as fetal stem-cell research.

The hurdle they have to jump with the religiously active voters is simple: how to convince them to pull the lever for a candidate who will not, for example, vote to ban partial-birth abortion or who will not vote to confirm judges who appear pro-life. This is a hard sell. It was a hard sell at the U.S. Bishops Conference in the early 1980s, when Cardinals Law and O'Connor publicly objected to Catholic teaching on the "seamless garment" that was used to support the Mondale-Ferraro ticket.

This was the strategy used by the Religious Left to support Al Gore in 2000 and John Kerry in 2004. No doubt, it will be used to support Democratic nominees in the future. Part of the equivalence strategy is numerical. Create a large number of positions on a range of issues from health care to poverty and global warming, and assign each a single point. Abortion receives one point, fetal stem-cell research another point. A conservative, usually a Republican legislator, can vote against abortion, against fetal stem-cell research, and find himself with two points against ten on the other side. The Bishops Conference facilitates this strategy by issuing a voting guide to each election, listing issues without any indication of priority. This allows left-wing dissenting groups such as Catholics in Alliance for the Common Good to pass out the bishops' voting guides in support of pro-abortion Catholic candidates.

Pro-abortion Catholics in the Senate and the House have used the numerical form of the equivalence argument to justify their votes on abortion. One such document produced by Senator Dick Durbin (D-Illinois) before the 2004 election rated Senator Rick Santorum (R-Pennsylvania) as the least Catholic of all the senators, while pro-abortion Catholic senators, such as Durbin, were rated higher. The Bishops Conference unfortunately allows this strategy by taking numerous positions on prudential matters, usually right in line with the Democratic Party leadership.

The more common use of the equivalence strategy is an argument from causality. Abortion is caused by unjust social conditions; eliminate those conditions, and you will lower the number of abortions.

During the 2004 campaign, another common strategy was to say that the Religious Right is inconsistent—it doesn't care about babies after they are born. If the principle behind antiabortion is the "sanctity of life," then why doesn't the GOP propose policies that "improve" the lives of those in need?

Wallis believes that more than equivalence can be established from Scripture. "The Gospels," Wallis argues, "speak more about the poor than any other social issue." [23] After reading *God's Politics,* one concludes that the most important work for a Christian, the "work" that evinces the presence of faith, is to help the poor. Wallis never addresses the issue of whether or not any of these references to poverty include the poverty "of

---

23. Jim Wallis, *God's Politics: Why the Right Gets It Wrong and the Left Doesn't Get It* (San Francisco: Harper San Francisco, 2005), 212.

spirit" explicitly mentioned in the Beatitudes. No, for Wallis and other members of the Religious Left, salvation is always, first of all, about improving the material conditions of life. Everything else comes second.

WHAT'S WRONG WITH US

Much ink has been spilled by the Religious Left over the years to discredit the Religious Right. In dozens of books and articles, many in preparation for the 2006 election, the Religious Left cited ten basic grievances:

1. The Religious Right gets religion wrong.
2. The Religious Right ignores the biblical teaching on relieving poverty and helping the poor.
3. The Religious Right ignores the biblical teaching on nonviolence.
4. The Religious Right opposes abortion and gay marriage, for which there is no biblical warrant.
5. The Religious Right has an unhealthy and repressive emphasis on sexual matters, which is the result of its adherence to patriarchy.
6. The Religious Right has transposed its racism into different political issues, such as school vouchers.
7. The Religious Right supports corporate capitalism and tax cuts for the rich at the expense of helping the poor.
8. The Religious Right supported the war in Iraq because of its interpretation of the Book of Revelations.
9. The Religious Right wants to impose its version of religious morality on everyone else without concern for tolerance and pluralism.
10. The Religious Right ignores the social and economic causes and solutions for abortion.

Most of these complaints are long-standing—racism, imposition of morality, ignoring poverty—and go back to the first critiques of the Religious Right published in the early '80s. Others, such as the charge of patriarchy, reflect a change in the dominant ideology of the left. It's highly unlikely that the Religious Left is going to persuade anybody but themselves, and sympathetic secularists, to accept their view of religion. The steep decline in membership among mainline Protestant denominations can be traced to embracing precisely the religious perspective recommended by Wallis, Lerner, and their colleagues. And the Evangelicals they would like to woo away are products of churches that have consciously avoided making the mistake of trading supernatural salvation for a political platform.

The Religious Left constantly pounds away on the issue of poverty and how the Republican Party and its religious supporters ignore the gospel on this subject. The difference between them is not one of caring; both sides care. Religious conservatives, such as Jim Towey, former head of Bush's faith-based initiative, advise to not look to government programs as the solution to this problem. The solution is getting out of the way of markets and letting a strong economy employ as many people as possible. More people will have the means to help the poor, not out of obligation to pay taxes but directly and charitably. On this score, it looks as if religious conservatives have done better than their liberal counterparts.

Syracuse University professor Arthur Brooks published a book in November 2006 comparing the giving of liberals and conservatives that rocked the pundit world. *Who Really Cares: The Surprising Truth about Compassionate Conservatism* is one of those books that explode a stereotype once and for all. Brooks cites extensive data demonstrating that religious conservatives are three and a half times more generous than liberals. In other words, conservatives do more than verbally tout their preferences for charitable social services over government ones. They put their money into charities at a much higher rate than liberals, who ideologically defer the role of giving to the poor to the government. "For too long," Brooks writes, "liberals have been claiming they are the most virtuous members of American society."[24] Liberals have avoided

24. Arthur Brooks, *Who Really Cares: The Surprising Truth about Compassionate Conservatism* (New York: Basic Books, 2006), 178.

taking personal responsibility for relieving poverty by demanding that government redistribute the nation's wealth. Brooks writes, "In essence, for many Americans, political opinions are a substitute for personal checks."[25]

Brooks's documentation and analysis show that religious conservatives give away more money than secular conservatives, secular liberals, or religious liberals—more than $1,000 per year more per family than the nation as a whole.[26] Religious conservatives are more likely to volunteer, give blood, and return change to merchants when mistakenly given back too much—regardless of their income level. Liberals, who give less to charity and spend less time doing volunteer work, talk about conservatives, and especially religious ones, as if they had no concern for those who suffer from economic and emotional need. It is the liberals who have the "charity deficit." Brooks concludes that the Democrat antipathy toward religion will only make the deficit worse: "If liberals persist in their faith in government and antipathy to religion, the Democrats will become not only the party of secularism but also the party of uncharity."[27]

The Religious Left shifts responsibility from the individual to government on a variety of fronts, always under the banner of having greater compassion. On abortion, for example, the cause of abortion is not a woman's choice but the social conditions that lead to that choice. The Religious Left employs this argument to accuse the Religious Right of hypocrisy on abortion—they ignore the life of the child once he or she has been born! For the Religious Left, therefore, there is no need to get tangled up in the debate to overturn *Roe* v. *Wade*. A new law preventing abortion cannot be effective when the economic causes remain unchanged. The analogy to Brooks's analysis of charitable giving would go like this: Abortion as an issue of public policy can only be addressed at the federal level. If you are against abortion, don't make demands on an individual woman not to abort her baby; make your demands on the

25. Ibid., 72.
26. Ibid., 47.
27. Ibid., 181.

government to change society in such a way that the same woman would never make that decision.

The Religious Left wants to change economic conditions but without compromising its sacred icon of personal choice. The economic changes, it is claimed, could lower the abortion rate among the poor. If Democratic Party strategists think such arguments are going to win them many new voters, they are mistaken. All they have succeeded in doing is adding one more reason to support entitlement programs, and they already have the voters who rally to that cause. The religious voter who cares enough about abortion to change his vote or to join a grassroots fight believes it is murder and should be against the law. Whatever sympathy the Religious Right may have with the Religious Left over this issue is overshadowed by the intensity felt toward the life being taken. Adding "Religious" to "left" adds an additional justification that the left does not care about or, more precisely, doesn't really need.

The Religious Left is bound by its compact with the feminist movement, so it must promote female liberation or lose an essential interest group, not only from its politics but from its religion. The same holds true for the marriage issue. Suddenly, the Bible has become unclear and ambiguous on the subject of marriage between a man and a woman. Wallis and Lerner both argue that the Bible is not clear or prescribed on the subject. Gay liberation, like feminism, controls the outcome of its exegesis. Wallis goes so far as to say that "protection of *civil rights* should be a bottom line in the debate,"[28] meaning that wherever the authority of Scripture is troublesome, it can be ignored. Early in *God's Politics*, Wallis writes, "The words of Jesus are either authoritative for Christians, or they are not."[29] Wallis won't admit that he wants it both ways, the Bible when it teaches about helping the poor, liberal ideology when it teaches about the rights of women and gays. This would be acceptable if he was honest about it and established a principle of some sort that explained why he was switching from one to the other. If he thinks the biblical teachings on marriage should not be applied to public policy, he

28. Wallis, *God's Politics*, 333 (emphasis added).
29. Ibid., 13.

should just say so. Instead, he resorts to pop psychology. The most important thing for Wallis is that "we should be able to look back and *feel good* about the way we conducted our dialogue and our relationships in the process." [30] Religious conservatives, along with most human beings, share Wallis's desire to feel good about how they conduct themselves in public life. The question that always looms around locutions like this is what are we feeling good *about?* It's a safe generalization to make, unsupported by polling of any kind that religious conservatives don't feel good about compromising with secularism. They also don't feel good about letting ersatz civil rights trump the meaning of marriage as it has been understood for centuries, across all cultures and religious traditions.

Though the Religious Left is relatively small, its lineage is clear. It stretches back to its golden days of the civil rights movement through the Vietnam War and antinuclear protests to women's rights, the prochoice movement, gay rights, and homosexual marriage. The leaders of the Religious Left, though they attempt biblical exegesis, find their authority elsewhere: for policy, the liberal wing of the Democratic Party; for ideology, the civil rights of "oppressed" groups; for philosophy, postmodernism.

What about the civil rights movement? Yes, it was a genuine religious movement, founded and led by black ministers, joined later by white Protestant, Catholic, and Jewish clergy and laypeople. This is the golden age to which the Religious Left wants to return. This movement, which morphed into antiwar protest, produced the greatest names of the Religious Left: William Sloane Coffin, the Berrigan brothers, Martin Luther King, Jesse Jackson, and Dorothy Day.

The Religious Left views the Religious Right with condescension because the Evangelical South resisted the civil rights movement. Many religious conservatives have admitted they came late to support civil rights, just as many of them came late to support Catholics on the abortion issue. The Religious Right has not been primarily interested in matters

---

30. Ibid., 335 (emphasis added).

of justice. It seeks to protect its faith communities and is wary of court-ordered social transformations.

In this way, the Religious Right and the Religious Left talk past each other. They employ different first principles and seek different objectives. The Religious Right wants a politics and culture that are friendly to living a Christian life and raising a Christian family, not ones that promote sin. The Religious Right wants a society that will help its members get to heaven, or at least not make it unreasonably difficult. The Religious Left, on a completely different track, wants to erase all human inequality based on its view of human rights.

The Religious Left ultimately cannot help the Democratic Party very much, because its message adds nothing and challenges nothing in the Democratic platform or on the political left. All it can really change is the perception that the Democratic Party is unfriendly to religion. Even then, the Religious Left will only mobilize those who fear the Religious Right and want to end its influence.

The Religious Right, on the other hand, cannot get its message from secular conservatism. It does not seek to baptize traditional conservatism. The Religious Left could lose its faith and its politics and not change its message at all. That's why it cannot have much influence over the long run. If the Religious Right were suddenly to go out of business, the Religious Left would disappear overnight.

With the death of Jerry Falwell, many farewells were written to the Religious Right. But it isn't going anywhere. The marriage debate that ignited with the 2004 *Goodridge* decision on gay marriage guarantees another generation of political engagement. Religious conservatives refuse to let their children grow up in an atmosphere where it makes no difference how children are born and raised. They also refuse to accept their children being taught that homosexual sex is just another way of expressing one's sexuality. They will fight to create a local community that protects their efforts to live a Christian life and raise their children in the faith.

8

"HELLO, THIS IS KARL ROVE"

WHEN KARL ROVE CALLED ME IN DECEMBER 1998, I DIDN'T know who he was. He called me as a consequence, one might say, of having a convert's perspective. Three years earlier, I had been invited to an event at the Republican National Committee. The former ambassador to the Vatican, Thomas Melady, had organized a panel to discuss the Catholic vote and the Dole presidential campaign. Melady, at the time, was chairman of what was called the Catholic Task Force at the RNC. Melady had been appointed to the Vatican post by President George H. W. Bush and, after Bush's defeat in 1992, had been asked to create an ongoing effort inside the RNC to court Catholic voters.

The meeting was sparsely attended, although RNC Chairman Haley Barbour did show up at the end to shake the hands of the attendees. The panel included Ambassador Melady and future RNC chairman Ed Gillespie, who was then on staff. The central focus of Dole's outreach to Catholics, we were told, was to be the candidate's attendance at Catholic ethnic events such as St. Patrick's Day and Columbus Day. The Catholic voters discussed that day were the "Reagan Democrats," who, the panelists explained, were ripe for GOP picking once again because of the Clinton scandals and his veto of the ban on partial-birth abortion. The key to bringing the Reagan Democrats back to the GOP was the candidate connecting with them through their various ethnic identities.

Having taught at Fordham in the Bronx, I was aware of the importance of recognizing the ethnicity that unites Catholics among Irish, Italians, Eastern Europeans, Hispanics, and so on. In fact, I had attended many Catholic dinners in Manhattan that seemed more a celebration of being Irish than of being Catholic. It seemed that every left-wing priest in the city had a bank of Pat-and-Mike jokes that set the crowd to nodding and laughing. The Catholic faith itself was rarely discussed, but sentimentality was everywhere.

The idea of courting Catholics at these feast days made sense but only limited sense. It didn't have much to do with being Catholic in the way I understood it as a convert. However, you certainly would connect with Catholics at some level. The Irish suffered badly before and after they immigrated to America in the nineteenth century. There are good reasons their memories are long and deep. But the celebration of Catholic ethnicity can become an end in itself. It can be used as a substitute for core Catholic beliefs, and I was concerned that the GOP was buying into it. Thus, the ethnic outreach to Catholics had limited usefulness, and it treated obliquely the reasons Catholics should support certain kinds of candidates.

I also wondered how Republicans were going to connect with Catholics who had been troubled by the Clinton presidency but did not have a strong identification with any Catholic ethnic group. This kind of Catholic may belong to an ethnic group but does not invoke ethnicity as integral to his religious faith. Atlanta, Georgia, is the locale of my ten-year journey into the Catholic faith, and its Catholic communities are not demarcated by Irish, Italian, and so forth. But enter any of the older Catholic cities of the Northeast and the Midwest, and the evidence of ethnic background is everywhere, from the placement and names of the parishes, based on the old neighborhoods, to ongoing grudges and rivalries. Yes, these are the places where the immigrant Catholic Church in the United States first took root, grew, and eventually prospered. However, the migration of Catholics to the suburbs diminished the vitality of these neighborhoods long ago.

The RNC strategy understood what should attract Catholics to Bob Dole but didn't understand where to find them. They seemed to have no inkling that there was an Evangelical movement under way in the Catholic Church under John Paul II. That movement was led, in large part, by converts—Scott Hahn, Jeff Cavins, Father Richard John Neuhaus, Father George Rutler, and Pat Madrid, to name a few. They were a small percentage, to be sure, but an increasingly potent one. And the growing influence of the Catholic television network, EWTN, was making the converts' enthusiasm and determination more acceptable among its Catholic audience.[1]

Converts are people who choose their faith, who are not born into it, and they usually have a fairly explicit understanding of Church teaching. The Evangelical support of the GOP is based on principled convictions about life, the family, and moral values. Why should Catholic outreach be any different? Perhaps a better way of describing a convert's perspective is to call it Evangelical. Converts are Evangelical by definition. They have a point in time when they decide to believe and to join a religious denomination. Some have as much of a "born-again" experience as any Protestant Evangelical. An entire literature of Catholic converts, led by popular speaker and writer Scott Hahn, has sprung up over the past twenty years.[2]

Thus, the ethnic outreach to Catholics had limited usefulness, and it treated indirectly the reasons Catholics should support certain kinds of candidates. Why not, I thought, reach out to Catholics because of what they believe, what they hear at mass, what the Holy Father teaches them, and what they can read in the *Catechism?* It seemed to me at the time that those Catholics who had the strongest beliefs in the teaching of the Church, and were free from dissent, would be the most likely to feel attracted to a pro-life Republican candidate to take the place of Bill Clinton.

I asked a few friends and associates of mine who were familiar with

1. My own television show, *Church and Culture Today,* was broadcast weekly on EWTN from 1996 to 2004.

2. Pat Madrid, for example, edited three volumes titled *Surprised by Truth,* published by Sophia Institute Press, which contained dozens of conversion stories. Marcus Grodi hosts a weekly TV show, *The Journey Home,* on EWTN, where he interviews notable converts.

politics and polling—Steve Wagner, Dan Casey, and Ann Corkery to meet. Over lunch, I told them about my reaction to the meeting at the RNC. They all agreed with my basic supposition. Several of them had had the same idea for some years. They thought that this direction should have been taken long ago, but the RNC just didn't feel comfortable with it. The staff and leadership inside the RNC, I was told, was already fed up with Evangelicals. The last thing they wanted to put up with was another group of religious conservatives insisting on opposition to abortion, and so on. Out of these conversations came the idea for a "Catholic Voter Project" to be published in *Crisis* magazine well before the 2000 election. The problem was going to be funding. I was barely keeping *Crisis* afloat, and the $50,000 I needed for the polling, research, and writing seemed like a pipe dream.

After a year of looking, we found a donor in Atlanta, Frank Hanna, who immediately saw the need for the project. Hanna had long been involved in politics, particularly with the Church. He was adamant that this would not be a Republican or Democratic project but rather a response to John Paul II's call for the laity to be involved in culture and politics. Hanna wanted the Catholic Voter Project to help debunk the media stereotype of Catholic voters being no different from voters at large. By then, Senator Dole had been beaten badly, and Catholic support for the GOP had dropped sharply. Thirty-seven percent of all self-identified Catholics voted for Dole, but his percentage of mass-attending Catholics was a more respectable 45 percent. Dole had lost narrowly to Clinton in the heavily Catholic states of Wisconsin, Ohio, Pennsylvania, Missouri, and Kentucky. Fifty-seven percent of his vote came from those voters who attended religious services regularly. These results boded well for my basic assumptions when I asked Steve Wagner of QEV Analytics in Washington, D.C., to undertake the project.[3]

I asked Wagner to focus on a few basic questions. If we distinguished between Catholic voters who attended mass once a week or more and those who didn't, how would the story of the Catholic vote be different?

---

3. The polling was done between February 26 and March 10, 1998. The survey consisted of 1,001 telephone interviews with self-identified Catholics. A survey of this size has a sampling error of 3 percent, plus or minus.

In other words, if we looked at the Catholic vote only as copying from the voters who are active Catholics, what would we find out about their voting patterns and their issue priorities? In short, were Catholics who attended mass at least once a week more likely to vote for a pro-life, pro-family candidate?

My principal aim was to start a public conversation about "Who is the Catholic voter?" That conversation might cause the political parties to focus more on what Catholics believe rather than what kind of last names they have. The first survey results were published in the November 1998 issue of *Crisis*, including the lead article by Wagner and a commentary by Bob Novak.[4] The second group of results was published in June 1999 with additional commentary by William McGurn, then at the *Wall Street Journal*, now a White House speechwriter. The central findings were as follows:

- There are, as Bob Novak put it, "two Catholic votes—just as there are two kinds of Catholics in America, active and inactive religiously."[5]
- Active Catholics constitute most of the Catholics who have left the Democratic Party after the election of John F. Kennedy in 1960. Why? Active Catholics accept the existence of an absolute moral standard, a standard that was challenged by the Democrats' embrace of the anti-American, feminist, and homosexual ideology. As Wagner explains, "This is, perhaps, the most profound, yet subtle, of all their characteristics, leading to a certain moral confidence, less confusion about the difference between pluralism and tolerance, and a greater reluctance to the claim of a moral right to do wrong, a central tenet of contemporary liberalism."[6]
- Active Catholic issue priorities can be summed up under what Wagner called the "social renewal" agenda of the GOP, as opposed to the "social justice" agenda of the Democrats.[7] Wagner determined that the reason for that migration is the preference of a majority of Catho-

4. Steve Wagner, "The Heart of the Catholic Voter Project," *Crisis* (November 1998).
5. Robert Novak, "The Catholic Vote: Does It Swing?" *Crisis* (November 1998).
6. Steve Wagner, "The Heart of the Catholic Voter," *Crisis* (November 1998).
7. Steve Wagner, "Social-Renewal Catholics," *Crisis* (June 1999).

lic voters for a "social renewal" agenda as opposed to the "social justice" agenda. These social-renewal Catholics care about the moral
decline in American culture, caused in part by an intrusive federal
government and a decadent popular culture.

- Perhaps the most unexpected finding: At the time of the survey, what
  Wagner saw as reliable Republicans among Catholics outnumbered
  dependable Democrats, 23 percent to 21 percent. This strongly confirmed the exodus from the Democratic Party, with 38 percent of Independent and Republican Catholics reporting they were former
  Democrats.

- Of the Catholics in Wagner's survey, 62 percent supported bishops
  and priests who express their views on political issues, while only
  27 percent opposed. This showed a clear reversal in the findings of the
  Weyrich survey of 1979, which showed that Catholics, along with
  mainstream Protestants, wanted to stay on the political sidelines.
  Social-renewal Catholics were more supportive of this involvement
  than the social-justice Catholics. Sixty-two percent of all Catholics
  reported "taking to heart" what the pope has to say.

- Catholic opposition to abortion was confirmed, with 55 percent saying it is always immoral and 26 percent saying it is usually, but not always, immoral.

- Catholic issue priorities were not strictly conservative. Catholics are
  unusually patriotic, strongly in favor of welfare reform, hostile to affirmative action, and socially conservative. But Catholics are sensitive
  to the conditions of the poor, distinctly tolerant, and not particularly
  antigovernment. They also favored raising the minimum wage, protecting personal privacy, enforcing television standards, protecting
  religious expression, and opposing gay marriage. Surprisingly, Catholics were ambivalent on support for school vouchers (once the central Catholic issue), restrictions on gambling, and ending no-fault
  divorce.

My hope that the Catholic Voter Project would create a new conversation about the Catholic vote was realized sooner than I expected. Father

Andrew Greeley, an established sociologist at the University of Chicago, offered his critique of the *Crisis* survey in *America* magazine.[8] Greeley immediately took issue with the emphasis on church attendance, arguing, probably tongue in cheek, that "sterner measures" could have been invoked, such as positions on birth control, premarital sex, or abortion. He scolded the surveyors for ignoring demographic facts such as age, remarking that the sample was mostly older adults. In making these comments, Greeley chose to ignore the central finding of the survey results: there was a dramatic difference between the voting patterns of mass-attending Catholics and nonactive Catholics. His assertion that Catholics "swing from Democratic to Republican candidates and back along with the national trends" is true only if you limit your analysis to self-identified Catholics. Active Catholics voted against McGovern in 1972, for Carter in 1976, against Mondale and Dukakis in 1984 and 1988, against Clinton in 1992 and 1996. As it turned out, active Catholics voted against Gore and Kerry by large margins as well. Greeley also chose, strangely, to ignore the fact that participation in the sacramental life of the Church is the central reality in the life of a Catholic. Our criterion of what distinguished a Catholic voter was both true to the teaching of the Catholic faith and accurate insofar as establishing a correlation between mass attendance and Catholic support of the GOP and its socially conservative agenda.

Bill McGurn summarized the Catholic Voter Project by describing active Catholic voters as part of a "counterculture" of the type revealed by a *Reader's Digest* poll in 1992 showing a vast difference in attitudes between families with children and those without.[9] This description explains why our findings surprised many in the mainstream media. They had missed the existence of this large subgroup among Catholics who clung to the moral teachings of the Church and wanted a leader, not necessarily a Catholic, who represented those principles. In George W. Bush, active Catholics recognized the leader they had been waiting for.

As I said earlier, Karl Rove called in December 1998. He had just read

8. Andrew Greeley, "The *Crisis* 'Survey,'" *America* (October 30, 1999) 6.

9. William McGurn, "Style Counts," *Crisis* (June 1999).

the Catholic Voter Project articles in *Crisis* and asked me if I had any plans to be in Austin, because he would like to meet with me and introduce me to Governor Bush. We met in Austin a month later at his office before the Bush campaign opened its office on Congress Avenue in front of the state capitol. Karl and I talked for several hours, and it was clear he had grasped the basic findings of the report and agreed with them. Fairly early in the conversation, Karl told me that he thought the Catholic vote was going to be the key to winning the presidency in 2000. I pressed him to make sure he understood what the report meant: Catholics should be approached on the basis of the "moral decline" issues, which meant that the governor would have to be forthright on abortion. He said, "You need to meet him. You can see for yourself how he handles that question." Rove took me to the governor's mansion for lunch. We met with Bush briefly, and then I sat down with the South Carolina legislators who had been invited to hear Bush talk about his positions on key issues.

The only thing I found missing in his remarks was an emphasis on the family. He had clearly stated his desire to lower the number of abortions, because "abortion is bad for America." He talked a lot about the limits of government, what it can and cannot do. He made the remark, repeated many more times in support of his faith-based initiative, that the "government cannot love." He talked about the importance of empowering mediating structures to deliver social services more effectively to those who needed help. But nowhere had Bush mentioned the centrality of the family, its prerogatives and privileges. I suggested to Rove that Bush should talk about the family as the institution that naturally limits the government, as the place where individuals receive love and learn to love. I suggested that John Paul II's language of the family as society's "first church," "first school," "first community"[10] should be introduced into Bush's political vocabulary.

Rove came to D.C. in a few weeks, and we talked through most of an afternoon. When he asked if I would be the principal outside advisor on Catholic outreach, I answered yes but with a few conditions. First was

10. See John Paul II's apostolic exhortation *"Familiaris Consortio"* ("The Role of the Christian Family in the Modern World") issued December 15, 1981.

that he would accept that I act as a Catholic first and a Republican second. Next was that Bush would remain consistently pro-life. My final condition was that the vice-presidential choice also be pro-life. Rove said that I should have "no worries" on any of those counts, and the work began.

Rove asked me to choose some Catholic leaders for meetings with Bush in Austin. There was some trepidation among those I invited to the first meeting that we could be "selling out" to partisan interests. Vatican diplomat John Klink, who had represented the Holy See at the Cairo and Beijing conferences, was particularly insistent that Bush be told what we expected. The evening before the meeting, we met in Austin to draft a memo of the goals Catholics would want him to achieve as president. That morning, I read the following list at the beginning of the meeting:

1. Sign the partial-birth abortion ban.
2. Encourage the states to demand parental-notification bills be passed.
3. Support federal legislation banning abortion in the third trimester.
4. End abortions conducted at federal facilities here and abroad.
5. Disallow federal funding for including abortion as an option in family-planning initiatives both domestically and under UN auspices.

Bush, in a characteristic way, told me with a laugh that I could sit down and proceeded to call the list a "no-brainer." The discussion covered a variety of topics, including Bush's own religious convictions and his vision of the faith-based initiative.

It was only when the conversation turned to economics, specifically to the capital-gains tax and marginal tax rates, that disagreements arose. This moment was, no doubt, a foreshadowing of Bush's falling out with economic conservatives over issues such as entitlement spending. However, I knew Bush had made a good impression when Bill Donohue of the Catholic League said to me, just as the meeting broke up, that Bush was the first Republican who had convinced him that he "cared about the poor." It was also clear to me that Bush was inclined to commit federal funds to address the compassion concerns he had discussed at length.

These Austin meetings, which were the Catholic component of a multitude of groups visiting the governor's mansion, established an initial network of Catholic leaders, donors, grasstops (leaders of grassroots organizations), and journalists to launch the Bush Catholic outreach effort. In addition to Klink and Donohue, leaders attending the meeting included Helen Alvare of the USCCB, Raymond Arroyo of EWTN, Father Robert Sirico of the Action Institute, Father Frank Pavone of Priests for Life, Dr. Robert George of Princeton University, and Carl Anderson of the Knights of Columbus. Anderson was perhaps more aware than anyone of the significance of these meetings. He had been a pro-life stalwart in the Reagan White House during the '80s. People like Alvare, Arroyo, Anderson, and Donohue made it clear they would not get involved in any campaigning, but I thought it was important for them to meet Bush and for Bush to meet them and hear what they had to say to him. The businessmen and financiers included in these first meetings provided the initial funding for the Catholic effort, and grasstops helped in gathering the Catholic lists from the battleground states, resulting in an overall list of more than 1 million names.

John Klink had distinguished himself in the pro-life community for his negotiations on behalf of the Vatican at international conferences such as those on children in New York (1990), on environment and development in Rio de Janeiro (1992), on population in Cairo (1994), and on women in Beijing (1995). When I called to invite him to the Austin meeting, he told me that just "at that moment," he'd been thinking about how to get involved in politics. During his years of negotiating on behalf of the Vatican, he had realized that the support of the United States against the proposed international right to abortion was crucial. With the election of Bill Clinton in 1992, the Vatican had lost the United States as an ally on life issues. The Cairo conference in 1994 became a showdown between the Vatican and the United States.

Klink recalled that just before the conference, the Vatican was made aware of a fax that went out from the U.S. State Department to all its diplomatic missions, saying the United States was supportive of an international right to abortion. "The Holy Father was gravely concerned. Joaquin Navarro-Valls [the pope's official spokesman] held a press conference saying that Vice President Gore's office had denied this was United States policy. Navarro-Valls reportedly then held up a copy of the fax."

According to Klink, Gore, who was head of the U.S. delegation, then invited the head of the Vatican delegation, Archbishop Renato Martino, to a meeting in Cairo at the beginning of the conference. At the meeting, Gore thanked Martino for coming and asked if the Vatican would sign off on the Cairo document. Martino said, "As we did in Rio de Janeiro [1992], we intend to negotiate in good faith and achieve a true consensus document." [11] The next day, Gore issued a press release with two misrepresentations, first that the U.S. delegation had *accepted the Vatican's invitation* to meet that morning, and, second that he was more convinced than ever that the Vatican *would not sign* the Cairo document. As Klink says, "The United States was trying to start a media blitz to show that the Vatican was fundamentalist, a part of the Religious Right."

For Klink, the conflict reached a breaking point at the 1999 Cairo +5 Conference at the United Nations. In its document, the UN wanted to stipulate that in cases where abortion was legal, all medical professionals should be trained to perform them. Klink realized that this meant that pro-life physicians could be fired for not complying. He introduced a conscientious objection clause that both the United States and the European Union opposed. It was then that Klink said, "I decided to get involved in politics. I could see the handwriting on the wall. If another Democratic administration was elected, the battle would be lost."

Klink played a vital role in helping Bush get elected in 2000 and then saw to it that key members of the Vatican Curia understood the strong

11. At the beginning of the conference, each delegation receives a draft document with disputed language in brackets. Conference negotiations focus on these bracketed sections until consensus is reached.

affinities between Bush and Catholic social teaching. As a result of Bush's presidency, Klink says, there is *still* no international right to abortion.

Klink's attitude was representative of almost all of the Catholics who joined the Bush effort. They were committed to stopping the drift of the United States, not just toward secularism but also toward an open hostility to their Catholic faith.

My next objective was to connect Governor Bush with some of the bishops. Meetings were arranged with most of the U.S. cardinals, including O'Connor, Maida, Law, and Hickey. I also made sure that the governor met with important bishops such as Chaput of Denver, Baker of Charleston, Donoghue of Atlanta, and Wuerl of Pittsburgh. Pro forma meetings with unfriendly bishops in battleground states were set up. Our networks of grasstops and media were used to get the news of these meetings through the grassroots. Most of these visits were kept private and away from the media. The bishop who got his picture taken with Bush along the campaign trail was, surprisingly, one of the Church's leading liberals, Cardinal Mahony of Los Angeles.

Some of the prominent Catholics I asked to meet with Bush refused and told me, "You are being used." When I relayed to them the assurances I had that the governor would be strongly pro-life, the response was that I was "naïve" and that the "son would turn out to be just like the father." At the time, I wasn't aware how much animosity lingered in D.C. among the Reaganites who had fought Vice President Bush's staff over life and foreign-policy issues. Throughout the first few years of Bush's presidency, I was reminded by those same skeptics that I would be let down. Bush never let me down, until he, unfathomably, approved before the election in 2006 the distribution of the Plan B morning-after pill. Other than the Plan B decision, Bush's record on life and related concerns, such as judges, was exactly what had been promised.

Even his decision to allow federal funding on existing stem-cell lines was made in his first nationally televised address (August 9, 2001), in which he said to the nation: "I also believe human life is a sacred gift from our Creator. I worry about a culture that devalues life, and believe as your president I have an important obligation to foster and encourage respect for life in America and throughout the world." This was the kind of president I had hoped the governor of Texas would be and why I took the step to help him meet Catholic voters.

By the end of the first term, I noticed that nearly all of the Bush skeptics had come around to admiring the president's leadership on life and family issues. What I learned from those skirmishes is that the initial reaction to candidates has as much to do with what has happened in Washington in the previous twenty years as the candidate's record and what he stands for. As a newcomer to politics, I had little idea where the mines were planted—who had "history" with whom—and how to avoid them. I stepped on more than one. I would have stepped on more, but Rove put several advisors close to me who were seasoned in the ways of political campaigns.

Easily the most dramatic moment of the entire campaign for me came the day I asked Cardinal O'Connor if he would meet with Bush. I met with him at his residence in New York on Madison Avenue just behind St. Patrick's Cathedral. In preparation for the meeting, he had read the Catholic Voter Project material in its entirety, and, true to his reputation, he had it practically memorized for our discussion. There was something so welcoming about that conversation with O'Connor that I decided to ask him about a growing misgiving I had about being so deeply involved in a political campaign. I asked him, "Eminence, as you know, I am a Catholic publisher and editor, the head of a small nonprofit. Should I be getting this involved in the Bush campaign?" His reply stunned me: "You not only have to be involved in this campaign, you have to win." Knowing that O'Connor had come from a Democratic background, I was not prepared for this. I expected at least some shred of sympathy for the Democratic Party, but he had none. He went on to explain that he feared for the future of America if Gore were elected. He added that he would be delighted to meet with the governor because he knew his father well and respected him. O'Connor added, "President Bush did more to protect life than Ronald Reagan, so I am sure we will get along" (an interesting comment, given what I had heard from Bush skeptics). The very next day, Cardinal O'Connor was diagnosed with the brain tumor that eventually took his life.

The relationships I forged on behalf of the campaign became strategically important later on, when Bush came under attack as anti-Catholic from John McCain for his speech at Bob Jones University. McCain's campaign in the Michigan primary sent out recorded messages to thousands of Catholic voters, telling them that Bush had spoken at Bob Jones University, which had explicitly anti-Catholic statements on its Web site. McCain's win in Michigan sent the Bush campaign into a tailspin, leaving South Carolina a do-or-die primary. Bill Donohue immediately issued a press release defending Bush and excoriating McCain for his attempt to manipulate Catholic voters. From Rove I learned that the candidate had decided what he wanted to do, and it was just the right thing. Bush had decided to write a personal letter of apology to Cardinal O'Connor. After their recent meeting in New York, Rove told me that Bush "felt he owed it to him." His letter, dated February 22, 2000, reads in part: "I have profound respect for the Catholic Church—a sympathy beyond mere tolerance. I have argued that our prosperous society must offer answers for the poor—and, on this issue the Catholic Church helps to shape our country's conscience." Later, at the Al Smith dinner on October 19 in New York City, Bush devoted much of his speech to paying tribute to O'Connor.

Catholic Outreach was also able to wrangle a skybox at the Philadelphia convention and to make use of that venue to raise the profile of the Catholic Outreach effort. Priests and nuns supporting Bush were seen on the convention floor. (Why was it that the Democrat mayor of Philadelphia, Ed Rendell, was in the Catholic box every night? *He* is a very smart politician and is now *Governor* Ed Rendell of Pennsylvania.) Every time I led a group of religious around the floor, they expressed surprise at their friendly reception, with delegates stopping them to chat and thanking them for being there. Most of the priests and nuns, predominantly from the Philadelphia area, had been lifelong Democrats and assumed they would be unwelcome on a Republican convention floor. During the nominee's acceptance speech, and in violation of a strict prohibition, we unfurled a homemade "Catholics for Bush" banner from our perch atop the convention center.

After the Republican National Convention, the Catholic Outreach operation moved out of its Austin headquarters to the RNC. This was somewhat ticklish, because inside the RNC, we encountered some resistance to our efforts. Several of the staff did not want to spend money on a Catholic-specific effort. Others did not have confidence in reaching Catholic voters based on their mass attendance. The old habit of Catholic ethnic outreach clearly lingered. Some of the staff were not comfortable addressing religiously active voters on issues of moral decline. I sensed that the presence of the Evangelicals in the RNC was all the religious coalition they could handle. They weren't all that happy about adding conservative Catholics to the mix. But, with Rove's backing, these conflicts were overcome, and we did two complete mailings to our list, as well as two phone calls to Catholic voters in all the battleground states.

Relations with the Evangelical effort were friendly but not coordinated. I was kept abreast of the Evangelical effort through Ralph Reed, who headed that outreach effort for the campaign. It was clear they were better funded and staffed, but they had been part of the GOP coalition since the Reagan years. Catholics were the new kids on the block. Almost everything I asked of Rove I received, which helped keep our mission in a forward trajectory. We had no field staff in 2000, so the effort was entirely through the candidate, his message, his events, RNC mailings, phone messages, and our networking and media. Our surrogates were seen and heard frequently in friendly Catholic media and organizations.

The results of the 2000 election were a clear vindication of the *Crisis* Catholic Voter Report, as well as Rove's decision to make it the blueprint for Bush's Catholic effort. Bush improved on Dole's overall Catholic vote by 10 percent and his active Catholic vote by 7 percent. The swing in the Catholic vote provided what Rove was looking for: the addition of a large bloc of voters to make Bush competitive. But the 78 percent of the Evangelical vote going to Bush certainly didn't hurt.

It is significant that our focus in the 2000 campaign was introducing George W. Bush and his message to active Catholics. Al Gore hardly ever entered the picture, unlike the Democratic nominee four years later. We assumed from our first meeting in Austin that if active Catholics could "meet" Bush, they would very likely choose him over Gore and the Democratic Party. If the Gore campaign had a Catholic vote effort, we never noticed it.

After the success of the election, Rove asked me to form the Catholic Working Group. The CWG held a weekly phone meeting with the White House and were often invited inside for meetings with the president and other members of the administration. For the first time in history, the White House had a formal relationship with a group of lay Catholics, outside the Bishops Conference, to advise them on matters of importance to Catholics. It stung the left that the Catholic Working Group consisted of orthodox believers who supported a Republican administration. *Boston Globe* columnist Ellen Goodman, for example, wrote, "Letting Hudson define Catholicism is like letting Osama define Islam." But Goodman's willingness to stretch her hyperbolic license (at least, I hope she was using hyperbole) was evidence that liberals were no longer in charge of the Catholic Church. They had hoped that the sex-abuse scandal that erupted in Boston would force the Church to change its commitment to celibacy, the male priesthood, and homosexuality. The left hoped that the renewal of the Church led by John Paul II would be undone by the scandal, but it didn't happen. A group called Voice of the Faithful arose in Boston to carry this, cleverly packaged under the banner of "structural change," but ran into a roadblock of bishops who would not let them meet on parish property.

The existence of a Catholic Working Group at the White House sent out a message that an alliance existed between faithful Catholics and a president willing to articulate these values as public policy. This was a nightmare come to pass for the left. For years, they had been able to depend on their Catholic allies to protect their ideology. Goodman and her allies had been so successful in keeping Catholicism from baring its pro-life teeth that they were shocked when faithful Catholics began to get public attention. But the leadership of in-name-only Catholics was crumbling, and a new generation was setting the agenda—Bill Donohue, Mother Angelica, Scott Hahn, Rick Santorum, Chris Smith, George Weigel, and others. Goodman should have been worried; she could no longer count on notable Catholics to do the bidding of the liberal elites.

It came as no surprise when President Bush received letters from both the president and the executive secretary of the USCCB protesting the CWG. They asserted that the sole prerogative of the Bishops Conference was to communicate with the White House and the Congress on Catholic issues. In truth, all we were doing through the CWG was what was taught by Vatican II, making our lay expertise available to the Church for the more effective evangelization of the culture and politics.

FINDING HISPANIC CONNECTIONS

When I took over as chairman of the RNC Catholic Outreach, we began immediately to increase our national leadership network and gather more lists. We hired our first full-time Catholic Outreach staff in the RNC, and by the time we started on the 2004 campaign, we had more than 68,000 team leader names, addresses, and e-mails. Clearly, the Bush White House and the RNC started working for reelection the day after the inauguration. One of the constant frustrations at the RNC was finding ways to connect with Hispanic Catholics. The White House was always having events with Hispanic leaders, but they were always Evangelical, not Catholic.

The problem was simple: there was no established network of conservative Hispanic Catholics through which we could reach that audience. All of the existing Hispanic Catholic organizations were controlled by the left. The explosion in the size of Hispanic Catholic communities across America made it clear that if the GOP did not find a way of attracting a significant portion of Hispanic voters, it would be destined to become a minority party.[12] Hispanics make up 9 percent of the electorate but are growing faster than any other group. Already, the 29 million Hispanic Catholics outnumber the 22 million white mainline Protestants. With only 23 percent of Hispanics belonging to Protestant

12. S. G. Liaugminas, "Catholicism with a Latin Beat," *Crisis* (September 2001).

churches, it was necessary to find a way to get into a community that has a natural affinity with Republican religious conservatives. Even without an organized outreach to Hispanic Catholics, Bush has done well in both elections: 35 percent in 2000, 44 percent in 2004. Political strategist Dick Morris credited Hispanic support for Bush as the decisive factor in his election: "The biggest reason for Bush's victory was that he finally cracked the Democratic stranglehold on the Hispanic vote."[13]

The 2004 election results showed that the president had succeeded in connecting with the Hispanic community. Sixty-three percent of Hispanic Protestants voted for Bush, even though only 37 percent identified themselves as Republican. Thirty-one percent of Hispanic Catholics voted for Bush, and only 13 percent identified themselves as Republican. These numbers, significantly up from the 2000 election, were bad news for the Democratic Party, which had depended on the loyalty of ethnic minorities for its base. In 2000, the Democrats saw the Catholic vote slipping away, and in 2004, they saw Hispanics falling away.

But the caustic debate over immigration put a sudden stop to the GOP success with Hispanics and threatens to ruin the GOP's relationship with Hispanic voters for years to come. "Republicans face the prospect, not only of fractured unity on immigration policy, but also the possibility of an explicitly anti-immigration candidate running for the presidential nomination."[14] The future was foreshadowed by the sharp drop in Hispanic support in the 2006 midterm election (30 percent, according to CNN exit polls). The number of Hispanic voters went from 4.7 million in 2002 to more than 6.5 million (8 percent of the total vote), an increase of 1.8 million votes, and that number will only get higher.

Steve Wagner told me he was particularly concerned about whether the GOP is going to "find a way to squander the natural advantage it has with Hispanics over Democrats." The immigration issue, he fears, will spur the rise of a "nativist, anti-immigration rhetoric that will kill the

13. Dick Morris, "The Hispanic Vote Elects Bush," NewsMax.Com, November 5, 2004, www .newsmax.com/archives/articles/2004/11/4/203450.shtml.

14. Thomas B. Edsall, *Building Red America: The New Conservative Coalition and the Drive for Permanent Power* (New York: Basic Books, 2006), 219.

GOP with Catholics." Wagner views immigration as a life issue. "The immigration issue is, at root, about whether you see people as an asset or not—that's the essence of the life issue. If Republicans say no to that, they will find they offend not only Catholics but many voters of faith." Some find this assertion tenuous, but consider that one of the two central arguments in favor of abortion is overpopulation and all the problems supposedly caused by it (the other main argument being women's "choice").

In the run-up to the 2008 election, Wagner's prediction has already come true. The nomination of Senator Mel Martinez of Florida to chair the RNC led to a "Stop Martinez" movement, including a banner ad on National Review Online. The wall being built between portions of the Texas-Mexico border will stand as a reminder of Republican grassroots hostility toward illegal Mexican immigrants. The challenge for Republicans is to address legitimate security issues, the strain on social services, and upholding the law without a rancor that will alienate Hispanics for decades to come.

CAMPAIGN 2004

Catholic Outreach in the 2004 campaign was a quantum leap beyond 2000. It was the culmination of three years of constant work. As James Moore and Wayne Slater commented about the collective religious outreach effort of the Bush White House, "By the 2004 reelection, Rove, Ralph Reed, and Deal Hudson had assembled the most effective religious political machine ever in presidential politics." [15] It was effective because it wasn't top-heavy. No one pretended that being close to some bishops, Catholic members of Congress, and lay leaders was going to get the job done. The years 2001 to 2003 were filled with regularly scheduled conference calls and coalition meetings. Catholic Outreach sought to tap every network of conservative, pro-life Catholicism, from the college campuses to the Catholic radio and television audience. The Catholic

15. James Moore and Wayne Slater, *The Architect: Karl Rove and the Master Plan for Absolute Power* (New York: Crown, 2006), 100.

Outreach e-mail list reached more than 100,000, with thousands of those volunteering to work actively in the campaign as team leaders.

As the campaign started, the RNC employed more than thirty field staff in addition to the volunteer team leaders. Savvy leadership came from Martin Gillespie, director of Catholic Outreach at the RNC. Campaign director Ken Mehlman supported the Catholic effort completely, as did Ed Gillespie, chairman of the RNC. It was quite a tribute to Gillespie that the RNC suddenly came up with the budget for the field staff. Gillespie, after all, had been one of the panelists at the RNC meeting in 1996 that led to the Catholic Voter Project. Gillespie became the perfect embodiment of both approaches to the Catholic vote. Himself a cradle Irish Catholic, he was also a smart strategist who embraced without reservation an innovative approach.

The Catholic Outreach field staff and volunteers, organized by Martin Gillespie, took GOP Catholic activism to an entirely new level. Gillespie and his team were able to pass out voter guides at 80 percent of the Catholic parishes in the battleground states. Never in the history of American politics had the Catholic vote been so systematically targeted by a political party. These young men and women received extensive training regarding the legality of handing out voter guides on church property. They were told, correctly, that they were perfectly within their rights. These volunteers knew the Catholic Church well enough to know that they were headed for confrontation. Bishops and priests, even in 2004, were predominantly aligned with Democrats. Many bishops issued directives telling priests to intercept any campaign workers attempting to hand out voter guides. Some priests policed parking lots on their own. Interviews with other campaign workers and volunteers in Florida, Ohio, New Hampshire, Michigan, and Pennsylvania revealed a pattern of confrontation during "lit drops."

The most heated incidents occurred at parishes that hosted Senator John Kerry during the campaign. Volunteers recounted an incident at a parish in South Orlando. A janitor drove up to some campaign workers who were distributing voter guides in the parish parking lot. As they attempted to leave in their vehicle, the janitor blocked their exit. The volunteers, now trapped by the janitor's car, phoned their supervisor. At this point, the pastor came into the parking lot and, rather than tell the janitor to move his car, began to disparage the volunteers. One of them, who was speaking to his supervisor, handed the phone to the pastor, who threatened the supervisor with a lawsuit and demanded his name. The local supervisor, who was also an attorney, informed the pastor that he could be charged with false imprisonment by not allowing them to leave the premises. Eventually, the campaign workers were allowed to leave the parking lot. Senator John Kerry attended mass and received communion at the very same parish the next morning.

This story is important because it exemplifies how the Catholic left was particularly resentful of the GOP's historic effort "on the ground" in 2004 to reach Catholic voters. They could mount nothing of any consequence to combat the momentum. This resentment was expressed in a report to a national meeting of diocesan social action leaders by a professor of religious studies at the Catholic University of America. He accused Bush campaigners of exhibiting "uncivil behavior, characterized by confrontation, harassment and attempts at intimidation." He reported a marked lack of civility among some groups and individuals who, according to the CNS account, "sought to get the entire Catholic community to make the election hinge on the issues of abortion and embryonic stem-cell research." [16] He accused the Bush campaign of causing "polarization" among Catholics in the wake of the 2004 election. That polarization was really the spectacle of the Democratic Party once again losing its hold on the Catholic vote.

Prior to the 2004 election, in late August, I stepped down from my role as Catholic advisor to the White House and the RNC. A left-wing Catholic newspaper that supported John Kerry published a lengthy exposé about me on its Web site. The article contained documents from a supposedly sealed file at Fordham University, where, as a philosophy professor, I had had a sexual encounter with a female undergraduate in February 1994. My wife already knew about it, but the public disclosure

---

16. Jerry Filteau, "Catholic Polarization Reached New Peak in 2004 Election, Speaker Says." Catholic News Service, February 22, 2005.

was devastating to my family, and to those with whom I worked at *Crisis* magazine. I acknowledged then, as I do now, that I was completely responsible for this incident, which I deeply regret. Needless to say, I did not want this revelation to harm the president, so I departed as quietly as the press would allow.

A few months later, after ten years as publisher of *Crisis,* I chose to resign that position as well. There was no way I was going to let further harm come to the magazine I had spent a decade nurturing and growing. I took another job with the same organization that publishes *Crisis.* As executive director of the Morley Institute for Church and Culture, I continued writing and speaking.

In the aftermath of this horrific experience, I can see why I was personally attacked. The stakes were very high. The Catholic vote was one of the determining factors in the close election of 2000 and undoubtedly would play a significant role—against a Catholic candidate—in 2004. I was at the vanguard of a sea change in political and religious history. Catholics were ripe to switch from the Democratic to the Republican Party. They were following in the footsteps of Evangelical voters of the '70s and '80s because issues of life and family values were on the brink of judicial extinction. A coalition of Catholic and Evangelical voters could successfully elect any national candidate they united to support—in sheer numbers, such a coalition was simply too large and too strategically placed to defeat. As I said earlier, the stakes were very high.

9

WHEN PHILOSOPHY GOES BAD

GEORGE W. BUSH ENTERED THE WHITE HOUSE AS AN EVANGEL-ical, but somewhere along the line, he evidently became a Manichaean. What is that, you ask? Manichaeanism, named after its Persian founder, Mani, was one of the most popular and influential religions of the ancient world. It rivaled Christianity. Saint Augustine was a devotee before his conversion. According to Google, there are 40,000 references on the Web to "Bush" and "Manichaean."

Take, for example, the comment of Kenneth T. Walsh in *U.S. News & World Report:* "The roots of Bush's Manichaean ideas may be found in several places. His born-again Christianity reinforces his desire to draw bright lines around what he considers right and wrong. His background in the oil industry of Midland, Texas, gives him the sense that simple solutions are best and that the intelligentsia tend to overly complicate things. His natural instinct is to find a mission and drive inexorably to accomplish it." [1]

Let's see, a clear sense of "right and wrong," "simple solutions," and a strong "mission" orientation. Those qualities, according to Walsh and dozens of other commentators, mean Bush can be *responsibly* described

---

1. *U.S. News & World Report,* November 9, 2003.

as a Manichaean. Did any of them ever take a look at what ancient Manichaeans actually believed? Along with the transmigration of souls, Mani taught that the entire world exists as a result of a primal conflict between two cosmological principles: light and darkness or good and evil. Mani's distinctions are cosmological; they describe the most extreme of metaphysical dualisms. Bush's distinctions are nothing more than the traditional moral distinctions between good and evil. By this measure, every Evangelical and every conservative Catholic must be channeling Mani as well.

It's silly, really. To call Bush Manichaean is not acceptable even as hyperbole. The massacre at Virginia Tech on April 16, 2007, was called evil by every major news commentator, and they are no more Manichaean than Bush. There is *no connection at all* between ancient Manichaeanism and Bush, or anyone who espouses a traditional morality.

The reason such nonsense has become a commonly accepted way of talking about President Bush is bad philosophy. Infused throughout popular culture is the denial of the ability to distinguish good from evil. So many are convinced that all traditional morality is rubbish that anyone who is so unenlightened as to talk about good and evil must be, well, a Manichaean. (George W. Bush as a follower of Mani is in good company with other leaders who fought against evil for the sake of good: Abraham Lincoln, Gandhi, Martin Luther King, Nelson Mandela, to name only a few.)

Our public discourse has completely deteriorated, because in our *postmodern* world, words have no fixed meanings, history has no authority, and nature does not exist. Nothing outside of us measures the truth of what we say. Where nothing can be established as true or rejected as false, any assertion is seen as plausible. There is nothing that restrains us from making any assertion that suits our purposes. In the case of all those references to Bush as a Manichaean, postmodern journalism has substituted bald assertion for reasoned reporting. The aim is swaying the reader one way or another—*exerting power*, in other words, rather than laying out the facts.

It's entirely predictable in a culture where reason and rationality

have been corrupted that people of faith would turn to their religious traditions to restore the basis for knowledge, morality, and politics.
The attacks on these efforts as theocratic or Manichaean usually make
reference to Enlightenment rationality as a standard of how people
ought to think and the morality they should espouse. The reliance on
faith to guide politics, the argument goes, is a rejection of reason and a
rejection of the Enlightenment idea upon which the United States was
founded.

MY REASON IS YOUR FAITH

It's always impressive to be on the side of reason and to invoke the
company of the great philosophers from the seventeenth and eighteenth
centuries—Adam Smith, Voltaire, Hume, Leibniz, Rousseau, Locke, and
so on. But most of these philosophers would not recognize themselves in
the words of the contemporary secular left that claims their patronage.
Indeed, the "reasoning" of the critics who proclaim the superiority of
their secular postmodern reason over faith is a simple case of bad philosophy, a philosophy that dehumanizes and demeans as it proclaims
justice, rights, and the demand for mutual recognition.

It's a misconception that people of faith care nothing for reason
and rationality. Catholics still rely on a centuries-old tradition called
natural-law reasoning, often referred to as Christian philosophy. Most
often associated with the influence of Saint Thomas Aquinas, this tradition within the Catholic faith views reason as absolutely essential to the
defense of basic values.

Jacques Maritain, one of the leading proponents of that tradition in
the twentieth century, wrote while he was teaching at Princeton University in the '50s: "A time will come when people will give up in practice
those values about which they no longer have any intellectual conviction. There are a certain number of moral tenets—about the dignity of
the human person, human rights, human equality, freedom, law, mutual
respect and tolerance, the unity of mankind, and the ideal of peace
among men—on which democracy presupposes common consent;

without a general, firm, and reasoned-out conviction concerning such tenets, democracy cannot survive." [2]

In other words, piety alone, and prayer alone, will not be enough to defend the principles and values that belong to the people of faith. To have a voice in culture and in politics, those who are religious must craft logic in a secular way. The starting point common to both cannot be the Bible; it must be reason.

Catholics can draw on an established tradition of natural law. Evangelicals, however, are heir to the Protestant distrust of reason—Martin Luther famously called reason "the devil's whore." The Reformation principles of "faith alone" and "Scripture alone" make Evangelicals suspect of natural-law reasoning, much less a Christian philosophy.[3] Yet, in spite of their theoretical stance against the use of reason to present a religious point of view, the Evangelical entrance into the political sphere made it practically necessary. Nowadays, it is quite common for an Evangelical arguing publicly against homosexual marriage to spend more time citing social-scientific studies than quoting Scripture.

The charge that religious conservatives reject reason is wrong on many grounds. Not only is the role of reason in religion misunderstood, but so is faith itself. To most people, even many believers, faith is conceived as some kind of feeling or emotional state. Looking at the passion displayed by some Evangelicals, especially Pentecostals, it's easy to see how faith can be identified with these emotions. But, whatever strong feelings are associated with religious faith and practice, faith itself cannot be one of those feelings or one of those emotions. Faith does not give believers emotions; it gives them intellectual content for their minds. When a Catholic, for example, recites the creed (a term derived from the Latin for "I believe," *credo*), a whole series of intellectual propositions are affirmed, beginning with God exists and created the world, Jesus Christ his only son was born of a young virgin, lived, suffered, died, and was

2. Jacques Maritain, *On the Use of Philosophy* (Princeton, N.J.: Princeton University Press, 1961), 12.

3. A flourishing branch of philosophy exists among Evangelicals making use primarily of analytic philosophy and phenomenology as it basis. Leading figures include the late Paul Holmer, Alvin Plantinga, Nicholas Woltersdorf, and Merold Westphal.

resurrected from the dead. Volumes of religious content has been gleaned from the Bible constituting the fundamental beliefs, or creed, for the believer. To have faith is the mind's affirmation of those ideas, which is called a "sacred deposit."

Faith has a content that can be put in sentences, and those sentences can be put in a creed or a catechism. The meanings of those sentences are recognizable to anyone who understands language, even someone who does not *believe* they are true. In this way, faith itself exists as a form of reason and rationality. Faith is capable of being communicated, capable of entering into rational dialogue, capable of converting people who consider its meaning and its claims to ultimate truth.

Faith is a way of knowing, a knowing that begins with the acceptance of revelation. So, when critics of religious conservatives claim a monopoly on reason, they are making a mistake that any truly observant person should never make: the failure to recognize the basic characteristics of what is being described. They ignore the respect for reason found in religious traditions and its direct impact on the development of Western rationality.[4]

In earlier chapters, we saw how the Religious Right was born out of a series of struggles defending the traditional family. These conflicts in the mid- to late '70s were against the attack of the IRS on Christian schools and against the imposition of gay-rights ordinances such as in Dade County, Florida. The right also opposed the adoption of multiculturalism curricula in Kanawha County, West Virginia, and the imposition of the feminist agenda by the ERA. All of these struggles underlined the need to defend the prerogatives of religious parents to raise their children according to their values. In every case, the values being defended were religiously based; they were, in fact, Christian values.

It is necessary to look at the opposing arguments, the *reasons* used by the left to bring this threat against the family and against the prerogatives of parents to raise their children and control their education. I am not talking about the instrumental means used by the left—the courts,

---

4. Rodney Stark, *The Victory of Reason: How Christianity Led to Freedom, Capitalism, and Western Success* (New York: Random House, 2005).

the judges, the media, the entertainment industry. I am talking about the ideas that have been employed to sway the American public.

The ideas employed by the secular left have gained traction in challenging the traditional family as the basic unit in society. Three traditional ideas—freedom, law, and rights—have been co-opted by the left in challenging the core values and worldview of the Religious Right. These ideas, in their postmodern form, are the prime culprits of what made philosophy go bad.

MADE TO MEASURE

When Benedict XVI walked out the doors of St. Peter's Basilica as the new pontiff, there was a collective groan heard from the secular and religious left in Europe and the United States. For twenty-five years, John Paul II had exposed the crooked thinking of secular liberalism, and now his doctrinal counsel and personal confidant was taking his place.

As prefect of the Congregation of the Doctrine of Faith, Cardinal Ratzinger was known not just as a churchman but as one of the preeminent European intellectuals. Like John Paul II, Benedict XVI was trained as a philosopher, a theologian, and a biblical scholar and was well prepared to meet any intellectual challenger. Again like John Paul II's, Benedict XVI's writings are likely to be a rich blend of Scripture, theological reflection, cultural analysis, and sometimes straight philosophical critique. Such was the case in his first encyclical on the nature of love in theology, philosophy, and politics, issued December 2005, *Deus Caritas Est* ("God Is Love").

The same level of intellectual breadth and penetration is seen in Cardinal Ratzinger's now famous "Doctrinal Note" on Catholics in politics from 2002. Father Drinan labeled this document "Inquisition stuff." Coming on the heels of Bush's 2000 election and during the preparation for 2004, then-Cardinal Ratzinger's words were very bad news to left-wing Catholics who hoped to capitalize on the secularizing tendencies among Catholics. Ratzinger, in the following passage, summarized the case against the "cultural relativism" that "sanctions the decadence and disintegration of reason and the principles of natural moral law":

> [I]t is not unusual to hear the opinion expressed in the public sphere that such ethical pluralism is the very condition for democracy. As a result, *citizens claim complete autonomy with regard to their moral choices, and lawmakers maintain that they are respecting this freedom of choice by enacting laws that ignore the principles of natural ethics and yield to ephemeral cultural and moral trends, as if every possible outlook on life were of equal value.* At the same time, the value of tolerance is disingenuously invoked when a large number of citizens, Catholics among them, are asked not to base their contribution to society and political life—through the legitimate means available to everyone in a democracy—on their particular understanding of the human person and the common good. The history of the twentieth century demonstrates that those *citizens were right who recognized the falsehood of relativism, and with it, the notion that there is no moral law rooted in the nature of the human person,* which must govern our understanding of man, the common good, and the state.[5]

Cardinal Ratzinger made it absolutely clear where the Vatican stood on the interface of religion and politics. It's not just about a defense of moral values; an entire "understanding of man" must be proclaimed and defended, because moral law is "rooted in the nature of the human person." The regulating function of human nature in regard to moral terms such as freedom, law, and rights is precisely what postmodernism rejects. There are no fixed natures in postmodern thought; there is only the meaning and significance we assign to things.

Ratzinger stressed reason and natural law because Catholics should participate in politics by using philosophical arguments from the natural law. The argument has been made before the courts that religious

---

5. Joseph Cardinal Ratzinger, "Doctrinal Note on Some Questions regarding the Participation of Catholics in Political Life," II.2, emphasis added.

values don't belong in politics *even if* they have independent secular or philosophical justification. In other words, natural law is crypto-religion and constitutes a threat to the separation of church and state. Thus far, the Supreme Court has rejected the most radical threat to the continued presence of religion in the public sphere. At least twice, lower courts have ruled that policies regarding abstinence education that comport with religious teaching do not constitute a violation of the separation of church and state. There is ongoing litigation, much of it filed by the ACLU, challenging abstinence programs around the nation. All of these lawsuits charge that abstinence education and faith-based social services in general contain religious content that violates the establishment clause of the Constitution. The ACLU would like to get a Supreme Court ruling that any moral content that comports with religious teaching must be considered religious regardless of any secular arguments that justify it.

According to Jim Bopp, general counsel for National Right to Life since 1978, the real turning point was the Supreme Court decision *Harris* v. *McRae,* regarding the Hyde Amendment case in 1980. "It could have gone either way," Bopp recalls. Carter's solicitor general successfully defended Health and Human Services Secretary Joseph Califano. The Court rejected the argument that the mere coincidence of a philosophical justification with a religious viewpoint made the former a form of religious argument. However, a strictly religious principle lacking a philosophical justification is at risk before the Court. But, as Bopp says, "Only religious teachings like the Resurrection lack secular justification."

"That is why the left has to go a step farther," says Bopp. "They now want to argue that it doesn't matter if there is a secular point of view; it only matters if it is *consistent* with religious belief." The Supreme Court in the *Lawrence* decision didn't take that step, but it took another dangerous step forward. The decision, written by Justice Anthony Kennedy, said that you cannot abridge a right because of moral concerns. "They said that morally based justifications are illegitimate. One of the justifications for the homosexual sodomy law in Texas is that it was immoral.

That is why James Dobson called Kennedy "the most heinous man in America," says Bopp.

Justice Kennedy appears to have no clue about the history of rights as a moral term. No one has a right to do wrong. A person has the *ability* not the right. Rights represent the human capacity to seek the basic goods of life. They are defined in terms of what human beings need (not want) in pursuit of a happy life. Rights don't guarantee happiness, as Jefferson made clear in the Declaration of Independence. They provide the opportunity for its pursuit. But those rights are limited by what is morally permissible in the pursuit of happiness.

Such arguments linking rights to a fixed human nature and happiness are foreign to Justice Kennedy as to all postmodernists. Kennedy, after all, is the author of the "mystery of life" passage in *Planned Parenthood* v. *Casey* (1992): "At the heart of liberty is the right to define one's own concept of existence, of meaning, of the universe, of the mystery of human life. Beliefs about these matters could not define attributes of personhood were they formed under the compulsion of the State." Kennedy cited this passage in his *Lawrence* v. *Texas* (2003) decision striking down the state law against homosexual sodomy on the grounds that moral concerns were not legitimate.

Notice how Kennedy finds "right to define one's concept of existence" at "the heart of liberty," as if human liberty had no objective reference points. Freedom in Kennedy's postmodern universe implies sheer randomness. The individual must make sense of it all by an act of self-definition. It's Nietzsche on steroids—but he, at least, had a "will to power" to ground his choices. Kennedy has nothing but the arbitrary choice of individual will. This view of the human will, known as voluntarism, combined with the notion of rights leads to a moral viewpoint where there is an absolute lack of standards except individual choice—the postmodern paradise toward which the most extreme of secular liberals yearn.

Justice Kennedy, however, does remind us that rights themselves have always been understood in terms of potential "compulsion," from the power of either religion or the state. The modern natural-rights arguments originally came from Dominican theologians in Spain who pro-

tested the harsh treatment of Indians in Mexico by Spanish explorers.[6]
Human rights provide an inviolate space for human action that church
and state are obligated to respect. But "a right to define one's own concept of existence" means that an individual has a right to come to the
conclusion that human rights don't exist, and both church and state have
no obligation to respect them, or that a nation's laws don't apply to him.
The absurdities of Kennedy's position can be multiplied endlessly. Unfortunately, one of them showed up in the *Lawrence* decision that severed human rights from moral considerations.

A version of Justice Kennedy's nihilism is seen in the latest blast at religious conservatives from Damon Linker, a former assistant editor to
Father Richard Neuhaus at the journal *First Things*. Linker begins with
an accurate portrayal of what he terms Neuhaus's "theocon" project of
providing a nonsectarian public language for communication of Christian values. He views that act of translation, however, as a threat against
secular politics. Linker supports the view that secular politics and democracy are the best, "that liberal democratic government works perfectly well (and perhaps best), without any religious or metaphysical
foundation at all."[7]

Linker adds, "The theocons endorse policies that are indefensible outside a universe of Catholic assumptions that are shared (and will likely
continue to be shared) by only one segment of the nation's citizenry—
namely, its more conservative Christians."[8] Linker relies on the bogus
account of the establishment clause; he writes, "Under our system of
government, religious believers are required to leave their theological
passions and certainties out of public life."[9] He further argues, "The
privatization of piety creates social space," and "This is the liberal bargain that secures social peace and freedom for all Americans."[10]

6. Bartolomé de Las Casas, *In Defense of the Indians,* trans. and ed. Stafford Poole (Dekalb:
Northern Illinois University Press, 1992).

7. Damon Linker, *The Theocons: Secular America under Siege* (New York: Doubleday, 2006),
218.

8. Ibid., 216.

9. Ibid., 224.

10. Ibid.

The liberal bargain, it hardly needs to be said, has killed millions of innocent children and threatens the lives of the infirmed elderly as well. Linker should rethink which party it is that constitutes a danger to democracy, the theocrats or the secular enthusiasts who define existence in terms of individual preferences.

EVERYONE HAS A BOTTOM LINE

Linker is just the latest critic to ignore the remarkable closeness of faith and reason in the Western tradition. First of all, the moral values held by the average person are inevitably grounded in some sort of worldview, whether faith-based or not, and it is natural for anyone who is explaining his position, or answering questions about his position, to have recourse to his "bottom line," so to speak. "All men," as Aristotle says, "desire to know." And the natural inclination to examine the basis of one's own morality is an expression of that fundamental desire to know.

Second, moral values for most of Western civilization, and, indeed, in civilizations outside the West, have long been grounded in religious traditions, which have provided their content and their larger worldview. Someone who has made a list of these teachings is Christian apologist C. S. Lewis in addenda to his classic work, *The Abolition of Man*. He calls it the "Tao," representing all the ethical teaching of the major religious traditions redacted into basic principles.[11]

Third, the so-called Enlightenment ideal, invoked by the secular critics of the Religious Right, is bogus. Most Enlightenment philosophers were not secularists or atheists. In fact, that was a minority position during the seventeenth and eighteenth centuries. Enlightenment philosophers enlisted religious arguments to justify their forms of rationalism and utilitarianism. One only has to read the central work of Enlightenment philosophy, John Locke's *Essay Concerning Human Understanding*,

11. C. S. Lewis, "Illustrations of the Tao," *The Abolition of Man,* new ed. (San Francisco: Harper San Franciso, 2001).

to see how closely he links his grasp of human understanding and action with the human desire to enjoy eternal happiness with God.

Fourth, the Founding Fathers were not uniformly pious by any means, but what they all had in common, without a single exception, was a deep respect for and belief in the moral values taught in the Christian tradition. Jefferson, for example, rejected the miracles, but he embraced Jesus of Nazareth as a moral teacher. Their instruction by Enlightenment philosophers reflected the same variety of religious views found in those philosophers themselves, most of whom embraced religion in one form or another, if only as a set of moral teachings.

Finally, Christian tradition has produced a philosophy that can stand on its own. In the Catholic tradition, it is called Christian philosophy. This is a form of philosophy that provides a coherent moral perspective that may be inspired by faith but can live a rational life of its own without being propped up by appeals to Scripture and tradition.

All of these single arguments are good enough, by themselves, to refute the secular objection if the secularists were really interested in a rational exchange. But the political terrain suggests they are not. Secular liberals are neither interested in rational consistency, that is, arguing from admitted first principles to their conclusions and engaging objections about their process of reasoning, nor in taking objections seriously. Sloganeering has replaced rational discussion. Or, as Thomas Sowell has put it, their voice is "The Voice of the Anointed," where any objection to their arguments is met not with counterargument but with the assumption that those who disagree must be morally deficient in some fundamental way, or they would agree.[12]

So, what remains to be done? If the voice of the people of faith is dismissed as a private belief that has no right to be made public, then how can they proceed?

Religious conservatives have to put aside the religiously based arguments and engage the "bad philosophy" of the left on its own terms. Conservatives who do not have the ability to address social issues without recourse to religious language are at a disadvantage. It's one thing to

12. Thomas Sowell, *The Vision of the Anointed: Self-Congratulation as a Basis for Social Policy* (New York: Basic Books, 1995), 5.

affirm the freedom to express one's faith in public, as our current president has done (and we applaud that), but another thing to meet the opponent on grounds that he cannot dismiss as faith-based.

NOT STARTING WITH OURSELVES

In the Western Judeo-Christian tradition, law, in all its meanings, has long been understood as an *extrinsic measure*. That is, law is something that measures *from the outside*, which makes perfect sense, since law is intended to measure a thing, to determine whether or not it falls within the appropriate boundaries.

Saint Thomas Aquinas, in his "Treatise on Law," discusses four kinds of law: eternal, divine, natural, and positive, all of which are extrinsic measures of different kinds.[13] Eternal law is that law within the being of God Himself, unknowable to us and something that belongs to God alone. Divine law is that which God has revealed to us through His revelation and is contained in Scripture. Natural law is the law revealed by the observation and study of nature. Natural law is known through reason, although it comports with revelation in some cases. Positive law is the law passed by government to rule its citizens. In a democracy, it is based on the will of the governed through the election of representatives who make the laws.

In each case, the extrinsic measure changes. In the first two cases, it is God; in the case of natural law, it is nature; and in the case of positive law, it is the state. What happens when the only remaining extrinsic measure is the state's is addressed by Reverend Martin Luther King in his "Letter from the Birmingham Jail." When quoting Thomas Aquinas, he wrote that one was not bound to obey a civil law that is positive law that was not found in natural law.[14]

Where there is no extrinsic measure transcending the authority of the state, there is no moral measure by which one can decide for or against

13. Thomas Aquinas, *Summa Theologica*, ed. Thomas Gilby (New York: McGraw-Hill, 1966), I.2, Q. 90–97.

14. Martin Luther King, "Letter from the Birmingham Jail," *I Have a Dream: Writings and Speeches That Changed the World*, ed. James Melvin Washington (San Francisco: Harper San Francisco, 2006), 89.

obedience to those laws. For example, Cold War arguments concerning the addition of "one nation under God" to the Pledge of Allegiance appealed to the desire to distinguish the children of the United States from the children of the Soviet Union, who pledged their allegiance to the state and not beyond it.

It is easy to see how the elimination of any extrinsic measure other than the state completely negates the vision of the Founders as found in the Declaration of Independence and the Constitution. Consideration of an extrinsic measure is missing from Justice Kennedy's "mystery of life." A mystery, by the way, is not something that is unknowable; it is something *not yet known,* as any reader of Sherlock Holmes knows.

The Founders were of one mind in viewing basic human rights as something that was not merely being conferred upon American citizens by the state but were *rights by nature.* These rights, therefore, were not something that could be invented in order to espouse a particular cause. They had to be inferred from the fundamental rights "endowed by the Creator" and "Nature's God."

The universality of human rights was reaffirmed in the 1949 Universal Declaration of Human Rights. But in June 1993, the famed UN document was challenged by the new postmodern elite. That summer, the United Nations World Conference on Human Rights met in Vienna to assess progress on human rights since the Declaration. Two months before the meeting, thirty-four Arab and Asian countries issued the Bangkok Declaration, stating that the notion of human rights is relative to the cultural, religious, and historical diversity of nations and that the Western powers should not use human rights "as an instrument of political pressure." [15]

During the conference, these countries invoked a "right to development" without interference. The conference was a battleground between universalists and relativists, with the conference ultimately taking the universalist position: "Human rights and fundamental freedoms are the birthright of all human beings . . . all human rights are universal, indi-

---

15. "Universality of Rights Is Defined by U.S.; Protest over Dalai Lama Mars Vienna Talks," *Washington Post* (June 15, 1993) A15.

visible, and interdependent and interrelated." It also said that the "right to development" can never justify the infringement of human rights.[16] Notice that "human being" is used as an objective measure, as a way of measuring laws and customs in every nation.

But the countries that protested against the Universal Declaration of Human Rights were protesting the oppression they felt by the Declaration's extremely long list of human rights. The postmodern protest against the universality of rights was also a practical way of rejecting the *use* of that list of rights to pummel countries that did not conform to the socialist fashion of the day. What began in the Universal Declaration as a defense of universal human nature had been twisted into a political tool for the imposition of "justice," as defined by the far left. The list of rights gave the states the responsibility of providing to their citizens all those goods that—it once was thought—were their individual responsibility. If, for example, there is a right to health care, does that mean that society must provide it without any cost to the patient, without demanding any payment for services rendered? If so, why should anyone pay for health care at all?

The problem goes back to the fact that rights were originally conceived in a negative, not positive, sense. A right was a special kind of human ability of obtaining basic goods—life, liberty, and the pursuit of happiness. They were abilities the state pledged not to obstruct or violate. When rights became positive, the obligations placed on the state changed. No longer did the state simply make sure it did not obstruct the pursuit of these goods; the state was now obliged to supply these goods on demand. As positive rights multiplied, the confusion mounted, because there is no practical way the state can supply what each right demands for a citizen. Those on the far political left treat rights as a laundry list of what government should provide to every citizen—food, clothing, shelter, education, and health care. But goods such as education and health care cannot be obtained in this way. A person has to *participate* in his education, has to study and attend class. An individual cannot be

16. *World Conference on Human Rights: The Vienna Declaration and Programme of Action, June 1993* (New York: United Nations Department of Public Information, 1993), 28–30.

healthy merely by having access to a doctor. He must eat, exercise, and take the medicine required for good health.

Thomas Sowell argues that "rights claims" have become substitutes for arguments about public policy. "Rights to anything mean that someone else has been yoked to your service involuntarily, with no corresponding responsibility on your part to provide for yourself, to compensate others, or even to behave decently or responsibly. Here the language of equal rights is conscripted for service in defense of differential privileges." [17] As Sowell illustrates, there is a big difference between rights *from government inference* and rights *to have something provided* for you by the government. In short, the left's assertion of a right means that somebody has to pay for and provide something that another person *cannot or will not secure for himself.*

Viewed in this way, human rights serve a deeper ideological purpose. They open the door to the government imposing moral standards on its citizens in the name of respecting rights.

An example is the so-called *right of equal respect,* most often associated with one of the left's leading philosophical apologists, Ronald Dworkin. [18] Equal respect is a right that has the power to trump all other rights, in particular religious liberty. To demand equal respect means that you are obliged to regard others in a way that does not "demean" them in relation to you or anyone else. The moral judgment that a person's behavior is immoral or sinful constitutes a violation of the right to equal respect. This puts a particular burden on religious conservatives who think their moral values should inform law and public policy. For Dworkin, obviously, this attempt violates equal respect that is the fundamental principle of political rights.

IS IT ALL ABOUT FEELING GOOD?

Charles Taylor, a Catholic philosopher from Canada, views the right of equal respect as the first principle of what he calls the contemporary

17. Sowell, *The Vision,* 100.

18. Ronald Dworkin, *Taking Rights Seriously* (Cambridge, Mass.: Harvard University Press, 1977).

"culture of authenticity." The ideal of authenticity replaces the traditional categories of moral virtue, good and evil, right and wrong.

For Taylor, this appeal eliminates any type of significance. "Even the sense that the significance of my life comes from its being chosen—the case where authenticity is actually grounded on self-determining freedom—*depends on the understanding that independent of my will there is something noble, courageous, and hence significant in giving shape to my own life.*"[19] Even the ideal of authenticity demands some sort of measure external to the self, some measure of what is authentic and what is not. Without an external or preexisting measure of worthwhile choice, no one direction appears better than any other.

The culture of authenticity relies upon an external measure in spite of a determination not to. That measure is the right of equal respect, which Taylor calls the "mutual recognition" of others. Thus, what seems a highly individualistic perspective, the search for authenticity, *becomes dependent on recognition by others* to validate one's identity. Consequently, a denial of recognition creates a barrier to achieving authenticity.

The demand for mutual recognition thus becomes problematic, because recognition cannot be honestly given where there is no shared view of what counts for being human. Taylor writes, "A favorable judgment on demand is nonsense . . . no one can really mean it as a genuine act of respect. As a result, the recognition that any self or community, its values and artifacts, is equal in worth to any others can only be a deception."[20]

Equal respect and mutual recognition is the unspoken agenda of the political left as is the demand for difference, diversity, and multiculturalism. These programs, having dominated the corporate and academic worlds for twenty years, have assumed that enforced recognition of a person's differences from other people, such as sexual orientation, will result in the suppression of traditional religious values. The hope is that

19. Charles Taylor, *The Ethics of Authenticity* (Cambridge, Mass.: Harvard University Press, 1992), 39.

20. Charles Taylor, *Multiculturalism and the "Politics of Recognition"* (Princeton, N.J.: Princeton University Press, 1992), 70.

people will give up their inclination to moral judgments in such matters and embrace the new "tolerance."

The gay-rights movement is currently the ideology of choice among secularists. The demand for gay marriage and the demand that homosexual acts be recognized as morally licit go hand in hand. It is homosexuals' right, not just to have the economic benefits of married couples but also to aspire to have their sexuality receive equal respect in the eyes of their fellow citizens. This is a dynamic that has already played out in the feminist movement. Working women, women who aborted their babies, women who left their families, and women who loved women not only demanded civil rights but also demanded that everyone else recognize that they were right in doing whatever they wanted to do.

Both feminists and gay activists have demanded that religious conservatives cease making judgments according to their traditional moral values. It makes no difference whether those judgments remain private, because private judgments are a denial of recognition. Were feminists and gay activists to succeed in eliminating the moral perspectives that produce negative assessments of their lifestyles, then, as Taylor argues, everyone would be equally recognized by everyone else, leaving no true recognition at all.

BATTERED BY BAD PHILOSOPHY

Scott Bloch came to Washington, D.C., from Lawrence, Kansas, to work in the Bush administration in 2001. For more than two years, he worked in the Department of Justice's Task Force for Faith-Based and Community Initiatives, serving as deputy director and counsel. The president then appointed him and the Senate confirmed him to head up the U.S. Office of Special Counsel, a small independent watchdog agency.

In some ways, Bloch does typify the kind of Bush appointee who elicits the charge of theocracy from the secular left. A Catholic with seven children, he attended the University of Kansas, going through the Pearson Integrated Humanities Program, a now-defunct but legendary Great

Books program. Bloch became a devotee of Catholic writers such as Hilaire Belloc and G. K. Chesterton. His vision of public service was shaped by his legal training, not only at the University of Kansas but also by his exposure to the Great Books, including Catholic philosophers such as Boethius, Saint Augustine, and Saint Thomas Aquinas.

Bloch had no preexisting ties to the ideological trench warfare that pervades the nation's capital—as he puts it, "I only wanted to serve the public trust." In Washington, however, politics would find him. A colleague of Bloch's in the Faith-Based and Community Initiative pointed out his own observation that "a surprising number of lawsuits against the faith-based organizations that the Justice Department monitored turned on the issue of gay rights." It was an observation that seemed anomalous, but it was no mere series of coincidences.

One such case the colleague described involved a Christian orphanage in Georgia that was a recipient of a state block grant. The mission of the orphanage includes giving children a solid foundation in Christian teachings in order to provide inner strength and virtue. With these tools, they claim (and empirical data support), the children have the lifetime tools to make the right choices in accordance with Christ's teachings.

The hiring of employees is, naturally enough, in keeping with their mission. When an employee threatened the formation of the children by disavowing the Christian mission and principles of the orphanage, she was fired. The woman, a lesbian, filed a lawsuit arguing that the Christian orphanage was receiving government funding and therefore could not have employment policies based on religious principles.

However, it is well established that the 1964 Civil Rights Act exempts religious groups from religious discrimination law. They are permitted to hire based on their beliefs to better fulfill the objectives of their mission. So the lawsuit could not succeed, but religious-liberty advocates were concerned. Was this a new front in the same war that had resulted in *Roe* v. *Wade*—a series of legal assaults designed to allow liberal and moderate judges to overturn the principle of religious liberty, just as they did with the sanctity of human life in 1973?

A trend was emerging: lawsuits about the First Amendment religion clause. Sometimes the more contentious ones were filed by gay or lesbian employees. Other cases had homosexual issues at their core, even when it was not apparent on their surfaces. In one such case, the Boy Scouts were denied the right to use public accommodations in retaliation for their refusal to allow homosexuals into leadership in the Boy Scouts.

According to Bloch's colleague at the Justice Department, "The gay agenda is in direct conflict with religious liberty, and whether it's welfare reform, Head Start, drug treatment funding, faith-based funding, or the Boy Scouts—'gay rights' trumps everything."

It is generally understood that the CARE Act, which would have given support to the Faith-Based and Community Initiative, failed because Democrat and moderate Republican legislators wanted to force religious organizations to give up their Title VII exemption under the Civil Rights Act. This would have forced these groups to hire or retain those who might sabotage their mission by disagreeing with principles of their faith in the workplace. At the heart of the bad philosophy is this coercive element of the left to require religion to toe the line of a politically correct view of sexuality. It is intolerance of faith masquerading as tolerance of everything.

"That was certainly eye-opening for many of us in the initiative," said Bloch's colleague, "but I wouldn't have thought Scott would encounter the same issues at OSC."

Yet shortly after taking office as the new special counsel in early 2004, Bloch was surprised to see that the gay agenda was creating significant subterfuge. A member of his staff brought to his attention that the OSC Web site contained erroneous information and asked if it should be removed. Bloch's predecessor, a Clinton appointee and an openly gay activist, had added "sexual orientation discrimination" to ethnic, race, and religious protections on the Web site.

One of OSC's major responsibilities is protecting federal workers from discrimination. However, nowhere in any of OSC's laws does "sexual orientation" appear as a protected group.

When Bloch researched the case law, he found a 1996 court decision that specifically rejected the claim that sexual orientation is a group protected by OSC. As Bloch says, "this wasn't a close call. My statutes are written by Congress and signed into law by the president, and the wording is fairly plain in this regard. I would be violating my oath to uphold the Constitution if I followed any other path."

Bloch removed the "sexual orientation" language from the Web site, and a public controversy ensued. He was assailed by activist groups and members of Congress, furious that he would challenge the Clinton interpretation of sexual-orientation discrimination. He was attacked as a Catholic and accused of "anti-gay bigotry." Congressional and White House investigations followed, and that scrutiny continues.

Astoundingly, there was even opposition to and ridicule to Bloch's hiring of two Catholic attorneys from an orthodox Catholic law school (Ave Maria University) established by Tom Monaghan, the founder of Domino's Pizza. Up to that point, upward of twenty other attorneys from a wide variety of law schools had been hired under Bloch's authority. To date, as special counsel, Bloch has hired almost forty attorneys and investigators maintaining that diversity of education and background.

Jeffrey Ruch, the head of Public Employees for Environmental Responsibility and a leading Bloch critic, entered the fray. In an interview with National Public Radio, he described Bloch's hiring of Ave Maria graduates as "personnel practices . . . taken straight from *The Da Vinci Code* rather than the civil service manual."[21]

The situation escalated after Bloch reassigned twelve employees to various field offices. The reassignments were part of a successful effort to improve the agency's functioning and prevent recurrent backlogs that had been resolved for the first time in a decade.

Anonymous employees who later claimed they were gay accused Bloch of targeting them in the transfers. Leading gay-rights groups demanded Bloch's resignation. Bloch denied targeting anyone and denied knowing about the sexual preference of any of the transferred

21. Interview with Bob Garfield, National Public Radio, March 25, 2005.

individuals. So far, there is no proof to the contrary despite a full-blown Senate hearing, staff investigations, GAO investigations, and an inspector general investigation.

Bloch had unknowingly stepped into an effort by gay activists to force states, and eventually the federal government, to recognize sexual orientation as a protected group. Legislative efforts to add sexual-partner preferences as a protected class (Senator Kennedy's Employment Non-Discrimination Act, or ENDA) have failed twice. The public policy of recognition could not be secured by statute, so the Clinton administration arbitrarily secured it by executive fiat—until Bloch reestablished the rule of law. The ENDA is at the top of the gay lobby's agenda to ram through Congress in the future.

The Human Rights Campaign, the leading pro-gay organization and a group with enormous power even within Republican bastions, led the charge against Bloch to have him investigated, hoping to drive him from office.

When studying the ferocity and tenacity of gay activists, it is clear that they want to be recognized as homosexuals without any negativity attached to the judgment. They want to be seen as what they are and affirmed in their lifestyle. Their ultimate goal is to eliminate any criticism of their orientation or sexual activity—they want to be included in what is called "normal."

The OSC controversy shows how gay activists abuse public policy to enforce federally protected immorality. As Jim Bopp, general counsel for National Right to Life, has pointed out, "The gay-marriage decision in Massachusetts set back their cause for several years because the backlash was so great."

The use of public policy by gay activists as a way of normalizing their lifestyle in the midst of a culture deeply informed by religion has brought about an inevitable showdown between the gay-rights movement and people of faith. This is true whether it is Scott Bloch at OSC, a Christian orphanage in Georgia, Dr. James Dobson at Focus on the Family, or parents preserving their children's religious worldview.

This conflict poses an interesting challenge to religious prudence.

Most people have a basic desire to be fair. Bigotry is rightly condemned. But where does decency get bent into forcing all of humanity to give up a normative understanding of human sexuality? In an excess of politeness, society has become vulnerable to losing religious freedoms. The group to whom they extend kindness demands they stop viewing them through a moral lens that sees their sexual acts as contrary to nature and God's law. Gay activists have taken advantage of the Christian desire to be tolerant and are exercising their own intolerance in return.

A senior aide (also Catholic) to a Republican senator explains it this way: "Gay rights has become the barometer of an acceptable worldview. If you think homosexuality should be stigmatized, you yourself will be stigmatized—gay activists will make it so painful and so unacceptable for you that there will be no debate, no discussion—you will be ostracized."

Asked why he stuck with his policy at OSC, given his awareness of the potential fallout, Bloch said, "I am an enforcer of law, not a maker of law. There was nothing in the intent, nothing in legislative history, and nothing in case law that would allow me to leave 'sexual orientation discrimination' in our materials and on our Web site. After finishing my legal review and consulting many lawyers, I concluded that I would be violating my oath to uphold the law and the Constitution if I allowed that material to have an official stamp of approval."

Bloch's experiences demonstrate why religious conservatives will continue to resist the bad philosophy of gay marriage, abortion rights, and other faux rights movements. Already in the Netherlands, it is considered "hate speech" to express negative moral judgments about homosexuality. An eminent Catholic philosopher and confidant of John Paul II, Rocco Buttiligione, was deprived of his position in the European Union because of his views on homosexuality. Canada is considering legislation to criminalize expressions of moral views condemning homosexuality. Religious liberty may fall victim to a criminalizing of religious speech, if not religious thinking itself.

Says Bloch, "What hurt was that people who know me know I'm not the bogeyman depicted in the press. They know I have no history of hatred toward groups. They know I'm a reasonable person who would befriend anyone of goodwill, regardless of their faith, viewpoint, or even private behavior. I had no history of prejudice or activism against any group."

Scott Bloch did not come to Washington looking for a fight; he came to serve an administration with which he shares basic values about the rule of law. His principled stand was answered by a tyrannical, unreasoning attack from the gay-rights movement. But the pervasiveness of bad philosophy made reasoned conversation impossible and personal destruction the tactic of choice.

10

PERSECUTION, ACCOMMODATION, AND TRIUMPH

B EFORE THE 2004 CAMPAIGN OF CATHOLIC SENATOR JOHN KERRY, there were three iconic moments that shaped the attitudes of American Catholics toward the presidency. The first two demonstrated the persistent fact of anti-Catholic prejudice in U.S. culture and politics. The third reveals the truth of the ongoing reference to the "slumbering giant," the potential power of Catholic voters to determine elections.

In 1928, a Catholic was nominated for president for the first time since the nation's founding. Al Smith, the four-term governor of New York, endured a barrage of relentless anti-Catholic vitriol. At the Houston Democratic Convention, after Smith was nominated on the first ballot, members of the KKK slit the throat of an Al Smith effigy on the convention floor and then splashed fake blood on its chest, while a mob chanted, "Lynch him."[1]

Throughout the campaign, Smith was assaulted by anti-Catholic attacks in the mainstream press. The Klan made sure he could see crosses burning next to the train tracks as he traveled the country, and they passed out leaflets at his campaign stops. Even the mainstream Protes-

---

1. Thomas J. Carty, *A Catholic in the White House? Religion, Politics, and John F. Kennedy's Presidential Campaign* (New York: Palgrave McMillan, 2004), 28.

tant denominations—Presbyterians, Methodists, Lutherans, and Episcopalians made no attempt to disguise their contempt for the candidacy of a Catholic who dared to dream of the presidency. They argued that in political and moral matters, the Catholic Governor Smith was subject first to the authority of the Church, making him unable and unfit to lead a democratic nation.

In short, Smith was considered a threat to democracy, a politician whose Catholic faith inevitably would lead him to impose—theocratically—his "papist" beliefs on a Protestant nation. The Protestants who made this charge against Smith are now on the receiving end. The anti-Catholic prejudice that once elicited accusations of theocracy has been replaced by a broader prejudice toward any form of conservative Christianity in politics.

If Smith's critics had been more attentive to the politics of the Vatican at the time, they would have found some justification for their concern about theocracy. In state agreements, called concordats, negotiated by the Vatican with Italy and Germany, Pope Pius XI agreed to disband the Catholic political parties of those countries, even though they were counterweights to the rise of totalitarianism in both countries. The joke going around after the election was that Smith sent Pius XI a one-word telegram: "Unpack."

Americans did not need any extra prodding from current events in Europe to manifest their anti-Catholicism. It was a prejudice that was born with America itself. The very notion of freedom in the thirteen colonies had been forged in the struggle against Catholic power in Europe. Catholics, as a result, were not welcome in many of the original colonies. The United States, whether or not it can be called a Christian nation, can certainly be called a Protestant one. Its Protestant elite not only shaped its culture and politics but also inserted a fear of Roman Catholics. After the tide of Catholic immigration came ashore in the mid-nineteenth century, the Protestant majority of the state of New York sought to impose its beliefs on the immigrant students enrolled in its newly created public schools.

The same religious leadership, faced in the 1920s with the growing influence of the Catholic voter, was determined to exclude a Catholic from the nation's highest office. There was nothing they wouldn't say about Smith. He was accused of being in league with bootleggers, gamblers, and prostitutes. At least one Christian newspaper reminded its readers that Roman Catholics had assassinated Lincoln, Garfield, and McKinley.[2]

The Republican Herbert Hoover won more than 58 percent of the popular vote to just more than 40 percent for Smith. The vote of the Electoral College was an overwhelming 444 to 87. The election demonstrated that the United States was not ready for a Catholic president.

KENNEDY'S NET LOSS

The second moment of particular significance to Catholics regarding the presidency is, of course, the candidacy and election of Senator John F. Kennedy in 1960. The Democratic Party had considered Kennedy as its vice-presidential nominee, along with another Catholic, Mayor Robert Wagner of New York City, to run with Senator Adlai Stevenson in 1956. Kennedy thought that a Catholic nominee would help boost the party's image as being opposed to Communism, as well as soften the negative image of the divorced Stevenson.[3] But the memory of Al Smith's defeat was still fresh in the minds of party leadership. To overcome their resistance, the chairman of the Connecticut Democratic Party sent around a memorandum under his name, although it was written by Kennedy advisor Ted Sorensen. The Bailey Memorandum argued that Al Smith had not lost the election because of anti-Catholic prejudice but because of other issues such as prohibition. The memo also argued that Catholic support for Eisenhower would return to the Democratic Party if it nominated a Catholic. Kennedy was not nominated but began laying the groundwork for a run in 1960.

2. George J. Marlin, *The American Catholic Voter: 200 Years of Political Impact* (South Bend, Ind.: St. Augustine's Press, 2004), 185.

3. Mark S. Massa, *Catholics and American Culture: Fulton Sheen, Dorothy Day, and the Notre Dame Football* Team (New York: Crossroad, 1999), 133.

In spite of the memo's downplaying of anti-Catholicism, much of Kennedy's campaign was designed to deflect the prejudice still prevalent around the nation. Ted Sorensen, who became Kennedy's chief counsel, remarked later that anti-Catholicism was the candidate's most serious problem in gaining the White House.[4] No longer, however, were mainline Protestant denominations the only cause of concern. The growing number of Evangelicals in the Southern states and the West were barriers as well. Billy Graham's form of revivalism was already increasing the numbers of Evangelical believers, often at the expense of mainline denominations.

The Protestant establishment had not lost its reservations about a Catholic president. Reverend Norman Vincent Peale, the author of many best-selling books, including *The Power of Positive Thinking*, made very public and eventually very embarrassing comments about the danger of a Catholic president. As in the '20s, major magazines and newspapers were not reluctant to provide space to Catholic bashers such as Peale. Even Billy Graham, pushed by Peale to oppose Kennedy publicly, came very close to publishing a cautionary article about Kennedy in *Life* magazine. However, Graham was saved from a loss of prestige by the candidate. Kennedy prevailed upon editor Henry Luce to have the article altered. Graham ended up writing about the need for Christians to vote, rather than the reasons not to vote for a Catholic.

From the beginning of the campaign, Kennedy and his advisors debated how to handle the attacks on Kennedy's religion. Should he respond directly, or should he deflect the issue? Kennedy's friends did not think him a very religious man. Sorensen, a close friend for eleven years, never heard him pray or ever discuss his personal views of religion.[5] But the intensity of Kennedy's piety was not the issue, and reminding the public that he was Catholic was a risk. Al Smith had goaded his critics by participating in high-profile Catholic events, such as serving as an acolyte at a mass in New Jersey during his campaign. No matter how much Kennedy wanted the issue to die, he and his advisors knew it would be

4. Carty, *A Catholic*, 2.
5. Massa, *Catholics*, 129.

front and center until Election Day. Several attempts to defuse the issue failed, including a high-profile interview in *Look* magazine in March 1959. The *Look* interview set a strong separationist tone for the entire campaign: "Whatever one's religion in private life may be, for the office holder nothing takes precedence over his oath to uphold the Constitution in all its parts—including the First Amendment and the strict separation of church and state."[6] Kennedy, therefore, did not intend to undo the fears of a Catholic president by admitting to his tepid faith but by insisting that the Constitution protected the country from presidential piety.

The decision to address 300 Protestant ministers at the Houston Ministerial Association on September 12, 1960, was a gamble that had been forced on Kennedy by a meeting five days earlier at the Mayflower Hotel in Washington, D.C. At the invitation of Norman Vincent Peale, 150 Protestant ministers met and issued a five-point statement condemning the political activity of the Catholic Church and Kennedy as a presidential candidate. The meeting and statement of the "Peale Group" forced Kennedy to take on the attacks directly and, at least, calm the waters of the debate. Shortly thereafter, he told a group of Houston ministers, "I believe in an America . . . where no Catholic prelate would tell the president—should he be Catholic—how to act, and no Protestant minister would tell his parishioners for whom to vote." Kennedy's awkward use of the word "parishioners" to Protestant ministers in Texas belies the gulf that lay between him and his audience. But, in spite of some discordant word choices, Kennedy convinced the ministers and much of the nation that his Catholic faith did not pose a danger of theocracy. Kennedy's Catholicism would effectively be put on the shelf while he was president of the United States.

Years later, with the coming of the culture wars, Kennedy's speech would appear to orthodox Catholics like Peter's denial of Christ the night of his crucifixion. But the media coverage during the campaign, such as *Time* magazine portraying Kennedy "in the lion's den of the

6. Ibid., 134.

Houston Protestant preachers," made Kennedy look courageous and his critics bigoted. Attempts forty years later to make Kennedy look like the proto–John Kerry failed to appreciate that the cultural attitudes he faced were much closer to those of Al Smith's generation than ours. Kennedy had compromised, no doubt, but it was a compromise in the face of anti-Catholic bigotry, not a policy debate over abortion or euthanasia. Without the compromise, Kennedy would not have convinced enough suspicious Protestant voters he needed to win.

It was the compromise of a man who was, by all accounts, a cultural Catholic of his generation. Kennedy did not face the sharply drawn battle lines presented by the debates over abortion, feminism, bioethics, and gay rights of later generations. Yet, as Mark S. Massa argues in his perceptive study of the 1960 election, the treatment of religion in the Kennedy campaign greatly accelerated the trend toward secularization and the "privatization" of religious faith.[7] It was only a few years before academic writers began making headlines with the announcement of the death of God, the creation of the secular city, and situation ethics.

There were plenty of contemporary critics on hand to point out how Kennedy was misrepresenting his Catholic faith. Editorials in diocesan newspapers, *America* magazine, and *Commonweal* expressed shock at the lengths to which Kennedy had gone to distance himself from his faith. Cardinal Spellman of New York stated that Kennedy had committed himself to a policy course that, if consistent, would be disastrous for the Church's interests. Spellman supported Nixon, a stance that must have required an enormous strength of will. This foreshadowed the dynamics that led Catholic voters to support an Evangelical candidate over the Catholic senator from Massachusetts in 2004. Today, Kerry, Ted Kennedy, and Nancy Pelosi are ducking an entirely different set of issues, all of which involve Catholic moral principles they refuse to apply to public policy.

John F. Kennedy's ability to soften his image as a Catholic may have been aided by the public image of Pope John XXIII. Although at heart a

7. Ibid., chapter 6.

conservative on doctrinal matters, John XXIII had adopted a completely different public style from his predecessors Pius XI and Pius XII. He was the kind grandfather rather than the strict father. He tried to decrease the sense of distance between himself and the common man, including non-Catholics. Where Pius XII had been a cold warrior, John XXIII sent candy to the niece of the Soviet Union's premier, Nikita Khrushchev. John XXIII, whether he knew it or not, was making it easier for Catholics like John F. Kennedy to be viewed without Gothic shadows of Romanist conspiracy theories.

In spite of their efforts, the best the Kennedy campaign could do was to limit the damage of anti-Catholic animus. The most comprehensive study of the Kennedy campaign concluded that the Massachusetts senator lost more votes than he gained because of his Catholicism.[8] An MIT computer model estimated his loss at 1.5 million votes (2.3 percent of the total). Kennedy's margin of victory over Nixon in the popular vote was 150,000 votes. There is little doubt that if Kennedy had not adopted the strategy and tone manifested at the Houston meeting, he would not have won the presidency. Some historians have concluded that the election of Kennedy represents the climax of Catholic assimilation into the American culture that began after World War II. That may be. Catholics were assimilating into American culture, moving to the suburbs, attending public schools, getting college degrees, pursuing successful careers, and entering politics. But the 1960 election certainly does not represent the public acceptance of a chief of state *as Catholic*. The comment by one scholar that "Kennedy's election broke down the last major American barrier to full Catholic political equality" is entirely wrong.[9] Had Kennedy not backed away from his Catholicism, he would have surely lost. In 1960, the American electorate was still not ready for that. Kennedy's election represented the assimilation of Catholics into American culture, but it did not provide evidence that American culture had substantially gotten over its fear of Catholic power and influence. A specific fear

8. Carty, *A Catholic*, 156.

9. Eric O. Hanson, *The Catholic Church in World Politics* (Princeton, N.J.: Princeton University, Press, 1987), 167.

remained that the pope would demand Kennedy's first loyalty be to him. The nation, however, was not yet familiar with the kind of Catholic Kennedy was—assimilated, cultural, respectful, and not afraid of Father or Sister So-and-so. Regardless of JFK's Catholic bona fides, the fact that Catholics voted more than 82 percent for Kennedy after having voted for Eisenhower showed that the 1960 election "almost certainly played a part in checking what might well have been a more rapid drift toward the GOP." [10]

The multiple failures of Catholic candidate Senator Eugene McCarthy in 1968 and 1972 to gain the Democratic nomination (he ran as an independent in 1976) underline the limits of a Catholic's appeal to the national electorate. However, McCarthy, who made no attempt to hide his Catholicism, was far more socially liberal than Kennedy and had little tact and no gift for political compromise.

JOHN PAUL II'S PRESIDENT

The third iconic moment, before the Kerry campaign, was the fall of the Berlin Wall in 1989. In the eyes of the American public, and particularly Catholics, the wall fell because of the special relationship between John Paul II and Ronald Reagan. Reagan had told Gorbachev to take down that wall and it came down ten months after he left office. John O'Sullivan writes in his book on Reagan, Margaret Thatcher, and John Paul II: "The breach of the Berlin Wall was the real climax of the Reagan presidency." [11] American Catholics, who had always been at the forefront of anti-Communist fervor, saw it just that way. To them, it was the culmination of decades of efforts led by Francis Cardinal Spellman, Bishop Fulton Sheen, James Francis Cardinal McIntyre, Senator Joseph McCarthy, and Father Edmund Walsh, founder and dean of Georgetown University's School of Foreign Service. Other longtime leaders included Clarence

10. Mark A. Noll, *Religion & American Politics: From the Colonial Period to the 1980s* (New York: Oxford University Press, 1990), 362.

11. John O'Sullivan, *The President, the Pope, and the Prime Minister* (Washington, D.C.: Regnery, 2006), 304.

Manion of Notre Dame Law School, William F. Buckley, Brent L. Bozell Jr., and Phyllis Schlafly, along with diocesan publications such as the *Brooklyn Tablet* and *Los Angeles Tidings.* Catholic organizations such as the Knights of Columbus, the Ancient Order of Hibernians, the Holy Name Society, the Cardinal Mindszenty Foundation, Catholic Boy Scouts, New York's Policemen's Benevolent Association, and the Catholic Veterans Association all played a part. Many Catholics still recall how the fall of the Soviet Union was at the heart of popular devotion to Our Lady of Fatima, represented by the Blue Army.

One reason for the gradual shift of Catholics out of the Democratic Party, as evidenced by Catholic support for General Dwight D. Eisenhower in 1952, was the perception that Democrats, then led by Adlai Stevenson, had gone soft on Communism. Recall that JFK thought a Catholic on the ticket in 1956 would help to offset that image. Though Eisenhower did not receive a majority of the Catholic vote, only 46 percent, it represented a switch of more than 3 million votes from the Truman victory of 1948. In 1956, Eisenhower's biggest gain came from Catholic voters. Senator John F. Kennedy, to his advantage, held strong anti-Communist credentials that helped him bring Catholics back to the Democratic Party. His election was the high point of Catholic support for Democrats, more than 70 percent. An amazing 67 percent of the Catholics who had voted for Eisenhower came back to the Democratic Party to vote for Kennedy.[12] To this day, there is no "Catholic vote," in the strict sense of a voting bloc that can be relied upon by a specific party to support its candidates. Since World War II, no one has owned the Catholic vote; it switches back and forth between political parties depending on the candidates and circumstances. In the 2006 congressional election, for example, the steady increase of Catholic support for the GOP took a step backward, from 50 percent for congressional candidates in 2004 to 44 percent.

Karol Cardinal Wojtyla became pope in the midst of a flailing Carter administration. On social issues, Carter had been a disappointment to

---

12. Marlin, *The American Catholic Voter*, 257.

the Evangelicals who supported him. Even more damaging was his inability to deal forcefully with the Soviet Union and the Middle East. Carter reinforced the image of Democrats as weak and ineffective in the face of a Soviet threat. In his 1977 speech at Notre Dame, Carter announced, "We are now free of that inordinate fear of Communism which once led us to embrace any dictator who joined us in our fear." [13] Carter would very likely regret these words countless times in the years to follow. Case in point: in late 1979, the Soviet Union invaded Afghanistan. As O'Sullivan puts it, "Carter was not un-American or anti-American; he was 'post-American,' in the sense that Carter believed the United States had lost it preeminent role in global politics." [14]

Carter's genuine piety had made him a man of the left, not the right. As O'Sullivan notes, Carter had succeeded in making the lack of respect for human rights in the Eastern bloc a point of embarrassment for the Soviet Union. [15] But beyond that, Carter's piety led him toward agreeing with the left's critique of American culture as decadent and the U.S. government as an "imperialist power."

Catholics had joined Evangelicals in voting for Jimmy Carter over Gerald Ford in 1976. Ford had been leading in the polls among Catholics during the campaign, until he committed a gaff comparable to Carter's at Notre Dame in 1977. In a televised debate one month before the 1976 election, Ford stated, "there was no Soviet domination of Eastern Europe" and the "Poles [did not] consider themselves dominated by the Soviet Union." Ethnic Catholic voters, like many others, were horrified and lost their enthusiasm for Ford. Evangelicals and Southerners were undoubtedly swayed by the prospect of having one of their own in the White House. This was in spite of where Carter stood on the cultural and social issues that were rapidly emerging as crucial to socially conservative voters. Catholics were evidently ready to continue their support of the Republican nominee, as they had backed Nixon in two previous elections. That is, until President Ford convinced them he just "didn't get it."

John Paul II was the first pontiff to visit the White House when Carter

13. O'Sullivan, *The President*, 48.
14. Ibid.
15. Ibid.

welcomed him in 1979. Carter met with the pope the following year in the Vatican.

Ronald Reagan, who had been a Cold Warrior since his days as president of the Screen Actors Guild, was perfectly suited to take advantage of Carter's foreign-policy problems. Reagan spoke with a black-and-white moral and spiritual clarity about the role of the United States in challenging atheistic totalitarianism. Like John Paul II, Reagan viewed the threat of Communism as a spiritual evil as well as a political one.[16] Both John Paul II and Reagan believed they had been saved from the assassin's bullet in order to bring an end to the Soviet Union. As reported by Carl Bernstein, this mutual understanding is something they shared with each other during their meeting at the Vatican in June 1982. According to George Weigel, however, Bernstein exaggerated the coordinated effort they agreed on to support Solidarity and liberate Poland from Soviet occupation.[17] The Holy Father himself, when asked about it, replied it was an "a posteriori hypothesis."

Given the level of agreement between Reagan and John Paul II on the Soviet threat, it is easy to see how Bernstein came to this conclusion. William Clark, a close Reagan advisor, an even closer friend, and an ardent Catholic, said they shared "a unity of spiritual view and a unity of vision on the Soviet Empire; that right or correctness would ultimately prevail in their divine plan."[18]

Reagan met with John Paul II four times, twice in the Vatican and twice in the United States. He thought the relationship with the Vatican so important that he ignored Protestant fears and established formal diplomatic relations. When Evangelicals got upset about this decision, Reagan sought help from Billy Graham to calm them down. Having his own man in the Vatican was a great help to Reagan in offsetting his troublesome relationship with the U.S. Catholic Conference.

16. Paul Kengor, *God and Ronald Reagan* (New York: Regan, 2004), 86–87.

17. George Weigel, *Witness to Hope: The Biography of Pope John Paul II* (New York: HarperCollins, Inc., 1999), 441.

18. "The Pope and the President: A Key Advisor Reflects on the Reagan Administration," *Catholic World Report* (November 1999).

PRESIDENT REAGAN'S POPE

John Paul II, the former cardinal of Krakow, survivor of both Nazi and Communist occupations, became symbolic of everything Reagan stood for and Carter did not. The combination of gravitas and intellectual power projected by John Paul II made President Carter, and his sentimentalized Evangelicalism, look small of stature on the world stage. The candidacy of Ronald Reagan with its uncompromising challenges to the Soviet Union and its Eastern bloc resonated in the public mind with the pope's historic trip to Poland in June 1979. During that trip, one-third of Poland's population turned out to see the first Polish pope, and this visit resulted in a weakening of the Soviet regime and generated the creation of the Solidarity movement. Ten years later, the Berlin Wall would fall, and Mikhail Gorbachev would agree to free elections in Poland.

John Paul II's anti-Communism was only the first way he had an impact on American politics. His impact on foreign policy eventually reached beyond Europe into Central America and the Caribbean, where Reagan confronted Marxist insurgencies in Nicaragua, El Salvador, and Grenada. Before his summer visit of 1982, two Reagan advisors, both Catholic, CIA director Bill Casey and Ambassador Vernon Walters, had briefed John Paul II on the administration's plans for opposing the spread of Marxism in these regions. The pope was well acquainted with the influence of Catholic Marxists in those areas who taught liberation theology. He had already fired a warning shot at liberation theology on his first pilgrimage to Mexico in his Puebla speech in January 1979. He called atheistic humanism "the drama of people severed from an essential dimension of their being." He followed this with a clear reference to liberation theology and Marxist dictators: "Faced with many other forms of humanism, which frequently are locked into a strictly economic, biological, or psychological view of the human being, the Church has the right and the duty to proclaim the truth about the human being that it received from its teacher, Jesus Christ. God grant that no external coercion will prevent the Church from doing so."

John Paul II's rejection of liberation theology was internationally broadcast in his rebuke of Ernesto Cardenal on the airport tarmac in Managua. Cardenal was a monk and a "poet" of liberation theology who had been enlisted by the Sandinistas to serve as their minister of culture. The videotape and photography of the Holy Father lecturing him and refusing to allow the kneeling Cardenal to kiss his ring sent a clear message around the world. The new pontiff was not making any compromise with the Marxism that had slain millions in his homeland and Eastern Europe.

That image no doubt helped Reagan win the support of American Catholics for his anti-Communist initiative in Central America. Catholics had been made wary of Contra groups funded by the administration when a right-wing guerrilla group killed four Maryknoll nuns. Still, the Religious Right to this day has ambivalent feelings about the presidents they have helped to elect. The inability of George W. Bush to win the war in Iraq after four years has left some religious conservatives disappointed, not in his policy but in his ability to respond effectively to terrorism. His father, George H. W. Bush, going into the 1992 election was considered "squishy" on issues such as gay rights.[19]

Even Ronald Reagan, whom many call the greatest president of the twentieth century, comes in for criticism. Ralph Reed commented that under Reagan, there was not a "day-to-day direction of policy" in the social-conservative direction. Paul Weyrich said, "Reagan was not terribly effective, and he did not accomplish much." For Phyllis Schlafly, "He was not ideological but was genuinely pro-life. Mexico City was his only legislation for the pro-life cause; on ERA he did nothing." Steve Wagner, author of the *Crisis* Catholic Voter Project, told me, "Reagan did not systematically engage in crafting an articulation of social renewal agenda, and that was disappointing. The Mexico City Policy was extremely important, but there was not an aggressive approach to life issues or broader social issues." I asked Richard Viguerie what he thought of Ronald Reagan: "In my opinion, he basically delivered symbolism. I think, privately, most Religious Right leaders would acknowledge that." Most of the lead-

19. Lawrence I. Barrett, "Pulpit Politics," *Time* (August 31, 1992).

ers I interviewed admitted that Reagan's greatest contribution was his personal support of the movement, not what he delivered in the way of policy and legislation."

What's remarkable about the legacy of Reagan is that he is so admired and, at the same time, is considered to have delivered very little on issues important to the Religious Right. Viguerie's "symbolism" seems too weak to explain the gratitude that movement leaders have for Reagan. Weyrich told me a story, and evidently there are many of these, that explains the continuing respect for the Reagan presidency. It cannot be added to the policy column or the legislative column, but it had a huge impact on bringing religious conservatives into the GOP and empowering the Religious Right. "Just before he was shot, Reagan held a lunch for over twenty social conservatives in the White House. The staff told him not to bring up the abortion issue. The president walked in and said, 'I want to talk to you about the abortion issue. I made a mistake in California, and it has led to some terrible things, and I want to rectify it.' The staff was horrified. He had an inherent belief." This difference of opinion in the Reagan White House regarding religious conservatives created a formidable barrier for staff aligned with the new Religious Right.

KNOCK-DOWN, DRAG-OUT

The Reagan White House was a place where the newly emerging movement of religious conservatives could connect with the president, meet with his staff, speak their minds, and, for the first time in modern history, feel part of an American presidency. What was predicted for the Carter years came to pass with Reagan. As seen in Weyrich's story, the relationship that was built over the two terms of Reagan's presidency was not without its detractors inside the White House. The coalition with the Religious Right was established in the face of internal resistance from members of Reagan's inner circle. "Every day was a knock-down, drag-out struggle," says Faith Whittlesey, who headed Reagan's Office of Public Liaison from 1983 to 1985.

Whittlesey was experienced in grassroots politics before taking the job in the Reagan administration. She held the highest elected position of any woman in Pennsylvania and was cochair of the state campaign for Reagan. She took the job of public liaison because of "a profound sense of obligation to the grassroots voters who had elected Reagan believing him to be a man of deep principle and traditional faith."

Whittlesey used her office to promulgate Reagan's social conservatism, including the pro-life message. She earned the nickname the "Joan of Arc of the Reagan White House," in spite of, as she admits, her somewhat fallen-away Protestant condition at that period in her life. "We had briefings in Room 450 every day. We gave the choir its music. We gave this music to the activists in the Religious Right to go out and sing across the country." (Room 450 is the large meeting space in the Old Executive Office Building adjacent to the West Wing used for large group briefings.)

From her first day on the job, Whittlesey met with opposition from members of Reagan's staff loyal to Vice President Bush and connected to Washington insiders. These included James Baker, Ken Duberstein, David Gergen, Jim Ciccione, Frank Donatelli, Fred Fielding, Ed Rollins, Craig Fuller, and Dick Deaver. Others wanted the president to pursue social and life issues: Ed Meese, Bill Clark, Bill Casey, Robert Reilly, Bruce Chapman, Michael Horowitz, Carl Anderson, Mona Charen, Josh Gilder, Morton Blackwell, Ken Cribb, Stephen Galebach, and Ben Elliot.

Whittlesey says of the opposition's motives: "Baker and his allies were fearful of Reagan being marginalized. They were trying to protect Reagan from the antipathy of the Washington establishment." This group did everything it could to sideline initiatives about pro-life, aid to parochial schools (tuition tax credit), and school prayer. The same group thought Reagan would be viewed as a warmonger if he promoted SDI (Strategic Defense Initiative) and the fight against Communism in Central America. Whittlesey found the daily bureaucratic infighting to be fierce.

In 1983, she hired a young Catholic from Chicago working in United States Information Agency, Robert Reilly, to take over the Catholic portfolio under her direction. Reilly's job was outreach to the bishops, the Bishops Conference, and lay organizations such as the Knights of Columbus. "The whole public liaison because of Faith Whittlesey's leadership was really animated by one thing—the moral worth of the objectives we were pursuing. So there was an enormous sense of motivation to do the right thing."

Their zeal was particularly evident in the VHS copies they made of the antiabortion movie *The Silent Scream* to send to every member of Congress. In 1985, Reilly and Whittlesey planned on screening it for pro-life leaders in Room 450 on Lincoln's birthday. Former abortion doctor Bernard Nathanson was to speak to those gathered. When the Baker group found out, they tried to block the screening by saying it was "too contentious." The screening was held, and Reilly eventually got Congressman Henry Hyde to send out the videos to members of Congress.

Reilly recalls, "We were fully cognizant of the fact that if it were shown in the White House, it would create an enormous uproar. We prepared a letter from the president to each member of Congress about the film and its significance. It went to legal affairs, and we got a phone call saying we could send the videos. We went ahead with the event anyway. Faith, with her brilliant sense of theater, constructed two giant pyramids of the videos on either side of the stage from which Bernard Nathanson gave his speech, and the film was shown. The cameramen were on their knees filming the pyramids, and the story led the network news that night."

Going into the 1984 election, Reagan made his support for Whittlesey clear and his support for the pro-life position clear to Whittlesey. Ed Meese, Bill Clark, and Bill Casey did the work of protecting her from White House politics. Whittlesey recalled a time when she, Baker, and Reagan were riding in a limo together, and "Baker was telling the president about poll numbers on his pro-life position with the implication that his views were hurting him. It was one of the few times I saw Reagan express a twinge of irritation. He said to Baker, 'Jim, I do not care what the polls say. This is the right thing. Do it.'"

At that point, the Religious Right was thought to consist largely of Evangelicals. Catholics who had voted for Reagan were seen as Reagan Democrats, not a part of the Religious Right. Whittlesey points out that Evangelicals were credited for electing Reagan. However, it was mostly Catholics such as Bill Clark, Bill Casey, Richard Allen, General Vernon

Walters, Ambassador William Wilson (first Vatican ambassador), Constantine Menges, John Lenczowski, Bob Reilly, and Carl Anderson who drove foreign policy and lobbied for social issues inside the White House. (Speechwriter Ben Eliot, who converted later to Catholicism, also helped with the social agenda.) She explains that these people shared Reagan's understanding of the "spiritual nature" of the struggle with the Soviet Union. "Without the Catholic impetus, it is unlikely that Reagan would have won the Cold War. There was a Catholic vision informing Reagan's foreign policy. Catholics always seemed to be at the forefront of anti-Communism."[20]

These were also the people in the White House who supported the policy of resisting the expansion of Communism into Central America exported from Cuba. Whittlesey was puzzled by the lack of cooperation from officials at the Bishops Conference and the active opposition from the Jesuits and Maryknolls. She was also surprised to realize how many priests and nuns in the United States supported "liberation theology" armed struggles in Central America.

It was Reilly's task to stay in close touch with the Catholic Church in Nicaragua. "I knew in excruciating detail about the persecution of the Church in Nicaragua, and I thought it was a scandal that the Church in the U.S. was not speaking out about this more forcefully. It was no secret that the Bishops Conference staff in Washington was completely dominated by left-wing Democrats. We did get phone calls from several senior Church officials who expressed their embarrassment and their sorrow that this abuse had taken place. For example, the very brave Bishop Gracida from Corpus Christi actually came to the White House and gave a very stirring speech against the Sandinistas' persecution of the Church. I remember when I was talking with Cardinal Obando of Managua about the extent of the persecution. I said to him, "Why don't your brother bishops in the United States know about this and speak

20. Her contact with Catholics during these years eventually led Whittlesey to become a Roman Catholic. As she told me in the interview, "I saw in the pro-life movement how active Catholics were, how they were fighting against the UN, the Catholic Church, and why we need authority and hierarchy as protection from the flock."

about it?" He said very wryly, 'They must not be getting their mail.' I will never forget that."

NOT THE BISHOP'S PRESIDENT

I asked Reilly who was responsible for this deaf ear at the Conference at that time. "The intellectual guiding light at the Conference was Father Bryan Hehir." Hehir had been a fixture at the Conference from 1973. Between that time and 1992, he held positions as director of the Office of International Affairs, secretary of the Department of Social Development and World Peace, and counselor for social policy. In 2001, Hehir was made head of Catholic Charities USA, and in 2003, his ordinary, Archbishop Sean O'Malley, asked him to return to Boston to run Catholic Charities in the archdiocese. Reilly continues, "We brought Hehir over for a private chat, and I clearly remember Father Hehir's mantra that violence can never be used, regardless of the circumstances. No matter what sort of argument you would present him with, this was always the response. So there really wasn't much of a way to have a conversation with him."

Reilly continues, "You can contrast that with our meeting with Bishop Antonio Troyo Calderon from Costa Rica. I took him in to meet with the president. He was on edge and somewhat nervous, and Reagan was a Christian gentleman of the first order. He sat the archbishop in the wing-chair across from him by the fireplace in the Oval Office, and you could see within thirty seconds, he had turned him into an old friend. The archbishop was completely at ease in his presence." Calderon told Reagan that from his point of view, it was required to do whatever was necessary to prevent the Sandinistas from consolidating their control. As usual, the staff at the Bishops Conference was livid over his meeting with the president, grousing that Reilly had "sort of smuggled the bishop around them," as though they should be the exclusive port of entry.

I asked Reilly if he had any allies at the Conference. "No," he said.

Reilly's attempt to work with the Bishops Conference came to a frustrating end with a White House meeting between the Executive Committee of the Bishops Conference and the president on nuclear deterrence and disarmament. The Conference had already issued its statement "The Challenge of Peace," but Whittlesey and Reilly thought it best for the president to make his case to them directly. Reilly remembers that after the meeting, which covered a range of issues, the president of the Conference, Archbishop John May, in response to questions from the press, pulled out a piece of paper and read from it. "He gave a statement that had been written before any of the meetings had taken place. We considered that a betrayal. To say we considered that bad manners would be an understatement. You could have at least responded to what you had heard instead of giving a predigested tract that had been written at the Bishops Conference. In fact, that was typical. That was sort of our last straw in dealing with them. I don't believe we ever invited anybody from the Bishops Conference or staff again. We simply didn't trust them. The whole thing was a setup." Two of the most senior members of the U.S. bishops, also at the meeting, later called to apologize to Reagan.

Whittlesey was "surprised at some of the naïveté of the bishops," Cardinal Bernardin, in particular. "Bernardin was there, asking questions betraying a substantial lack of relevant military facts. It appeared that the bishops had never been briefed by a knowledgeable person—many had already taken negative positions."

Reagan's White House may not have had any allies at the Bishops Conference, but they had one in the Vatican: John Paul II. Emblematic of Reagan's building of relationships with religious conservatives was his decision that the United States should finally offer official recognition to the Vatican. This had been a hot-button issue in politics for many years, with mainline Protestants and Evangelicals strongly opposing it. Nixon had gotten close to offering recognition but pulled back under pressure. Whittlesey recalls being asked to hold a meeting at which she and Bob Reilly were tasked with telling Evangelical leadership that Reagan was sending an ambassador to the government of the Holy See. Reilly got the message from the leadership "that they couldn't embrace this, but they were not going to undertake any activity to oppose it." It was the dawning realization on the part of the Christian Right that Catholics were necessary as allies in real-life political struggles over abortion, pornography, and school prayer. Evangelicals realized a Protestant president was spending political capital to get something vital for Catholics so they could unify their effort to address the moral decline of the nation.

Things had gotten so bad in the 1970s that people who politically never worked together and may not have socialized together found themselves overcoming sectarian barriers. Whittlesey says of the meeting with Evangelicals about Vatican recognition, "It was quiet and cordial. There were absolutely no objections voiced. At the time, Evangelicals and Catholics were converging on the pro-life issue. We explained to the leaders that the president hoped that this would not be an issue because there were larger issues to address. We needed to join forces to defend our values against the aggressive secularism being imposed on our children by the courts. Whittlesey recalls being especially impressed with Jerry Falwell. "He understood the spiritual nature of the Cold War and how vital it was to our long-term national interests. For him, I had the very highest respect and admiration."

Like Whittlesey, Reilly was left deeply impressed by his years working with Reagan, "He was the real thing. He was a great man." As an example, he tells of a meeting in the Oval Office about school prayer. It was basically an opportunity to greet the president and get a picture taken. The press left the room. Reilly found himself in the Oval Office with ex-football player Rosey Grier, a few other former athletes, secret service agents, and Reagan. "Rosey Grier says, 'Let's not just talk about prayer, let's pray,' and as if on cue, they submerged the president under their huge paws. The secret service didn't quite know what to do. These athletes had the president submerged with their hands on his shoulders and head. Rosey Grier started praying, 'Lord God, thank you for bringing forth in this nation in this great time of need, this great man who is'— and he extemporized and went on and prayed for Reagan. It was profoundly moving and so well done. Then Rosey Grier stops, and all their hands melt away, and they step back. I'm looking at the president, and he raises his head, and tears are streaming down his face. There was no press—it was the real thing. That is what he evoked in people."

Whittlesey summarized the reasons she thinks Reagan was the greatest president of the twentieth century: "moral leadership; a commitment to principles; good humor in the face of attacks; did not create a list of enemies; and always thought the best of people." The most powerful moment she personally witnessed with Reagan was his 1985 meeting with then-president of the Switzerland Federation, Kurt Furgler, before his meeting in Geneva with Gorbachev. "Both were devout Christians, and they had a short exchange about the differences between the Soviet Union and the United States. They agreed that human rights in the nations of the West were believed to be conferred by God, while in the Soviet Union they were privileges granted by the state. On that occasion, Reagan confirmed for me his deep awareness of the spiritual struggle between the atheistic Soviet Union, and the United States."

The popularity of Ronald Reagan with Catholic voters in the face of hostility from the Catholic Conference signaled a loss of influence for the bishops and their staff in Washington. Through their two Conferences, founded in 1966, the bishops had hoped to amplify their voice in politics and increase their influence on policy and legislation. By pursuing agendas directly opposed to Reagan, who had the visible support of John Paul II, the Bishops Conference and the Catholic Conference made it obvious that they were closely aligned with the left wing of the Democratic Party. The Catholics who identified with the emerging movement of religious conservatives had found their leadership, and it wasn't at the Catholic Conference. He was in the White House.

11

SEPARATED BRETHREN NO MORE

RONALD REAGAN UNITED AND EMPOWERED RELIGIOUS CON-
servatives with a patriotism and religiosity that appealed
equally to cradle Catholics and Evangelicals. His vice president and successor, George H. W. Bush, was a different kind of political
figure. Bush was the epitome of the mainstream Protestant WASP, an
Episcopalian, a country-club Republican, and an avid golfer. In fact, the
"W" in his name stood for an ancestor named Walker who founded the
Walker Cup matches between the best amateur golfers of Great Britain
and the United States. He was called a Texan, but his entire demeanor
screamed Connecticut. Compared with the common-man appeal of
Reagan, Bush seemed aloof. As Reagan's second term wound down, Bush
faced the same problem that befell Pope Benedict XVI when he was
elected after the death of the charismatic John Paul II.

Given the differences between Reagan and Bush, it is remarkable that
the religious conservative movement continued to flourish as it did
under the forty-first president. Inside the Reagan White House, infighting divided the staff between the pro-lifers, mostly Catholic, and the
Bush loyalists who wanted to downplay the social issues, especially abortion. But Bush broke ranks with close advisors by converting on the pro-
life issue during the 1980 campaign. When the news of this conversion

spread through the pro-life community, it meant that the movement would continue the trajectory forward inside the GOP and continue to grow and mature with the help of the political party in the White House.

A MEETING IN KENNEBUNKPORT

When Dr. Jack Willke was elected president of National Right to Life in June 1980, his organization was small but influential. NRTL, founded seven years earlier, had a small staff and a budget of only $500,000 a year. As president, Willke commuted from his home in Cincinnati to his Washington, D.C., office every week and made regular visits to Reagan campaign headquarters in Arlington, where he met Reagan and got acquainted with close associates such as Ed Meese.

When Reagan chose the pro-abortion George H. W. Bush as his running mate, concern mounted in the pro-life ranks. Willke decided to do something about it. He went to the Pontchartrain Hotel in Detroit, where the Republican convention was being held, and knocked on the door of Bush's hotel room. Bill Casey, the future CIA director, answered and brought Willke in to meet Bush, who was sitting with several friends. Willke told the vice-presidential nominee, "We would like you to clarify your position on abortion." Bush chuckled and started to answer, but Willke held up his hand and interrupted: "I don't want to hear your position now." He asked if he could set up a time to brief him on the issue. Bush agreed to a thirty-minute meeting to be arranged when he returned to Washington.

"I need four hours," Willke responded.

"What?" Bush said with surprise.

Willke explained, "Please understand that we are not going to be able to support this ticket if you are directly opposed to Reagan."

Bush sat quietly for a moment, thinking. "Okay," he said, and invited Willke to meet him a few weeks later at the Bush family home in Kennebunkport.

In September 1980, Willke arrived in Kennebunkport with his PAC director Sandy Faucher, and set up his slide projector adjacent to a room where Barbara Bush was knitting. He went through his slides for three hours, showing Bush the stages of fetal development and the medical details of the abortion procedure. Willke responded to questions from Bush and one question from his wife ("What if she's raped?").

They took a break for lunch with Bush and his staff, where they discussed other political matters. When lunch was over, Willke reminded Bush about the question in Detroit that he wouldn't let him answer. "Now is the time for you to answer that question. Where are you on abortion and, particularly, on the Human Life Amendment?"

Willke remembers that Bush sat back in his chair and replied, "Well, I was not there before, but I am now. I will support an amendment to the Constitution to overturn *Roe* v. *Wade*. But it will have to be a *state's rights* amendment. I can't support a federal amendment." Willke reported the news of Bush's change of position in his NRTL newsletter and the Reagan-Bush ticket got the full support of the pro-life movement.

Eight years later, in June 1988, when Bush was running for president, Willke met with him again. This time Willke got almost all of what he wanted. Bush agreed to support for a *federal* version of the Human Life Amendment with exceptions for rape, incest, and the life of the mother. That, too, was announced in the National Right to Life newsletter in time to bolster to candidates pro-life credentials for the November election.

Once he was elected, Willke asked the new president for a thirty-minute meeting in the Oval Office. Bush asked him what he wanted to discuss. "I want to talk you out of that rape exception," said Willke. Bush met with Willke in February 1989. At the meeting, Willke spent the first twenty minutes trying to persuade him to change his mind on the rape exception. By the end of the meeting, Bush said, "You're probably right, Doc, but I'm still going to hold to the rape exception. I guess you might say it's a gut feeling of compassion for that woman."

Dr. Willke, though, was not yet through. He asked the president if he would agree to narrow the exception to "assault rape." He agreed, and Willke knew Bush had gone as far as he could go.

It was a determined Midwestern Catholic, brought up with the Baltimore Catechism, who convinced a WASP vice president from Connecticut to become pro-life.

With that decision, Bush made himself the legitimate successor to Ronald Reagan in the eyes of religious conservatives. Growing in number and influence, pro-lifers were having trouble connecting with Bush, the country-club Republican, but they could identify with his basic decency and his opposition to abortion. The Southern wing of the Religious Right embraced Bush, in part, because Dr. Willke, a Catholic active in the pro-life movement for ten years, doggedly pursued George H. W. Bush to change his mind. He did it by presenting the scientific facts about the life of the unborn child in the womb. It's a story of remarkable solidarity on a contentious issue, dividing not only political parties but religious denominations as well.

The Willke story illustrates one aspect of the advantage spawned by a Catholic-Evangelical coalition. It's a virtual reuniting of Christendom, wedding the use of reason in the Catholic tradition to the passionate commitment of Evangelical Christians. If an Evangelical had met with Bush to review the scriptural evidence condemning abortion, the result might not have been the same. While the Religious Right focused on Scripture for its message, Catholics such as Dr. Willke pushed the movement in the direction of employing more scientific and philosophical means of making public arguments. As one young Evangelical leader, Drew Ryun, told me, "The intellectual part of our movement comes from Catholics. This is gradually changing, but it is Catholics who have made us intellectually appealing."

This new Catholic-Evangelical alliance surprised me, given the experiences I had while attending a Southern Baptist church in college during the late '60s. The first Sunday-school class I attended in my Fort Worth church was taught by a student from Southwestern Baptist Theological Seminary. Using the blackboard, he illustrated the "idolatry" of Roman Catholic beliefs. Catholics, we were told, are not "saved." They worship Mary, not the true God. This kind of teaching, I found out, was often encountered in conservative Evangelical churches at that time, particularly among Fundamentalists. "Catholics are going to hell" was commonly heard in those days. Anti-Catholic pamphlets could be found in the vestibules of many Fundamentalist churches. The close ranks of Catholics and Evangelicals during the decades of the pro-life movement suppressed this attitude.

American Catholics had their own unhealthy attitude toward Evangelicals. In the '50s and '60s, Catholics, raised in urban areas with high concentrations of Italian and Irish immigrants, were taught to look at Protestants much the same way Fundamentalists looked at them. Catholics lived in close subcultures, and their children, almost without exception, attended Catholic schools. Well-intended nuns forbade any discussion of the Protestant faith, other than describing those practicing it as sadly separated from God and condemned to hell. Some nuns would instruct the students to turn their heads in the opposite direction when passing a Protestant church, so as not to be spiritually contaminated. (Most younger students were actually afraid of Protestants, because, though it was never said out loud, they got the distinct impression that Protestants were cursed by God.) Protestants deeply resented the implication that they were separated from the "true Church."

For Irish Catholic families whose parents and grandparents were born in Ireland, historical accounts of the centuries of enmity and anti-Catholic discrimination at the hands of the Protestant Parliament of Ireland continued to cause bitterness toward Protestants in heavily Irish-populated cities. This explains why John F. Kennedy's Irish heritage was just as important as his Catholicism in galvanizing the Catholic vote. But in the past forty years, much has happened to heal those divisions.

This moment of political collaboration between a Catholic obstetrician and a Protestant vice president signaled the diminution of a feud that began in the American colonies and came to a head in the aftermath of World War II. The religious culture of the postwar period holds the key to understanding the religious conflict the Evangelical and Catholic resurgence would later have to overcome.

HEAD CATHOLIC VERSUS
FIRST LADY WASP

In 1949, there was a very public fight between former first lady Eleanor Roosevelt and Cardinal Spellman, the archbishop of New York City. Catholics began challenging the accepted anti-Catholicism among Protestants after many years of "Catholics need not apply" signs. Catholics had been disproportionately represented in the armed services during World War II and in its aftermath were determined to pursue their piece of the American dream. After witnessing the death of so many sons and daughters of the Church, American Catholics just weren't going to countenance anti-Catholic habits of an earlier generation. When the moment came, it pitted Eleanor Roosevelt against the venerable Cardinal Spellman.

Spellman's willingness to take on an old friend, the imposing Mrs. Roosevelt, in a public shouting match was a turning point for American Catholics. In the late '40s, Mrs. Roosevelt was easily the most admired and influential woman in America. Cardinal Spellman, archbishop since 1939, was one of the two best-known religious leaders (the other being the young evangelist Billy Graham).

The brief but intense battle over the allocation of federal money to educate Catholic children exposed the prejudice and resulting social inequities that Catholics needed to overcome if they ever hoped to reach social parity with their Christian brethren.

In fact, public money was first allocated to the earliest public schools (called "common schools") in the 1840s, when discriminatory attitudes of the Protestant majority became embodied in public policy. The discriminatory policy of denying public money to Catholic schools was particularly upsetting, because the curriculum of the common schools contained undisguised bias against Catholic immigrants.

In his 1948 presidential campaign, Harry Truman called for federal aid to public schools. For Democrats, it was a repeat of its position in 1944 under President Roosevelt, when the Democratic Party called for allocating federal money to education (FDR died April 12, 1945). In

their 1948 platforms, both parties had expressed support for the principle of federal aid to education.[1]

On January 9, 1949, a federal aid-to-education bill was introduced in
the Senate with a bipartisan report. It requested $300 million to equalize
educational opportunities among states and territories, including an option for states to allocate funds to private or parochial schools. Equitable
distribution was also mandated for segregated African-American
schools. The bill passed the Senate 58-15 on May 5 and went to the House
Committee on Labor and Public Welfare (a nearly identical bill had
passed in the Senate nine months earlier). Support for the bill came from
both parties and from both Protestant and Catholic senators. This level
of bipartisanship is surprising given that only 7 of 98 Catholics in the
81st Congress were Republican. One of the two Catholics opposing the
bill was Senator Joseph R. McCarthy of Wisconsin.

On the same day, an amendment that would have eliminated aid to
parochial schools was defeated 71-3. The Senate clearly supported federal funding for parochial schools. The committee chair was a Catholic
from Michigan, John Lesinski. His home district of Detroit had the highest percentage of parochial-school children in the nation. Lesinski appointed Graham A. Barden, a Presbyterian from North Carolina, to chair
a subcommittee to conduct hearings on the bill. Barden's district was
rural and Protestant, devoid of a Catholic constituency. His subcommittee revised the bill, eliminating the requirement for segregated schools
and the limiting of federal funds to public schools.

No one seemed to notice the subcommittee's changes until June 19,
when Cardinal Spellman, speaking at Fordham University, named
Barden as the "new apostle of bigotry."[2] Spellman said those who refused
federal aid to parochial schools were part of a "craven crusade of reli-

1. *National Party Platforms,* ed. Donald Bruce Johnson (Urbana: University of Illinois Press,
1956), 433, 453.
2. Philip A. Grant, Jr., "Catholic Congressmen, Cardinal Spellman, Eleanor Roosevelt and the
1949–1950 Federal Aid to Education Controversy." *American Catholic Historical Society of Philadelphia Records* 90 (1979), 4.

gious prejudice against Catholic schoolchildren and their inalienable rights."[3]

Spellman's outburst got the attention of Chairman Lesinski. Eight days later, Lesinski accused Barden of writing an "anti-Catholic" and "anti-Negro" bill "dripping with bigotry and racial prejudice." The Catholic House Majority leader, John W. McCormack of Massachusetts, vowed to lead opposition to the bill, calling it "grossly unfair," and predicted it would die in committee. It was at that moment the presidential widow, Eleanor Roosevelt, chimed in. In her newspaper column on June 23, she insinuated that the cardinal, not Congressman Barden, was responsible for starting the controversy. American citizens, she wrote, were being accused of prejudice because "We do not want to see public education connected with religious control of our schools."[4]

Mrs. Roosevelt was publicly opposing the position of her own party and indirectly criticizing members of Congress from her home state. She reiterated on July 8 that she did not want "church groups controlling the schools of our country." But a week later (July 15), she backed away from her earlier criticism, saying she had not read the Barden bill carefully. What she meant to say was that she was not arguing for or against any particular bill.

Cardinal Spellman was not satisfied with Mrs. Roosevelt's half-hearted retraction. On July 21, Spellman sent a seventeen-paragraph letter to Mrs. Roosevelt that was released by the chancery the following day. Spellman wrote that Catholic children have the right to qualify for federal aid and added: "Your record of anti-Catholicism stands for all of us to see—a record which you yourself wrote on the pages of history which cannot be recalled—documents of discrimination unworthy of an American mother." The cardinal concluded the letter by saying, "I shall not again publicly acknowledge you."[5] Spellman's gutsy leadership

3. Ibid.

4. Eleanor Roosevelt, *My Day: The Best of Eleanor Roosevelt's Acclaimed Newspaper Columns, 1936–1962*, ed. David Emblidge and Marcy Ross (Cambridge, Mass.: Da Capo Press, 2001). Her newspaper column was published six days a week from 1935 to 1962, with an audience of more than 4 million readers.

5. Grant, "Catholic Congressmen," 5.

ushered in a new era. Bigotry against Catholics would no longer be tolerated. Catholics were grateful that the cardinal had the courage to acknowledge Roosevelt's acumen as discrimination. This "calling out" by a Catholic prelate of a public figure, the widow of the United States' most revered president, had never been done before—and it has rarely been done since.

The ensuing debates in the House started on June 28, with Congressman Charles A. Buckley of New York commending Spellman on the House floor. Three other Catholic congressmen introduced an alternative bill, including the young Congressman John F. Kennedy of Massachusetts. His compromise version guaranteed auxiliary services for children in parochial schools, such as bus transportation. The executive session of the committee convened in August but was completely deadlocked between the Barden and Lesinski factions. Hearings did not resume until January, and the committee steadily met until mid-March.

On March 6, Mrs. Roosevelt and Barden made a joint appearance at an education conference in New York City. Barden accused the Catholic hierarchy of injecting the religious issue and branded Spellman a "cruel authoritarian" for insulting the former first lady.[6] Roosevelt reiterated her opposition to the funding, including that for the auxiliary services supported by Congressman Kennedy.

Spellman, on an extended visit to the Vatican at the time, returned to questions from reporters on March 22 about Barden's remarks. The cardinal kept it candid: "It was un-American that any Federal law be passed disposing of Federal monies for auxiliary services and depriving American children of these public facilities."[7]

Spellman was aware of Kennedy's attempt to forge a compromise and added, "Now they are attempting to keep Catholic children off public transportation facilities. Tomorrow they will keep us out of the public libraries, the public gardens, and perhaps off the sidewalks if they continue using the same logic they are using in the manner of bus transportation."

6. Ibid., 7.
7. Ibid., 9.

The committee defeated the Kennedy proposal 16–9, as well as Barden's version 21–3, denying both aid to parochial schools and a mandate for segregated schools. Eventually, on March 14, the committee defeated the Senate version 13–12, with, of all things, Lesinski voting with Barden against the bill. When all was said and done, the federal aid-to-education bill never made it to the floor.

The spat between Spellman and Roosevelt ended with a reconciliation of sorts. Roosevelt's niece recalls visiting her famous aunt at the Val-Kill Cottage in Hyde Park. Niece and aunt, both named Eleanor, were sitting together when a black limousine pulled up to the front door. The only scheduled appointment that morning was with the pest exterminator. A knock came at the door, and when the butler opened it, there stood a chauffer announcing the arrival of Cardinal Spellman. The niece was well aware of the feud over Catholic schools in the previous months. To have the cardinal appear unannounced at her doorstep must be a statement of truce. Eleanor Roosevelt graciously received the cardinal, taking him into the living room for coffee and conversation. "She later reported they spoke of trivialities for an hour before he took his leave and the long, black limousine slid out of the narrow country road that served as driveway to the simple abode of the first lady of the world."[8]

A PROTESTANT NATION

It must not have been easy for Cardinal Spellman to knock on Eleanor Roosevelt's door. Protestant families of wealth and influence had been the main obstacle to the integration of Catholics into American society since the colonial period. President Roosevelt himself had consciously brought Catholics into his political coalition and his administration.[9] It may have been FDR's record that took Spellman out to Hyde Park that day.

8. "Eleanor Roosevelt's Niece Eleanor Roosevelt II Remembers Val-Kill," http://www.nps.gov/archive/elro/what-is-vk/family-memories/roosevelt-eleanor-2.htm

9. George Q. Flynn, *American Catholics & the Roosevelt Presidency, 1932–1936* (Lexington: University of Kentucky Press, 1968).

Spellman was the leader of America's Catholics at a time when they enjoyed their first moment of ascendancy in a Protestant nation. Anti-Catholic prejudice had been brought to the colonies with the very first settlers who were deeply entrenched in the culture that would become the United States of America. Most of the early inhabitants of the New World were from Great Britain, where violence and hatred against Catholics was two hundred years old. Even though many of the early settlers were themselves targets of religious persecution, their own desire for tolerance did not extend to welcoming those practicing "popery." The American idea of freedom was born in the crucible of suspicion toward Catholics in the New World.

In 1776, Catholics made up a small percentage of the population. Where they were most numerous, in the middle colonies, Catholics represented only 4.2 percent of the population. In New England and the Southern colonies, the numbers fell below 1 percent. There were 56 Catholic parishes, compared with 668 Congregational churches, 533 Presbyterian, 497 Baptist, 495 Episcopal, and so on. Quakers had 310 congregations.[10] In that same year, only one Catholic signature, among the fifty-six, could be found at the bottom of the Declaration of Independence, attorney Charles Carroll of Maryland.[11]

As long as the Catholic community remained small in number, the imported fear of Catholics was accepted more as a fact of life than a heated public issue. But with the huge influx of nineteenth-century Catholic immigrants, predominantly Irish, anti-Catholicism became a rallying cry used by social and political leaders to check the potential power and influence of the new immigrants. The public-school movement itself, launched in the 1840s, was an undisguised attempt to sub-

10. Roger Finke and Rodney Stark, *The Churching of America, 1776–2005: Winners and Losers in Our Religious Economy* (New Brunswick, N.J.: Rutgers University Press, 2005), 33.

11. Maryland had, in fact, been founded by Lord Baltimore, the former Cecilius Calvert, a Catholic convert, as refuge for Catholic settlers who were not welcome in the other colonies. Through the Toleration Act of 1649, Lord Baltimore ensured that Maryland provided Protestants, even Puritans, the same religious freedom Catholics enjoyed. This is not to say Maryland was a paradise of tolerance by contemporary standards. Anyone who did believe in the Trinity could be put to death.

vert the growing power of immigrant Catholics. Protestants wanted to place their children in an educational environment saturated with Protestant culture and anti-Catholic jibes.

Horace Mann, the godfather of American public schools, wanted to protect the dominant Protestant culture from the influence of newly arrived Catholics and their "priestcraft." [12] For the first time, however, the Catholic minority did not remain silent. Two public debates arose over money and the Bible. State funding was denied to Catholic schools on the grounds that they were "sectarian," the obvious irony being that the first "common schools" of New York City were explicitly Protestant in their outlook and curriculum. [13] (Federal funding for elementary and secondary schools did not begin until a century later.)

The second debate, and by far the loudest, was over which translation of the Bible would be used in the common schools. The Protestants who controlled New York City's common schools insisted that all students read the King James translation, which had been the standard English version among Protestants for two centuries. [14] Having been translated under a Protestant regime, the King James version was prepared with an eye to disproving the authority of the Catholic Church. Catholics, however, used the Douay-Rheims translation. This translation was completed by English Catholics, all graduates of Oxford, after they had fled to Europe during the sixteenth-century persecution and founded an English college in Douay, Flanders. (Because of political conflicts, the scholars were forced to work in Rheims for a time, thus the complete title of

12. Charles Leslie Glenn, *The Myth of the Common School* (Amherst: University of Massachusetts Press, 1988), 83.

13. The powerful Protestant elites who controlled the public funding through the Public School Society and denied financial support to the Catholic Christians did not recognize their own "sectarian" interests in educating Catholic children according to their view of the Christian tradition. Catholics objected that they had the right to teach their children according to their own values. But that was exactly what the leaders of the common schools wanted to avoid. They made no attempt to hide their intention to instill Protestantism into the children of immigrant parents.

14. The Supreme Court of Maine in *Donahoe* v. *Richards* (1854) ruled that a school board had the legal and constitutional right to expel a child from school for refusing to read the Bible used by the school.

the translation.) Their source was the Latin version of the Scriptures called the Vulgate, not the original Greek and Hebrew texts.

The Douay-Rheims New Testament was published in 1582, but both testaments did not appear together in English until 1609. This makes it older than the King James Version, which was not published until 1611. The Douay-Rheims translators appended their work with a series of articles intended to answer the charges of the Reformers against Catholics.

The King James translators responded by making reference to the earlier version in their preface: "We have shunned the obscurity of the Papists." As a side note, it should be added that not all Protestants objected to the work of the Catholic scholars in exile. Protestant editions of the Douay-Rheims translation appeared, one as early as 1589, as well as one in the United States in 1834.

Bishop John Hughes of New York City led the fight against the Protestant-dominated common schools and, specifically, the use of the King James translation. "Dagger John," as he was called, was successful in forming an alliance with Governor Seward that led to stripping the Public School Society of its control over public funding. However, the board of education and the school board taking over from the Society were also dominated by Protestants. Anti-Catholic policies remained in place, including the required reading of the King James translation.

The ensuing riots in New York were mild compared with those in Philadelphia over the same issue. Bishop Francis Patrick Kendrick had requested that Catholic students be exempted from reading the King James Version. The local school committee agreed, leading to a series of riots in 1884 by anti-Catholic leaders. These riots killed thirteen people, burned five churches, and forced the bishop to leave the city.

The beginning of the public schools led directly to a surge in the number of parochial schools. The Catholic hierarchy moved to protect children from the evangelical techniques of these public schools. By 1840, there were eight Catholic schools in New York City, serving about 5,000 children.

The Second Plenary Council of Baltimore (1866) mandated that Catholic parents must send their children to parochial schools if they were available, and if they were not, should provide catechism to those children who attend public schools. It was a requirement for lay trustees of a parish to send their children to Catholic schools.

The Catholic subculture, sometimes called a "ghetto," of newly arrived immigrants thus received ecclesial sanction in an attempt to avoid government-supported Protestant proselytizing through public schools.

In spite of Catholic protest, the evangelical mission of public schools to reeducate Catholic children, while denying Catholic schools public funds, soon became institutionalized in law by the so-called Blaine Amendment. Congressman James B. Blaine was speaker of the U.S. House of Representatives in 1875, when he proposed an amendment to the Constitution that would prohibit the use of state funds for "sectarian" schools. The amendment passed the House 180-7 but failed in the Senate by four votes.

Supporters of the Blaine Amendment rallied in the individual states and succeeded in passing amendments to thirty-seven state constitutions ensuring that public funds would be denied to Catholic schools. New states that subsequently entered the Union were required to have the "Blaine language" in their proposed constitutions. Sixteen states still have Blaine amendments, in spite of Catholic efforts to eliminate them.

Anti-Catholicism of the sort seen in the public-school movement and the Blaine amendments was not an anomaly of American life. And it was not confined to the nineteenth century. The public-school riots were only the beginning of the high tide of anti-Catholic discrimination that lasted from 1850 to 1930. In 1854, the Know-Nothing or American Party formed, evolving from the Order of the Star Spangled Banner, a secret patriotic association. The American Protective Association was created in 1887, and the second founding of the Ku Klux Klan in 1915 was directed against Catholics as well as African-Americans.[15]

After World War II, with the surge of confidence among American

15. The Ku Klux Klan boasted of having 5 million members and was a serious factor in the presidential election of 1928 between Herbert Hoover and the Catholic Al Smith. At its peak in the mid-1920s, its membership was estimated at 4 million to 5 million. Although the actual figures were probably much smaller, the Klan nevertheless declined rapidly to an estimated 30,000 by 1930. The Klan spirit, however, was a factor in breaking the Democratic hold on the South in 1928, when Smith became that party's presidential candidate.

Catholics, anti-Catholicism was forced to take a different turn. The specifically Protestant objections to the Catholic faith were transposed into the advocacy of secularism and opposition to the specter of the pope exercising political power in the United States through a Catholic voting bloc. The most influential example of this is Paul Blanchard who founded Americans United for the Separation of Church and State in 1947 and published his widely read *American Freedom and Catholic Power* in 1929. Catholics were no longer on the outside of powerful institutions, no longer an oppressed minority. Blanchard called for a "resistance movement" to prevent the Catholic hierarchy from "imposing its social policies upon our schools, hospitals, government, and family organization," which sounds as if it could have been written today.[16] Like today's critics of the Religious Right, Blanchard claimed he was protecting democracy.

PRACTICAL AGREEMENT, THEORETICAL FRUSTRATION

A milestone in the acceptance of Catholics in American culture was the popularity of Pope John Paul II. The old Protestant objections to the Catholic Church were taken over by Evangelical Fundamentalists in the postwar period. But John Paul II started to make headway in breaking down even these barriers. He spoke with the zeal of an evangelist, in the language of a biblical scholar, and with the depth of a Catholic intellectual. He appealed to everybody, except the secular left. His leadership energized the pro-life movement, the religious conservatives who supported Reagan and the Bushes, and the growing cooperation between Evangelicals and Catholics. Where theologians had limited success in building consensus, John Paul II broke down the barriers with the rallying cry to build a "culture of life."

As noted previously, one of the reasons given by Evangelicals for their late entrance into the debate over *Roe* v. *Wade* in 1973 was their view that abortion was a "Catholic issue." At the moment John Paul II became

---

16. Paul Blanchard, *American Freedom and Catholic Power* (Boston: Beacon Press, 1949), 303.

pope, the Evangelical community began to engage in the pro-life movement, joining forces with Catholics who had led the movement from the beginning. The Evangelicalism of the new pontiff greased the skids of that political cooperation.

John Paul II, elected to the papacy at the age of fifty-eight, was athletic, energetic, and beloved. He traveled to 129 countries, more than any pope in the 2000-year history of the Church. His genuine affection for youth inspired and anchored an entire generation. Hundreds of thousands of young people would travel from all over the world to participate in the series of International World Youth Days, sleeping outside, worshiping the Blessed Sacrament, praying the rosary, and participating in the closing liturgy with John Paul II.

Through the inspiration and leadership of the pope, many lay theological and political initiatives were made between Catholics and Evangelicals, bound by their shared impatience with the cultural rebellion against God, both outside and inside Christendom. John Paul II empowered the growing voice of religious conservatives in the public square by addressing theology of the body, sexuality, marriage, family, chastity, celibacy, and prohibitions against contraception and abortion.[17]

Symbiosis between Catholics and Evangelicals was further nurtured when Evangelical leaders spoke openly about their respect for John Paul II. Billy Graham was quoted in *Time* saying, "Pope John Paul II will go down in history as the greatest of our modern Popes. He's been the strong conscience of the whole Christian world."

If it were not for the growing allegiance of so many Catholic and Evangelical groups, the left would have much less to fear. Nothing terrifies the left as much as the prospect of Evangelicals and conservative

17. At the United Nations General Assembly in October 1995, John Paul II spoke about the binding relationship of freedom to truth. "Freedom is not simply the absence of tyranny or oppression. Nor is freedom a license to do whatever we like. Freedom has an inner 'logic' which distinguishes it and ennobles it: freedom is ordered to the truth, and is fulfilled in man's quest for truth and in man's living in the truth. Detached from the truth about the human person, freedom deteriorates into license in the lives of individuals, and, in political life, it becomes the caprice of the most powerful and the arrogance of power. Far from being a limitation upon freedom or a threat to it, reference to the truth about the human person—a truth universally knowable through the moral law written on the hearts of all—is, in fact, the guarantor of freedom's future."

Catholics joining forces in politics. The prospect of 30 million voters consistently supporting the GOP is exactly what forced Democrats into taking a new approach to religious outreach in the 2006 election. Catholics and Evangelicals have slowly learned to work together over the past forty years. They have, in large measure, put aside their theological disagreements to pursue practical ends. This process began during the ERA fight and the pro-life movement when they were told by leaders such as Phyllis Schlafly and Reverend James Robison to just "get over it."

Thus far, no explicitly cooperative effort on a national scale has emerged between Evangelicals and Catholics. (Prospective initiatives are always being discussed.) It has been what Southern Baptist theologian Timothy George calls an "ecumenism of the trenches."[18] Since the Second Vatican Council, Catholics have been taught to look upon Protestants as Christian brethren but *separated* brethren.[19] When Catholics walk alongside Evangelicals in the annual March for Life in Washington, D.C., "separated" seems to be a misnomer.

Although there has been no organizational melding of the two Christian communities, there has been an ongoing effort to resolve their theological differences. Father Richard Neuhaus, a Lutheran who converted to Catholicism, and Chuck Colson, an Evangelical of Prison Fellowship, led a group of twenty-one Evangelicals and twenty Catholics in an attempt to define areas of practical and theological agreement. They produced three documents under the name Evangelicals and Catholics Together in 1994, 1997, and 2002. The first ECT statement called for cooperation and an end to the antagonism and suspicion dividing the

18. Laurie Goodstein, "How the Evangelicals and Catholics Joined Forces," *New York Times,* May 30, 2004, 4.4.

19. "It is the urgent wish of this Holy Council that the measures undertaken by the sons of the Catholic Church should develop in conjunction with those of our separated brethren so that no obstacle be put in the ways of divine Providence and no preconceived judgments impair the future inspirations of the Holy Spirit. The Council moreover professes its awareness that human powers and capacities cannot achieve this holy objective—the reconciling of all Christians in the unity of the one and only Church of Christ. It is because of this that the Council rests all its hope on the prayer of Christ for the Church, on our Father's love for us, and on the power of the Holy Spirit. And hope does not disappoint, because God's love has been poured into our hearts through the Holy Spirit, who has been given to us." "Unitatis Redintegratio" (Decree on Ecumenism, 1964), par. 24.

major bodies of Christendom: "The two communities in world Christianity that are most evangelistically assertive and most rapidly growing are Evangelicals and Catholics. In many parts of the world the relationship between these communities is marked more by conflict than by cooperation, more by animosity than by love, more by suspicion than by trust, more by propaganda and ignorance than by respect for the truth."[20]

ECT was a tough sell in the Fundamentalist wing of the Evangelical movement. Respected ministers such as F. James Kennedy, John MacArthur, R. C. Sproul, and John Ankerberg criticized the initiative as a flawed attempt at consensus to debunk the Reformation as a needless conflict, saying, "We wish they would discard it."[21] While agreeing that political collaboration on moral and social issues is attainable, they felt the statements were ambiguous affirmations made to appear as though the dispute over the doctrine of "justification by faith alone" (*sola fide*) was ancillary to the objective of theological unity between Catholics and Evangelicals. Other theological differences between Evangelicals and the teachings of the Catholic Church which must not be minimized include: justification involves faith, human effort, and merit; water baptism as a sacrament of regeneration; the authority of the pope has equal validity with the Bible; and the Virgin Mary, saints, and clergy are mediators between the faithful and God.

Even if the ECT effort has exposed the divisions that still remain, it also has helped support further cooperation on the practical level. In both of George W. Bush's presidential campaigns and terms in the White House, lobbying for the federal marriage amendment, and the furor over Bush's nomination of Supreme Court justices, there were levels of cooperation between Catholics and Evangelicals that were far more deliberate than in the past. In other words, it wasn't a matter of gathering anti-ERA or antiabortion activists and finding out later that they were one denomination or the other. These efforts were deliberately designed

20. "Evangelicals and Catholics Together: The Christian Mission in the Third Millennium," *First Things*, April 1994, introduction.

21. "Evangelical-Catholic Pact Questioned," *The Christian Century*, March 15, 1995.

to bring the combined influence of Catholics and Evangelicals to bear on the same goal. The presence of a religious conservative in the White House took religious coalition building to an entirely new level.

THE COALITION OF THE FUTURE

Manny Miranda, a Catholic and a graduate of Georgetown University, was working in a senior staff position for Senator Orrin Hatch when the debate over judicial nominations began in earnest. The debate was particularly infuriating for religious conservatives. Judge Charles Pickering, who had been president of the Mississippi Southern Baptist Convention, was accused of being "too pious." Leon Holmes, a Catholic nominated for a district court in Arkansas, was ridiculed for citing the "Letter to the Ephesians" in an article on marriage for a Catholic publication. Judge William Pryor, a Catholic from Alabama, was a member of the Knights of the Holy Sepulchre of Jerusalem, an organization supporting Christians living in the Holy Land. When it came time for his hearing before the Senate Judiciary Committee, Democratic staffers were passing around a printout on pro-life from the Web site of the Knights of Columbus. As Miranda said, "Evidently, they couldn't keep the different Knights straight, or it didn't make any difference as long as they were Catholic and pro-life."

Miranda says what really ignited the effort was the attack on Pickering. It led to the unprecedented act of the Southern Baptist Convention to pass a resolution on March 15, 2002, calling for an up or down vote on judicial nominees. The White House initiated a series of conference calls led by Tim Goeglein to create a coalition of support for judges. But Miranda wanted to do more. He irritated the White House when he started holding these calls on his own. "We needed to function on our own. There was no way we could influence the White House or Senate without being independent." In the spring of 2003, working with other conservative leaders, Miranda created the Umbrella Group. "We took our Evangelicals, who were already engaged, added a Catholic list, and publicly raised the issue of a religious test for judges."

The controversy around Leon Holmes provided the perfect opening. Holmes had already been through an uneventful Senate hearing when the attacks by Senators Durbin, Feinstein, and Schumer started. They ridiculed his article defending the husband as the "head" of the wife in a Christian marriage. It made no difference that Holmes was regarded as perhaps the most intellectually gifted of all Bush's nominees at the time. He was going to be branded as an extremist. That's when Miranda held his first Umbrella Group phone call in March 2003, with Bill Donohue, head of the Catholic League, as the host. Groups within the Umbrella Group began fighting back. The Committee for Justice and the Ave Maria List published some print ads with the banner "Catholics Need Not Apply," which Senator Feinstein described as "diabolical." Feinstein took those ads, blew them up, and had them placed behind her in the Senate hearings. "She gave us $100K to $200K worth of free press. Feinstein and the Democrats made the mistake of engaging us on this issue."

Under Miranda's leadership, the Democrats' attempt to undermine the credibility of Bush's nominees on the basis of religion backfired. But Miranda was going to pay a price. In what he called his "Memogate," Miranda was accused of hacking into the computers of Democratic legislators. Senator Frist asked Miranda to leave his staff, and the judicial effort, as Miranda says, "fell apart."

Miranda went home but did not give up. Working out of his house, he put to use the large e-mail list he had compiled while working in the Senate. He started to network all the conservative groups with an interest in judicial nominations. In early 2005, he created the National Coalition to End Judicial Filibusters, which he soon renamed Third Branch Conference. It was one of the largest single coalitions ever formed, with leaders from 200 organizations—Catholic, Evangelical, and Jewish. He used regular e-mail blasts to keep these leaders educated and to keep their message unified.

Miranda did not realize that his most important effort was still ahead of him. On October 3, 2005, at 6:12 A.M., he received an e-mail of an Associated Press story. At 8:00 A.M., President Bush was going to announce the nomination of Harriet Miers, his choice as justice for the Supreme Court. At 8:06 A.M., even before Bush had finished his announcement, Miranda had sent out a five-sentence e-mail stating, "The reaction of many conservatives today will be that the President has made possibly the most unqualified choice since Abe Fortas, one of President Lyndon Johnson's lawyers. The nomination of a nominee with no judicial record is a significant failure for the advisers that the White House gathered around it." According to Miranda, this has become "the most famous e-mail in the history of the Bush administration," and there is no reason to disagree. At 11:00 A.M., Miranda held a conference call with more than one hundred members of his Third Branch Conference.

White House counsel and personal friend of the president, Harriet Miers was the first Evangelical nominee to the Supreme Court. The confirmation of Catholic John Roberts as chief justice meant there were now four Catholic justices. Yet no one was representing the Evangelicals, who were arguably the most powerful political force in the country at that moment. James Dobson, the most influential of all Religious Right leaders, had been presold on the Miers nomination and had quickly given a public endorsement. Evangelicals were expected to fall in line behind Dobson and the other leading Evangelical, Richard Land, chief lobbyist for the Southern Baptist Convention. Miranda remembered, "There was a lot of tension on the call. A number of Evangelical leaders were defensive about Miers, and some of the Catholics were very hesitant. It was very uncomfortable. The Evangelicals were saying, 'She is one of us—she's been born again.' Catholics responded by saying, 'Just because she attends church doesn't mean she can be counted on.'"

The bottom line was that there were two reasons to mistrust Miers. She was not on any of the lists known by conservatives to contain the names of all qualified candidates in the country for the Supreme Court. More important, Miers did not have a known track record supporting the sanctity of life. That she had been "born again," the White House's main selling point, wasn't working for Catholics or for some Evangelicals, either.

When a pro-abortion speech given by Meirs in 1993 to the Executive

Women of Dallas came to light, the objections to her nomination in the pro-life community became vocal. The White House was genuinely surprised that religious conservative leaders were not willing to believe Miers's opinion had changed since the 1993 speech. This was the first time the religious conservatives who supported Bush through two national elections were not going to take his word for it.

Miranda says that by the second week of the four-week controversy, most of the Evangelicals, with the exception of leaders from the Southern Baptist Convention, had abandoned Miers. Miranda kept the pressure on the nomination with his daily e-mail blast containing all the press coverage and his own commentary. Nina Totenberg, a reporter from PBS, told him she found the e-mails so interesting that when she opened them up, "she felt like getting popcorn." Miranda told me the press was fascinated because they had never seen that kind of internal debate among conservatives.

After four weeks of controversy, the White House withdrew the nomination. Miranda's mission of creating an independent coalition of Catholics and Evangelicals to engage judicial nominations had proven effective in a way he had not foreseen. Starting as a staunch ally of the president's nominee, he had turned into a foe, albeit a friendly one. As Miranda said, "The winner in the Miers nomination was the conservative movement; this is how we have to function. We have to replicate this effort in other areas to exert our influence."

The growing internal strength of Catholic and Evangelical unification for political activism is relying less on the traditional structures of the Republican Party and the White House. This trajectory toward independence coexists with the deliberate networking of Catholics and Evangelicals. It may be that the additional strength derived from the collaboration makes an independent strategy possible. Along with Manny Miranda's Third Branch Conference, the best example is the Alliance for Marriage, founded in 1999 by Matt Daniels, an Evangelical attorney from Queens, New York. Daniels understands the importance of building a coalition with Catholics.

Daniels knew he had to get Catholics involved: "The success or failure of the effort to protect marriage in America rests on the shoulders of the Catholic community. There is no community in the United States equal in size, magnitude, or political force to the Catholic community on the right side of this issue, at least in terms of the teaching of the Church. The single biggest unplayed political card, without any question, is its leadership and voice on this issue—as goes the leadership of the Roman Catholic Church in America, so goes the debate."

When Daniels created his organization, he was extremely careful in putting together his board of advisors. It is a model of effective diversity. His board includes not only four Catholic bishops and several lay leaders but also influential Evangelicals on the left and right, African-Americans, Hispanics, mainline Protestants, and women leaders. "I reached out to board members who share the understanding of a natural-law approach to social issues as found among thinking Roman Catholics and among Evangelicals in the reformed tradition."

Unlike some Evangelicals who work with Catholics on the political front, Daniels understands the limitations of purely lay involvement. Catholic bishops must be brought into play. Daniels's ability to do this has been a key ingredient in his success. "I think it's going to take the bishops speaking individually, particularly in key states where senators are on the wrong side of the electorate. The bishops need to individually approach the Senators in their states and make their personal voices heard as leaders of the community."

Daniels faced this issue head-on after the Alliance for Marriage announced the introduction of the Federal Marriage Amendment in May 2002. The constitutional amendment was designed to protect marriage as a union between one man and one woman but was opposed by every Catholic Democrat in the Senate. Daniels knew that if the bishops could prevail over the Catholic Democrats, the marriage amendment would pass. "The margin of victory that we need in the Senate can easily be made up from senators in states that are heavily Catholic. We have enough senators in heavily Catholic states who are currently on the wrong side of this issue, and if the Church reaches them in time, we can win."

After patient lobbying at the USCCB, Daniels got the support he needed. He stood with the executive secretary Monsignor William P. Fay and other members of the Alliance of the USCCB at a press conference on the day of the first Senate vote on the marriage amendment. Daniels recalls that day very well: "Monsignor Fay was reading from a beautifully worded, thoughtful statement about the truth of marriage between a man and a woman, about their complementarity, and how this can be known not just by the light of faith but by natural law, when the African-American part of the coalition, about 200 of them, all shouted, 'Amen.' At first, Monsignor Fay looked shocked, but as the 'Amens' continued, he started enjoying it and was beaming from ear to ear." Fay's reaction is a repetition nearly thirty years later of Paul Weyrich's hearing "Amen" shouted at him from the group of ministers gathered in a Senate hearing room to protest the IRS.

Daniels told me in our interview that he became a Christian in part because of the witness of a Catholic layman who worked with the homeless on the streets of New York City. "He had such tremendous credibility, I had to take his witness seriously." During his years of building the Alliance for Marriage, Daniels took five trips to the Vatican to meet with members of the Curia. "I was profoundly changed and influenced by meeting with Cardinals Arinze, Martino, Lopez-Trujillo, Re, and others. I took away a global perspective on this debate, which is so easy to lose when you are an Evangelical. They told me that everything is riding on what happens in the U.S."

The efforts between Catholics and Evangelicals are becoming more and more seamless, and there is no doubt that their common causes are gradually dissolving the centuries-old animus.[22] However,

22. Another coalition that was formed to help coordinate religious conservatives is the Arlington Group. In 2002, Reverend Don Wildmon of the American Family Association recruited leaders such as Dr. James Dobson as chairman, and other powerful names include Gary Bauer, Richard Land, Paul Weyrich, Shannon Royce, Tony Perkins, Richard Viguerie, Jerry Falwell, Chuck Colson, and William Bennett. In the beginning, the Arlington Group competed with Alliance of Marriage over the language of the marriage amendment but eventually learned to cooperate amiably. The Arlington Group remains a potent force uniting many religious conservative leaders on a variety of issues. And it is willing to challenge the Republican White House. In January 2005, the Arlington Group wrote a letter to Karl Rove expressing concerns regarding statements made by President Bush

it may be many years before the "ecumenism of the trenches" helps the Neuhaus-Colson Evangelicals and Catholics Together initiative persuade Fundamentalist Christians to drop their theological guard.

---

that gave the impression that he endorsed civil unions for same-sex couples, that "nothing would happen" on the marriage amendment due to the lack of support from the Senate, and the apparent focus of the administration on Social Security privatization. Coming from a group that had been highly supportive of the Bush administration, the letter made it clear that they were going to keep their independence.

12

ALTAR BOYS AND CATHOLIC GRANDMOTHERS

O N September 2, 2003, in Mount Pleasant, South Carolina, Senator John Kerry announced his candidacy to become the Democratic Party's nominee for president of the United States. He made no comments about his personal faith or about any religious tradition, but he did reiterate his support for abortion.

Kerry announced, "George Bush has sought to undo guarantees enshrined in the Constitution, not by amending it but by subverting it with his judicial nominees. As president, I will only appoint Supreme Court justices who will uphold a woman's right to choose and the right to privacy in America. A just America demands a Supreme Court that honors our Constitution, and it demands an attorney general whose name is not John Ashcroft."

Kerry, the Catholic candidate for the Democratic nomination, decided at the beginning to make his support for abortion and judicial nominees a major focus of his campaign. Did he realize at the time that the prospect of at least two resignations from the Supreme Court was already energizing the foot soldiers of the Religious Right in their effort to reelect President Bush? Did he intentionally make his announcement in the heartland of religious conservatism and in the state where Bush had an early primary victory over John McCain in 2000, securing the nomination?

Such a gesture at the outset of his campaign was a mark of either great bravura or simple incompetence; I would opt for bravura. I would argue that based on his subsequent botched attempt to garner the Catholic vote. Kerry believed that he was the man for the age, not Bush, and he was sure that the age was predominantly secular. Bush, the 2000 election, and the power of traditional Christians were all anomalies, waiting for a secular champion to return things to normal. Kerry's problem became twofold when he assumed the Church had made a lasting covenant with the secularists. That was probably closer to being true in the Archdiocese of Boston, especially after the departure of Cardinal Law, than any other diocese in the country (with the possible exception of Rochester, New York). I'm sure that after it was all over, Kerry wished he had campaigned in 1960 rather than forty-four years later.

During the early days of Kerry's campaign, there were inevitable comparisons with Senator John F. Kennedy—a senator from Massachusetts, a Catholic candidate for president, a full head of dark hair, lean, athletic, independently wealthy, and bearing identical initials. Kerry initially gave Catholics in the Democratic Party hope for a return to the days of Camelot and, more important, the reaffirmation that Catholics had truly been accepted into the mainstream of American culture and politics. "It is almost as though the Democratic Party decided to run a controlled experiment to compare the electoral fortunes of a Catholic candidate in 1960 and 2004." [1]

But John Kerry did not run for president as John F. Kennedy; he ran as Ted Kennedy. This was inevitable. Too much had changed since 1960. The changes in American politics, the Catholic Church, and the Democratic Party made 1960 and 2004 incomparable. Some of those changes Kerry understood; others he did not.

The central political issue facing a Catholic was abortion, and Kerry recognized this. The looming Catholic issue for a Catholic presidential

---

1. David E. Campbell, ed., *A Matter of Faith: Religion in the 2004 Presidential Election* (Washington, D.C.: Brookings Institution Press, 2007), 8.

candidate in 2004 was not the anti-Catholicism that defeated Al Smith and nearly defeated JFK. Kerry faced the impact of Pope John Paul II and his bishops. The Church in the United States itself had changed under the leadership of John Paul II. Bishops such as John Cardinal O'Connor, Bernard Cardinal Law, Archbishop Charles Chaput, and Archbishop Raymond Burke openly challenged politicians who condoned abortion. There was no indication that Kerry anticipated the rebellion that would come from Catholic voters, educated for more than twenty years under the leadership of John Paul II. Kerry was a byproduct of Boston's Paulist Center, a Jesuit bastion of dissent, and a Democratic Party that gradually became the party of abortion, gay rights, and feminism led astray with Ted Kennedy's 1972 departure from the duty to protect unborn children. Kerry's Democratic Party remained willfully ignorant of the reasons it was steadily losing its base of loyal Catholic voters.

The children and grandchildren of the Catholic Democrats who had elected FDR three times, Truman in 1948, and Kennedy in 1960 were steadily migrating to the Republican Party when Kerry began his run for office. As the announcement of his candidacy clearly reveals, Kerry was out of touch with the concerns that were keeping Catholics away from the party of their ancestors.

Since Catholics make up approximately 30 percent of those who vote in national elections, a Catholic candidate should have a natural advantage. They are a powerful swing vote, especially in states with large numbers of electoral votes such as Michigan, Pennsylvania, Florida, Ohio, Illinois, and California. Bush won 10 percent more (47 percent) of the self-identified Catholic vote than Robert Dole (37 percent), barely beating Al Gore in 2000. The loss of the Catholic vote to Kerry would have been disastrous to Bush's reelection.

Kerry's campaign was constructed on the counsel of Catholic strategists such as Father Robert Drinan, who still looked at Catholic voters through the lens of the so-called post–Vatican II Church. They devised an outreach on the assumption that American Catholics liked John Paul II personally but did not like his message, particularly his condemnation of abortion. Kerry's campaign sought to appeal to Catholics on symbolic associations and hoped the lack of substance wouldn't be noticed. Kerry and his advisors felt that American Catholics would respond to a reinvention of the FDR Democratic Party coalition: soft-pedaling "divisive" issues such as abortion and gay marriage and reasserting the moral equivalence of a broad range of social issues emphasizing help for the poor and minority groups. This strategy, they thought, would be aided by the enormous sex scandal in the Catholic priesthood that dominated headlines throughout 2003. The "loss of moral authority" of priests and bishops, they assumed, would dampen the receptivity of Catholic voters to the moral teaching of the Church on abortion.

NOT IN BOSTON ANYMORE

There was at least one good reason Kerry assumed his Catholic strategy was workable. At the time of his campaign, of the 150 Catholic members of the Senate and House of Representatives, more than 70 had pro-abortion voting records. Looking at this record, it's no stretch to assume that a pro-abortion Catholic could be elected president. His pro-abortion Catholic colleagues in the Senate and the House had been elected, why not him? Kerry's Senate colleagues obviously agreed with this inference and tried to help boost the Catholic bona fides of their presidential nominee in the face of growing criticism from the bishops.

On June 6, 2004, Illinois Senator Richard Durbin (D-Illinois) announced that Senator John Kerry was the "most Catholic" member of the Senate. Senator Durbin released an analysis of the voting record of Catholic Senators, scoring them by their adherence to the list of legislative priorities of the United States Conference of Catholic Bishops (USCCB). Kerry was ranked first at 60.9 percent, followed by Durbin himself (60.5 percent), and Ted Kennedy (60.4 percent). Pat Leahy (D-Vermont) and Barbara Mikulski (D-Maryland) were four and five on this list. Pro-life Senator Rick Santorum (R-Pennsylvania) was twentieth out of twenty-four. The top five, with the exception of Leahy, all voted to oppose the partial-birth abortion ban. Not only that, but all five voted against the Human Cloning Prohibition Act sponsored by Senator Sam Brownback, another Catholic.

In creating his scorecard, Durbin looked at twenty-four issues on which the USCCB took a position, such as the minimum wage, the right to unionize, the Iraq war resolution, and global AIDS funding. If a senator voted in agreement with the USCCB, he was given a point. In the end, the points were added up, and the senators were ranked. In other words, in Durbin's view, all the issues were of equal moral value. So a vote for the Collins Mercury Reduction Act (which limits the use of mercury fever thermometers) was equal in weight and importance to a vote for the partial-birth abortion ban. Likewise, a vote for the Dorgan Joint Resolution (which rejects "the rule submitted by the Federal Communications Commission with respect to broadcast media ownership") was of equal importance to a vote banning human cloning.

Senator John Kerry, who voted against the partial-birth abortion ban, against the Born-Alive Infant Protection Act, and against the Unborn Victims of Violence Act, was now crowned the most Catholic member of the Senate.

It was astonishing that the Kerry campaign went along with the Durbin scheme. The outcry against it was so loud that the Bishops Conference had to distance itself from the ranking. The USCCB staff, however, had to be considered complicit in the Durbin scheme. The lobbying arm of the USCCB had been taking positions for years on prudential matters, such as the restriction on thermometers and broadcast media ownership. Frustrated Catholics had been asking, "How can there be an official Catholic position on issues such as these?" Informed Catholics realized they were free to differ with the prudential judgments of the USCCB. There was widespread realization that to rank Catholic senators in this manner was just as much an indictment of the USCCB as Durbin and his pro-abortion Catholic colleagues in the Senate.

But the enabling of the USCCB was not yet over. Shortly after the Durbin affair, the USCCB sent its Presidential Questionnaire to each candidate. (This was the same questionnaire they had allowed in 2000 to let Al Gore describe himself as "pro-life" without any editorial correction.) In spite of distancing itself from the Durbin ranking, the USCCB questionnaire was little different. It contained a long list of questions about prudential matters and only a few on crucial life issues. The questionnaire found its way into the hands of several bishops who were not happy about it.

On August 10, 2004, Bishop Rene Henry Gracida, the bishop emeritus of Corpus Christi, Texas, published a statement in which he wondered about the usefulness of a questionnaire that didn't make a distinction between life issues and debatable social-policy issues. (Gracida was one of the American bishops who publicly denounced Communist incursions into Central America in support of Ronald Reagan.) He wrote:

> I have had an opportunity to review a copy of the 2004 Presidential Questionnaire submitted by the United States Conference of Catholic Bishops to President George Bush and Senator John Kerry. I am disappointed that the questionnaire is so broad and covers so many issues that are before the American public today that its value in helping to show the differences between the positions of the two candidates on the really important issues will be minimal.

From the perspective of the Church's teaching, some issues far outweigh others in importance. For instance, there is no moral equivalence between the issue of abortion-on-demand and farm subsidies. The questionnaire should have been much shorter and should have been limited to questions on those issues on which there is a clear unequivocal teaching of the Church, e.g., abortion, cloning, assisted suicide, embryonic stem-cell research, and marriage." [2]

After some weeks of internal debate at the White House and during the campaign, the campaign declined to fill out the questionnaire. Even

2. The remainder of Bishop Gracida's statement: "There is no clear unequivocal position of the Church on such issues as the minimum wage, immigration, farm subsidies, etc. The inclusion of questions in the questionnaire can only result in confusion in the minds of Catholic voters who do not understand that there is no moral equivalence between these two groups of issues. I can only hope that both presidential candidates will refuse to reply to the questionnaire, or, if they do reply, that the leadership of the United States Conference of Catholic Bishops will recognize the danger to Catholic voters and will publish those replies with a clear teaching on the greater importance which should be attached to the replies to the first group of questions I have listed above that have far greater moral implications for the nation."

though it did not directly create a numerical ranking, it could have been spun by the media and pro-Kerry Catholic organizations to accuse President Bush of being weak on Catholic issues, just as Santorum was portrayed by the Durbin ranking. Kerry did not fill out the questionnaire, either, presumably for different reasons.

GETTING PRIORITIES STRAIGHT

Senator Rick Santorum (R-Pennsylvania) has unambiguous opinions about the USCCB lobbying to the Congress and the White House. Until his defeat in the 2006 election, he was *the* national leader of politically active conservative Catholics and had developed a large following among Evangelicals as well. Santorum was not especially liked at the USCCB. He had publicly denounced Catholic Charities for getting most of its money from state and federal governments. Santorum also represented precisely the kind of Catholic politician who insisted on the priority of life issues and rejected the equal weight given to a broad range of social issues.

"The biggest problem with the Catholic bishops," he said, "is that they speak on things which have very little moral authority, such as agriculture or trade issues. Every issue has a moral component, but from the standpoint of Church teaching, they don't derive moral authority on issues like agriculture subsidies, broadband legislation, or Canadian lumber."

When I pointed out to Santorum that the USCCB had put a huge amount of resources into lobbying on immigration policy, he replied, "I think immigration is a legitimate place for them to weigh in, just as it is legitimate for them to weigh in on education. They are providers of education. But I think areas of foreign policy are best left to the secular world, and I don't believe that the bishops should be getting involved."

"What about the bishops issuing public letters on the war in Iraq?" I asked.

"This is a perfect example of the Church not speaking from a standpoint that cannot point to a clear Catholic doctrine to support its position," Santorum said.

"As we had this debate leading up to war, the question was, 'Do civil servants have a right to make prudential judgments based upon Catholic teachings?' The answer is yes. They can lay out ground rules by which we are to make those decisions, and they can make sure we are thinking through these consequences. But the Church must leave it up to civil servants to make that call while continuing to remind them about the basis on which they should make the call without trying to make it for them."

Santorum told me that he viewed the USCCB as having significant lobbying influence on life issues in the years he served in the Congress. "This is clearly part of their domain. In my opinion, it's the only part of the Church's lobbying here that has any impact. I wish I could say that lobbying for educational vouchers has an impact; it doesn't much because the teachers union is much more influential. But the USCCB has been one of the most clear and consistent voices for life. They have been effective there, but they would be much more effective if they focused on those things instead of trying to lobby on so many things outside of their moral authority."

The only way to overcome the kind of Catholic culture that produced Kennedy, Kerry, and Pelosi is "re-Evangelization." Santorum tells me, "We are risking souls by not preaching the truth and laying out the full truth in the Catholic Church. It is scandalous that our clergy would allow that to continue. Part of the problem is that priests themselves have not been properly formed. Re-Evangelization would have a huge political impact in the culture. I hate to put this in political terms, because political terms are obviously less important than religious ones. But in political terms, the reestablishment of the Church in its fullest sense in areas where Catholics are a significant voting percentage would have huge implications for the country."

Santorum is no doubt right. The consistent story line of the Catholic vote in the last fifty years has been the correlation between religious activism and support for the GOP. The best thing that can happen for Republicans is for the Catholic Church to insist upon its social teachings *in their proper priority.* The coverage after the 2006 election on Speaker Nancy Pelosi constantly referred to her Catholic background but only made passing mention of her 100 percent pro-abortion voting record. The media delighted in her description of herself as a "Catholic grandmother" and ignored her years of dissent from the core issues of Catholic social teaching. One story (from the official Catholic News Service, no less) quotes the director of the Office of Public Policy and Social Concerns for the Archdiocese of San Francisco, saying, "I think she gets half of Catholic social teaching; the half she gets she does well."[3] This is Santorum's point. If all the social issues are treated as having equal importance, they can be neatly divided into two halves, so that someone with a 100 percent pro-abortion voting record such as Speaker Pelosi can be congratulated.

Pelosi celebrated her ascent to the speaker's post by holding a mass on January 3, 2007, at her alma mater, Trinity University, in Washington, D.C. Present at the mass to congratulate her was the architect of the pro-abortion movement of Catholic Democrats, Father Robert Drinan. His comment on Pelosi, "She's the first mother in the seat," was meant to be laudatory. Instead, it succeeded in underlining the irony of Pelosi's attempt to spotlight her Catholic faith as she ascended to the speaker's position. Judi Brown at the American Life League issued a press release calling on the recently installed archbishop of Washington, D.C., Donald W. Wuerl, to deny communion to Pelosi, but Wuerl refused, saying that Trinity University was under the control of the Sisters of Notre Dame, not the archdiocese. In a subsequent interview with a reporter, Wuerl said he would not be using his "faculty" to deny communion to Pelosi and, presumably, other pro-abortion Catholic politicians.[4]

Archbishop Wuerl took the same tack as his predecessor, Cardinal McCarrick. This means that Catholic Democrats such as John Kerry and Nancy Pelosi will continue to pronounce their "Catholic" view of things

---

3. Patricia Zapor, "Madame Speaker: Anticipating How Pelosi Will Run the House," CNS, January 5, 2007.

4. www.lifesite.net/ldn/2007/jan/07011604.html.

political without fear of reprimand from the local ordinary.[5] This works to their disadvantage, as Kerry has already learned the hard way. As a Catholic, John F. Kennedy downplayed his Catholicism to defuse anti-Catholic prejudice. Kerry, like Ted Kennedy and so many others, did not downplay his Catholicism at all; he tried to claim to be a good Catholic while rejecting several of its infallible teachings. He rejected the option of admitting "I'm not a very good Catholic." Instead, he expected people to believe he was a Catholic in good standing while rejecting the Church's teaching articulated by a sitting pope who happened to be the most popular and influential pope of the modern era. Indeed, Kerry went to Iowa and told Catholics there that he "believed that life began at conception" but added the now-familiar Mario Cuomo qualification.

KERRY STUMBLES, AGAIN

There was one moment on the campaign trail with Kerry when he met face-to-face with the Catholic Church that he evidently knew nothing about. On September 4, 2004 he arrived in Steubenville, Ohio, for a campaign rally at Old Fort Steuben with Senator John Glenn and Ohio gubernatorial candidate Ted Strickland. Kerry's agenda that day was for Strickland to set the record straight on his military service in the face of the Swift Boat Veterans' book, *Unfit for Command.*

Steubenville is one of those Rust Belt towns that Democrats assume are still in their pockets—blue-collar, ethnic, Catholic, 5-1 registered Democrat, and suffering economically. Kerry probably had never heard of the Franciscan University of Steubenville, the small but vital Catholic institution nursed back to financial health and orthodoxy more than twenty years ago by Father Michael Scanlon. Under Scanlon's leadership, Franciscan had become a powerhouse among orthodox Catholics, utilizing its weekly program on EWTN and the popularity of its faculty on the lecture circuit, especially best-selling author Scott Hahn.

It's poetic justice, in a way, that the awaiting protest was organized by

5. "Ordinary" refers to a bishop's authority over his diocese, in this case the cardinal is the archbishop of Washington, D.C.

one of Hahn's sons, Gabriel, who was working for RNC Catholic Out-reach. Kerry, Glenn, and Strickland were by a wall of pro-life signs held aloft by 500 Franciscan University students and another 500 Bush sup-porters. Nearly half of the 3,500 gathered for the rally were there to tell Kerry he wasn't welcome. Before the candidate arrived, Kerry's advance staff tried to keep the protesters from attending the rally. Jefferson County Sheriff Fred Abdallah refused to bar them, saying, "They have a right to do whatever they want to do as long as they don't interfere." It was reported to me that the local firemen and policemen who were there for security were more than glad to let the student protesters behind the rope line.

The "Steubenville Meltdown," as it came to be known, turned out to be the biggest anti-Kerry protest the candidate met during his entire campaign. Calling themselves Catholics for Life, the Franciscan students held up pro-life signs that put a visibly angry look on Kerry's face. (All candidates have advance men who are supposed to make sure such things do not take place.) Senator Glenn attempted to introduce Kerry, but the protesting yells of the students and faculty spoiled the moment and left the candidate stumbling for words.

Martin Gillespie, head of Catholic Outreach for the Republican Na-tional Committee for both the 2002 and 2004 elections, was chief insti-gator of protests such as the one Kerry experienced in Steubenville. He agrees that politicians such as Kerry, Pelosi, and Kennedy would be much better off to say, "Look, I'm a Catholic, and my faith means a lot to me, but I disagree with the Church on abortion." Then people would not have thought he was misusing the label.

I asked Gillespie to describe Kerry's use of the Catholic faith in 2004: "It was a photo-op strategy; he showed up at mass and got his picture taken. In Cleveland on Ash Wednesday, he came out of mass with ashes on his forehead, and hundreds of media were waiting for him. I wonder how they knew he was going to be there? Media was everywhere." Kerry's publicity stunts at parishes and schools failed to bolster his credibility as a Catholic.

At the grassroots level, Kerry's strategy backfired; he was like a member of the family who was using the family name in a bad way. Gillespie told me that Catholic voters were highly motivated to organize against Kerry's dissent on the life issues. "No question about it, Kerry passing himself as Catholic was a great recruiting tool. I recruited thousands of people at the parish level who had never been active; they were looking for practical ways to get involved because Kerry was misrepresenting the Catholic faith," Gillespie said.

THE "MOST CATHOLIC" SENATOR

Using Senator Durbin's office to pronounce Kerry the "most Catholic" senator did not comport with moments such as the second debate. It backfired in exactly the same way as his military salute before his acceptance speech at the Democratic National Convention.

Well aware of Bush's success with Catholics and Christian Evangelicals in 2000, Kerry and the DNC thought they could clone Bush's Catholic outreach. But Bill Donohue of the Catholic League exposed numerous radical credentials belonging to their outreach directors that were unfriendly to orthodox Catholics. The Democrats were then forced to hire one religious advisor after the other. One of the most offensive to orthodox Catholics, Mara Vanderslice, went on to found her own initiative, Common Good Strategies, which advises Democrats about Catholic outreach. Kerry's own Catholic advisory committee was a Who's Who of the Catholic left. All of them were convinced that the Ted Kennedy form of dissenting Catholicism that had kept him in the Senate for so many years would convince Catholics around the nation that the Democratic nominee was as much a man of faith as the Evangelical president.

Left-leaning strategists ignore basic facts about religious voters. In the wake of the 2000 election, many analysts confirmed what the *Crisis* Catholic Vote Project established, that the genuine Catholic voter is a religiously active voter who does not vote the same as those who never, or rarely, attend worship services. The trend lines of the *Crisis* report were confirmed by the 2000 election. Pundits recognized that regular church attendance had become one of the most reliable indicators of voting behavior among Evangelicals as well as Catholics. The religiously active voter cares deeply about social issues, not abortion exclusively, and looks for moral leadership and integrity in elected officials.

For politicians to represent themselves as good Catholics while obviously dissenting from Church teaching on life issues sends the wrong message to the religiously active voter. John Paul II and his bishops had made sure of that. The 2004 presidential campaign was very much a contest between the two sides of the Catholic Church in the United States; those who hoped Vatican II would lead to changes in teaching about sexual morality and the priesthood and those who rallied to the orthodox leadership of John Paul II. John Kerry, as a Catholic, was not merely running against Bush, he was facing off against John Paul II.

Kerry, like the other pro-abortion Catholic Democrats, tried to ignore the increasing number of lay Catholics and bishops who publicly criticized "Catholic" politicians for rejecting the fundamental moral and social teachings of their Church. Of course, it's one thing to ignore the laity but another to ignore the bishops. When they started publicly to affirm Catholic teaching, Kerry's attempt to label pro-life Catholics "right-wing extremists" suddenly fell flat.

Under the leadership of bishops such as Weigand (Sacramento), Burke (St. Louis), Myers (Newark), Cupich (Rapid City), Chaput (Denver), Keleher (Kansas City), Sheehan (Colorado Springs), and Morlino (Madison), the pro-life Catholic community struck out hard at pro-abortion politicians, most of whom were Democrats. Bishop Weigand of Sacramento was actually the first in this line, challenging California's Gray Davis to withhold himself from communion in 2002. Just as the bishops gave the laity backing, the Vatican solidly backed these bishops. Joseph Cardinal Ratzinger, prefect for the Congregation of the Doctrine of the Faith, issued his "Doctrinal Note" on political participation, which clearly specified the priority of life issues. In this document, which the Catholic left spun in the media as lacking authority, Ratzinger had distilled the political implications of John Paul II's call to a culture of life.

On January 9, 2004, Bishop Raymond Burke, then of Madison, Wisconsin, unwittingly ignited the communion controversy that would slowly burn and finally surround the Kerry campaign in the spring of the campaign. Burke quietly published a "Notification" in the La Crosse diocesan newspaper that Catholic legislators who steadfastly supported abortion or euthanasia should be denied communion until they publicly renounced their positions.

"Catholic legislators who are members of the faithful of the Diocese of La Crosse and who continue to support procured abortion or euthanasia may not present themselves to receive Holy Communion," the notification said. "They are not to be admitted to Holy Communion, should they present themselves, until such time as they publicly renounce their support of these most unjust practices."

Burke said he felt compelled to issue the statement because of his failure to persuade three state legislators to change their positions on these issues. He made this statement within weeks of being installed as archbishop of St. Louis. Shortly after his installation on January 31, Burke was asked a question about communion in a television interview. The interviewer asked, "If Senator John Kerry were to stand in Archbishop Raymond L. Burke's communion line Sunday, Burke would bless him without giving him communion?" Burke's reply was, "I would have to admonish him not to present himself for communion." Burke's statement ignited a controversy that lasted until Election Day. Burke himself was vilified for months but never backed down.

The USCCB naturally moved in to throw a blanket over the fire that was doing obvious damage to the Kerry campaign. A Task Force on Political Participation was formed, headed by Theodore Cardinal McCarrick of Washington, D.C., to study the matter of denying communion to pro-abortion Catholic politicians. A preliminary report was to be issued at its 2004 summer meeting in Denver. Many fellow bishops were horrified at Burke's comments. They were especially horrified when he was backed up by statements from fellow bishops: Archbishop Chaput on April 14, Cardinal Arinze in the Vatican on April 23, Bishop Sheridan on May 1, Archbishop Myers on May 6, and Bishop Cupich on May 18, among others. Kerry's response to all this was, once again, classic Mario Cuomo, classic Ted Kennedy: "My oath is to uphold the Constitution of the United States in my public life; my oath privately between me and God was defined in the Catholic Church . . . which allows for freedom of conscience for Catholics with respect to these choices, and that is exactly where I am."[6]

Kerry's fellow Catholic Democrats tried to come to his defense. On May 20, the press announced that the so-called Letter of 48 had been delivered to Cardinal McCarrick, who was chairing the task Force. "As Catholics we do not believe it is our role to legislate the teachings of the Catholic Church," the letter said. "Because we represent all of our constituents, we must, at times, separate our public actions from our personal beliefs." Durbin's ranking of the most Catholic senators followed a few weeks later.

During McCarrick's deliberations, he received a three-page memo from Cardinal Ratzinger on the meaning of Canon 915, which had supplied some of the authority for Burke's January notification. Cardinal Ratzinger replied with a memo directly to McCarrick, who did not share the entire memo with his fellow bishops but only a summary of its contents.

According to McCarrick, Ratzinger had authorized the individual bishops latitude in how to apply Canon 915. The public statement on the issue of communion published by the bishops at their Denver meeting reflected McCarrick's version of the Ratzinger memo. The entire Ratzinger memo was published in an Italian magazine a few days later, clearly showing that McCarrick had misled the bishops about its contents. Needless to say, McCarrick was embarrassed, and many bishops were furious. Ratzinger's June 2004 memo said that Canon 915 must be applied by the bishops; they should not apply their individual judgment. Burke gave an interview later in the summer where he expressed his disappointment with McCarrick's handling of the memo. Whatever McCarrick's motives, all he did was to succeed in keeping the issue before the public eye, especially to Catholics who were now following the

6. Maria L. La Ganga, "Kerry's Take on Catholicism 'Typical, '" *Los Angeles Times,* May 2, 2004, A24.

debate closely in the press. (McCarrick's resignation in 2005 was quickly accepted by Pope Benedict XVI.)

Liberal Catholics tried to offset the avalanche of bad publicity for Kerry. A consortium of 200 Catholic pro-Kerry groups bought ads in diocesan newspapers in Ohio, Pennsylvania, and West Virginia with the slogan "Life Does Not End at Birth." Bishop Gabino Zavala, auxiliary bishop of Los Angeles and president of the liberal Pax Christi USA, who helped create the statement, commented to the *New York Times*, "If you look at the totality of issues as a matter of conscience, someone could come to the decision to vote for either candidate."[7] The weakness of his comment shows how far back on their heels the Catholic left was by the time Election Day arrived.

BISHOPS BREAK RANKS

The U.S. bishops issued their traditional statement on political responsibility in advance of the election, but it was the individual bishops who made the most difference and got the headlines. The 2004 election marked the end of an ongoing struggle since the early '80s between the voice of the Conference and the voice of individual bishops who wanted to underline the single issue of abortion. What Cardinals O'Connor and Law did in 1983 more than a dozen bishops did in 2004. Archbishop John J. Myers of Newark, the former archdiocese of Cardinal McCarrick, issued a pastoral statement on May 6, 2004, titled "A Time for Honesty." In it, the archbishop explained the Church's uncompromising support of life and the responsibility to be in full communion with the Church and its teachings before receiving the Eucharist:

> There is no right more fundamental than the right to be born and reared with all the dignity the human person deserves. On this grave issue, public officials cannot hold themselves excused from their duties, especially if they claim to be Catholic. Every faithful

7. David D. Kirkpatrick and Laurie Goodstein, "Group of Bishops Using Influence to Oppose Kerry," *New York Times*, October 12, 2004.

Catholic must not only be "personally opposed" to abortion, but also must live that opposition in his or her actions. Catholics who publicly dissent from the Church's teaching on the right to life of all unborn children should recognize that they have freely chosen, by their own actions, to separate themselves from what the Church believes and teaches.[8]

That Myers spoke from a major archdiocese on the East Coast, in a state where Catholics had long voted for pro-abortion Democratic candidates, ensured that his *Wall Street Journal* op-ed would get some notice.

Bishop after bishop backed up Burke on the issue of denying the Eucharist to a pro-abortion politician, without mentioning Kerry by name. One of the most important of these, Archbishop Chaput of Denver, penned a very humorous comment in his diocesan newspaper:

> If it quacks like a duck and looks like a duck and walks like a duck, it's probably a duck. A fox can claim to be a duck all day long. But he's still a fox. . . . I remembered this last week as I read yet another news report about candidates who claim to be Catholic and then prominently ignore their own faith on matters of public policy. We've come a long way from John F. Kennedy, who merely locked his faith in the closet. Now we have Catholic senators who take pride in arguing for legislation that threatens and destroys life— and who then also take Communion. . . . The kindest explanation for this sort of behavior is that a lot of Catholic candidates don't know their own faith."[9]

---

8. Archbishop Myers continued: "To receive communion when one has, through public or private action, separated oneself from unity with Christ and His Church, is objectively dishonest. . . . Because the Eucharist is the source and summit of our faith, the most sacred action of our Church, to misuse the Eucharistic symbol by reducing it to one's private "feeling" of communion with Christ and His Church while objectively not being in such union is gravely disordered." Archbishop John J. Myers, "A Time for Honesty," Pastoral Statement, May 5, 2004.

9. Archbishop Charles Chaput, "How to Tell a Duck from a Fox: Thinking with the Church As We Look Toward November," *Denver Catholic Register,* April 14, 2004.

Many in the media would later blame these bishops for Kerry's poor performance with Catholics. But Martin Gillespie disagrees: "In Missouri, where the communion debate was the loudest, Bush lost Catholic votes. And the exit polling was clear; 70 percent of Catholics did not want Kerry denied communion. That the bishops defeated Kerry among Catholic voters is a media myth."

Myth or not, Kerry's strategy on abortion wasn't working. Catholics may not have wanted to deny Kerry communion, but they were being made constantly aware that he was out of sync with the Church. He was out of sync because he was in sync with the Democratic Party, whose Catholic legislators had become accustomed to taking the "personally opposed" approach to the abortion issue. His quote from the *St. Louis Post-Dispatch* during the primary was typical: "What I believe personally as a Catholic as an article of faith is an article of faith. And if it's not shared by a Jew, or an Episcopalian, or a Muslim, or an agnostic, or an atheist, or someone else, it's not appropriate in the United States for a legislator to legislate your personal religious belief for the rest of the country."

The changes in the Democratic Party resulting from the chaos of the 1968 Chicago Convention and the 1972 McGovern campaign have often been told. The loss of voter loyalty among Catholics in the Northeast and the Midwest along with Southern Evangelicals also has been documented. The loss of Evangelical support, as discussed earlier here, is correctly linked to cultural decline and the mistakes of the Democratic Party and the Carter administration in the late '70s. But the alienation of Catholics, and specifically pro-lifers, is less well documented.

For example, the public controversies surrounding Cardinal O'Connor's disagreements with vice-presidential candidate Geraldine Ferraro and the Notre Dame speech of Mario Cuomo were manifestations of a change in the Democratic Party that had occurred a decade earlier.

Mark Stricherz explained that not only did social liberals join the Democratic Party in the late '60s and early '70s, but they rewrote the rules. "In 1969, they changed the way the delegates were chosen. This change affected the party's presidential nomination. Southerners and

Catholics began leaving the Democratic Party, while African-Americans, students, and feminists started joining it." [10]

The man who was tapped to head the commission to rewrite the rules for choosing delegates became the man the Democrats nominated for president in 1972, Senator George McGovern. The rules that McGovern's commission put into effect in 1969 mandated a quota system for choosing delegates, with the result that 43 percent of the 1972 delegates were women (up from 18 percent in 1968). Since all the women coming into the Democratic Party at that time were pro-abortion, as Stricherz points out, "A generation of Democratic female officeholders became almost uniformly pro-choice." So it is not surprising that Senator Ted Kennedy turned in his pro-life position to make common cause with the abortion advocates who had taken power in his party. Senator Kennedy, after all, had presidential aspirations, and he had to take a position for or against the 1973 *Roe* v. *Wade* decision.

Before *Roe*, Kennedy followed the Church's opposition to abortion. In a letter to Tom Dennelly of Great Park, New York in 1971, Kennedy wrote, "It is my personal feeling that the legalization of abortion on demand is not in accordance with the value which our civilization places on human life. Wanted or unwanted, I believe that human life, even at its earliest stages, has certain rights which must be recognized; the right to be born, the right to love, the right to grow old."

TEDDY'S BURDEN

Mike Schwartz, a longtime pro-life Democrat who now works for Senator Tom Coburn, maintains that it is impossible to overestimate the impact of Kennedy's decision on the Democratic Party, the Church, and politics in general: "He changed everything. Had Ted Kennedy maintained his pro-life posture, I don't think American liberalism would have said that it is a good thing to butcher the unborn."

But Kennedy's decision, it turns out, was not an impromptu response

10. Mark Stricherz, "Casey's Heirs: The Plight of the Pro-Life Democrat," *Crisis* (May 2002).

to the Supreme Court decision invalidating the state's antiabortion laws. The "personally opposed" argument had been percolating through the Kennedy clan and the Catholic Democratic establishment for years.

In 1964, there was a weekend meeting at the Kennedy compound in Hyannisport hosted by Senators Robert and Ted Kennedy. Robert Kennedy was running for the New York Senate seat, "and their political advisors wished to discuss the position a Catholic politician should take on abortion." Present at the meeting were Jesuit novice Albert Jonsen, Father Joseph Fuchs, Father Robert Drinan, Father Richard McCormick, and Father Charles Curran of Catholic University of America. All of the theologians were Jesuits, except for Curran, who was a diocesan priest. The theologians worked together at a hotel nearby and met with the Kennedy clan in the evening. After a day and a half of discussion, they reached the conclusion that "Catholic politicians in a democratic polity might advocate legal restrictions on abortion; but in so doing might tolerate legislation that would permit abortion under certain circumstances if political efforts to repress this moral error led to greater perils to social peace and order." "This position," according to Jonsen, "seems to have informed the politics of the Kennedys."[11]

There was a follow-up meeting at Hyannisport in 1968, hosted by Senators Robert Kennedy and Sargent Shriver. The purpose of the weekend meeting was identical, and many of the participants were the same. Shriver, of course, was chosen in 1972 as the vice-presidential running mate to George McGovern.[12] The line of thinking coming out of these conversations with the Kennedys was the same one formalized by Governor Mario Cuomo in his September 13, 1984, speech at Notre Dame. By 2004, the Church of John Paul II and his bishops was no longer willing to ignore that challenge.

On April 23, 2004, Kerry addressed NARAL Pro-Choice America at its rally leading up to that Sunday's pro-abortion March for Women's

11. Albert Jonsen, "Theological Ethics, Moral Philosophy, and Public Moral Discourse," *Kennedy Institute of Ethics Journal* 4, no. 1 (1994).

12. Sargent Shriver, it should be noted, was evidently not convinced by the meetings at the Kennedy compound; he never abandoned his pro-life beliefs.

Lives in D.C. A few days earlier, after meeting with Cardinal McCarrick, he had announced that he was a Catholic "in good standing" who received the Eucharist at Easter. Even Bill Clinton never addressed a pro-abortion rally. Kerry's speech at the rally, just a few days after meeting with McCarrick, was perceived by Catholics loyal to the pro-life teachings of John Paul II, devotees of EWTN, and readers of conservative Catholic publications as an affront to the cardinal. Anticipation mounted that McCarrick and other bishops who had formed the committee and the task force to "examine" Canon 915 would hijack and misrepresent Canon Law to give constructive permission to reject the directives of the Deposit of Faith and the hierarchical structure of the Church. After all, what was there to examine? Pope John Paul II and Cardinal Arinze had made the duty of the bishops unequivocally clear. Canon 915 is the Church's law to protect Christ's communion from sacrilegious entrapment into the soul of an unrepentant sinner, where he endures suffering.

John Paul II's encyclical *Ecclesia de Eucharistia* ("Church and Eucharist," 2003) gives clear guidelines: "However, in cases of outward conduct which is seriously, clearly and steadfastly contrary to the moral norm, the Church, in Her pastoral concern for the good order of the community and out of respect for the Sacrament, cannot fail to feel directly involved. The *Code of Canon Law* refers to this situation of a manifest lack of proper moral disposition when it states that those who 'obstinately persist in manifest grave sin' are not to be admitted to Eucharistic Communion." [13]

The pope explains the communion between the invisible dimension of the sacrament ("through the working of the Holy Spirit, unites us to the Father and among ourselves") and the visible dimension, "which entails communion in the teaching of the Apostles, in the Sacraments and in the Church's hierarchical order. The profound relationship between the invisible and the visible elements of ecclesial communion is constitutive of the Church as the sacrament of salvation. Only in this context

---

13. *Ecclesia de Eucharistia*, 4.37.

can there be a legitimate celebration of the Eucharist and true participation in it. Consequently, it is an intrinsic requirement of the Eucharist that it should be celebrated in communion, and specifically maintaining the various bonds of that communion intact."[14]

The damage of Cardinal McCarrick's task force wasn't limited to the further eroding of the relationship between the educated Catholic laity and the U.S. Bishops Conference. It taught, by way of example, how to twist the words of the Church to create excuses for bishops who ignore the pro-abortion Catholic politicians in their dioceses. What conclusion were Catholics supposed to draw from their actions? And what about Evangelicals who had grown used to John Paul II's leadership in this area? Most important from a historical perspective is seeing this as a reply on a larger scale to the conflict between Cardinals O'Connor and Law in the 1984 presidential election. This time around, a score of bishops risked speaking out without the consent of the USCCB; they led the public discussion, not the staff at the USCCB or the bishops who toe its line.

Adding fuel to the debate, the November 18, 2003, *Goodridge* ruling from the Massachusetts Supreme Court on homosexual marriage could not have come at a worse time for Kerry. Already caught up in a debate over his receiving communion, Kerry didn't know how to respond to his state's decision on homosexual marriage. The Federal Marriage Amendment, restricting marriage to a man and a woman, which had floundered in the Congress, was immediately elevated to the forefront of the campaign. The FMA was put before the Senate on July 15 before the election. The lobbying arm of the USCCB, the Office of Government Liaison (OGL), directed for decades by Frank Monahan, finally got behind it but failed to deliver any of the sixty-seven senators needed for passage. Fifteen of the twenty-four senators opposed to the bill were Catholic. Only one in five of the Catholic senators supported FMA. The "most Catholic" senators, according to Senator Durbin, all opposed it: Kerry, Durbin, Kennedy, Leahy, and Mikulski.

Catholics in 2004 eventually voted for George Bush at the historic

---

14. Ibid., 4.35.

level of 51 percent overall and 55 percent for regular mass attenders. Kerry had not convinced America's Catholics that he was the reincarnation of JFK. In fact, he had not convinced Catholic voters that his faith meant much to him at all. This shift in political support provides further evidence of the changes in the Catholic Church in this country. Most evident is the growing split between the John Paul II Catholics and those who fashion themselves as the true heirs of Vatican II and the papacy of John XXIII. Although informed Catholics realize that neither Vatican II nor the pope who called for it would justify the kind of open dissent from Church teaching that pours out of dissenting Catholic institutions.

Along with the challenge to Church institutions itself, this generation of lay Catholics who have been inspired by John Paul II will not be intimidated by the demonization of religious beliefs so widespread during the campaign and in the aftermath of Bush's election. The name calling and labeling of Catholics and Evangelicals by the media elite have done nothing but create a formidable backlash.

Some Catholics thought that the bishops were the big losers in this election, that in the failure of many of them clearly to delineate the difference between an issue such as fetal stem cells and Arctic drilling, they abdicated their responsibility. In reality, it was the Bishops Conference that lost.

The winners in this election, from a Catholic perspective, were the Catholic laity and the individual bishops who spoke out in defense of life and the integrity of the Eucharist. Their unprecedented level of participation and their commitment to protecting life and marriage, as expressed through their vote, demonstrate that the bishops recognized the scandal and harm Kerry's claim to be a Catholic in good standing would do if left uncontested.

13

WILL THE DEMOCRATS
GET RELIGION? WILL THE
REPUBLICANS KEEP IT?

THE IMMEDIATE REACTION OF THE DEMOCRATIC PARTY TO THE 2004 election was "We better get some religion, fast." Democratic National Committee chairman Howard Dean and Senator Hillary Clinton, the leading contender for the 2008 nomination, quickly began publicly reaching out to religious voters.[1]

On January 24, 2005, Senator Clinton's speech to 1,000 pro-abortion activists in Albany, New York, received national news coverage. She publicly challenged them to open communication with leaders of the pro-life movement. (It hasn't happened.) She exclaimed, "We want every child born in this country to be wanted, cherished and loved." She affirmed the influence of "religious and moral values" and cautioned against the charge of religious extremism that is so often hurled against men and women of faith who participate in public life. This speech, paired with another one in Boston, where she affirmed the constitutional legitimacy of Bush's faith-based initiative, was notable for Clinton's will-

---

1. See analysis by Democratic strategists Stan Greenberg and Matt Hogan, "Reclaiming the White Catholic Vote," www.democracycorps.com/reports/analyses/Democracy_Corps_March_2005_Catholic_Analysis.pdf, who counsel Democrats to "reach across to more traditional Catholics."

ingness to risk alienating the more ideological segments of the Democratic Party.

Her speeches of January 2005 came in the wake of having compiled a 100 percent pro-abortion record during her time in the Senate. Clinton voted against the ban on partial-birth abortion, the Born-Alive Infant Protection Act, and the Unborn Victims of Violence Act. Her voting record no doubt pleased the ideological wing of the Democratic Party and made her gesture toward religious voters appear purely political.

A few days later, Clinton made an attempt at religious outreach more in keeping with her voting record and ideology. At a Jesuit College in Buffalo, she gave a speech on "The Governmental Role in Caring for the Sick." When Democrats talk about caring for the poor and the sick they are playing to their strength with religious voters. Candidates such as Clinton may try to sound conciliatory on family issues, but they will convince nobody when their voting records tell an entirely different story. They will be more successful by presenting antipoverty and universal-health-care programs as getting to the root cause of abortion, saying these factors are the true causes of abortion in America. Whether or not this is really true is not the point for Democrats: It's the only consistent way for them to address the abortion issue.

Democrats, therefore, can portray themselves as concerned about "lowering" the number of abortions but are forced to ignore the core issue, which, ironically, is choice. Every voter will be familiar with personal decisions about abortions in the middle and upper class that are not economically driven. They also will be aware of cases where mothers under economic duress heroically did not choose the abortion "solution." If Clinton and the Democrats want to get a piece of the religious conservative vote, they will need to break free from the influence of Emily's List, NOW, and Planned Parenthood, whose money and influence ensure perfect conformity in supporting abortion.

The sponsoring organization of Clinton's speech in Buffalo was a Catholic dissident group named Call to Action. For Clinton to associate publicly with CTA demonstrates the same problem that plagued John

Kerry. Call to Action has been the leading proponent of married priests, female priests, and the end to both priestly celibacy and the ban on contraception for the past forty years.

EXORCISING LIBERAL DEMONS

The public association of Call to Action with Senator Clinton is typical. When Democrats appear in public to express their religious "credo," they surround themselves with representatives of the far left. This is hardly helpful if Democrats want to reach into the religious conservative community, which can't be fooled by politics masquerading as religion. (Their skepticism, admittedly, has become so pronounced that they probably would not recognize a sincere confession of belief.)

The left's incomprehension of religion, as in the case of calling Bush a Manichaean, can manifest itself unintentionally in humorous ways. Case in point: A few months after Bush took the White House in 2001, I got a call from someone on Karl Rove's staff asking if I could bring a priest to bless his new office. I didn't consider this an unusual request. I had a priest bless my office in Washington and my home in northern Virginia, and I had worked closely, practically on a daily basis, with Rove for more than a year. It was time for the White House to deliver on Bush's campaign promises. It seemed entirely appropriate that he wanted a blessing as he began his new work. So I asked a parish priest from Alexandria, Virginia, and Carl Anderson, supreme knight of the Knights of Columbus, to join us. We had a fifteen-minute ceremony that asked for God's blessing and protection on the people, places, and projects we were undertaking. Prayers of protection and blessing are very much a part of Catholic and Christian tradition.

Rove had taken over Hillary Clinton's office. Naturally, we were all aware that we were blessing her old office, but this was definitely not why we were there or why Rove had asked us to be there. Years later, I was interviewed about my involvement with the Bush White House, and I told this story to coauthor of *The Architect* Wayne Slater. When his book came out, it portrayed the incident as though our Christian tradition was an insult to Hillary Clinton.[2] Admittedly, I told the author that there was a lighthearted discussion about the differences in political viewpoints between the previous occupant, Hillary, and Karl. (Big mistake.)

On the day of the book's release, a blogger having a little fun, as bloggers do, described the account in the book as an "exorcism of Hillary Clinton's White House office by Deal Hudson and a Catholic priest." Within a few days, national newspapers on the left characterized the Catholic and Christian tradition of blessing as secularly insulting and intolerable, with me as a leading exorcist of the Religious Right. One article even named me as a "conservative Catholic priest," and another referred to two additional Catholic priests and me as doing "the exorcism." All of a sudden, we had another chapter of *The Da Vinci Code* being written at Rove's expense. The White House was finally able to get the story quashed with the help of Brit Hume on Fox, who humorously clarified what really happened.

This incident, which fortunately was only a matter of temporary heartburn (along with multiple phone calls from colleagues and friends entertaining themselves by requesting appointments with the exorcism crew for their offices), is an example of how the left and the media see everything that is done by religious conservatives in purely political terms. If they view it as religious, they think it must be darkly conspiratorial and paranoid, calling upon the power of God to turn out the leftover demons of Hillary Clinton, or worse, that we view Clinton as the incarnation of the devil. This is the exact kind of mockery and mischaracterization of the Religious Right that evidences an irretrievable breakdown in political collaboration. Any attempts that follow by the left to promote respect for our religious values and traditions seem duplicitous.

Howard Dean, chairman of the DNC, is going to have a hard time convincing religious voters that Democrats are not hostile to their faith. At a June 2005 speech in San Francisco, he said Republicans are "a pretty monolithic party. They all behave the same. They all look the same. It's

2. James Moore and Wayne Slater, *The Architect: Karl Rove and the Master Plan for Absolute Power* (New York: Crown, 2006), 95. There is no mention of an "exorcism" by Moore and Slater.

pretty much a white Christian party." This was seven months after Bush had received a historic 44 percent of the Hispanic vote and more African-American (11 percent) and Jewish support (25 percent) than anyone expected. Dean's obvious hostility to conservative Christians won't help Democrats return to their winning ways. As pointed out by *Washington Post* reporter Thomas Edsall, "The two Democrats who won the presidency since 1968, Jimmy Carter and Bill Clinton, ran as moderates, each maintaining some independence from the traditionally liberal social agenda. Both were Southern Baptists supporting the death penalty, and both conveyed certain cultural values through the cadence and rhetoric of the southern vernacular."[3] For the chairman of the Democratic Party to speak so condescendingly about "white Christians" ensures that figures such as James Dobson and Bill Donohue will retain their visibility and power. Religious conservatives demand that their leaders confront anti-Christian bigotry.

GOOD NEWS FOR DEMOCRATS

If the Democrats at the beginning of 2005 were nervous about Dean's further alienation of religious voters, the end of 2005 brought the Democratic Party some good news. A Catholic Democrat, Tim Kaine, was elected governor of Virginia. He defeated an ardent pro-life Evangelical, Lieutenant Governor Jerry Kilgore. A central theme of Kaine's campaign was his experience as a Catholic college student working with the poor in Progreso, Honduras, and how the experience developed his passion for social justice. Left-wing pundits and Republicans wary of life issues used this election as an opportunity to describe the Kaine victory as a defeat of the Bush-Rove political strategy of wooing the Religious Right. But Kilgore's defeat was largely a result of his own clumsy attempts to attack Kaine on the death penalty. His strategists did not understand the dynamics of religious voters, especially Catholics.

Kilgore succeeded in first dividing and then alienating his religious

---

3. Thomas B. Edsall, *Building Red America: The New Conservative Coalition and the Drive for Permanent Power* (New York: Basic Books, 2006), 246.

support. He began by attacking the Catholic Kaine on his opposition to the death penalty. By doing this, Kilgore succeeded in alienating many Catholics who had changed their attitude toward the death penalty since Pope John Paul II's *Evangelium Vitae* of 1995. In defending himself against Kilgore's attack, Kaine was given the opportunity to witness publicly to his Catholic faith in a way not seen in a Democratic candidate in a long time. In taking on Kaine's opposition to the death penalty, Kilgore was taking on John Paul II. As John Kerry had just found out, this is not a good political strategy.

On abortion, Kaine espoused the Drinan-Cuomo line about the difference between his private belief and his public responsibility. But under harsh attack by Kilgore on a matter of religious belief, Kaine was provided the opportunity to tell the story about his conversion to political action while on a Jesuit mission trip. Kilgore ended up strengthening Kaine's religious credentials, making him more attractive to Catholic voters. Then Kilgore, unbelievably, waffled on the very question that was most important to his remaining religious supporters: abortion. By the end of the campaign, he had effectively dismantled the base support that should have energized his candidacy—Evangelical and socially conservative Catholic voters.

Misunderstanding the religious voter is not what defeated Ralph Reed in July 2006. No one arguably knows them better. Reed probably knew what was coming when he saw the first returns coming in on Election Night in his race for lieutenant governor in Georgia. Reed knew that the political coalition of religious conservatives that he, as much as anyone, had helped to create had strong opinions about issues of character and judgment.

The Georgia Republican primary had been in the national news since Reed, former executive director of the Christian Coalition, had announced his intention to run for office. To the national media, Reed symbolized not only the political power of religious conservatives but also the potent marriage between those same conservatives and the Republican Party that had resulted in the election of George W. Bush in 2000 and 2004.

In both national elections, Reed played a key role as political advisor and grassroots organizer for Bush. Between those elections, as chairman of the Georgia GOP, Reed found the time to lead the state Republican Party to control of the state house and the governor's mansion in 2002 for the first time since Reconstruction.

But only four years after the historic 2002 success in his home state, Reed lost the election to a little-known state senator, Casey Cagle. For more than a year, the scandal surrounding Reed's dealings with lobbyist Jack Abramoff had consumed Washington, the *Atlanta Journal-Constitution*, and the radical left. Cagle had relentlessly labeled Reed a hypocrite. Cagle's message against Reed was amplified not only by the media but also by half a million dollars of attack ads and direct mail paid from out-of-state sources such as billionaire Democrat George Soros.

Neither the media nor the U.S. Senate committee looking into the matter found that Reed had engaged in any wrongdoing. But his critics' attacks, especially the barrage of articles in the *Atlanta Journal-Constitution*, poisoned the atmosphere of the Georgia electorate against Reed. Unable to clear the air, his campaign struggled to make up ground in the final days of the campaign, only to lose by 12 percentage points.

During the campaign, Reed repeatedly admitted his mistake of not ensuring the source of the money he was paid to lobby against casino gambling. That money, it turned out, was provided by the gambling revenues of rival casino owners. By Election Day, only one newspaper in the state, the *Waycross Journal-Herald*, had endorsed him.

It was predictable that the media would make Reed's defeat a referendum on the power of the Religious Right. The *Atlanta Journal-Constitution*'s front-page story the following morning (July 19) contained the following: "Reed's defeat has set a limit on the influence of Christian conservatives in Georgia's growing Republican Party," said Charles Bullock, a political scientist at the University of Georgia. "They may be the tail now, but they're not the dog anymore," he said.[4]

4. Jim Galloway, "Cagle Tops Reed for GOP Nomination," *Atlanta Journal-Constitution*, July 19, 2006.

But the real lesson of the Reed defeat, as with Kilgore's in Virginia, was quite different from the way it was spun in the media. The Religious Right demands a great deal from its leaders. The Religious Right was doing what could be expected from a movement that values moral character and prudent behavior. As James Dobson found out after his endorsement of Harriet Miers, the rank and file of the Religious Right rarely keep their disapproval to themselves. Dobson, they thought, should have demanded the White House produce Miers's record on key issues rather than taking the administration's word for it. But there was no documentation and no clear evidence of qualifications for the Supreme Court. Dobson had to withdraw his support because the Religious Right, led by Manuel Miranda's Third Branch Coalition, considered his action as stepping outside their circle.

Reed also fell victim to growing fatigue within the relationship between the Bush White House and leadership in the Religious Right. When Bush suddenly approved the Plan B emergency contraception pill, religious leaders did not say much out loud, but privately they were disappointed. As Jim Bopp, chief counsel to National Right to Life, said to me, "What good does it do if you eliminate abortion on demand but allow a pregnant woman to abort her baby with an over-the-counter pill!" Some in the grassroots of the Religious Right saw the allegations against Reed as an example of how leadership had sought to profit from their place in the GOP network. It didn't matter that Reed had announced publicly that he was leaving the Christian Coalition and going into business, presumably to make a profit. In the eyes of many religious conservatives, Reed was still doing "the Lord's work," and his relation to the Abramoff scandal came as a shock.

Only a month after Reed's defeat, a Pew Forum poll delivered the Republican Party some more bad news. The survey found that the number of Americans saying the Republican Party is friendly to religion fell 8 percentage points, from 55 percent to 47 percent in the past year. Among Catholics and white Evangelicals, the decline was 14 percentage points. Democrats and those on the Religious Left were flushed with excitement with the likelihood that the 2006 election would mark a significant reversal in the voting patterns of religious voters. Most of them failed to notice that Democrats had fared no better in the survey.[5]

BAD NEWS FOR REPUBLICANS

On the morning after the 2006 election, there was good news and bad news. Democrats won back the House and the Senate, but overall gains for the Democrats among religious voters were rather small, with one exception. The GOP remained the party of the religiously active voter. White Evangelicals remained loyal to the GOP nearly at the same level as 2004, and a majority of religiously active white Catholics joined their Evangelical brethren in voting for GOP congressional candidates.

Self-identified white Evangelicals remained with the GOP, voting 72 percent versus 75 percent in 2004. Since this group makes up 22 percent of the total vote, even 3 percent can be significant. Among active white Evangelicals, the percentage went down from 78 to 76 percent, meaning the GOP lost hardly any of their support.

The bigger change came among self-identified white Catholic voters, where the percentage that voted Republican dropped from 54 to 49 percent. The GOP still won the active Catholic vote, but it went down from 58 percent in 2004 to 52 percent. Among all religiously active voters, the Republican vote decreased from 57 to 53 percent but kept an 8 percent lead over the Democrats.

The biggest loss was the white unaffiliated voters, with a drop from 35 percent to 25 percent in voting for the GOP. Additionally, among the least actively religious voters, Democratic support jumped from 60 to 67 percent. As John Green of the Pew Forum put it, "If anything, the 2006 election showed that the majority of the religiously active voters are still in the GOP column, and Democrats still have the greatest appeal to those voters who declare themselves unchurched."[6] Democrats' outreach

5. Amy Sullivan, "Not God's Party," *Slate*, August 29, 2006.

6. "Understanding Religion's Role in the 2008 Election," event transcript, Pew Forum on Religion & Public Life, December 5, 2006.

worked, in other words, with those who were already disposed to favor them.

Green added a comment that is well worth Republicans' noticing: "The 2006 election shows the special relationship that President Bush has with the active religious voters, a connection that will not likely be repeated by the GOP in the future. This is why the choice of presidential candidates is so crucial for the party that wants to attract religious voters—the issue of identification is central."

Where the GOP really suffered serious losses was in the number of prominent religious conservatives in Congress who were defeated, including Rick Santorum (Pennsylvania), Mike DeWine (Ohio), Melissa Hart (Pennsylvania), Ann Northrup (Kentucky), Mike FitzPatrick (Pennsylvania), John Hostlettler (Indiana), Mark Kennedy (Minnesota), Jim Talent (Missouri), Conrad Burns (Montana), and Jim Ryun (Kansas). The pro-life leadership of the Republican Party in Congress was decimated.

In spite of the small percentage increases of religious support for Democrats, reporters and pundits have given much credit for the results to the religious outreach among Democrats. This outreach was headed primarily by Jim Wallis, editor of *Sojourners* and founder of Call to Renewal, and Mara Vanderslice, a political consultant with Common Good Strategies.[7] It's clear that the 2006 election marked the beginning of a new kind of coordinated religious outreach in the Democratic Party. There were no official leaders for this effort, but the public messenger was certainly Jim Wallis.[8] Wallis claims, "I don't consult with or collaborate with Democrats on their strategy." But on December 2, 2006, one month after the election, he was chosen by his friend Senator Harry Reid to give the Democrats' weekly radio address. In all the years of the much-touted relationship between the GOP and the Religious Right, no reli-

7. Alan Cooperman, "Democrats Win Bigger Share of Religious Vote," *Washington Post*, November 11, 2006, A1.

8. David Paul Kuhn, "The Gospel according to Jim Wallis," *Washington Post Magazine*, November 26, 2006, W20.

gious leader had ever been given the chance to deliver the Republican radio address.

Wallis called it a "difficult decision," because "I work hard to maintain my independence and nonpartisanship, and [don't] want to be perceived as supporting one party over the other."[9] It would be hard to imagine anyone knowledgeable in the world of religion and American politics believing that Wallis did not support the Democrats over the GOP. He might state that if the GOP became the party of social justice and concern for the poor he would change his party preference—that would be believable. But to pretend that he personally has no party preference is simply nonsense and does not contribute to his credibility.

As I learned from my own experience working with the White House and the RNC, the moment you do anything under the banner of an administration or a political party, you cannot pretend to be personally nonpartisan any longer. Wallis can respect the nonprofit status of his magazine and his organization by avoiding partisan endorsements of candidates or parties, but he would be better off not pretending to be above the political fray. Unlike some, I don't think it is a mistake for a religious leader to declare a personal preference for one party over the other. This is how the game is played in American politics, how candidates are elected, how legislation is passed, and how agendas are driven. Anyone, with a few a notable exceptions, who has an interest in making a real impact on politics will find themselves in one corner or the other. And there is no shame in that. Wallis may be suffering from the Evangelical post-*Scopes* view that politics is a dirty enterprise and wants to keep his distance from it. As the point man for Democratic religious outreach, his pretence of independence was never necessary.[10]

Mara Vanderslice makes no attempt to hide her agenda. She and

9. Jim Wallis, God's Politics: A Blog, December 1, 2006.

10. On June 4, 2007, Wallis and his organization Sojourners hosted a televised forum at George Washington University with Senators Clinton, Obama, and Edwards, the front runners for the Democratic presidential nomination. "The people of God should never be in the pocket of any political party or candidate," Wallis said at the forum. Christina Bellatoni, "Top Democrats Open Up to Faith," *Washington Times*, June 5, 2007.

her colleagues helped to organize the religious outreach of the 2006 election on the ground in six states. Vanderslice, a former religious advisor to Howard Dean and John Kerry, is on record as saying that her advice to Kerry was routinely ignored in 2004. She was also criticized during the election by Bill Donohue of the Catholic League for her participation in an ACT UP rally. This was the homosexual group that desecrated a mass at St. Patrick's Cathedral while Cardinal O'Connor was celebrating in 1989. Vanderslice wanted to respond to Donohue but was muzzled by the Kerry campaign.

Out of her frustration, Vanderslice created Common Good Strategies in the summer of 2005, along with Eric Sapp, whose father is a Presbyterian minister, to help "Democrats reclaim the debate on faith and values." Their 2006 clients included Bob Casey in Pennsylvania, Reverend Ted Strickland and Sherrod Brown in Ohio, Jennifer Granholm in Michigan, and Kathleen Sebelius in Kansas. All were elected, and exit polls indicated they did 10 percentage points better than Democrats did nationally among religious voters.[11] Some of the races appeared to be carefully chosen to maximize the result of their efforts, a wise move. Casey kept a huge lead over Santorum from day one. Strickland was an ordained Methodist minister in a state poisoned by GOP scandals, and Sebelius was already a popular governor.

Vanderslice and Sapp copied the Christian Coalition playbook. They advised their candidates to speak openly and unapologetically about their faith and its relation to their political positions. Their candidates met with members of the clergy in person and by conference calls. The campaigns bought air time on Christian radio and sought events at religious schools. They had Catholic sisters running phone banks in Michigan and Ohio to urge Catholic voters to vote for Democratic pro-abortion candidates.[12] Anyone who is shocked by this is not well acquainted with the religious and political convictions of most American nuns.

Most important, they wisely told their candidates not to talk about

11. David Kirkpatrick, "Consultant Helps Democrats Embrace Faith, and Some Are Not Pleased," *New York Times,* December 26, 2006.
12. Ibid.

the "separation of church and state" and not to talk about abortion except in terms of reducing the number. As Sapp said after the election, "All the Democrats who made strong gains were talking about abortion reduction. If you reduced poverty in the country by 10 percent, you'd see a 30 percent reduction in abortion." [13]

No one from Common Good Strategies is expecting a revolution in religious voting patterns. But they believe that 2006 showed that by taking a slice, even a small one, from the religious voting bloc of the GOP, the Democrats can keep the Congress and win the presidency. As Sapp explained, "If the Democrats learn the lessons from '06 and implement them, they're going to be in good shape because . . . when you're talking about the Evangelical vote or the Christian vote, there are massive numbers. . . . If the Democrats had won 3.5 percent of the Evangelical vote Bush won, in real numbers that would have been the same as guaranteeing 100 percent African-American turnout at the polls. Small swings can have huge effects on Election Day." [14] This sounds a lot like Karl Rove on the eve of the 2000 election.

Brent Bozell, head of the Media Research Center and chairman of the 1992 Pat Buchanan presidential campaign, sees an opportunity for the Democratic Party to make inroads into the religious conservative community. "The Christian community has been taken for granted for twenty-five years by the GOP. In the eyes of the Republican Party, the Christian community is a source of money, troops, and boats, but good God, don't you dare sit at our table, or go have dinner with servants. I have always felt that insulting, and I don't know why the right-to-life movement has put up with this."

While the marriage between the GOP and religious conservatives is perennially fragile, Bozell added that it may be a "metaphysical impossibility" for the Democrats to understand the need to solve their problems with religious voters. "They would realize the vulnerability and take advantage of it. If the Democratic Party could ever break the chokehold

---

13. "Religious Voters and the Midterm Elections," event transcript, Pew Forum on Religion & Public Life, November 13, 2006.
14. Ibid.

that the pro-abortion movement has on it and reach out to pro-lifers, I think it would find a lot of recruits."

THREE STRATEGIES

Presuming that the Democrats cannot overcome the "metaphysical impossibility" that Bozell mentioned, the likely message of the Democratic Party to Evangelicals in coming elections will be:

1. Republicans talk about family values, but they only pass laws that favor the rich.
2. The Republicans only listen to Religious Right Evangelicals like Dobson and Robertson; they are not listening to you or to your broader concerns for the poor, health care, and the environment.
3. The Religious Right has "hijacked" the gospel and turned it into something angry, divisive, and violent.
4. Our candidates talk about their faith in a way that you, the voter, can identify with more easily than you can with those fanatics on the Religious Right.
5. Religious faith should work to unite people and create compassion for the needy, rather than promote condescension and judgmentalism toward those who choose different values and lifestyles.

Catholics, of course, are the voting group Democrats would most like to woo back into the fold. The historic selection of a woman, the Catholic Nancy Pelosi, as speaker of the House, has given the Democrats at least a two-year window to sell themselves to the Catholic voters who have drifted away. Their message to Catholics in coming elections will be:

1. Democrats will focus on attracting the religiously inactive Catholic voter using the message of social justice, freedom of conscience, and "the spirit of Vatican II."

2. Question the priority of life issues in Catholic social teaching by reviving the "seamless garment" as a political paradigm.

3. Demonize Catholic Republican activists, and build a virtual fence around parishes before elections to eliminate the distribution of voter guides.

4. Showcase some arguably pro-life legislator such as Pennsylvania Senator Bob Casey Jr., son of the late governor, to prove that the party is inclusive.

5. Create an echo effect in the media to enhance the image of pro-abortion Catholic Democrats, for example, by using the 213 diocesan newspapers in the United States and Canada reaching an audience of 6,637,512 readers.

The biggest problem Democrats will have is convincing their feminist and gay supporters to allow any kind of religious outreach to continue. Many will see this as a threat to the moral relativism enabling their on-going pursuit of "rights" that counteract the traditional family and sexual roles.

Fearing the reentry of traditional believers into the Democratic ranks, some Democratic activists may embrace the new proponents of atheism," such as Sam Harris, Richard Dawkins, Daniel Dennett, and Christopher Hitchens.[15] Their books are best-sellers, not because of their attacks on God and religion per se but because they are targeting a favorite enemy, the Religious Right. These atheists, like the religionists on the left, are really interested in politics, not God.

Harris, for example, used the 2004 Republican National Convention as the launching pad to promote his breakthrough book *The End of Faith*. And his *Letter to a Christian Nation* was published just in time to take advantage of the debate on politics and religion before the 2006 election. Harris writes in a way reminiscent of the atheistic philosopher

15. Sam Harris, *The End of Faith* (New York: W. W. Norton, 2004), and *Letter to a Christian Nation* (New York: Alfred A. Knopf, 2006); Richard Dawkins, *The God Delusion* (Boston: Houghlin Mifflin, 2006); David Dennett, *Breaking the Spell: Religion as Natural Phenomenon* (New York: Viking Adult, 2006); Christopher Hitchens, *God Is Not Great: How Religion Poisons Everything* (New York: Twelve, 2007).

Bertrand Russell, who wrote similar tracts in the '50s. Harris, however, shapes his argument to fit the media stereotype of the Religious Right: "There is, in fact, no worldview more reprehensible in its arrogance than that of a religious believer: *the creator of the universe takes an interest in me, approves of me, loves me, and will reward me after death; my current beliefs, drawn from scripture, will remain the best statement of the truth until the end of the world; everyone who disagrees with me will spend an eternity in hell.* . . . An average Christian, in an average church, listening to an average Sunday sermon has achieved a level of arrogance simply unimaginable in scientific discourse—and there have been some extraordinarily arrogant scientists."[16]

Harris may have had the "extraordinarily arrogant" Richard Dawkins in mind, but I don't think so. Dawkins has become Harris's chief ally in the attack on faith. Dawkins quotes him often and approvingly. A professor at Oxford, Dawkins made his name in the United States defending evolutionary biology against the attacks of creationists and proponents of intelligent design. His *The God Delusion* became a best-seller after it was published in late 2006. Like Harris, Dawkins is not just interested in refuting basic credal beliefs; he wants to show why people of faith are fanatical and bigoted. After Dawkins is finished dismissing proofs for the existence of God, he makes sure everyone knows where he stands on Pat Robertson: "Pat Robertson would be harmless comedy, were he less typical of those who today hold power and influence in the United States."[17]

Both Harris and Dawkins represent the protest of intellectuals against the fact that God never died and the secular city was never established. Their evangelical atheism will have a powerful appeal to the secular liberal wing of the Democratic Party. But if they are lured in this direction, Democrats will lose all hopes of capitalizing on their gains of 2006.

There's not much chance of atheism infiltrating the GOP ranks. Republican leadership is likely to embrace the demands of religious conservatives, even if their heart really isn't in it. The GOP, however, should beware of the reemergence of religion among Democrats, as represented

16. Harris, *Letter*, 74–75, emphasis added.
17. Dawkins, *The God Delusion*, 239.

by the "Catholic grandmother," Speaker Nancy Pelosi. Democrats will use their religious outreach to pummel the GOP on poverty, war, and global warming. Republicans are most vulnerable, and will continue to be, when seen through the eyes of Catholics and Evangelicals as the white-only party of the rich, uncaring toward the poor, too quick to employ America's military might, and dismissive of environmental issues. To reinvigorate its coalition of religious conservatives, it would be a mistake for Republicans to spend all of their energy trying to convince the electorate that the Democrats are wrong.

If the GOP tries to reinvent itself as the party of social justice, it will lose. It's much more important to stick to the basics:

1. Consistently defend the family by keeping the marriage amendment alive and continue to work on passing admendment to protect *all* unborn life.
2. Embrace a larger range of social issues from a religious perspective by endorsing faith-based, rather than governmental, solutions.
3. Emphasize judicial appointments and the historic problem of left-wing judges legislating from the bench.
4. Pick the right presidential candidate. Any nominee without a pro-life and pro-family record will split the GOP and hand the election to the Democrats. (The argument "Where else can they go?" does not work, because religious conservatives are religious first and Republican second. They will stay home or form a third party.)
5. Remind voters of George W. Bush's accomplishments in defense of life and the family—that he did more for religious conservatives than any other president, including Ronald Reagan.

The GOP needs to remember what earned it the support of religious conservatives in the first place and stay the course in the midst of the tremendous pressure to "moderate" its message. Religious conservatives know that in politics, "moderate" is a code word for being sold out. "Moderate" need not become synonymous with a leader or candidate who has concerns, say, for the HIV/AIDS epidemic in Africa. Pastor Rick Warren is not a moderate simply because he has included among his priorities the AIDS epidemic in Africa.

The importance of the GOP picking the right candidate was reinforced by my interview with Matt Smith, who worked in the White House Office of Public Liaison during the first six years of the Bush administration. His job, along with Tim Goeglein, was religious coalition building with Catholics and Evangelicals. I asked him what motivated religious conservatives to support Bush and the GOP. "What I heard constantly was that 'the president understands us; he is one of us,'" Smith explained. "He let himself and faith be seen, for example, when he said during the Iowa caucus, 'Jesus is my favorite philosopher.' That helped him, even though the media made fun of him." Smith told me that from his experience working in the White House, religious conservatives could identify with Bush because of their desire to make faith part of their lives and the lives of their children. "Bush is not afraid to talk about that." Smith added that religious voters could not identify with either Gore or Kerry. "Do you wind-surf or own a vacation home in Idaho?"

RENDER UNTO CAESAR

Religiously active voters have developed a nose for distinguishing sincere piety from political messaging. The only religious outreach that will work consistently is one that does not seek to mislead and manipulate people of faith with candidates scripted in religious rhetoric and deft at making symbolic connections with the religious imagination. Religious outreach will be successful only when fundamental religious rituals and maxims are respected and not reconfigured to conform to party pressures.

This is easier said than done. "Politics is about compromise; the kingdom of God is about conviction and eternal truth," says Cal Thomas. One of the nation's leading political and cultural commentators, Thomas once worked as communications director for Jerry Falwell at the Moral Majority. He left in 1985, after he decided what he was doing, and what the Moral Majority was doing, was bad for his faith and hurting his church. Together with Ed Dobson, Thomas wrote *Blinded by Might,* as an account of their involvement with the Religious Right and their reasons for leaving it behind.[18] "I just think the church always loses in these things, and the church ends up compromising for access."

Thomas remembers when he went on *Nightline* and raised questions about Reagan's nomination of Sandra Day O'Connor to the Supreme Court. "I got chastised by one of the top leaders at Moral Majority. He said, 'Yeah, but we have to maintain access to Reagan.' That was a great message. This was our premiere issue. Abortion is called the number one sin in America, but we were willing to trim our sails in order to keep access to Reagan, in order for people to think we were having influence so they would send money."

I asked Thomas what he thought of the argument used by religious conservatives that it's important they keep their "place at the table." Thomas said it is preferable for the people of faith to stay on the "outside." He continued, "During my years in this game, I always heard the argument that it's better to be at the table having influence than it is to be outside being a harping critic. This is certainly not the attitude of Jesus or the disciples. These guys were outside like you wouldn't believe. They were outside of the Roman government, and they were outside of Jewish leadership. I remember visiting the prison in Rome where Paul was held. You come up out of the prison. Just 50 to 100 yards away are the ruins of the Roman Forum in an empire that was going to envelop the world and last forever. What came up out of that prison is what has changed the world, not the Roman Forum. I remember Ralph Reed's line the year *Time* magazine put him on the cover. He said that Evangelicals had finally found a place at the table. I wrote a piece at the time asking, is this why Jesus died? So we could find a place at the table with the teachers unions? Is that what gospel is all about?"

18. Cal Thomas and Ed Dobson, *Blinded by Might: Can the Religious Right Save America?* (Grand Rapids, Mich.: Zondervan, 1999).

I reminded Thomas about "incrementalism," the political approach recommended by John Paul II in *Evangelium Vitae*. That encyclical was a powerful call to build a culture of life, but John Paul II included a section on the legitimate tactic of supporting policies that stop short of completely outlawing abortion and euthanasia. He urged Catholics to seek incremental progress, when it was impossible to be successful in securing the final goal. "I have a problem with that. It's like co-belligerency. I'm for speaking truth to power, speaking about justice for the unborn, poor, and a lot of other things. In a wicked generation, to borrow another line from Scripture, without the power of the life-changing word of God, you are a 'sounding brass and tinkling cymbal.'"

Thomas then told me a story about George H. W. Bush. "He came to a religious broadcasters convention in Washington, and he talked about his favorite Bible verse, John 16:3. I said I didn't know he suffered from dyslexia. Obviously somebody said, 'Quote this, and they'll vote for you.' It's cynical, it's manipulative, but it's politics. They all do it. A white guy goes into an NAACP meeting and quotes MLK. Just name your group, a Protestant goes before a Catholic group and quotes the pope. That's what politicians do; they try to give the idea that maybe he is one of us. But maybe he is, and maybe he isn't."

The possibility of hoax is always there. Politics, after all, is partly about image making, partly about the art of creating a sense of identification between the voter and the candidate. The GOP will continue to cultivate religious conservatives, and the Democrats will extend the religious outreach strategy that bore fruit in 2006. There will be sincere expressions of faith from social-justice and social-conservative candidates. And there will be a repackaging of secular candidates who will end up looking foolish when they stumble over their scripts. But there will be conversions, too. Once the glamour of campaigning gives way to the responsibility of public service, especially in the White House, I believe it can soften even the hardest heart. Seemingly forgotten prayers, learned by rote as a child, can come back with an unexpected force of meaning in the face of decisions about the life and health of our nation.

David Barton, the influential head of WallBuilders, doesn't agree with

Cal Thomas. Shortly after the publication of *Blinded by Might*, Senator Sam Brownback (R-Kansas) organized a debate on the issue at the Library of Congress. Barton was one of the Religious Right leaders invited to take the position contrary to Ed Dobson and Cal Thomas. When it was Barton's turn to speak, he said, "Christ gave forty-nine commands, and one of those is to render unto Caesar the things that are Caesar's. Government is ordained by God, so as a Christian I have to be involved."

Barton remembers that the debate went back and forth until Ed Dobson told the audience that at his church, he didn't talk about voting but was active in street ministries, such as handing out free lunches. Pat Nolan from Prison Fellowship said, "Dobson, I am really glad you are doing that, but what about the minister in San Diego who got five years for doing the exact thing you are doing?" According to Barton, Dobson didn't say anything for the rest of the debate. "You have to protect your rights, or you will have them taken away," warns Barton.

In spite of the cynical uses of religious outreach in politics, Barton is exactly right. If the people of faith walk away from politics, religious liberty itself will be threatened. As in the case of Scott Bloch, head of the Office of Special Counsel, the gay-rights movement is provoking a head-on collision with the religious liberty of traditional Christians. That threat is not going to subside.

There are many in the GOP who don't want to engage issues such as gay marriage, just as they didn't want to take on the feminists over the ERA in the '70s. They will argue that such issues are divisive and stand in the way of a GOP victory. This is a formula for defeat. They will argue, like the Democrats, that any use of religion in politics should help "move us to the center." The success of religious conservatives ensures that religion and the spectrum of family-related issues will be front and center in future presidential campaigns. But the challenge posed to religious conservatives as they survey the field of candidates requires political prudence, not heavy-handed dismissal. Prudence guides legitimate compromise, and courage discerns the right moment to draw a line and say, "Enough."

How much trust should be shown to politicians who make socially conservative statements when they have no discernible track record? As in the case of the Harriet Miers nomination, religious conservatives have come to a point where they need more than promises, more than a "born-again" experience to give their support. Yet again, there is the example of George H. W. Bush, who, once presented with scientific facts, changed his mind on abortion and never looked back.

Religious outreach in politics, as Cal Thomas argues, is fraught with temptations. Part of that outreach is to politicians, not just to voters. Politicians can be converted, too. It's cynical to assume all expressions of a candidate's faith as opportunistic political marketing. Candidates don't help, of course, when they talk about their religious faith as if they're reciting stump-speech boilerplate.

Campaigns are long, drawn-out affairs and becoming more so. The candidates, especially presidential nominees, are thrown under a very bright light. Under that glare, religious conservatives inevitably will recognize candidates overselling their religiosity, whether it's "I was an altar boy" or "I am a Catholic grandmother." The same is true for the political parties, as a whole.

At present, the Democrats can honestly tout their social-justice agenda and hope that voters believe it will reduce the number of abortions. This is a plausible, if unproven, position. Republicans should keep faith with the religious conservatives in their ranks by reaffirming core values about the family, marriage, and life. The grassroots desire for social renewal in American society brought religious conservatives into politics, but renewal will not be accomplished by the mere fact of having a "place at the table." Accepting anything less than inclusion at the top tier of policy concerns and legislative priorities is a step backward.

Future presidential campaigns will reveal whether or not the GOP considers religious conservatives indispensable. They also will provide a test for the Religious Right. Have its leaders become so used to a White House welcome that they will settle for any candidate who can win? Will religious conservatives make their support contingent on continued commitment to their core issues? The Republican Party will do only what is demanded of it.

The answers to these questions will determine the future of religious conservatives in politics, and the GOP. The Catholics who found their way into the Republican Party have not been there long enough to feel deep loyalty. Evangelicals fall in line less and less when a Robertson or a Dobson issues a call to arms. Politics exists in a flux of ever-changing contingencies. Engaging that flux with the people of faith requires both political savvy and commitment to the first principles that faith provides. The Catholics and Evangelicals of the Religious Right gained political power because they were numerous enough to force the GOP to take a stand on life and the family. Their continued power will depend on both the vitality of their religious communities and the principled translation of that vitality into political action.

BIBLIOGRAPHY

Aikman, David. *A Man of Faith: The Spiritual Journey of George W. Bush.* Nashville, Tenn.: W Publishing Group, 2004.

Aitken, Jonathan. *Charles W. Colson: A Life Redeemed.* Colorado Springs, Colo.: Waterbrook Press, 2005.

Alexander-Moegerle. Gil. *James Dobson's War on America.* Amherst, Mass.: Prometheus Books, 1997.

Allen, Brooke. *Moral Minority: Our Skeptical Founding Fathers.* Chicago: Ivan R. Dee, 2006.

Allen, John L. *The Rise of Benedict XVI.* New York: Doubleday, 2005.

Allison, Jim. "The 'Christian Nation' Decision and Rebuttal." http//members.tripod.com/~candst/holytrin.htm.

———. "The NRA (National Reform Association) and the Christian Amendment." www.candst.tripod.com/nra.htm.

Allitt, Patrick. *Religion in America Since 1945: A History.* New York: Columbia University Press, 2003.

Altizer, Thomas J. *The Gospel of Christian Atheism.* Philadelphia: Westminster Press, 1966.

Alitzer, Thomas J. and Hamilton, William. *Radical Theology and the Death of God.* Indianapolis: Bobbs-Merrill, 1966.

American Religious Identity Survey, 2001. www.gc.cuny.edu/faculty/research_briefs/aris/aris_index.htm.

Aquinas, Thomas. *Summa Theologica.* Thomas Gilby, ed. New York: McGraw-Hill, 1966.

Arroyo, Raymond. *Mother Angelica: The Remarkable Story of a Nun, Her Nerve, and a Network of Miracles.* New York: Doubleday, 2005.

Balmer, Randall. *Thy Kingdom Come: An Evangelical's Lament.* New York: Basic Books, 2006.

Baptist Joint Committee on Public Affairs, "Critique of David Barton's 'America's Godly Heritage.'" http://candst.tripod.com/bjcpa1.htm.

Barrett, Lawrence I. "Pulpit Politics." *Time,* August 31, 1992.

Beasley, Maurine H. Holly C. Shulman, and Henry R. Beasley, eds. *The Eleanor Roosevelt Encyclopedia.* Westport, Conn.: Greenwood Press, 2001.

Begala, Paul, and James Carville. *Take It Back: A Battle Plan for Democratic Victory,* New York: Simon & Schuster, 2006.

Bellatoni, Christina. "Top Democrats Open Up to Faith." *Washington Times,* June 5, 2007.

Bernstein, Carl and Marco Politi. *His Holiness: John Paul II and the History of Our Time.* New York: Penguin Books, 1997.

Black, Alida M., ed. *Courage in a Dangerous World: The Political Writings of Eleanor Roosevelt.* New York: Columbia University Press, 1999.

Black, Earl and Merle Black. *The Rise of Southern Republicans.* Cambridge, Mass.: Belknap Press, 2002.

Blake, Mariah. "Stations of the Cross: How Evangelical Christians Are Creating an Alternative Universe Faith-Based News." *Columbia Journalism Review* (May–June 2005).

Blanchard, Dallas A. *The Anti-Abortion Movement and the Rise of the Religious Right: From Polite to Fiery Protest.* New York: Twayne, 1994.

Blanchard, Paul. *American Freedom and Catholic Power.* Boston: Beacon Press, 1949.

Boston, Robert. *Close Encounters with the Religious Right: Journeys into the Twilight Zone of Religion and Politics.* Amherst, Mass.: Prometheus Books, 2000.

———. *The Most Dangerous Man in America? Pat Robertson and the Rise of the Christian Coalition.* Amherst, Mass.: Prometheus Books, 1996.

———. *Why the Religious Right is Wrong about Separation of Church and State.* Buffalo, N.Y.: Prometheus Books, 1993.

Bozell Jr., L. Brent, and William F. Buckley. *McCarthy and His Enemies.* Chicago: Regnery, 1954.

Bozell III, L. Brent. *Mustard Seeds: A Conservative Becomes Catholic.* Manassas, Va.: Trinity Communications, 1986.

Brooks, Arthur. *Who Really Cares: The Surprising Truth About Compassionate Conservatism.* New York: Basic Books, 2006.

"Brothers and Sisters to Us." U.S. Catholic Bishops Pastoral Letter on Racism, 1979. www.nccbuscc.org/saac/bishopspastoral.shtml.

Brown, Candy Gunther. *The Word in the World: Evangelical Writing, Publishing, and Reading in America 1789–1880.* Chapel Hill: University of North Carolina Press, 2004.

Brown, Ruth Murray. *For a "Christian America": A History of the Religious Right.* Amherst: Prometheus Books, 2002.

Bruce, Steve. *The Rise and Fall of the New Christian Right: Conservative Protestant Politics in America, 1978–1988.* Oxford: Clarendon Press, 1988.

Bruce, Steve, Peter Kivisto, and William H. Swatos, Jr. *The Rapture of Politics: The Christian Right as the United States Approaches the Year 2000.* New Brunswick, N.S.: Transaction Publishers, 1995.

Buckley, James L. *Gleanings from an Unplanned Life: An Annotate Oral History.* Wilmington, Del.: ISI, 2006.

Buckley, William F., Jr. "The Catholic Church and Abortion." *National Review.* April 5, 1966: p. 308.

———. *God and Man at Yale: The Superstitions of "Academic Freedom."* South Bend, Ind.: Regnery/Gateway, 1977.

———. *Nearer My God: An Autobiography of Faith.* New York: Doubleday, 1997.

Budziszewski, J. *Written on the Heart: The Case for Natural Law.* Downer's Grove, Ill.: InterVarsity Press, 1997.

Butler, Jennifer S. *Born Again: The Christian Right Globalized.* Ann Arbor, Mich.: Pluto Press, 2006.

Byrnes, Timothy A. *Catholic Bishops in American Politics.* Princeton, N.J.: Princeton University Press, 1991.

Campbell, David, E., ed. *A Matter of Faith: Religion In the 2004 Presidential Election.* Washington, D.C.: Brookings Institution Press, 2007.

Campolo, Tony. *Letters to a Young Evangelical.* New York: Basic Books, 2006.

Carlin, David. *Can a Catholic be a Democrat? How the Party I Loved Became the Enemy of My Religion.* Manchester, N.H.: Sophia Institute Press, 2006.

———. *The Decline and Fall of the Catholic Church in America.* Manchester: Sophia Institute Press, 2003.

Carter, Dan T. *From George Wallace to New Gingrich: Race in the Conservative Counterrevolution.* Baton Rouge, La.: Louisiana State University Press, 1996.

———. *The Politics of Rage: George Wallace, the Origins of the New Conservatism, and the Transformation of American Politics.* New York: Simon & Schuster, 1995.

Carty, Thomas J. *A Catholic in the White House? Religion, Politics, and John F. Kennedy's Presidential Campaign.* New York: Palgrave MacMillan, 2004.

Castelli, Jim. *The Bishops and the Bomb: Waging Peace in a Nuclear Age.* Garden City, N.Y.: Image Books, 1983.

———. *The Emerging Parish: The Notre Dame Study of Catholic Life Since Vatican II.* Cambridge, Mass.: Harper & Row, 1987.

————. *A Plea for Common Sense: Resolving the Clash Between Religion and Politics.* Cambridge, Mass.: Harper & Row, 1988.

Clarkson, Frederic. *Eternal Hostility: The Struggle Between Theocracy and Democracy.* Monroe, Me.: Common Courage Press, 1997.

Conway, Flo, and Jim Siegelman. *Holy Terror: The Fundamentalist War on America's Freedom in Religion, Politics, and Our Private Lives.* Garden City, N.Y.: Doubleday, Inc., 1982.

Cooney, John. *The American Pope: The Life and Times of Francis Cardinal Spellman.* New York: Times Books, 1984.

Cooperman, Alan. "Democrats Win Bigger Share of Religious Vote." *Washington Post,* November 11, 2006; A1.

Corrin, Jay P. *Catholic Intellectuals and the Challenge of Democracy.* South Bend, Ind.: University of Notre Dame Press, 2002.

Coulter, Ann. *Godless: The Church of Liberalism.* New York: Crown Forum, 2006.

Cox, Harvey. *Fire from Heaven: The Rise of Pentecostal Spirituality and the Reshaping of Religion in the Twenty-First Century.* Reading, Pa.: Addison-Wesley, 1995.

————. *The Secular City: Secularization and Urbanization in Theological Perspective.* New York: Macmillan, 1965.

Critchlow, Donald T. "Mobilizing Women: The Social Issues." In *The Reagan Presidency,* eds. W. Elliot Brownless and Hugh Davis Graham. Lawrence, Kan.: University of Kansas Press, 2003.

————. *Phyllis Schlafly and Grassroots Conservatism: A Woman's Crusade.* Princeton, N.J.: Princeton University Press, 2005.

Crocker, Harry III. *Triumph: The Power and the Glory of the Catholic Church.* Roseville, Calif.: Prima Publishing, 2001.

Cross, Robert. *The Emergence of Liberal Catholicism in America.* Cambridge, Mass.: Harvard University Press, 1958.

Cuneo, Michael W. *The Smoke of Satan: Conservative and Traditionalist Dissent in American Catholicism.* Baltimore: Johns Hopkins University Press, 1997.

Danforth, Senator John. *Faith and Politics: How the "Moral Values" Debate Divides America and How to Move Forward Together.* New York: Viking Penguin, 2006.

"David Barton on the Foundation of American Freedom," *The 700 Club.* www.cbn.com/spirituallife/ChurchAndMinistry/ChurchHistory/David_Barton_Foundations0207.aspx.

Dawkins, Richard. *The God Delusion.* Boston: Houghton Mifflin, 2006.

Dennett, Daniel. *Breaking the Spell: Religion as a Natural Phenomenon.* New York: Viking Adult, 2006.

Diamond, Sara. *Not by Politics Alone: The Enduring Influence of the Christian Right.* New York: Guilford Press, 1998.

———. *Spiritual Warfare: The Politics of the Christian Right.* Boston: Southend Press, 1989.

"Dignitatis Humane." I.2.; Austin Flannery, ed. *Vatican Council II: Constitutions, Decrees, Declarations.* New York: Costello, 1996.

Dobson, James. *Dare to Discipline.* Glendale, Calif.: Regal Books, 1970.

Dobson, James, and C. Everett Koop. *Whatever Happened to the Human Race?* Old Tappan, N.J.: Fleming H. Revell Company, 1979.

Dolan, Jay P. *The American Catholic Experience: A History from Colonial Times to the Present.* New York: Oxford University Press, 1985.

———. *In Search of an American Catholicism.* Oxford: Oxford University Press, 2002.

Donohue, William A. *Twilight of Liberty: The Legacy of the ACLU.* New Brunswick, N.J.: Transaction Publishers, 2005.

Drinan, Robert F. *Can God & Caesar Co-Exist? Balancing Religious Freedom & International Law.* New Haven, Conn.: Yale University Press, 2004.

Dworkin, Ronald. *Taking Rights Seriously.* Boston: Harvard University Press, 1977.

Easton, Nina J. *Gang of Five: Leaders at the Center of the Conservative Crusade.* New York: Simon & Schuster, 2000.

Edsall, Thomas Byrne. *Building Red America: The New Conservative Coalition and the Dive for Permanent Power.* New York: Basic Books, 2006.

Edsall, Thomas Byrne, and Mary Edsall. *Chain Reaction: The Impact of Race, Rights, and Taxes in American Politics.* Reprint ed. New York: W.W. Norton, 1992.

Edwards, Lee. *The Conservative Revolution: The Movement That Remade America.* New York: Free Press, 1999.

———. *Goldwater: The Man Who Made a Revolution.* Washington, D.C.: Regnery, 1995.

El-Faizy, Monique. *God and Country: How Evangelicals Have Become America's New Mainstream.* New York: Bloomsbury, 2006.

"Evangelicals and Catholics Together: The Christian Mission in the Third Millennium." *First Things* (April 1994): Introduction.

Fabro, Cornelio. *God in Exile: Modern Atheism,* Trans. Arthur Gibson. Westminster, Md.: Newman Press, 1968.

Falwell, Jerry. *Falwell, an Autobiography.* Lynchburg, Va.: Liberty House Publishers, 1997.

Feeney, Mark. "Congressman-Priest Dies." *Boston Globe,* January 29, 2007.

Feldman, Noah. *Divided by God: America's Church-State Problem—And What We Should Do About It.* New York: Farrar, Straus and Giroux, 2005.

Filteau, Jerry. "Catholic Polarization Reached New Peak in 2004 Election, Speaker Says," Catholic News Service, February 22, 2005.

Finke, Roger, and Rodney Stark. *The Churching of America, 1776–2005: Winners and Losers in Our Religious Economy.* New Brunswick, N.J.: Rutgers University Press, 2005.

Fletcher, Joseph. *Situation Ethics: The New Morality.* Philadelphia: Westminister John Knox Press, 1967.

Flynn, George Q. *American Catholics & The Roosevelt Presidency 1932–1936.* Lexington: University of Kentucky Press, 1968.

Fowler, Robert Booth. *A New Engagement: Evangelical Political Thought, 1966–1976.* Grand Rapids, Mich.: William B. Eerdsmans, 1982.

Frank, Thomas. *What's the Matter with Kansas: How Conservatives Won the Heart of America.* New York: Henry Holt, 2004.

Froehle, Bryan T. and Mary T. Gautier. *Catholicism USA: A Portrait of the Catholic Church in the United States.* Maryknoll, N.Y.: Orbis Books, 2000.

Galloway, Jim. "Cagle Tops Reed for GOP Nomination." *Atlanta Journal-Constitution.* July 19, 2006.

Gallup, George Jr. and Jim Castelli. *The American Catholic People: Their Beliefs, Practices, and Values.* Garden City, N.Y.: Doubleday, 1987.

———. *The People's Religion: American Faith in the 90's.* New York: MacMillan, 1989.

Garry, Patrick M. *Wrestling with God: The Courts' Tortuous Treatment of Religion.* Washington, D.C.: The Catholic University of America Press, 2006.

Gelm, Richard J. *Politics and Religious Authority: American Catholics Since the Second Vatican Council.* Westport, Conn.: Greenwood Press, 1994.

George, Robert, and William Saunders. "The Failure of Catholic Political Leaderhip." *Crisis* (April 2000).

Gilgoff, Dan. *The Jesus Machine: How James Dobson, Focus on the Family, and Evangelical America Are Winning the Culture War.* New York: St. Martin's Press, 2007.

Glenn, Charles Leslie. *The Myth of the Common School.* Amherst, Mass.: University of Massachusetts Press, 1988.

Gold, Philip. *Take Back the Right: How Neocons and the Religious Right Have Betrayed the Conservative Movement.* New York: Carroll & Graf, 2004.

Goldberg, Michelle. *Kingdom Coming: The Rise of Christian Nationalism.* New York: W.W. Norton, 2006.

Goldstein, Warren. *William Sloan Coffin, Jr.: A Holy Impatience.* New Haven, Conn.: Yale University Press, 2004.

Goldwater, Barry. *The Conscience of a Conservative.* New York: MacFadden Books, 1960.

Goodstein, Laurie. "How the Evangelicals and Catholics Joined Forces." *New York Times,* May 30, 2004: 4.4.

Grant, Philip A. Jr. "Catholic Congressmen, Cardinal Spellman, Eleanor Roosevelt and the 1949–1950 Federal Aid to Education Controversy." *American Catholic Historical Society of Philadelphia Records* 90 (1979): 3–13.

Greely, Andrew. "The '*Crisis* Survey.'" *America,* October 30, 1999: 6.

Green, John C., Mark J. Rozell, and Clyde Wilcox, eds. *The Christian Right in American Politics: Marching to the Millennium.* Washington, D.C.: Georgetown University Press, 2003.

Greenberg, Stan and Matt Hogan. "Reclaiming the White Catholic Vote." www .democracycorps.com/reports/analyses/Democracy_Corps_March_2005_ Catholic_Analysis.pdf>.

Haberman, Aaron. "Into the Wilderness: Ronald Reagan, Bob Jones University, and the Political Education of the Religious Right." *The Historian,* 2005.

Hanna, Mary T. *Catholics and American Politics.* Cambridge, Mass.: Harvard University Press, 1979.

Hanson, Eric O. *The Catholic Church in World Politics.* Princeton, N.J.: Princeton University Press, 1987.

Hardisty, Jean. *Mobilizing Resentment: Conservative Resurgence from the John Birch Society to the Promise Keepers.* Boston: Beacon Press, 1999.

Harris, Sam. *End of Faith.* New York: W.W. Norton, 2004.

———. *Letter to a Christian Nation.* New York: Alfred A. Knopf, 2006.

Hart, Gary. *Religious Right: God and Caesar in America: An Essay on Religion and Politics.* Golden, Colo.: Fulcrum Publishing, 2005.

Hart, Jeffrey. *The Making of the American Conservative Mind.* Wilmington, Del.: ISI Books, 2005.

Hasson, Kevin Seamus. *The Right to Be Wrong: Ending the Culture War over Religion in America.* San Francisco: Encounter Books, 2005.

Hebblethwaite, Peter. *Paul VI, The First Modern Pope.* New York: Paulist Press, 1993.

Hedges, Chris. *Christian Fascists: The Christian Right and the War on America.* New York: Free Press, 2007.

Heft, James L. *A Catholic Modernity? Charles Taylor's Marianist Award Lecture.* New York: Oxford University Press, 1999.

Heineman, Kenneth J. *God Is a Conservative: Religion, Politics, and Morality in Contemporary America.* New York: New York University Press, 1998.

Hemming, Laurence Paul. *Benedict XVI: Fellow Worker for the Truth.* London: Burns and Oates, 2005.

Hendershott, Anne. *The Politics of Abortion.* New York: Encounter Books, 2006.

Hennesey, James. *American Catholics: A History of the Roman Catholic Community in the United States.* New York: Oxford University Press, 1981.

Hentoff, Nat. *John Cardinal O'Connor at the Storm Center of a Changing American Catholic Church.* New York: Charles Scribner's Sons, 1987.

Hewitt, Hugh. *Painting the Map Red: The Fight to Create a Permanent Republican Majority.* Washington, D.C.: Regnery, 2006.

Himmelstein, Jerome L. *To the Right: The Transformation of American Conservatism.* Berkeley, Calif.: University of California Press, 1990.

Hitchcock, James. "The Strange Political Career of Father Drinan." *Catholic World Report* (July 1996).

Hitchens, Christopher. *God Is Not Great: How Religion Poisons Everything.* New York: Twelve, 2007.

Hodgson, Godfrey. *The World Turned Right Side Up: A History of the Conservative Ascendancy in America.* Boston: Houghton Mifflin, 1996.

Holifield, E. Brooks. *Theology in America: Christian Thought for the Age of the Puritans to the Civil War.* New Haven, Conn.: Yale University Press, 2003.

Holmes, David L. *The Faiths of the Founding Fathers.* Oxford: Oxford University Press, 2006.

Hout, Michael and Andrew M. Greeley. "A Hidden Swing Vote: Evangelicals." *New York Times,* September 4, 2004.

Hudson, Deal W. *American Conversion: One Man's Search for Beauty and Truth in a Time of Crisis.* New York: Crossroad, 2003.

———. "*Crisis* Interview with Jim Towey," *Crisis* (June 2002).

———. *Happiness and the Limits of Satisfaction.* Lanham: Rowman & Littlefield, 1996.

Hunter, James Davidson. *Culture Wars: The Struggle to Define America.* New York: Basic Books, 1991.

Hynes, Patrick. *In Defense of the Religious Right: Why Conservative Christians Are the Lifeblood of the Republican Party and Why That Terrifies the Democrats.* Nashville, Tenn.: Nelson Current, 2006.

Jenkins, Philip. *Decade of Nightmares: The End of the Sixties and the Making of Eighties America.* New York: Oxford University Press, 2006.

———. *The New Anti-Catholicism: The Last Acceptable Prejudice.* New York: Oxford University Press, 2003.

Jonsen, Albert. "Theological Ethics, Moral Philosophy, and Public Moral Discourse." *Kennedy Institute of Ethics Journal,* vol. 4, no. 1 (1994).

Kaplan, Esther. *With God on Their Side: George W. Bush and the Christian Right.* New York: New Press, 2004.

Keller, Catherine. *God and Power: Counter-Apocalyptic Journeys.* Minneapolis, Minn.: Fortress Press, 2004.

Kelly, George A. *The Battle for the American Church.* Garden City, N.Y.: Image Books, 1981.

———. *The Battle for the American Church Revisited.* San Francisco: Ignatius Press, 1995.

Kengor, Paul. *God and Ronald Reagan: A Spiritual Life.* New York: Regan, 2004.

King, Martin Luther, Jr. "The Letter from Birmingham Jail." *I Have a Dream: Writings and Speeches That Changed the World* Ed. James Melvin Washington. San Francisco: HarperSanFrancisco, 2006.

Kirkpatrick, David. "Consultant Helps Democrats Embrace Faith, and Some Are Not Pleased." *New York Times,* December 26, 2006.

Kirkpatrick, David, and Laurie Goodstein. "Group of Bishops Using Influence to Oppose Kerry." *New York Times,* October 12, 2004.

Krannawitter, Thomas L., and Daniel C. Palm. *A Nation Under God? The ACLU and Religion in American Politics.* Lanham, M.D.: Rowman & Littlefield Inc., 2005.

Kuhn, David Paul. "The Gospel According to Jim Wallis." *The Washington Post Magazine,* November 26, 2006: W20.

Kuo, David. *Tempting Faith: The Inside Story of a Political Seduction.* New York: Free Press, 2006.

LaGanga, Maria L. "Kerry's Take on Catholicism 'Typical.'" *Los Angeles Times,* May 2, 2004: A24.

Land, Richard. "Francis Schaeffer and C. Everett Koop's Invaluable Impact on Pro-Life Evangelism." www.nrlc.org/news/2003/NRL01/land.html.

Lassiter, Matthew D. *The Silent Majority: Suburban Politics in the Sunbelt South.* Princeton, N.J.: Princeton University Press, 2006.

Lawrence, Michael, Ed. *The Best of Triumph.* Front Royal, Va.: Christendom Press, 2001.

Layman, Geoffrey. *The Great Divide: Religious and Cultural Conflict in American Party Politics.* New York: Columbia University Press, 2001.

Lerner, Michael. *The Left Hand of God: Taking Back Our Country from the Religious Right.* San Francisco: HarperCollins, 2006.

Lewis, C. S. *The Abolition of Man,* new ed. San Francisco: HarperSanFrancisco, 2001.

Liaugminas, S. G. "Catholicism with a Latin Beat." *Crisis* (September 2001).

Link, Richard. *American Catholicism and European Immigrants.* New York: Center for Migration Studies, 1975.

Linker, Damon. *The Theocons: Secular America Under Siege.* New York: Doubleday, 2006.

Linn, Jan G. *What's Wrong with the Christian Right.* Boca Raton, Fla.: Brown-Walker Press, 2004.

Locke, John. *An Essay Concerning Human Understanding.* Peter H. Niddith, ed. New York: Oxford University Press, 1975.

Lockwood, Robert, ed. *Anti-Catholicism in American Culture.* Bloomington, Ind.: Our Sunday Visitor Press, 2000.

Lynn, Barry W. *Piety & Politics: The Right-Wing Assault on Religious Freedom.* New York: Harmony Books, 2006.

Madison, James. "Memorial and Remonstrance Against Religious Assessments." *James Madison: Writings,* ed. Jack N. Rakone. New York: Penguin Putnam, 1999.

Madrid, Patrick. *Surprised by Truth 3: 10 More Converts Explain the Biblical and Historical Reasons for Becoming Catholic.* Manchester, N.H.: Sophia Institute Press, 2002.

Manion, Clarence. *The Conservative American: His Fight for National Independence and Constitutional Government.* New York: Devin-Adair, 1964.

Maritain, Jacques. *On the Uses of Philosophy.* Princeton, N.J.: Princeton University Press, 1961.

Marlin, George J. *The American Catholic Voter: 200 Years of Political Impact.* South Bend, Ind.: St. Augustine's Press, 2004.

Marsden, George M. *Fundamentalism and American Culture.* 2nd ed. New York: Oxford University Press, 2006.

————. "The Modern Period," In *Religion & American Politics: From the Colonial Period to the 1980s,* Mark Noll, ed. New York: Oxford University Press, 1990.

Martin, William. *A Prophet Without Honor: The Billy Graham Story.* New York: William Morrow, 1991.

————. *With God on Our Side: The Rise of the Religious Right in America.* New York: Broadway Books, 1996.

Massa, Mark S. *Catholics and American Culture: Fulton Sheen, Dorothy Day, and the Notre Dame Football Team.* New York: Crossroad, 1999.

McCarraher, Eugene. *Christian Critics: Religion and the Impasse in Modern American Social Thought.* Ithaca: Cornell University Press, 2000.

McGirr, Lisa. *Suburban Warriors: The Origins of the New American Right.* Princeton, N.J.: Princeton University Press, 2001.

McGreevy, John T. *Catholicism and American Freedom: A History.* New York: W.W. Norton, 2003.

McGurn, William. "Style Counts." *Crisis* (June 1999).

————. "The Heart of the Catholic Voter." *Crisis* (June 1999): 16–30.

McKenna, George. "Criss-Cross: Democrats, Republicans, and Abortion." *Human Life Review* 22 (2006): 57–79.

McMillan, Craige. "The Last Honorable Politician?" October 29, 1998. www.worldnetdaily.com/news/article.asp?ARTICLE_ID=19259.

Meacham, Jon. *American Gospel: God, the Founding Fathers, and the Making of a Nation.* New York: Random House, 2006.

Meehan, Mary. "Robert Drinan Under Siege." *Our Sunday Visitor,* September 8, 1996.

Melady, Thomas Patrick. *Public Catholicism: The Challenge of Living the Faith in a Secular American Culture.* Huntington, N.Y.: Our Sunday Visitor Publishing Division, 1996.

Meyer, Frank S. *The Conservative Mainstream.* New Rochelle, N.Y.: Arlington House, 1969.

Micklethwait, John, and Adrian Wooldridge. *The Right Nation: Conservative Power in America.* New York: Penguin, 2004.

Moore, James, and Wayne Slater. *The Architect: Karl Rove and the Master Plan for Absolute Power.* New York: Crown, 2006.

Morris, Charles R. *American Catholic: The Saints and Sinners Who Built America's Most Powerful Church.* New York: Random House, 1997.

Morris, Dick. "The Hispanic Vote Elects Bush." NewsMax.Com, November 5, 2004. www.newsmax.com/archives/articles/2004/11/4/203450.shtml.

Murray, John Courtney. "Memo to Cushing on Contraception Legislation." Murray Archives, Woodstock Theological Seminary, Woodstock Theological Center, Georgetown University, Washington, D.C.: File 1-43.

Nash, George H. *The Conservative Intellectual Movement in America Since 1945,* 30th Anniversary Edition. Wilmington: Intercollegiate Studies Institute, 2006.

Nathanson, Bernard. *The Hand of God: A Journey from Death to Life by the Abortion Doctor Who Changed His Mind.* Washington, D.C.: Regnery, 1996.

Neuhaus, Father Richard. "Truths and Untruths About the Catholic Alliance." *First things* (February 1996): 7.

Nicholson, Jim. *The United States and the Holy See: The Long Road.* Rome: 30 Days in the Church and the World, 2002.

Noll, Mark A. *Religion & American Politics: From Colonial Period to the 1980s.* New York: Oxford University Press, 1990.

Novak, Robert. "The Catholic Vote: Does It Swing?" *Crisis* (November 1998).

O'Reilly, Kenneth. *Nixon's Piano: Presidents and Racial Politics from Washington to Clinton.* New York: Free Press, 1995.

O'Sullivan, John. *The President, the Pope, and the Prime Minister.* Washington, D.C.: Regnery, 2006.

Patterson, James T. *Restless Giant: The United States from Watergate to Bush v. Gore.* Oxford: Oxford University Press, 2005.

Perlstein, Rick. *Before the Storm: Barry Goldwater and the Unmaking of the American Consensus.* New York: Hill & Wang, 2001.

Phillips, Kevin. *American Theocracy: The Peril and Politics of Radical Religion, Oil, and Borrowed Money in the 21st Century.* New York: Viking, 2006.

———. *The Emerging Republican Majority.* New York: Arlington House, 1969.

Placher, William C. *The Domestication of Transcendence: How Modern Thinking About God Went Wrong.* Louisville, Ky.: Westminster John Knox Press, 1996.

Ponnuru, Ramesh, *The Party of Death: The Democrats, the Media, the Courts, and the Disregard for Human Life*. Washington, D.C.: Regnery, 2006.

Press, Bill. *How the Republicans Stole Christmas: The Republican Party's Declared Monopoly on Religion and What Democrats Can Do to Take It Back*. New York: Doubleday, 2005.

Puryear, Elmer L. *Graham A. Barden, Conservative Carolina Congressman*. Buie's Creek, N.C.: Campbell University Press, 1979.

Ratzinger, Joseph. "Doctrinal Note on Some Questions Regarding the Participation of Catholics in Political Life," January 2003.

Ratzinger, Joseph, and Vittorio Messori. *The Ratzinger Report*. San Francisco: Ignatius Press, 1985.

Reese, Thomas J. *A Flock of Shepherds: The National Conference of Catholic Bishops*. Kansas City, Mo.: Sheed & Ward, 1992.

Reeves, Andree E. *Congressional Committee Chairmen: Three Who Made An Evolution*. Lexington: University Press of Kentucky, 1993.

Reichley, James A. *Faith in Politics*. Washington, D.C.: Brookings Institution Press, 2002.

"Religious Voters and the Midterm Elections." Event transcript. Pew Forum on Religion & Public Life, November 13, 2006.

Ribuffo, Leo P. *The Old Christian Right: The Protestant Far Right from the Great Depression to the Cold War*. Philadelphia, Pa.: Temple University Press, 1983.

Richardson, Michael. *Amazing Faith: The Authorized Biography of Bill Bright, Founder of Campus Crusades for Christ Int'l*. Colorado Springs, Colo.: Waterbrook Press, 2000.

Robinson, John A. T. *Honest to God*. Philadelphia: Westminster Press, 1963.

Robinson, Marilynne. "Onward, Christian Liberals." *American Scholar* (Spring 2006): 42–51.

Roosevelt, Eleanor. *My Day: The Best of Eleanor Roosevelt's Acclaimed Newspaper Columns, 1936–1962*. David Emblidge and Mary Ross, eds. Cambridge, Mass.: Da Capo Press, 2001.

Roosevelt, Eleanor II. "Eleanor Roosevelt's Niece Eleanor Roosevelt II Remembers Val-Kill." *National Park Service*. www.nps.gov/archive/elro/what-is-vk/family-memories/roosevelt-eleanor-2.htm.

Rudin, Rabbi James. *The Baptizing of America: The Religious Right's Plans for the Rest of Us*. New York: Thunder's Mouth Press, 2006.

Rusher, William. *The Rise of the Right*. New York: William Morrow, 1984.

Sager, Ryan. *The Elephant in the Room: Evangelicals, Libertarians, and the Battle to Control the Republican Party*. Hoboken, N.J.: John Wiley, 2006.

Sandbrook, Dominic. *Eugene McCarthy: The Rise and Fall of Postwar American Liberalism*. New York: Alfred A. Knopf, 2004.

Santorum, Rick. *It Takes a Family: Conservatism and the Common Good*. Wilmington, Del.: Intercollegiate Studies Institute, 2003.

———. "Subsidiarity at Work: A Catholic's Vision of Social Policy." *Crisis* (1999): 31–35.

Schaeffer, Francis A. *How Should We Then Live: The Decline of Western Thought and Culture*. Old Tappan, N.J.: Fleming H. Revell, 1976.

Schoenwald, Jonathan M. *A Time for Choosing: The Rise of Modern American Conservatism*. Oxford: Oxford University Press, 2001.

Schuler, Robert H. *My Journey from an Iowa Farm to a Cathedral of Dreams*. San Francisco: Harper Collins, 2001.

Schwartz, Michael. *The Persistent Prejudice: Anti-Catholicism in America*. Huntington, Ind.: Our Sunday Visitor, 1984.

Seaman, Ann Rowe. *America's Most Hated Woman: The Life and Gruesome Death of Madalyn Murray O'Hair*. New York: Continuum International, 2005.

Seger, Linda. *Jesus Rode a Donkey: Why Republicans Don't Have the Corner on Christ*. Avon, Mass.: Adams Media, 2006.

Sewell, Dennis. *Catholics: Britain's Largest Minority*. London: Penguin Books, 2001.

Sheen, Fulton J. *Peace of Soul*. New York: McGraw-Hill, 1969.

Shiflett, Dave. *Exodus: Why Americans are Fleeing Liberal Churches for Conservative Christianity*. New York: Penguin Group, 2005.

Sowell, Thomas. *The Vision of the Anointed: Self-Congratulation as a Basis for Social Policy*. New York: Basic Books, 1995.

Stark, Rodney. *The Victory of Reason: How Christianity Led to Freedom, Capitalism, And Western Success*. New York: Random House, 2005.

Steinfels, Margaret O'Brien. *American Catholics & Civic Engagement*. American Catholics in the Public Square, Vol. 1. New York: Rowman and Littlefield, 2004.

Steinfels, Margaret O'Brien, ed. *American Catholics, American Culture, Tradition and Resistance*. American Catholics in the Public Square, Vol. 2. New York: Rowman and Littlefield, 2004.

Steyn, Mark. *America Alone: The End of the World as We Know It*. Washington, D.C.: Regnery, 2006.

Stricherz, Mark. "Blood on Their Hands: Exposing Pro-Abortion Catholic Politicians." *Crisis* (May 2003).

———. "Casey's Heirs: The Plight of the Pro-Life Democrat." *Crisis* (May 2002).

Sullivan, Amy. "In Good Faith: The Real Meaning of Barack Obama's Speech on Religion and Politics." *Slate*, July 3, 2006.

———. "Not God's Party," *Slate*, August 29, 2006.

Sullivan, Andrew. *The Conservative Soul: How We Lost It, How to Get it Back.* New York: HarperCollins, 2006.

Sweetman, Brendan. *Why Politics Needs Religion: The Place of Religious Arguments in the Public Square.* Downer's Grove, Ill.: IVP Academic, 2006.

Taylor, Charles. *The Ethics of Authenticity.* Cambridge, Mass.: Harvard University Press, 1992.

———. *Multiculturalism and the "Politics of Recognition."* Princeton, N.J.: Princeton University Press, 1992: 70.

Taylor, Mark Lewis. *Religion, Politics, and the Christian Right.* Minneapolis: Fortress Press, 2005.

Texas Freedom Network. "The Anatomy of Power: Texas and the Religious Right in 2006." www.tfn.org/files/fck/SORR%2006%20ReportWEB.pdf>18.

"The Catholic Voter Project." *Crisis* (November 1998).

"The Pope and the President: A Key Advisor Reflects on the Reagan Administration." *Catholic World Report,* November 1999.

Thomas, Cal, and Ed Dobson. *Blinded by Might: Can the Religious Right Save America?* Grand Rapids, Mich.: Zondervan, 1999.

Tillich, Paul. *The Dynamics of Faith.* New York: Harper and Row, 1957.

Tucker, Todd. *Notre Dame vs. the Klan: How the Fighting Irish Defeated the Ku Klux Klan.* Chicago: Loyola University Press, 2004.

Tull, Charles J. *Father Coughlin and the New Deal.* Syracuse, N.Y.: Syracuse University Press, 1965,

"Understanding Religion's Role in the 2008 Election." Event transcript. Pew Forum on Religion & Public Life, Event Transcript, December 5, 2006.

United States Conference of Catholic Bishops. *Readings on Catholics and Political Life.* Washington, D.C.: USCCB Publishing, 2006.

"Universality of Rights Is Defined by U.S.; Protest over Dalai Lama Mars Vienna Talks." *Washington Post,* June 15, 1993: A15.

Vahanian, Gabriel. *The Death of God.* New York: George Braziller, 1961.

Varacalli, Joseph A. *The Catholic Experience in America.* Westport, Conn.: Greenwood Press, 2006.

Viguerie, Richard. *The New Right: We're Ready to Lead.* Falls Church, Va.: Viguerie Co., 1981.

Viguerie, Richard A. and David Franke. *America's Right Turn: How Conservatives Used New and Alternative Media to Take Power.* Chicago: Bonus Books, 2004.

Wagner, Steven. "Catholics and Evangelicals—Can They be Allies?" *Crisis* (2000): 12–17.

———. "Election 2000: A New Dawn?" *Crisis* (January 2000): 12–17.

———. "The Heart of the Catholic Voter." *Crisis* (November 1998).

———. "Social-Renewal Catholics." *Crisis* (June 1999).

———. "Will America Bury the Hatchet?" *Crisis* (January 2001): 10–16.

Wakefield, Dan. *The Hijacking of Jesus.* New York: Nation Books, 2006.

Wald, Kenneth D. *Religion and Politics in the United States.* Lanham, Md.: Rowman & Littlefield, 2003.

Wallis, Jim. God's Politics: A Blog, December 1, 2006.

———. *God's Politics: Why the Right Gets It Wrong and the Left Doesn't Get It.* San Francisco: Harper San Francisco, 2005.

Warner, Michael. *Changing Witness: Catholic Bishops and Public Policy, 1917–1994.* Washington, D.C.: Ethics and Public Policy Center, 1995.

Weigel, George. *Witness to Hope: The Biography of Pope John Paul II.* New York: HarperCollins Publishers, Inc., 1999.

"What Chalcedon Believes." www.chalcedon.edu/credo.php.

Wilcox, Clyde. *Onward Christian Soldiers? The Religious Right in American Politics.* 2nd ed. Boulder, Colo.: Westview Press, 2000.

Wilcox, Clyde, and Carin Larson. *Onward Christian Soldiers? The Religious Right in American Politics.* 3rd ed. Washington, D.C.: Georgetown University Press, 2006.

Willis, Clint and Nate Hardcastle, Eds. *Jesus Is Not a Republican: The Religious Right's War on America.* New York: Thunder's Mouth Press, 2005.

Wills, Garry. *Politics and Catholic Freedom.* Chicago: Regnery, 1964.

———. *Under God: Religion and American Politics.* New York: Touchstone, 1990.

———. *What Jesus Meant.* New York: Penguin Group, 2006.

Wilson, Matthew, J. "The Changing Catholic Voter: Comparing Responses to John Kennedy in 1960 and John Kerry in 2004." In David E. Campbell, ed. *A Matter of Faith: Religion in the 2004 Presidential Election.* Washington, D.C.: Brookings Institution Press, 2007.

Wolfe, Alan. "The Religious Rights' Last Rites." http://commentisfree.guardian.co.uk/alan_wolfe/2006/11/alan_wolfe_1.html.

Wolters, Raymond. *Right Turn: William Bradford Reynolds, the Reagan Administration, and Black Civil Rights.* New Brunswick, N.J.: Transaction, 1996.

Woods, Thomas E. *The Church Confronts Modernity: Catholic Intellectuals and the Progressive Era.* New York: Columbia University Press, 2004.

World Conference on Human Rights: The Vienna Declaration and Programme of Action, June 1993. New York: United Nations Department of Public Information, 1993.

Yee, Daniel. "Clinton, Carter Back Moderate Baptists." Associated Press, January 9, 2007.

Zapor, Patricia. "Madame Speaker: Anticipating How Pelosi Will Run the House." Catholic News Service. January 5, 2007.

Zoller, Michael. *Washington and Rome: Catholicism in American Culture.* Trans. Steven Rendall and Albert Wimmer. South Bend, Ind.: University of Notre Dame Press, 1999.

INDEX

Abdallan, Fred, 277

Abington Township School District v. Schempp (1963), 81

abortion: and Catholics, 12, 15, 16, 18, 20, 21–22, 47, 53–54, 127, 128, 130, 132, 134, 138–45, 149, 154–59, 173, 178, 180–82, 193, 240, 246, 256–58, 268–70, 286–88; and Christian nation debate, 113; and Christian Right-Catholic alliance, 240; and communion controversy, 287–88; and Congress, 140, 141, 236; and Constitution, 244; and democracy, 96; and Democratic Party, 33, 130, 151, 154–59, 161, 172, 269, 270, 284, 290–91, 302, 304; and economic conditions, 172; and elections of 1980, 242; and elections of 1988, 244; and elections of 1992, 184; and elections of 2004, 267–68, 276–77, 279–81, 284, 286–87; and elections of 2006, 151, 276; and emergence of pro-life movement, 53; and emergence of Religious Right, 150; and equivalence strategy, 168; and Evangelicals, 3, 4, 12, 54–57, 127, 138, 163, 240, 246, 256–57, 258; and faith-based initiatives, 79; and feminism, 64; funding for, 160, 183; international right to, 184–85; and "John Paul II priests," 147; and Kaine-Kilgore campaign, 295; and

Kerry, 151, 267–69, 276–77, 279–80, 284, 286–87; and liberalism, 59, 159; and Miers' Supreme Court nomination, 262–63; and ministers, 54–55; and Moral Majority, 13; and opposition as hate crime, 93; partial-birth, 145, 155, 158, 175, 183, 270, 271, 291; and philosophy-religion issues, 214, 219; and Protestants, 138; and racism, 72–73; and Reagan–Religious Right alliance, 308; and religious conservatives, 173; and Religious Left, 171–72; and Religious Right, 167, 171–72; and Republican Party, 168, 299; and secularism, 39; and Senate voting records, 270, 271; as sinful, 18; and theocracy, 92; and transition from anti-feminism to anti-secularism of Religious Right, 11; and what is wrong with the Religious Right, 169, 171–72. *See also* Human Life Amendment; Hyde Amendment; *Roe v. Wade; specific person or organization*

Abramoff, Jack, 296, 297

ACLU. *See* American Civil Liberties Union

ACT UP, 301

Action Institute, 184

"Action for Life," 130

activism, rise of, 12–16

Adams, John, 108

Franciscan University, 24, 276, 277
freedom: "basic," 101; and Catholics,
203; and Christian nation debate,
101, 113; individual, 113; and
philosophy-religion issues, 202, 203,
219
Friedan, Betty, 65
Frist, Bill, 103, 261
Fuchs, Joseph, 286
Fuller, Craig, 235
Fundamentalists, 3, 4, 8, 126, 138, 163,
164, 245–46, 256, 259, 265, 266
Furgler, Kurt, 241

Galeback, Stephen, 235
gay marriage: and Bible, 172–73; and
Bush administration, 89, 98; and
Catholics, 60, 180, 288; and Christian
nation debate, 113–14; debate about,
174; and democracy, 93; and
Democratic Party, 33, 161, 270;
and elections of 2004, 60, 89, 288;
and elections of 2006, 60; and
Evangelicals, 60, 163; as family issue,
60; and Kennedy (Ted), 288;
and liberals, 59; and marriage
amendment, 259, 264–65; in
Massachusetts, 60, 89, 218, 288;
opposition to, as hate crime, 93;
and philosophy-religion issues,
214, 218, 219; and reinvention of
Republican Party, 306; and religious
conservatives, 173; and Religious
Left, 173; and Religious Right, 55,
56, 167, 169; and Republican Party,
310; and Schlafly, 63; and theocracy,
93
gay rights: and Bloch case, 215–20; and
Bush (George H.W.), 233; and
Catholics, 127, 135; and civil rights,
172; and Clinton, 217, 218; and
culture, 218; and Democratic Party,
269; and feminism, 61, 64–65;
and Kennedy (John F.), 226; and
philosophy-religion issues, 201, 214,
215–20; and Religious Left, 173; and
religious liberty, 216–20, 310; and
Religious Right, 53, 65; and

Republican Party, 218; and Schlafly,
63; and theocracy, 92
generational interdependence, 95–96
George, Robert, 24, 131, 184
George, Timothy, 258
George Washington University
Hospital, Operation Rescue at, 130
Georgia: elections of 2002 in, 296; flag
of, 73; orphanage case in, 215, 218;
Reed as candidate for lieutenant
governor of, 295–97
Gergen, David, 235
Gilder, Josh, 235
Gillespie, Ed, 175, 194
Gillespie, Martin, 194, 277, 278, 284
Gingrich, Newt, 103
Glendon, Mary Ann, 24
Glenn, John, 276, 277
God: as central to culture wars, 49–50;
and Christian nation debate, 114–18;
and divine law, 209; in Pledge of
Allegiance, 136, 210
God and Politics (PBS TV), 81–82
Goeglein, Tim, 5–6, 260, 307
Goldberg, Michelle, 50
Goldsboro Christian School, 67, 69,
70
Goldwater, Barry, 33, 56, 62, 64, 127,
128, 131, 135
good and evil, 197–99, 213
Goodman, Ellen, 190–91
Goodridge decision (2004), 174, 288
Gorbachev, Mikhail, 228, 232, 241
Gore, Al, 167, 181, 185, 187, 189–90,
269, 271, 307
government: and rights, 211–12; role of,
73
Gracida, Rene Henry, 237, 272
Graham, Billy, 31, 39, 64, 70, 95, 163,
164, 224, 231, 247, 257
Granholm, Jennifer, 301
Grant, Robert, 8, 12
Gray, Nellie, 130
Great Awakening, 118
Greeley, Andrew, 181
Green, John, 298–99
Green v. Connally (1970), 67
Grier, Rosey, 240